AMERICAN BIG BANDS

D1155515

HAL•LEONARD®

AMERICAN BIG BANDS

Hal Leonard books are available at your local bookstore,
or you may order through Music Dispatch at 1-800-637-2852 or
www.musicdispatch.com

Published by Hal Leonard Corporation
7777 Bluemound Road
P.O. Box 13819
Milwaukee, WI 53213

Trade Book Division Editorial Offices
19 West 21st Street
Suite 201
New York, New York 10010

Library of Congress Cataloging-in-Publication Data

Lee, William F.
  American big bands / William F. Lee.-- 1st ed.
     p. cm.
  Includes bibliographical references (p.   ).
  ISBN 0-634-08054-7
  1. Big bands--United States. 2. Jazz musicians--United States. I. Title.
  ML3518.L44 2005
  784.4'80973--dc22
                              2005030166

Printed in the United States of America
First Edition
Book Designed by Hal Leonard Creative Services
Cover photo: Judd Binkert Orchestra, circa 1936
Interior photos courtesy of Down Beat Magazine.

HAL•LEONARD®
CORPORATION
7777 W. BLUEMOUND RD. P.O. BOX 13819 MILWAUKEE, WI 53213

Visit Hal Leonard online at www.halleonard.com

CONTENTS

INTRODUCTION

Big jazz bands were everywhere when I was growing up in Washington, D.C. I heard all the great jazz bands of the day on the radio, in the movies, in dancehalls, and in the theaters. I loved the music they played and I wanted to play with them but I was too young and too inexperienced. To prepare myself, I practiced hard, studied European classical music, listened to jazz recordings, and played with as many older and more experienced musicians as I could.

Bill Baldwin's band was a local dance band that played for many social events and I made friends with the members of the band. I made such a pest of myself that they would sometimes let me sit at the end of an evening just to get rid of me. There was another good big band in town, which was led by Tommy Myles. It featured a young singer named Billy Eckstine. Eckstine was so good that, despite his youth, Earl Hines hired him as a featured singer. That inspired all of us who were young and ambitious and made us practice much more earnestly.

I joined my first big band when I was a freshman in college and by the time I was a senior, I was the leader of the band. I had learned a lot, but this was only the beginning. After college, I worked with all kinds of small ensembles but I did not work regularly with another big band until I joined the legendary Don Redman as the pianist with the first American jazz band to tour Europe after World War II. Don Redman was not only a superb musician, he was the first jazz composer-arranger who had the inspiration, imagination, and conservatory training to organize big band playing in the way that came to define what jazz musicians meant when they said the music was swinging.

Though the Don Redman band was basically a "swing band," Don introduced his European audiences to bebop by, including a few examples of melodic, harmonic, and rhythmic devices being used in the style. Even in the 1940s, many of us were not content to limit our creative efforts to the parameters set by the big bands of the 1930s and Don was one of the "elders" who encouraged us to experiment. Bebop was the music and to play it well, a musician had to execute intricate spontaneous melodies as well as play extremely difficult preconceived melodic lines in strict unison with other instruments. This music demanded quite a lot from the listener as well as the player.

Many years later, when I was leading my own bands on TV shows hosted by David Frost, Tony Brown, and others, I was proud of the musicians I assembled and presented on a daily basis. I was also grateful for the "on-the-job training" I had been given during my formative years. I was determined to pass along as much as I could. Even then I realized that there were thousands of students studying and playing excellent jazz in exciting big bands. Now these ubiquitous have not only become an important part of academic programs worldwide, they have added new talent, imagination, and energy to contemporary music. Today, there is more information available on jazz than ever before and there is so much to be studied and learned that jazz has been given new life in schools, concert halls, and festivals all over the world.

—Billy Taylor

OVERTURE

For one-and-one-quarter century Americans depended, primarily, on music developed by their forefathers in Western Europe. With the advent of peoples emigrating from Africa, Asia, the Near East, Far East, South America, Central America, and the Caribbean, a new music culture was developing in the United States. This culture was demanding a change in melody, harmony, and rhythm and was impacting instrumental and vocal music throughout the states. By the turn of the century, all of the acoustic instruments, as we now know them, had been invented and tested. Concert and marching bands (including military bands) were playing at various venues, concert halls, gazebos, clubs, schools, and the recording industry was beginning to thrive. People hungered for music that would provide gaiety; music for dancing and celebrating. American musicians, too, hungered for a musical vehicle that would allow for more self-expression than the classical music Western Europe provided. The art of improvisation, which had once been at the forefront of musical creativity in Western Europe, was beginning to thrive in New Orleans and would work its way to St. Louis, Kansas City, Chicago, and New York City.

Many foreign operettas were brought to America before the 20th century. *The Red Mill, Naughty Marietta, Babes in Toyland, Mlle. Modiste*, and *Sweethearts* figured prominently in early American theater in the early part of the century. Early show composers in the 20th century included Sigmund Romberg, Rudolf Friml, and the popular George M. Cohan, whose patriotic songs were universally enjoyed by the American populace. Victor Herbert penned many popular shows, including *The Merry Widow, The Chocolate Soldier, The Sleeping Beauty and the Beast*, and *A Chinese Honeymoon*. Other composers for the music stage were Raymond Hubbell, Franz Lehar, Gustav Luders, Gustav Kerker, and Jean Schwartz.

Songs gained popularity in the early years through the sale of sheet music. Although the phonograph record was produced by Columbia and Edison, joined by Victor in 1901, and manufactured to play at 78-rpm, it was not until the late '40s and early '50s that the 33-rpm and 45-rpm records were produced, followed, of course, by the 8-track, cassette and CD. Vaudeville, headlined by Belle Baker, Fred and Adele Astaire, Sarah Bernhardt, Harry Houdini, Sophie Tucker, Lillian Russell, Rae Samuels, Lulu Blaser, and many others, gradually began to replace the early operettas as America's favorite form of entertainment.

In 1914, ASCAP (American Society of Composers, Authors, and Publishers) was formed by Victor Herbert, Raymond Hubbell, Jay Witmark, Louis Hirsch, George Maxwell, Nathan Burkan, and several others. The courts gradually recognized that a song was a product of the heart and brain and was a product. This resulted in hotels, restaurants, dance halls, bars, theaters, clubs, radio, phonograph records, television, etc. paying royalties for the use of copyrighted songs.

Prior to World War I, the entertainment industry was very strong. During the war, there were drives for the sale of war bonds, entertainers performing for the men and women in service and a number of patriotic songs such as "Oh, How I Hate to Get Up in the Morning," "Hinky-Dinky Parlez-Vous," "Good-bye Broadway," "Hello France," and "When the Boys Come Home." Some great songs were written at the end of the turmoil as well. "How Ya Gonna Keep 'Em Down on the Farm?" joined the postwar move toward Prohibition.

Musical theater developed in the '20s and names like George and Ira Gershwin, Vincent Youmans, Arthur Schwartz, and Jerome Kern came to the fore. These great talents were followed by writers Richard Rogers, Buddy DeSylva, Lew Brown, Ray Henderson, and the biggest name of all, Irving Berlin. *The Ziegfeld Follies* led the stage presentations.

By 1915, the dance bands of the period began to develop sophistication and the various styles that would pervade for the following 50 years were beginning to be defined. Some of the pioneers were Isham Jones, Paul Whiteman, Sam Lanin, Ted Lewis, Art Hickman, and Joseph C. Smith. By the early and mid-'20s, Fred Waring, Ben Pollack, Ben Bernie, Paul Specht, Roger Wolfe Kahn, Ray Miller, Vincent Lopez, Abe Lyman, George Olsen, Jean Goldkette, Ben Selvin, and others were considered great dance bands. In the '30s, other pioneers were contributing to the American big band effort. Some of the leaders were Russ Morgan, Woody Herman, Glenn Miller, Benny Goodman, Kay Kyser, Eddy Duchin, Freddy Martin, Count Basie, Duke Ellington, Lawrence Welk, Al Donahue, and, as you will note, many, many others. The '40s brought forth Stan Kenton, Billy Eckstine, Tex Beneke, Dizzy Gillespie, Claude Thornhill, and many others too numerous to mention. The '50s and '60s introduced us to Billy May, Sauter-Finegan, Maynard Ferguson, Hugo Montenegro, Gerry Mulligan, Peter Duchin, and Doc Severinsen. Although America's big bands began some activity at the turn of the 20th century and continued into the 21st century, the '20s, '30s, and '40s are usually considered the big band era.

Radio, which began in 1920, had a shaky start. Listening was done through a crystal set with earphones allowing for one person at a time to enjoy the "magic" sounds. In the mid-'20s electric radio sets were available, eliminating the need for earphones and allowing for various-sized audiences to listen together to a single radio. Programming was all done on a local level and most of the time was spent listening to recordings or the local music talent. One of the ways people passed time was to dial to various radio stations to see how many stations, and from what distance, they could receive programs. NBC (National Broadcasting Company) was formed in 1926 and CBS (Columbia Broadcasting System) in 1929. These network stations greatly improved the quantity and quality of broadcasting featuring network shows like *Amos 'n' Andy*, B.A. Rolfe and the Lucky Strike Orchestra, Rudy Vallée, and Jones and Hare, the Interwoven Pair, among others. During the early '30s, other stars emerged, including Ed Wynn, Bing Crosby, Kate Smith, Fred Allen, Eddie Cantor, Jack Benny, Will Rogers, Joe Penner, Fanny Brice, etc. Bands that were given much radio exposure in the early to mid-'30s included Wayne King, Ben Bernie, Guy Lombardo, Paul Whiteman, Fletcher Henderson, and Fred Waring; all of whom had network radio shows. By the mid '30s, the Lucky Strike Hit Parade (Your Hit Parade) was going strong followed by hit radio shows like *Lum 'n' Abner*, *Dick Powell*, *Fibber McGee and Molly*, *The George Burns & Gracie Allen*, and others. By the late '30s, bandleaders, including Kay Kyser, Tommy Dorsey, Hal Kemp, Phil Spitalny, and Benny Goodman, along with personalities Edgar Bergen and Bob Hope, all had radio shows of their own. During the '40s, radio features included Glenn Miller, Red Skelton, Garry Moore, Jimmy Durante, Milton Berle, and *Duffy's Tavern*'s Ed Gardner.

In 1927 Al Jolson starred in the first talking motion picture, *The Jazz Singer*. By 1929, many movie musicals were born, including *The Love Parade*, *Sunny Side Up*, *Innocents of Paris*, *Broadway Melody*, *The Desert Song*, and *Broadway Revue of 1929*. Some of the top players in these early movies included Jack Oakie, Jeanette MacDonald, Cliff Edwards, John Boles, and Maurice Chevalier, among others.

During the Depression years radio and movies thrived; however, musical theater badly suffered. By 1943, things began to turn around for this medium with the offering of the Richard Rodgers/Oscar Hammerstein II production *Oklahoma*. During the remainder of the '40s and during the '50s songwriters Cole Porter, Irving Berlin, Burton Lane, Harold Arlen, Kurt Weill, Lerner and Lowe, etc., along with stars Nanette Fabray, Alfred Drake, Victor Moore, Ethel Merman, Gertrude Lawrence, Danny Kaye, Ray Bolger, Mary Martin, and others brought much vitality to the Broadway stage

World War II brought a number of hit songs to the repertoire of America's big bands, including such standards as "They're Either Too Young or Too Old," "The Last Time I Saw Paris," "When the Lights Go On Again," etc. During the second war, there was an attempt by the phonograph companies to get the public to turn in their old records as there was an extreme shortage of shellac, the material from which records were manufactured. This unfortunately resulted in the loss of many rare recordings. Also, in 1942, President James C. Petrillo of the AF of M (American Federation of Musicians) declared a musicians' strike against the record companies. This strike lasted until September 1943 (although Victor and Columbia did not commence until November 1944). During the strike, singers were able to record; which greatly boosted the careers of Dick Haymes, Bing Crosby, Frank Sinatra, Dinah Shore, and others. (They used vocal ensembles as their backgrounds.)

During the '40s great arrangers-composers began to write for America's big bands. Among these talented musicians were Gil Evans, Dizzy Gillespie, Stan Kenton, Johnny Richards followed in the '50s and '60s by Manny Albam, Don Ellis, Neal Hefti, Quincy Jones, Billy May, Gerry Mulligan, Shorty Rogers, and many others. Television became the country's main entertainment beginning in the '50s with *I Love Lucy* headlining the offerings. Game shows, quiz shows, talk shows, re-releases of movies, and shows "made for television" became America's principal entertainment in the latter half of the 20th century.

During 1900–1919, there were 40 bands; 1920–1929, 186 bands; 1930–1939, 217 bands, 1940–49, 147 bands; 1950-59, 43 bands; and 1960–1969, 17 bands. The total number of American bands formed from 1900 to 1970 was 650 bands. There were, no doubt, hundreds, perhaps thousands of local bands, and marching and military units, throughout the United States that never recorded, were never heard on radio, nor seen on television or in motion pictures, were considered hometown outfits, and are not included in this presentation.

During the century, bands were normally placed into three categories: swing bands (or jazz bands); Mickey Mouse bands (also referred to as commercial bands, hotel bands, tenor bands, or sweet bands); and studio bands, which were organized with the advent of records, radio, films, and television. In the case of the swing (or jazz) bands, the leaders had jazz backgrounds, but knew they had to play music for dancing; their music was energetic and well executed with a strong rhythmic feel; all of their arrangements made great allowances for featured soloists; singers were a vital part; and the leaders, arrangers, and soloists were innovative. The Mickey Mouse bands were characterized thusly: focus in the arrangements was always on the melody; the band's volume was always very controlled; tempos were planned carefully to fit the dance style of the tune; improvised solos were rare; each band had a very identifiable sound, instrumentally and vocally; these bands were extremely conservative and almost always played the posh hotels and society parties. The studio bands were organized to provide music for another medium—for recordings, radio after 1920, films after 1930, or television after 1945; the music directors (conductors), composers-arrangers, and sidemen were the top musicians in their field and were expected to sight-read music in any style and from any historical period; a great variation in instrumentation was experienced (from keyboard soloist to full symphony orchestra and beyond). Most of the best music composition in the 20th century came from studio composers.

Bands are introduced by section during the decade in which they were formed; within the sections they are listed chronologically. For example, some band leaders began their careers playing with other groups in the '20s and/or '30s but organized their own bands in the '40s. Those leaders are listed in the '40s. At the beginning of each section there is a brief mention of historical events that occurred during that particular decade in order to acclimate the reader to the period in which those bands were formed.

My gratitude to the many band leaders who took the time to talk with me and to my good friend Clem DeRosa for his insight, experience, and knowledge of America's big bands. Enjoy!

—William F. Lee III

Louis Armstrong: "I don't need words; it's all in the phrasing."

Pearl Bailey: "If I just sang a song, it would mean nothing."

Charlie Barnet: "I learned to play hot by fooling around with the Victrola. I was nuts about the Fletcher Henderson band."

Count Basie: "If there's going to be hope for the big bands they're going to have to play a little different music and meet the kids halfway and give it a little of their flavor."

Sidney Bechet: "The music, it's something you can give only to those who love it."

Eubie Blake: "Mama didn't allow no ragtime playin' at the Blake home."

Connee Boswell (of the Boswell Sisters): "You know what we did? We revolutionized trio and group singing!"

Les Brown: "There was an agent on the West Coast named Jimmy Saphier who was trying to sell Doris Day to Hope for his radio show, and so he brought him the records she had made with us. When Hope heard them, he asked Jimmy, 'How about that band?'"

Cab Calloway: I was always terrible at remembering lyrics and so I'd just shout 'Heigh-de-ho.'"

Frankie Carle: "I play a round of golf once or twice a week with Ede, my Mrs. Everyday I'm at the piano, keeping the fingers in shape, composing, and practically living a life of Riley."

Rosemary Clooney: "We had no music and when somebody asked us, 'What key?' we just looked wide-eyed and asked, 'What's a key?'"

Nat "King" Cole: "It's a shame when you're told you can't do something just because it's 'too good.'"

Eddie Condon: "We don't flat our fifths. We drink them!"

Bing Crosby: "As a kid, I had all the good phonograph records in town. I was strictly a follower of good jazz groups. My ambition was to be around those guys. I never wanted anything more than that."

Bob Crosby: "I'm the only guy in the business who made it without talent."

Xavier Cugat: "I would rather play 'Chiquita Banana' and have my swimming pool than play Bach and starve."

Jimmy Dorsey: "If you don't feel well, stop thinking about yourself and rise above it."

Tommy Dorsey: "My life's not my own. I want to get out to the ball park, but instead I'm stuck here in my dressing room all day."

Eddie Duchin: "If the crowd finds your music easy to dance to, you're a success."

Jimmy Durante: "The song gotta come from da heart."

Billy Eckstein: "When Duke and I worked on the same bill, neither of us wore the same suit twice. By the third week, people were buying tickets just to see the sartorial changes."

Duke Ellington: "If you're going to play good jazz you've got to have a plan of what's going to happen. There has to be intent. It's like an act of murder. You play with intent to commit something."

Ella Fitzgerald: "I used to think that people would think I was big-headed if I went into a record store and asked for my own records."

Helen Forrest: "I had to sing with a band."

Dizzy Gillespie: "I don't care if people say what I play isn't the greatest they ever heard. But I do want them to say it's not in bad taste."

Benny Goodman: "I'm completely absorbed in what I'm doing, and I expect other people to be, too."

Lionel Hampton: "I want to be remembered most for spreading happiness and good will."

Dick Haymes: "If you're going to be a male singer, don't be half a man!"

Ted Heath: "British bands have to play in all styles in order to survive."

Woody Herman: "You can do any damn think you want if you have the courage and the ability."

Earl Hines: "The young don't believe I'm me, and the old are too tired to come and see."

Billie Holiday: "I don't think I'm singing. I feel like I'm playing a horn; what comes out is what I feel. I have to change a tune to my own way of doing it. That's all I know."

Harry James: "I have a degree in mass psychology. I want to have a band that really swings and that's easy to dance to all the time."

Quincy Jones: "When they scraped my brain, they scraped all the BS out of me."

Louis Jordan: "I get tired but I love it. Just give me the chance to get tired."

Sammy Kaye: "From my observation, the dancing public, ninety-nine percent of it, comes to a place of dancing for dancing and romance."

Stan Kenton: "Some people with lots of nervous energy could feel what we were doing, but nobody else could."

André Kostelanetz: "I'd like to be remembered as a musician and conductor who has done a great deal to interest as many people as possible in music. That would make me happy."

Gene Krupa: "I succeeded in doing two things in my life. First of all, I made the drummer a high-priced guy, and secondly, I was able to project enough so that people were drawn to jazz."

Kay Kyser: "You might make a musician out of a gentleman, but you cannot always make a gentleman out of a musician."

Peggy Lee: "I learned more about music from the men I worked with in bands than I've learned anywhere else. They taught me discipline and the value of rehearsing and how to train."

Michel Legrand: "I just sit there, glued to the piano bench, and I don't move from it, even if I feel like an old lemon."

Guy Lombardo: "The place was so empty, we had to get four waiters and a guy out of the kitchen to clap."

Mantovani: "I wondered what I could do to make an impression in America."

Glenn Miller: "I milked cows, worked in a boot factory, and jerked sodas before settling on music as a career."

Mitch Miller: "If you don't reach your audience, you're nothing."

Vaughn Monroe: "The band business isn't an artistic thing, it's strictly a business."

Gerry Mulligan: "You've got to reach people on a personal level if you expect to reach them musically."

Red Nichols: "I was the businessman of the group. I always tried to get the best men I could."

Anita O'Day: "It gets to be so heavy, you just pack it all down and walk on top. You keep the spirit up and go right on."

Sy Oliver: "I decided to stick to music and see if I could make a nine-piece band sound like a fourteen-piece band."

Buddy Rich: "Did you come to see my teeth or hear me play?"

Sauter-Finegan: "If things are getting that bad, we'd better start our own band."

Artie Shaw: "I just didn't want to be just a half-assed human being in order to become a whole-assed musician."

Frank Sinatra: "I'm more conscious of the words in a song than I am of the melody. More than anything I expect and hope from people is kindness. If I don't get it, it upsets me."

Jo Stafford: "When I was with Tommy Dorsey's band, my sound was perfect—but boring, too. The notes meant more to me than the words. But that's the way I had been trained."

Claude Thornhill: "It seems to me that touch and tone are pretty much overlooked by pianists who are leading bands nowadays. You can get so many more and better musical effects if you pay attention to those little, shall I say, niceties."

Mel Torme: "Music began to be sung and played not for posterity, but for prosperity."

Rudy Vallée: "In some sort of reverse reasoning I have accomplished a feeling of satisfaction—to have become a popular figure when my appearance, to many people at least, in no way indicated that I might be the personality that had won their approbation through a microphone."

Sarah Vaughan: "As far as I'm concerned, an appreciative audience is the highest form of honor I can receive. It's their response that gets me going and keeps me going."

Fred Waring: "To join a band a musician has to be able to sing as well as play an instrument."

Lawrence Welk: "I'll roll up my sleeves for my wife and let her see the goose-pimples I get just watching myself."

Paul Weston: "Leading a classical orchestra is eighty percent acting. Leading a dance orchestra is a waste of time."

Paul Whiteman: "We were so scared; we postponed the date four times before we made the records."

Margaret Whiting: "I sang simply, and I sounded virginal."

Lee Wiley: "I always sang the way I wanted to sing. If I didn't like something, I just wouldn't do it. Instead, I'd take a plane to California and sit in the sun."

Joe Williams: "I'm not a blues singer, but a singer who sings the blues."

Teddy Wilson: "What I do for money is exactly what I do for pleasure."

AMERICAN BIG BANDS

William F. Lee III, Ph.D., Mus. D.

CHAPTER 1

A NEW CENTURY BEGINS
(1900–1919)

THE SCIENTIFIC AGE

The 19th century had come and gone. It had been an uncomfortable time to be alive. Famine, disease, and lack of proper medications had taken their toll on civilization. Transportation was by horse, surrey, wagon, or train. There were neither automobiles nor airplanes; they were yet to be invented. Indoor toilets were scarce. Slavery and the Civil War had done much to impede progress in the United States. There were few Hispanics, Asians, or African-Americans in the United States. Much of North America was still desolate and unoccupied. We had moved from savagery to barbarism, to civilization, and to enlightenment. Many immigrants were learning English and a new urban infrastructure was being built. Technology was becoming a high point of interest, many African-American sharecroppers moved to the big cities and industrialization and change were the orders of the day.

1900: More than 13 million Europeans were immigrating to the U.S., many seeking jobs in industries, creating great ethnic diversity and squalid living conditions. A few of the well-known personalities included Jule Styne, Bob Hope, Samuel Goldwyn, Charles Atlas, Claudette Colbert, Irving Berlin, Edward G. Robinson, Knute Rockne, and many, many others. There was a population of only 76 million in the U.S. (compared with more than 275 million today). The Boxer Rebellion took place in China. Music publishing grew (an estimated 100 songs sold a million copies each).

1901: President McKinley was assassinated. Teddy Roosevelt became president of the United States (he became the first president to travel outside the U.S. [to Panama]), and was known as "a steam engine in trousers!" The Victor Talking Machine Company was incorporated and developed 10,000 record dealers.

1902: Founding of the Ford Motor Company.

1903: The Wright brothers' first airplane flight.

1904: Many new foods were introduced at the St. Louis fair, including iced tea, the hamburger, and the ice cream cone. There was an anthropology exhibition inspired by Charles Darwin.

1905: Freud's psychoanalysis.

1906: San Francisco earthquake. The Auxetophone (an amplification system) was invented.

1907: The valve amplifier was developed.

1908: The Model T Ford was produced. The U.S. Congress passed the historic Copyright Law that provided published mechanical rights in recorded music.

1909: Marconi developed the wireless radio. Robert E. Peary reached the North Pole.

1910: More than $3 million was bet on the Jack Johnson–James Jeffries heavyweight-boxing match held in Reno, Nevada.

1911: The first electronic oscillator was produced. The year of the Mexican revolution.

1912: The *Titanic* sank.

1913: The Woolworth Building was constructed in New York. It was the world's tallest building at 60 stories!

1914: World War I broke out when British and Canadian forces battled German troops. Panama Canal, the "big ditch," was completed. European population grew from 50 million in 1890 to more than 300 million by 1914. Henry Ford's automobile plants produced 1,000 cars a day. Women were not allowed to vote.

1915: The *Lusitania* was sunk by a German submarine killing several American passengers. Einstein's theory of relativity. The Audion Piano, an electronic keyboard instrument to exploit the vacuum tube, was developed.

1916: The vibraphone was developed and manufactured by the Leedy Drum Company. The first jazz record was released.

1917: The U.S. entered World War I. Radio broadcasting for military purpose began. The Russian revolution began.

1918: The end of World War I: 1.8 million Germans were killed during the war; the Carnegie Endowment for International Peace announced that WWI had cost $337 trillion; a total of nearly 10 million people had died and 20 million were wounded during the war.

1919: Treaty of Versailles. The Neo-Bechstein-Flugel, an electronic piano, was manufactured by Bechstein and Siemens A & Halske in Germany. The Spanish Flu Pandemic, an unusually severe strain of the influenza virus, kills at least 25 million people worldwide.

BANDS FIRST ORGANIZED DURING
1900–1919

JACK "PAPA" LAINE

(Jack "Papa" Laine and His Orchestra). Born in New Orleans, Louisiana on September 21, 1873. George Vitelle Laine (aka: Jack "Papa" Laine) studied bass, saxophone, and drums in his early years. In 1888, he formed a band that specialized in playing "Shadow Rag" (written by Scott Joplin) and his band imitated other early Negro stomps. Prior to 1914, he led the Reliance Brass band, which included the cornetist Nick La Rocca. The Reliance Brass band was said to be the precursor to the Original Dixieland Jazz band, which was first fronted by Nick La Rocca. Laine's band claimed to be the first that played Ragtime music. When Laine was 77 years old, the New Orleans Jazz Club presented him with a certificate, which recognized him as the first White jazz musician. Laine was indeed a pionér in Big band history. He died in New Orleans on June 1, 1966.

ALPHONSE FLORISTAN PICOU

(Picou's Independence band) Born in New Orleans, Louisiana on October 10, 1878. Picou learned to play guitar by 1892, at the age of fourteen. He learned clarinet the following year. In 1894, he played in the Accordiana band and formed his own band in 1897, The Independence band. Records indicate that he played in the Oscar Duconge band in 1899 and the Excelsior band in 1900. In 1901, Picou joined the Olympia band led by Freddie Keppard. In the 1920s, in New Orleans he played with various bands, symphony orchestras, and small combos. Picou played with the Crescent City Orchestra in 1932 and went into retirement. Picou, coming out of retirement, recorded with Kid Rena in 1940 and in 1947 recorded with Papa Celestin. By 1960, he owned a bar and lived in the apartment over the bar. In 1961, he was still playing and spent much of his time performing with the Eureka Brass band in New Orleans, where he ultimately died on February 4, 1961.

EDWARD "KID" ORY

(Kid Ory's Original Creole Jazz band) Born in La Place, Louisiana on December 25, 1886. Ory is thought to be among the most famous New Orleans "tailgate" trombone players. When he was very young, he formed a four-piece "skiffle" orchestra and it was thought that Kid Ory's Sunshine Orchestra was the first Black New Orleans band to cut a record. Kid Ory played valve trombone in addition to slide trombone. He also played guitar, piano, banjo, bass violin, saxophone, clarinet, and trumpet. As a child, he built a banjo out of a cigar box, and by the age of ten learned to play banjo. When he was 13, he led his own band in his hometown of La Place, Louisiana and began to listen to many great musicians who toured through that area, including Buddy Bolden. As a teenager, he moved to New Orleans and organized a typical New Orleans brass band, which featured Joe "King" Oliver playing trumpet. Kid moved to the West Coast in 1919 where he remained for three years. Moving to Chicago, he formed a new band, which included Johnny St. Cyr on banjo, Johnny Dodds on clarinet, and Lil Hardin on piano. While in Chicago he recorded with Louis Armstrong's Hot Five and made the famous records *Muskrat Ramble* and *Heebie Jeebies* on Okeh Records. During 1929–30, he played with bands in Los Angeles, California and, at the end of 1930, quit the music business and opened a chicken ranch with his brother. For ten years he stayed out of music but in 1942 he joined Barney Bigard and his combo and, in 1943, played with Bunk Johnson and his combo. In 1944, Kid Ory formed a new band, which played for the Orson Welles broadcasts and, in 1946, was seen in a film with the Louis Armstrong Orchestra. In 1947, he appeared in the film *Crossfire* and, in 1950, the film *Mahogany Magic*. Ory won the All-Star Poll in 1951 and, in 1954, his original composition "Muskrat Ramble" was recorded by many artists, some featuring lyrics, which had been added to the piece. In 1956, Kid Ory appeared in the film *The Benny Goodman Story* prior to touring Europe that year. In 1957 he was featured at the Newport Jazz Festival in Rhode Island and again toured Europe. On January 23, 1973, Kid Ory died in Hawaii.

WILBUR C. SWEATMAN

(Wilbur C. Sweatman and His Orchestra) Born in Brunswick, Missouri on February 7, 1882. Wilbur Sweatman studied piano, violin, and clarinet and is credited with having organized the first dance band in 1912. He is remembered as the composer of "Old Folks Rag," "Boogie Rag," and "Down Home Rag." He was taught piano by his sister and taught himself violin and clarinet. He played in a circus band and with Mahara's Minstrels early in his career. In 1902, he organized an orchestra in Minneapolis, Minnesota. In 1910, he was music director at various theaters in Chicago and, in 1912, he led his own band at the Pekin Theater in Chicago. Sweatman was a songwriter and joined ASCAP in 1917. By 1922, he had a quasi-symphonic orchestra in New York; his young pianist was Edward Kennedy "Duke" Ellington. Other players in Sweatman's orchestra included Toby Hardwicke and Sonny Greer. Sweatman was thought of as the counterpart to Paul Whiteman in the Negro world. Sweatman died in New York City on March 9, 1961.

BUDDY BOLDEN

(Buddy Bolden and His Orchestra) Born in New Orleans, Louisiana in 1868. He was one of the first musicians who played the music we call Dixieland jazz although he was a barber by trade. By 1906, he was beginning to suffer periods of derangement, but continued playing until 1907 when he was committed to the Louisiana State Hospital. His last job was with the Allen Brass band, which played for funerals in and around New Orleans. He was a very popular band leader and at times led as many as seven bands in a single night traveling from one to the other playing his specialties which included "Funky Butt," "Take It Away," "Bucket's Got a Hole in It," and "Make Me a Pallet on the Floor." Bolden died in New Orleans, Louisiana on November 4, 1931.

OSCAR "PAPA" CELESTIN

(Oscar "Papa" Celestin's Tuxedo band) Born in Napoleonville, Louisiana on January 1884. Celestin traveled to New Orleans in 1906 where he played cornet. By 1908, he was playing with Henry Allen's Excelsior Brass band and, in 1910, led his own band, the Tuxedo band. Celestin was relatively inactive during the Depression years and worked in a shipyard during WWII. By 1947, he formed a band, which recorded for Deluxe Records. In 1953, he did a special presidential performance for Dwight D. Eisenhower. In 1954, the Jazz Foundation in New Orleans presented a bust of Oscar Celestin to the Delgado Museum commemorating his role as a jazz pionér. Celestin died in New Orleans, Louisiana on December 15, 1954.

JAMES REESE EUROPE

(Jim Europe and the Hellfighters) Born in Mobile, Alabama on February 22, 1881. When Europe was ten years old his family moved to Washington, D.C., where he took violin lessons. By 1904, he migrated to New York and directed an orchestra, which accompanied a show, *Shoo-Fly Regiment*, with which he traveled for three years. In 1909, he returned to New York, gave piano lessons, and organized a large stage band, which included 47 mandolins, 27 harp-guitars, 11 banjos, 8 violins, 10 pianos, and 1 saxophone. In 1912, he organized an 11-piece society orchestra, which appeared at the Clef Club, and, in 1915, his booking office processed $100,000 worth of contracts. In 1917, he enlisted in New York's Negro Regiment, the 15th Infantry. The group was known as the Hellfighters and was one of the best-known groups during WWI. After the war, they traveled from Europe to New York where they continued to perform. Jim Europe died on May 14, 1919 at the age of 40. He was buried with full military honors.

CHARLES A. PRINCE

(Charlie Prince and His Orchestra) Born in 1869. He made many recordings for Columbia Records, recording such tunes as "Poet and Peasant Overture," "On the Beautiful Blue Danube," "March of the Sharpshooters," "You Splash Me and I'll Splash You," "Harrigan's Reel," "Dodola," "White Cockade," and "Afghanistan." He also recorded children's songs, including "Two Little Tots," "Whistling Rufus," and "The Boys and the Birds," among others. During his lifetime, Charles Prince conducted the Columbia Records house band and recorded during the 1910s and '20s. Prince died in 1937.

CHARLIE ELGAR

(Charlie Elgar and His Orchestra) Born on June 13, 1885. Elgar was a leader and violinist, a classically trained musician, and led an old New Orleans band. The Elgar band played at the Tuxedo Dance Hall in New Orleans and his band appeared at the Fountain Inn in Chicago in 1911. He later led his band at the Savoy Ballroom and the Dreamland Ballroom in Chicago. His band was comprised of members with considerable talent and included Darnell Howard and Cliffor King, clarinet and alto saxophone; William Neeley, flute and tenor saxophone; Joe Sulder and William Randall, trumpets; Harry Swift, trombone; Bert Hall, euphonium; William Shelby, banjo and guitar; William Gossette, piano and organ; Walter Wright, bass; Leroy Bradshaw, drums, xylophone, and marimba; and Richard Curry, drums. After WWI, he became active in the union movement and began to book bands. Elgar died in 1973.

EARL DABNEY

(Earl Dabney and His Orchestra) The Dabney Orchestra was a Dixieland jazz-type band and played at Flo Ziegfeld's Roof Club in New York City in 1912.

ART HICKMAN

(Art Hickman and His Orchestra) Born in 1886. Hickman studied piano, and started his first band around 1913 in San Francisco. Prior to the Hickman band dances had been impromptu affairs. The theme song for the Hickman Orchestra was "Rose Room." He formed his first band to entertain the San Francisco Seals baseball team at their spring training camp. He then entered the St. Francis Hotel in San Francisco where he worked six nights a week. By 1915, he played at the San Francisco World's Fair. While playing at the St. Francis Hotel, Flo Ziegfeld invited the band to come to New York in 1919 to play at the Biltmore Hotel and the Ziegfeld Roof and, by 1920, they played at the *Ziegfeld Follies*. The band returned to the St. Francis Hotel in San Francisco during the later part of 1920. At that time he sent a second band to London, which played at the Roof Garden the Criterion Restaurant, with the title Art Hickman's New York London Five. In 1921, Hickman's band played at the Coconut Grove in Los Angeles. The personnel of the Hickman Orchestra included Ray Hoback, Hank Miller, Lou Marcasie, Earl Burtnett, Nick Noolan, Ed Fitzpatrick, Dick Winfree,

Forrest Ray, Juan Ramos, Roy Fox, Jess Fitzpatrick, Bela Spiller, Frank Ellis, Mark Mojica, Steve Douglas, Vic King, Ben Black, Bert Ralton, Clyde Doerr, Walt Rosener, Bert Ralton, and Fred Cofferman. Shortly thereafter, Hickman retired from the band business and turned his orchestra over to Frank Ellis. It is believed that Hickman led the first dance band to have ever played onstage in a Broadway show. The band was known as America's First Big Band. Hickman died in San Francisco, California in 1930. He was 44 years old.

ORIGINAL DIXIELAND JAZZ BAND

The ODJB was first formed in 1914 in New Orleans and was led by drummer Jerry Stein. In a few months, the band was booked into the Chicago Schiller Cafe. Soon after the opening, four of the sidemen left the band to join a group formed by Nick LaRocca. LaRocca was born in New Orleans in 1889 and had played with the "Papa" Laine band where he learned music. They met with great success and were eventually booked into New York's Reisenweber's Restaurant at Eighth Avenue and Columbus Circle. On the second floor of the building was located Reisenweber's Restaurant where the band played; on the third floor was Earl Coleman's orchestra that catered to dancers. Sophie Tucker was the featured singer with the Coleman group. The members of the ODJB listened intensively to the Joe "King" Oliver's Creole Jazz Band. Later in New York, the ODJB was the first to record the new jazz sounds at Victor's Studio. In 1917, they cut "Livery Stable Blues" and "The Original Dixieland One Step"; the record was an immediate smash hit. All of the top musicians in New York went to hear the Original Dixieland Jazz Band and they played the following tunes over and over every night: "At the Jazz Band Ball," "Sensation Rag," "Jazz Me Blues," "Tiger Rag," "Ja Da, Indiana," "After You've Gone," and "For Me and My Gal." Among the many famous people who listened to the band was the famous bandleader Vincent Lopez who said that "Dark Town Strutter's Ball" was his favorite tune that they played. In 1919, the ODJB sailed for London where they were proclaimed a big success. Among the people working at Reisenweber's Restaurant at that time was songwriter Irving Berlin (who wrote poetry on his tuxedo shirt cuffs), singer Sophie Tucker, and Al Jolson. Nick LaRocca remained in music until 1938 when he became a building contractor. His son, who still resides in New Orleans, carries on the tradition. The Original Dixieland Jazz Band stills plays as of this writing.

TOM BROWN

(Brown's Dixieland Jass band) Born in New Orleans, Louisiana on June 3, 1888. Tom Brown brought his band to Chicago from New Orleans in 1915. It was a Dixieland band and was originally called the Thomas Brown Orchestra; later, Brown's Dixieland Orchestra. The word "jass" connotated the "red-light" district activity. Trombonist Alcide "Yellow" Nunez who had been with the Original Dixieland Jazz band was the trombonist on Brown's Dixieland Jazz Band. Brown died in New Orleans on March 25, 1958.

WILL MARION COOK

(Will Marion Cook and His Orchestra) Born in Washington, D.C. on January 27, 1869. Cook was a violinist and composer who studied at Oberlin College and later traveled to Europe. He began composing for stage shows, which featured the great vaudevillian Bert Williams and, in 1898, composed the music for the all-Negro show *Clorindy* that opened in New York City and London. During 1919, he toured the United States and Europe with his group, the Southern Syncopaters Orchestra, which included such noted musicians as Sidney Bechet and included 16 banjo players. Will Marion Cook composed tunes such as "Mammy, Mandy Lou" and "I'm Coming Virginia." He died in New York City on July 19, 1944.

CHARLIE CREATH

(Charlie Creath and His Orchestra) Born in Ironton, Missouri on December 30, 1890. Creath was a trumpet player and led an orchestra, which was called by Andy Kirk "one of the incubators from which came the sidemen for a lot of great bands." The size of Creath's bands varied from time to time but remained viable from 1916 to 1940. The band made several records on the Okeh label. He is best remembered for the smaller group that he fronted which included Creath, trumpet; Charles Lawson, trombone; Margie Creath (Creath's sister), piano; Willie Rollins and Sammy Long, C-melody saxophones; and Zutty Singleton, drums. Creath died in 1951 at the age of 61.

TED LEWIS

(Ted Lewis and His Orchestra) Born on June 6, 1890 in Circleville, Ohio. Lewis was the son of a haberdasher. Ted Lewis (né: Theodore Leopold Friedman) was proficient on the clarinet during his teen years. His family wanted him to be a businessman but he chose music as his profession. In 1906, at the age of 16, he began working in vaudeville. While working in vaudeville, he teamed with a vaudevillian named Lewis and an erroneous billing listed the team as Lewis and Lewis. Ted Lewis thought it was a good idea and used that name for the remainder of his career. He eventually moved to New York City and continued to work in vaudeville stages and clubs. In 1916, as part of his comedy-vaudeville act, he formed his first band called Ted Lewis and His Nut Band. In 1917, he got a job playing clarinet in pianist Earl Fuller's band and got a chance to hear the Original Dixieland Jazz Band at Reisenweber's Restaurant and became enthralled with this new music. The restaurant rectors in New York City hired the Fuller band to lure customers away from their competitor, Reisenweber's Restaurant. Lewis did not have a natural voice but was able to sell a song and began to wear a disheveled top hat and use the catchy phrase, "Is everybody happy?" In 1918, he opened his own club with his own band. Following the flop of that idea, he went back on stage in a show called *The Greenwich Village Follies* and then financed his own production, *The Ted Lewis Follies*. The great producer Flo Ziegfeld hired Lewis to appear in *The Midnight Follies* at the New Amsterdam Theater's Rooftop Cafe. Lewis also appeared in the revue *Artists and Models*. In 1919, Columbia Records signed Ted Lewis and released his first single, "Wond'ring." "Blues My Naughty Sweety Gives to Me" was on the flip side of the record. In 1920, Lewis made the first recording of "When My Baby Smiles at Me," which was a big hit and became his theme song. Throughout the '20s and '30s, Lewis was famous and continued to lead his own band. Columbia Records joined Ted Lewis and Fats Waller together to record "Royal Garden Blues" and "Dallas Blues" and the Lewis band backed Sophie Tucker as she sang "Some of These Days" which became a million-selling record in the early days of radio and phonograph. When he visited England, his band played at the Hippodrome and the Kit Kat Club in London and the top venues in Europe. Columbia Records placed his top-hat silhouette on their record label. Ted called his own clarinet sound "gas pipe." In 1928, George Brunies, an ex–New Orleans Rhythm King trombonist, joined the Lewis band and, in 1929, famous cornetist Muggsy Spanier and Don Murray (reeds) were added. Some of the sidemen in the Ted Lewis Orchestra were George Brunis, Manny Klien, Harry Raderman, Walter Kahn, Dick Reynolds, Vic Carpenter, John Lucas, Frank Ross, Don Murray, Sol Klein, Tony Gerhardt, Nat Lobovosky, Sammy Blank, Sam Shapiro, Jack Aaronson, Hymie Wolfson, Al Podova, Harold Diamond, Moe

Dale, Jack Teagarden, and Rudy Van Gelder. Lewis could afford to pay his men well and did so as his December 1929 contract with Columbia guaranteed him $42,000 plus royalties on each record sold for two years. In 1929, while they were making their first film, reedman Don Murray was killed in an automo-

bile accident. His replacement was Frank Teschemacher, who would also die in a later automobile accident. Teschemacher's replacement in 1930 was Jimmy Dorsey. Songs such as "Aunt Hagar's Blues" and "Sobbin' Blues, Parts One and Two" were recorded in 1930. Shortly thereafter, Lewis announced his retirement. Columbia Records seduced him back in 1931, and replacing clarinetist Jimmy Dorsey was Benny Goodman. Lewis's records no longer sold as well as they had during the '20s. The Depression made it impossible for many people to own record players and Lewis was beginning to seem quite corny. In 1933, Lewis signed a contract with Decca Records but failed to meet his previous success. During the '30s, the Lewis band played the *Valspar Paint Program* and the *Merritt Beer Show*. In 1945, he hosted the *Coca-Cola Spotlight Show* but sound alone would not save Ted Lewis. He had to be seen wearing that crushed top hat to appreciate his corniness. During the '40s he appeared in movies such as *Hold That Ghost* with Abbott and Costello and the Columbia Pictures feature *Is Everybody Happy?* In the early '50s, he recorded "Blue Skies," "My Blue Heaven," and other tunes for Decca and, in the late '50s, recorded some dance music for the RKO label. In 1967, he was still wearing his trademark top hat at the Desert Inn in Las Vegas—50 years after he first played publicly. Ted Lewis was a prolific songwriter penning, such hits as "When My Baby Smiles at Me," "While We Danced 'Til Dawn," "Show Me the Way," "Walking Around in a Dream," and "Fair One." He died in New York City on August 25, 1971.

WILLARD ROBISON

(Willard Robison and His Orchestra) Born in Shelbina, Missouri on September 18, 1894. Robison formed his first band in 1917 called the Deep River Orchestra and toured featuring spirituals and Negro folk music. In the '20s, he recorded, singing and playing piano with his orchestra, and was heard on the radio with the show *Deep River Music*. In the mid '30s he had his own radio show, *Plantation Echoes*, and remained active in the '40s and '50s. Robison wrote a number of important songs, including "Old Folks," "A Cottage for Sale," and "Peaceful Valley." Willard Robison died in Peekskill, New York on June 24, 1968.

PAUL SPECHT

(Paul Specht and His Orchestra) Born in 1895. Specht began in Detroit in 1916 with a six-piece band. Specht was a violinist who is remembered as a true pionér in the dance band world. He soon enlarged the combo to 12 pieces and named the six-piece group within the 12 pieces the Georgians. Many famous musicians began as sidemen in the Specht orchestra, including Artie Shaw, Russ Morgan, Charlie Spivak, Bob Chester, Arthur Schutt, Orville Knapp, and Chauncey Morehouse. Among other initiatives, Specht's band was the first to be heard live on radio broadcasting on station WWJ in Detroit, Michigan in the late '20s. He wrote many songs, including "Moonlight on the Ganges," "Who Takes Care of the Caretaker's Daughter?" and others, which were recorded for Columbia and Okeh Records. Specht's theme songs were "Sweetheart Time" and "Evening Star." The band made at least one European tour. In the '40s, Specht formed a booking agency and discontinued leading his band. He died in New York in April 1954. He was 59 years old.

FRED WARING

(Fred Waring and His Pennsylvanians) Born in Tyrone, Pennsylvania on June 9, 1900. When Waring graduated from Penn State University in the '20s he started his own orchestra. Soon thereafter the band recorded for Columbia and Victor record companies, featuring Fred's brother Tom who sang and played piano. Fred, who had always been partial to vocal music, started his own glee club. Some of the participants in Waring's early glee clubs included movie stars Rosemary and Pricilla Lane and choral directors Robert

Shaw and Kay Thompson. Toward the end of his career in 1966 Fred had a 50th-anniversary party. The guests paid tribute to Fred Waring—a man who successfully conducted his own group, the Pennsylvanians, for 50 years, published the monthly magazine, *The Music Journal*, ran the 600-acre Shawné Inn in Pennsylvania, and also invented and sold the Waring blender. Fred Waring died on July 29, 1984. He was 84 years old.

W.C. HANDY

(Handy's Orchestra of Memphis) Born on November 16, 1973 in Florence, Alabama. Although Handy led a number of big bands, we remember him most as the composer of tunes such as "St. Louis Blues," "Beale Street Blues," and others. He is known as "The Father of the Blues." One of his bands, Handy's Orchestra of Memphis, recorded many records for Columbia Records. In the late '50s, though totally blind, Handy continued to run his music publishing business. In 1958, at the age of 85, Handy died.

VINCENT LOPEZ

(Vincent Lopez and His Hotel Taft Orchestra) Born in Brooklyn, New York on December 30, 1895. Lopez studied for the priesthood at an early age but decided to choose music as his profession. The pianist secured a job at the Taft Hotel in the early '20s. Since he played the dinner hour, he had to hire musicians who didn't play during the early evening hours. The theme song of the bands fronted by Lopez was "Nola." In New York he subcontracted several bands that played under his name. He also ran his own nightclub for three years, the Casa Lopez. Lopez had two sisters from Michigan (Marion and Elizabeth Thornburg) who sang with his band under the names Marion and Betty Hutton. Marion eventually sang with the Glenn Miller band and, of course, Betty Hutton became a star in her own right fronting her own band. Famous sidemen with the Lopez Orchestra included Jimmy Dorsey, Xavier

Cugat, and Tommy Dorsey. The band recorded for Bluebird, Okeh, Brunswick, and Paramount Records. Vincent Lopez died in Miami, Florida from a stroke in 1975 at the age of 80.

GEORGE OLSEN

(George Olsen and His Orchestra) Born on March 18, 1893 in Portland, Oregon. Olsen formed his first band while attending the University of Michigan. After graduation, Olsen took the band to New York where they played in vaudeville shows and in the theater pits for various musicals. The band featured the Williams Sisters doing the vocals. The band's theme songs were "Beyond the Blue Horizon" and "Music of Tomorrow." Around 1932, the George Olsen Orchestra was the official band for Jack Benny's first radio show, which was sponsored by Canada Dry. Some of the prominent sidemen on the band included Red Nichols, Orville Knapp, Leighton Noble, Fred MacMurray, Rudy Wiedoeft, and George Henkel. During the late '20s and early '30s, the band's personnel changed and two new singers, Fran Frey and Ethel Shutta, were added. Frey, a male vocalist, went on to become director of a radio station in

Chicago. Ethel quickly became Mrs. George Olsen, until divorce eventually broke up the relationship. Ethel Shutta was seen in Stephen Sondheim's *Follies* in New York in the '70s. Olsen retired as bandleader, started his own restaurant in New Jersey, using his own recordings as background music. He died in Paramus, New Jersey on March 18, 1971.

CHARLIE STRAIGHT

(The Charlie Straight Band) Born on January 16, 1891 in Chicago, Illinois. Straight was a piano player and led a New Orleans jazz group. The band appeared at the Rainbow Gardens in Chicago in 1911. Straight wrote the theme song "Mockingbird Rag" and had recording affiliations with Paramount and Brunswick records. A number of famous musicians worked with Straight over the years, including Bix Bierderbeck, Ike Williams, and Bob Strong. Other sidemen who worked with the Charlie Straight band were Johnny Jacobs, Jack Davis, Ralph Morris, Don Morgan, Joe Gist, Dale Skinner, Frank Stoddard, Randy Miller, Bob Conselman, Gene Caffarelli, Frank Shylvano, Wally Preissing, and Guy Carey. During the late '20s, his music was aired over Chicago's radio stations. Straight claimed that he started the style called swing, which became so popular during the '30s. Straight was killed September 21, 1940, when a car struck him in Chicago.

PAUL BIESE

(Paul Biese and His Novelty Orchestra) Biese was a tenor saxophone player and a highly regarded musician during his active years. His band played at some of the best places in Chicago, including the Edgewater Beach Hotel, Marigold Gardens, and the Bismarck Hotel. The band also worked several seasons in New York City and was active during the late 1910s and early '20s. The band's personnel included Ralph Williams, banjo; Arnold Johnson, piano; Lou Goldwasser, drums; Harry "Rags" Vrooman, trumpet; Lloyd Barber, trombone; and Paul Biese, tenor saxophone/leader. The band's specialties were "Carol," "I'm So Sympathetic," and "Yellow Dog Blues."

PERCY HUMPHREY

(The Crescent City Joymakers) Born on January 13, 1905. The Joymakers was a New Orleans orchestra, which played from the late teens to the early '20s. Percy played trumpet. His brothers, Willie and Earl, were also musicians who played clarinet and trombone respectively. Willie was born in 1900 and died in 1944; Earl was born in 1902 and died in 1971. In addition to the Crescent City Joymakers, Percy Humphrey also had an orchestra called the Eureka Brass band and in his later years Percy played at the Preservation Hall and Palm Court Café in New Orleans.

JIMMY DURANTE

(Jimmy Durante's New Orleans Jazz Band) Born in New York City on February 10, 1893. Durante led the New Orleans Jazz Band although he is thought of today as being the great vaudevillian and character in radio, television, and motion pictures. He is not really remembered as a person who started his career as a Dixieland musician in New York City. Around 1911, Durante was playing piano in a New York City club, billed as Ragtime Jimmy. By 1917, he heard the Original Dixieland Jazz Band at Reisenweber's in New York City. At the time he was booked in Harlem at a club called Alamo's. He got the ODJB to appear with him for a few nights. Dixieland was sweeping the city and the world and Jimmy, with his friend Johnny Stein, formed a novelty group called Durante's Jazz and Novelty band that played at the Alamo Club. In 1918, Okeh Records had them record two sides under the name of the New Orleans Jazz band and a few months later they recorded two more tunes for Gennett Records. This time they used the name Original New Orleans Jazz Band. In 1920, they recorded again for Gennett; this time using the name Jimmy Durante's Jazz band. In 1921, the singer, Mamie Smith recorded "Let's Agree to Disagree," a tune written by Jimmy Durante and Chris Smith. All during the early '20s, Durante played piano and recorded with several jazz bands, including Eddie and Sugar Lou's Orchestra, Phil Napoleon's Original Memphis Five, Ladd's Black Acesa, Eddie and Sugar Lou's Orchestra, and Lenin's Southern Serenaders. By the mid-'20s, Durante became a part of Clayton, Jackson, and Durante, a comedic vaudeville music team. Near the end of the '20s, his role in the show *Jumbo*, which was playing in New York City, made him a star. In the early '30s, he began acting in movies and also became a popular radio star. On one of his radio shows, he joked about writing a symphony that he would call "Inka Dinka Doo," and in 1934, he recorded a tune with that title, which became his theme song. He was an all-around entertainer and a good ragtime pianist who was influenced by Scott Joplin. He was one of the true pioneers of jazz in acoustic recording and had one of the most successful careers imaginable. He covered the rags era, the jazz era, records, vaudeville, Broadway shows, radio, and television. Jimmy Durante died on January 29, 1980. Ethel Merman and other great stars paid him homage by attending his funeral.

FREDDIE KEPPARD

(Freddie Keppard and His Olympia band) Born in New Orleans, Louisiana in 1889. By 1907, the cornetist played with the Olympia Brass Band and, in 1913, joined the Original Creole Band and went to Chicago in 1914 with the band. He assumed the leadership of the band in 1915 to 1916 and took it to New York City. By 1918, the Original Creole Band disbanded and Keppard went to Chicago and formed the Freddie Keppard Orchestra. He later played with Erskine Tate at the Vendome Theater. Among some of the musicians who played with Freddie Keppard in the Olympia band were Johnny Dodds, clarinet; Arthur Campbell, piano; Jasper Taylor, washboard and woodblocks (he also composed "Stockyard Strut"); and Papa Charlie Jackson, vocals. Freddie Keppard was considered one of the major musicians playing jazz in New Orleans before WWI. Keppard died in Chicago on July 15, 1933.

FLOYD RAY

(Floyd Ray and His Orchestra) Born on July 19, 1909. His first band was called Floyd Ray and the Harlem Dictators or just the Harlem Dictators. From 1918 to 1930, the band played at New York's famous Apollo Theater and the Cottonwood Club. Around 1925, he changed the name to Floyd Ray and His Orchestra and they played until 1950. During the tenure, there were three female singers and it is said that the Andrew Sisters derived their style from these three singers. Their names were Vern Whittaker, Willie Lee Floyd, and Ivy Jones. The male vocalist was Joe Alexander. Some of the tunes that they featured were "Coming on with the Blues" and "Three O'Clock in the Morning." A few of the people who played in the Ray band included Jimmy Lunceford, Dizzy Gillespie, Sir Charles

Thompson, and Joe Liggins. Between 1940 and 1950, the band played in a competition held in Los Angeles at the Hollywood Paladium competing against the Benny Goodman band. Ray played saxophone and bass and was an arranger and songwriter. During the '50s and '60s, Ray worked as a record promoter for King Records. In the early '60s, he opened a record store named Pico Records in Los Angeles. In the '80s, his music was compiled on the Golden Era Records. Ray died on November 15, 1985.

ERSKINE TATE

(Erskine Tate and His Band) Born in Memphis, Tennessee on December 19, 1895. Tate was a violinist. From 1918 to 1927, he played at the Vendome Theater, which fronted on State Street in Chicago midway between Thirty-first and Thirty-second streets. The theater was a movie palace with 2,700 seats. The band was called Erskine Tate and His Vendome Syncopaters. They played twice nightly—an hour long, each show between various feature films. It is said that they opened with light classical overtures and ended with jazz, featuring solos by various members of the band. By 1924, he had augmented the instrumentation from 12 to 15 pieces and during the band's life the personnel included Freddie Keppard, Louis Armstrong, Earl Hines, Fats Waller, Omar Simeon, and Buster Bailey. In 1926, he moved to the Metropolitan Theater, where he stayed until 1930. Tate was active until the mid '30s, when he became a music teacher and discontinued his big band.

PAUL WHITEMAN

(Paul Whiteman and His Orchestra) Born in 1887. Whiteman was known as "The King of Jazz"; his theme song was "Rhapsody in Blue." Included in the personnel in his various bands was Bing Crosby. Whiteman's father, Wilberforce Whiteman, was superintendent of music education in the Denver, Colorado public school system, where he was responsible for developing music talent and intro-

ducing other young people to music as well. Among his students were Jimmie Lunceford and other musicians. Whiteman formed his first band in 1918 for a venue in San Francisco but later became more active in the Los Angeles area. In 1920, his band began its Victor recordings and his fame became national. In 1923, a music instrument company called him "The King of Jazz," as part of a promotional event, and that title remained with him until his death. Whiteman was a 28-year-old viola player out of a San Francisco orchestra when he started his band in 1915; he was enraptured by the sound of jazz and wanted to play it. He joined the John Tate band but was fired by Tate after Tate discovered that Whiteman couldn't play jazz. While in Tate's band, he met pianist Ferde Grofe. In 1917, Whiteman tried to join the U.S. Army, but was turned down because of his weight; sometime later the U.S. Navy appointed him a band director. In 1918, he formed the first Paul Whiteman Orchestra for the Fairmont Hotel in San Francisco and then played dates in and around Los Angeles before settling in at the Hotel Alexandria in 1919. He picked up Ferde Grofe, whom he had met on the Tate band and Grofe played piano for him for three years before he became the band's full-time composer-arranger. Pianists who played after Grofe were Ray Turner, Roy Bargy, and Lenny Hayton. The Whiteman Orchestra was said to be the first to popularize arrangements; to utilize full reed and brass sections; to travel to Europe; to play in vaudeville; to feature a girl singer (Mildred Bailey); and to feature a vocal trio (The Rhythm Boys: Harry Barris, Al Rinker, and Bing Crosby). In 1924, Paul Whiteman introduced George Gershwin's "Rhapsody in Blue" at the Aeolian Concert Hall in New York City. A few of the various sidemen to have played in Paul Whiteman's band include Henry Busse, Ferde Grofe, Roy Matson, Bill Murray, Ray Tuner, Matty Malneck, Red Nichols, Jimmy Dorsey, Tommy Dorsey, Bix Biederbeck, Hoagy Carmicheal, Steve Brown, Lenny Hayton, Jack and Charlie Teagarten, Billy Butterfield, and others. Famous vocalists included the Rhythm Boys, Mildred Bailey, Red McKenzie, Johnny Mercer, Mable Todd, and Dollie Mitchel. The band played on a number of sponsored radio shows, including *The George Burns and Gracie Allen Show*, *The Kraft Music Hall*, and *The Old Gold Cigarette Show*. They appeared in several motion pictures, including *Rhapsody in Blue*, *Strike Up the Band*, and *The King of Jazz*. The Whiteman Orchestra had recording affiliations with Signature, Decca, Capitol, Columbia, and Victor records. Whiteman died in Doylestown, Pennsylvania on December 29, 1967, of a heart attack. He was 77 years old.

BERNIE CUMMINS

(Bernie Cummins and His Orchestra) Bernie Cummins started his first band in 1919. He was a former prizefighter and drummer. His band recorded frequently for such labels as Bluebird, Decca, Vocalion, Victor, Columbia, Brunswick, and Gennett. The band was well known for its live performances. They played many times at the Biltmore Hotel in New York City, the Hotel New Yorker, the Trianon, Blackstone, Aragon, and the Edgewater Beach Hotel in Chicago. The singer for the band was Bernie's younger brother, Walter. Other singers included Dorothy Crane and the Sophisticates, Scotte Marsh, and Belle Mann. In the late 1950s, Cummins took his band to Las Vegas, where he played until his retirement in 1959. Some of the famous sidemen who played in the Bernie Cummins Orchestra included Fred Benson, Chuck Campbell, Wally Smith, Charlie Callas, Paul Roberts, and his brother, Walter Cummins. The Cummins band played on radio shows, including the Fitch bandwagon and the Coca-Cola Spotlight Dance Program. The theme song of the band was "Dark Eyes." Cummins retired in Florida in 1959.

ARNOLD JOHNSON

(Arnold Johnson and His Paramount Hotel Orchestra) Born on March 23, 1893 in Chicago, Illinois. He began his career at the age of 14, playing piano in a Chinese restaurant in Chicago and later studied at the Chicago Music College and The American Conservatory of Music. As a songwriter, he wrote "Don't Hang Your Dreams on a Rainbow," "Good-bye Blues," "All for You," "Sweetheart," "Does Your Heart Beat for Me," "O," and Teardrops." He recorded for Brunswick and Vocalion records. Before leading his first band, Johnson worked in vaudeville playing piano as accompanist and soloist. He was also associated with Rudy Wiedoft in a New York venture called the Frisco Jazz band. He worked primarily in New York and the Chicago area with his own band. When he left music, he sold real estate for a while. Johnson is best known for his last dance band, which he led in the '20s, and he appeared in several Broadway musicals, including the *George White Scandals*. In the early '30s, he became a radio musical director and producer. Some of his notable sidemen included reed players Pete Pumigilo and Danny Polo; Scrappy Lambert, singer; Bob Chester, trumpet; and Vic Burton, drums. He also featured, from time to time, Harold Arlen, pianist and singer. After selling real estate in Florida, he returned to music in the late '20s and his band appeared in two Broadway musicals, *George White Scandals* and *Greenwich Village Follies*, in 1928. During WWII, his bands entertained U.S. troops in Europe.

ISHAM JONES

(Isham Jones and His Orchestra) Born January 31, 1894 in Coaltown, Ohio. He formed his first band when he was 20 years old and toured Michigan, where he played for many dances. He then went to Chicago where he studied and secured bookings for his band in several top places, including the Rainbow Gardens and the Green Mill. He then played at the College Inn for six years. One of his famous sidemen was Woody Herman who played saxophone and sang with the band; Gordon Jenkins was the pianist and arranger. Jenkins later became Frank Sinatra's music director. At that time, the Music Corporation of America (MCA) was just getting its start in Chicago and Isham Jones was one of the first bandleaders to sign a contract with them. They introduced him and broadened his operations through tours of many major cities throughout the country. Eventually, he made a trip to England where he found many fans who had heard his records and were waiting to hear the band live. Isham Jones was a saxophone player who apparently played it very well and he hired many well-known musicians to play in his band. He recorded for Brunswick, Victor, and Decca. In 1936, he retired due to poor health after playing his last engagement in Memphis, Tennessee. Within a few months, he was back in New York playing again with another band and competing with one of his former star musicians, Woody Herman, who was playing in another New York location with a band built around key men from the first Jones orchestra. Some of the outstanding sidemen were Louis Panico, Gordon Jenkins, Jiggs Novle, Saxie Mansfield, Walter Yoder, Sonny Lee, Al Elridridge, and Joe Bishop. His theme songs were "You're Just a Dream Come True" and "Spain." He again retired in the '40s for a short time before he returned to the music business and remained active until the big band decline after WWII. Jones wrote many popular tunes, including "It Had to Be You," "I'll See You in My Dreams," "The One I Love Belongs to Somebody Else," "There Is No Greater Love," "You've Got Me Crying Again," "On the Alamo," "You're Just a Dream Come True," and "Swinging Down the Lane." He died on October 19, 1956 in Hollywood, California.

FATE MARABLE

(Fate Marable and His Orchestra) Born on December 2, 1890 in Paducah, Kentucky. Marable was considered one of the great riverboat bandleaders. The riverboats operated on the Mississippi River and traveled out of New Orleans and St. Louis and featured such outstanding musicians as Louis Armstrong, Alphonso Trent, Dewey Jackson, and Charlie Creeth among many others. Marable went to St. Louis with a ten-piece band in 1919 called the Metropolitan Jazz Band, which included Louis Armstrong, Louis Brasheer, George "Pops" Foster, Norman Mason, Johnny Dodds, and Johnny St. Cyr. Marable started his career before WWI and remained active into the '40s. Marable was a pianist and played steam calliope. One of his outstanding bands included Henry Kimball, tuba; Sydney Desvinges, trumpet; Harvery Lengford, trombone; Barnett Bradley, violin; Walter Thomas, Norman Mason, Bert Bailey, saxophones; Willie Foster, banjo; and Zutty Singleton, drums. The Marable band played stock arrangements; however, Marable rearranged these stocks, which greatly enhanced the bands sound. Around 1923, Marable played on the Streffus Steamer "JS," which made day trips daily from St. Louis, Missouri to Alton,

Illinois and back. The boat contained a beautiful dance floor. Marable recorded several records for Okeh Records in New Orleans. In 1924, he cut "Frankie and Johnny" using drummer Zutty Singleton. Marable died in 1947.

GEORGE MORRISON

(George Morrison and His Orchestra) Born on September 9 1891 in Fayette, Missouri. The George Morrison Orchestra began between 1918 and 1920. His band toured from Arizona to New York. In 1920, the band played at the Albany Hotel. Personnel included future stars such as Andy Kirk and Hattie McDaniel. Other personnel included Eugene Montgomery, drums; Desdemona Davis and Mary Colston, piano; Cuthbert Byrd and Andy Kirk, saxophone; Leo Davis and Frank Handy, trumpet; Lee Morrison (brother of George), banjo; Edward Caldwell, trombone; and George Morrison, violin.

NEW ORLEANS RHYTHM KINGS

Founded in 1919, the New Orleans Rhythm Kings played in Chicago at the Friar's Inn. They recorded for Gennett Records. In 1917, the Original Dixieland Jazz Band in Chicago became an international success. Four years later, in 1921, the New Orleans Rhythm Kings opened on Chicago's Northside at the Friar's Inn and included Paul Mares, trumpet and leader; Leon Rappolo, clarinet; Steve Brown, bass; Lew Black, banjo; George Brunies, trombone; Frank Snyder, drums; and Elmer Schoebel, piano and arranger. Schoebel was the only member of the band who could read and write music. He composed a number of tunes, including "Nobody's Sweetheart," "Farewell Blues," "Bugle Call Rag," and "Tin Roof Blues." They played at the Friar's Inn for two years. By 1922, they were using the name Friar's Club Orchestra. By 1923, they changed the name back to New Orleans Rhythm Kings. They had a New Orleans style of upbeat, peppy ensemble playing, which inspired a number of very young Austin high school students, including Jimmy and Dick McPartland, Bud Freeman, Frankie Teschmacher, and Jimmy Lanigan. This group of students listened to the recordings of the New Orleans Rhythm Kings and taught themselves to play by emulating the recordings. They later played under the name of the Austin Blue Friars. Other young musicians in Chicago who learned by listening to this group included Benny Goodman, Gene Krupa, Mezz Mezzrow,

Joe Sullivan, Art Hodes, and Eddie Condon. At that time, they were only one of two American groups widely known by their initials ODJB (Original Dixieland Jazz band) and NORK (New Orleans Rhythm Kings). The only one who remained in Chicago and stayed active was George Brunies. The rest returned to New Orleans.

JOSEPH "KING" OLIVER

(King Oliver's Creole Jazz band) Born in Abend, Louisiana in 1885. In 1907, he began playing with the Melrose Brass Band. In 1912, he played with the Olympia band until around 1916 when he formed his first band. In 1917, he played at the 25 Cafe and began calling himself "King" Oliver. By 1918, he had moved to Chicago and worked as a sideman there until 1919. In 1922, he formed his King Oliver Creole Jazz Band with Louis Armstrong. Armstrong later told the world jokingly, "Oliver was my true mentor." In 1923, the Creole Jazz band was comprised of the following sidemen: Louis Armstrong, Lil Hardin, Honore Dutrey, Bill Johnson, and Johnny Dodds. In 1916, King Oliver and His Dixie Syncopators included George Field, trombone; Luis Russell, piano; Paul Barbarin, drums; Johnny Dodds, clarinet; Bobby Shoffner, trumpet; Joe "King" Oliver, trumpet and cornet; Albert Nicholas, clarinet and alto saxophone; Bert Cobbs, tuba; Darnell Howard, alto saxophone and clarinet; and Bud Scott, banjo. At that time, most musicians in Chicago would visit the club to hear King Oliver and his band play. In 1927, King Oliver was offered a job in New York City to play at the Cotton Club. He turned it down and after that his career began to disintegrate. King Oliver wrote "Sugarfoot Stomp," "Canal Street Blues," "West End Blues," and "Doctor Jazz." He recorded for Vocalion, Brunswick, Victor, Columbia, Okeh, Gennett, and Paramount records. His health started to fail and during the Depression, which started in 1929, the club business slowed down and the Creole Jazz Band was in Kansas City with no jobs booked. In the 1930s, King Oliver went into the fruit and vegetable business in Savannah, Georgia. He later worked as a pool hall janitor and had high blood pressure. In 1938, he died in Georgia. His body was returned to New York City and buried at the Woodlawn Cemetery in the Bronx.

PETE PONTRELLI

(Pete Pontrelli and His Orchestra) Pontrelli began with his first band in Los Angeles in 1919. He started as a barber but was always a musician and became a bandleader, beginning with a five-piece band in 1919. The band eventually grew to 15 pieces. Pontrelli was a saxophone player and was very popular in Southern California. He played for four years at the Palace Ballroom in Ocean Park and broadcast over radio station KTM. He then played for five years at the Palace Inn in downtown Los Angeles, broadcasting over CBS. He won an award from the Fox Theater chain, presented by Edward Arnold, for having the best dance band in 1937. In 1944, he became the operator of the Figuerora Ballroom, ran the operation, and featured his own band. He ran the ballroom for fourteen years. In the '60s, he worked at Myron's Ballroom in Los Angeles with a seven-piece band. When he turned 80 years old, he was still working in Southern California.

FESS WILLIAMS

(Fess Williams and His Royal Flush Orchestra) Born April 10, 1894 in Danville, Kentucky. Fess Williams (né: Stanley R. Williams) attended the Tuskegee Institute, where he learned to play many instruments but concentrated on clarinet and alto saxophone. He lived in Cincinnati from 1914 until 1923, where he taught for several years, formed his first combo in 1919, which toured the Midwest and South, and moved to Chicago, where he led a band in vaudeville. In 1926 to 1927, he led a widely popular band in 1929 at the Savoy Ballroom that made a lot of recordings for Victor Records, including some tunes like "Here 'Tis," "Hot Town," and "A Few Riffs." Other record labels were Brunswick and Vocalion. Some of the band's personnel included Williams, leader; Perry Smith and Felix Gregory, clarinet and tenor saxophone; David "Jelly" James, trombone; George Temple and Ken Roane, trumpets; Hank Duncan, piano; Andy Pendelton and Oliver Blackwell, banjos; David Emmanuel Casamore, tuba; and Ralph Bedell, drums. In the '40s and '50s, Fess Williams built a strong reputation as a composer and arranger.

These bands were directed by the following and were known to have existed but there is not sufficient historical information to include them: Allie Ross and Coon-Saunders.

CHAPTER

BATH TUB GIN AND RADIO RULES
(1920–1929)

THE JAZZ AGE

Technology produced radio, movies, the automobile, and the airplane. Prohibition, bootlegging, neon, skyscrapers, mass-produced products, the first motel (San Luis Obispo, California), the first traffic lights (New York City), the first shopping center (Kansas City, Missouri), and the first parking garage (Detroit, Michigan) were products of the decade. The concept of "buy now, pay later" was conceived and advertising gained more prominence. Many teenage girls drank, smoked cigarettes, dressed in suggestive clothing, and engaged in premarital sex. The rural South and Midwest remained largely untouched by the economic boon. The Ku Klux Klan had more than 4 million members. There were exploits of big time mobsters like Al "Scarface" Capone, "Machine Gun" Jack McGurn, and George "Bugs" Moran. People who were drunk were said to be "jazzed," "corked," "potted," "boiled as an owl," "loaded to the muzzle," "loaded for bear," "tanked," "burning with a blue flame," "pie-eyed," "slopped," "lit," or "oiled." People discussed evolution and witnessed the Scopes trial. By the early '20s, Rudolph Valentino starred in *The Sheik*, Clara Bow was the *It* girl, and people were playing mah-jongg and singing "Yes! We Have No Bananas." Babe Ruth changed the game of baseball. New magazines, such as *Time* and *Reader's Digest*, were published. People listened to the music of Duke Ellington, Louis Armstrong, and George Gershwin. New York's Harlem grew six times over and became an entertainment mecca.

1920: There were 8 million automobiles in America. The League of Nations was formed. The first radio broadcasting station was established at station KDKA in Pittsburgh, Pennsylvania. American Society of Composers Authors and Publishers (ASCAP) was established giving music publishers and writers income from performances of their music.

1921: Treaty of Berlin was signed between the U.S. and Germany. One hundred million phonograph records were produced in the United States.

1922: The year began with 28 radio stations; by the end of the year, there were 570. Benito Mussolini marched on Rome. Two electronic pianos were invented—the Thiring in Vienna and the Etherophone in Russia.

1923: Adolf Hitler wrote *Mein Kampf.* AT&T inaugurated the first radio network.

1924: Vladimir Lenin died at age 54. Bell Laboratories developed an electronic process for recording increasing the audible range to 100–5,000 Hz. The Theremin, a monophonic electronic instrument, was introduced.

1925: Scopes Trial. The first electronic amplifiers were developed. The Midgley-Walker Organ, an electronic organ, was developed. The first electronic amplifiers were developed.

1926: Ernest Hemingway wrote *The Sun Also Rises.* A Chickering Ampico player piano was electrified. The Radiano, a piano microphone, was developed. Electronic instruments Omnitonium, Pianorad, and Spharophon were invented.

1927: Charles Lindbergh flew *The Spirit of St. Louis* across the Atlantic to Paris. The Teapot Dome Scandal. The Cellulophone, Dynaphone, Ktronische Zaubergeige, and Superpiano—electronic instruments— were developed.

1928: First radio broadcast of the New York Philharmonic. Electronic instruments Electronic Monochord and Ondes Martenor were invented. An electric piano, Piano Electrique, was developed in France.

1929: There were 20 million automobiles in America. There were 32,000 speakeasies in New York City. The Speaker of the House had a private still. On October 24, 1929, Black Thursday, the stock market crashed and the Great Depression began. The meteoric rise of radio popularity slowed down progress in the recording industry. Sound film was introduced in the U.S. and the U.S.S.R.

BANDS FIRST ORGANIZED DURING
1920–1929

BUCKTOWN FIVE

The Bucktown Five was a quintet comprised of Mel Stitzel, piano; Muggsy Spanier, cornet; Bill Shelby, banjo; Marvin Saxbe, banjo, guitar, and cymbal; Volly De Fait, clarinet and alto saxophone; and Guy Carey, trombone. It was believed to be the most authentic white jazz band of the early '20s in New Orleans and played in a pseudo-Chicago style not unsimilar to the Original Dixieland Jazz Band. Bucktown was a settlement opening on the shores of Lake Ponchartrain after the closing of Storyville in New Orleans.

"LUCKEY" ROBERTS

("Luckey" Roberts and His Orchestra) Born August 7, 1887 in Philadelphia, Pennsylvania. Charles Luckeyth "Luckey" Roberts appeared on the New York stage at the age of three, where he acted in the play *Uncle Tom's Cabin*. His family had settled in New York shortly after his birth. Roberts studied piano and became an early ragtime soloist and composer writing "Pork and Beans Rag" and "Junk Man Rag." Between 1913 and 1923 Roberts wrote the music for 14 comedies on the New York stage. During the '20s, he fronted a popular band that worked in various resorts in Palm Beach, Florida, Newport, Rhode Island, and New York. During the '30s, he owned and operated a bar in Harlem called the Rendezvous on St. Nicholas Avenue, while continuing to lead his band. He appeared in Carnegie Hall in 1939 and Town Hall in 1941. During the '40s, he wrote "Massachusetts" and "Moonlight Cocktail" made famous by Glenn Miller. It is said that his piano playing influenced James P. Johnson and Duke Ellington. He assisted the Duke of Windsor in choosing his collection of jazz records. Roberts died in New York City on February 5, 1968.

JAN GARBER

(Jan Garber and His Orchestra) Born in Indianapolis, Indiana on November 5, 1894. Garber was a violinist who was termed "The Idol of the Airlanes." He was trained classically, studying at the Coombs Conservatory in Philadelphia. After graduation, he joined the Philadelphia Orchestra and remained until he was drafted into the U.S. Army in 1918. While in the army, stationed in Alabama, he formed a marching band, which whetted his interest in popular music. After his discharge, he joined the Meyer Davis band. At that time Davis had a number of bands under his auspices and he assigned one of them to Garber. In 1921, Garber combined his band with a band led by Milton Davis and the new group was called the Garber-Davis Orchestra. In 1924, Garber took over the band entirely when Davis had an affair with a married woman that led to a skirmish with the woman's husband who threatened to kill him. Garber paid $1,000 to buy out Davis's interest and the group became permanently known as the Jan Garber Orchestra. During the '20s, the band played jazz. The group switched to the more commercially sweet music style during the '30s, when Garber fired his entire band, keeping the pianist Rudy Rudisill, and taking over the Freddie Large Orchestra, a Canadian band. The band appeared briefly on *The George Burns and Gracie Allen Show*. The Garber theme song was "My Dear," a song that Garber wrote in collaboration with Freddie Large. In 1942, Garber lost most of his musicians to the draft and formed a new band featuring swing music. After WWII, Garber revamped his band and returned to the commercial style that remained. The personnel of the Garber Orchestra through the years included Jack Barrow, Frank MacCauley, Tony Briglia, Al Powers, Memo Bernabel, Vince Di Bari, Ernie Mathias, Frank Bettencourt, Jack Motch, Ted Bowman, Bill Oblak, Billy Hearn, Don Korinek, Walter Moore, Chelsea Quealey, Harry Goldfield, Harold Peppie, Benny Davis, Paul Weirick, Joe Rhodes, Freddie Large, Fritz Heilbron, Norman Donahue, Jerry Large, Rudy Rudisill, Don Shoup, Charlie Dord, Lew Palmer, Doug Roe, Buss Brown, and Bill Kleeb. In the 1950s, the Jan Garber Orchestra played in Las Vegas and continued to record on the Decca label through the '60s, when Garber retired and turned the band over to his daughter, Janis. The Garber Orchestra was disbanded in 1973 and Garber died in Shreveport, Louisiana on October 5, 1977.

SAM LANIN

(Sam Lanin and His Orchestra) Lanin started his band in New York City in 1920 playing at the Roseland Ballroom. He was one of the most often recorded bands of his time and recorded for Harmony, Paramount, Embassy, Camden, Banner, King, Decca, and Columbia Records. The theme song of the Sam Lanin Orchestra was "A Smile Will Go a Long, Long Way." The Lanin band was considered one of the most popular in the New York City area and used a number of recording names, e.g., Sam Lanin and His Famous Players, The Okeh Melodians, The Melody Sheiks, The New York Syncopators, The Broadway Broadcasters, The Ipana Troubadours, Lanin's Arcadians, Lanin's Southern Serenaders, Bailey's Lucky Seven, and Lanin's Roseland Orchestra. Some of the most famous sidemen who appeared with the Lanin Orchestra included Bunny Berigan, Glenn Miller, Phil Napoleon, Benny Goodman, Eddie Lang, Joe Venuti, Jimmy McPartland, Jack Teagarden, Manny Klein, Tommy and Jimmy Dorsey, and Miff Mole.

JOE RINES

(Joe Rines and His Orchestra) Born in Boston, Massachusetts on October 1, 1901. Rines began in 1921 on radio as an entertainer. He formed his own orchestra and played and directed on the Yankee Network. He also performed in New England and on WMCA, New York and the NBC network. He produced and directed the radio shows *Abie's Irish Rose*, *Judy Canova*, and *The Andrew Sisters*. In the '40s and '50s, he supervised the *Colgate Comedy Hours* and *The Shirley Temple Storybook* and collaborated on songs with Abel Baer. They wrote "Halo," "Everybody," "Halo and Ajax," and "The Foaming Cleanser."

CLYDE McCOY

(Clyde "Sugar Blues" McCoy and His Orchestra) Born on December 29, 1903 in Ashland, Kentucky. McCoy was a child when his family moved to Portsmouth, Ohio. By age nine, Clyde was marching with the Loyal Temperance Legion band and playing "The Brewer's Big Horses Can't Run over Me" on trombone. Switching to trumpet, he began playing in theaters and on riverboats during his teens. He formed his own band at the age of 16 and, at the age of 19, discovered his wah-wah trumpet sound that made him famous. By 1930, McCoy had formed his own band and was playing ballrooms and clubs. In 1931, he recorded "Sugar Blues," utilizing his muted wah-wah sound, which became his theme song. Columbia Records sold several million copies of the tune originally and Decca recorded another version at a later date, which also sold millions. While "Sugar Blues" remained his big hit, he also recorded "Wah-Wah Lament," "Smoke Rings," "The Gonna Goo," and "In the Cool of the Night." He added the singing group The Bennett Sisters to the band in 1937 and married the lead singer in 1938. His pianist was the future bandleader Jack Fina. In WWII, the U.S. Navy Special Services enrolled the band and singers until 1945, the end of the war, when McCoy reformed his big band. Shortly thereafter, McCoy took temporary retirement. In the '50s, he reformed his band into a Dixieland group and recorded "Tumbling Tumbleweeds," "Panama," and swing-era tunes like "In the Mood" and "Opus Number One." McCoy had recorded "St. Louis Blues" and "Basin Street Blues" in 1933 and re-recorded both tunes with his big band in the 1950s. At that time he worked in major concert halls, ballrooms, and clubs in the U.S. and Canada and continued performing with a small band until the mid-'80s when he retired. During his active life as a bandleader, he recorded for Capitol, Decca, and Columbia records. He died in Memphis, Tennessee on June 1, 1990 at the age of 87.

HARRY HORLICK

(Harry Horlick and His Orchestra) Born in Kiev, Russia. Horlick remained in Russia when his family immigrated to the U.S. at the beginning of WWI. As a violinist he played various venues until he was drafted into the Russian army and was a prisoner of war. The American Consul and his family helped free him and move him to the U.S. The A&P Gypsies, a group consisting of all Russian-born musicians played various cafés in the early '20s and they were heard on radio for the A&P food store chain. The theme song was "Two Guitars," written by Harry Horlick. The Gypsies recorded for Brunswick Records. Horlick soon took charge of the Gypsies and enlarged the group that was heard on a long-running radio series during the '20s to mid-'30s. When the group disbanded Horlick organized a group under his own name that recorded for Lion, Decca, and Vocalion records.

EMIL COLEMAN

(Emil Coleman and His Orchestra) Born on June 19, 1894. Coleman led a commercial society band that played at the famous Waldorf-Astoria Hotel. He and his music were well thought of by New York high society. During his lifetime, the Coleman Orchestra played for many debutante balls and social galas through the country. Emil Coleman died on February 3, 1965.

LUD GLUSKIN

(Lud Gluskin and His Orchestra) Born in Russia c. 1898. It is said that the Lud Gluskin Orchestra was the only American band that played in Europe continuously during the late '20s and early '30s. The band was actually a jazz band that recorded in a commercial style. Most of the musicians were from Detroit and the band was influenced by the Goldkette sound. Inasmuch as they spent most of their time in France, at least a quarter of the band's personnel had to be French. The band did their first recording on December 30, 1927, and the record label was Lud Gluskin and his Versatile Juniors. In 1980 record producer Warren K. Plath produced an album with the title *Black and White Jazz in Europe, 1929*, which featured three bands—Gregor, Sam Wooding, and Lud Gluskin.

Gluskin and Gregor played opposite each other in the summer of 1929 at Le Touquet Paris Plage. In the first part of 1929, the band was known as Lud Gluskin and The Ambassadonians as they played at the Ambassadors in Berlin and recorded for five record companies. They recorded "Tiger Rag," "That's My Weakness Now," "I Wanna Be Loved by You," and "That's a Plenty." Some of the Gluskin sidemen included Bart Curtis, drums; Arthur Pavoni, bass; Howard E. Kennedy, banjo; Paulie Freed, piano; Fred Zierer, violin; Spencer Clark, Serge Glykson, Mauricea Cizeron, Georges Charron, Gene Prendergast, reeds; Emile Christian, trombone; and Eddie Ritten and Faustin Jeanjean, trumpets. In 1937, Gluskin was director of music at CBS in Hollywood, California.

"WILD BILL" DAVISON

(William Edward "Wild Bill" Davison and His Commodores) Born January 5, 1906 in Defiance, Ohio. He was named "Wild Bill" because of his wild music and personal life, being strongly attracted to women and whiskey. The trumpeter started in the early '20s and worked with various groups, including Ben Meroff's Orchestra in Chicago. There, he met Eddie Condon, the guitarist, and they became lifelong friends. Davison possessed a photographic memory and great relative pitch, which assisted him greatly in his improvisation. Most of the '30s were spent in Milwaukee, where he was called "Trumpet King" Davison. In 1939, a flying beer bottle hit him in the mouth inflicting a severe lip injury, which caused him to quit playing temporarily. By 1941, he played at Nick's in New York. He also formed a version of the Original Dixieland Jazz Band for the *Katherine Dunham Radio Show* and recorded 12 records for the Commodore

Label in 1944. In 1945 he recorded with George Brunis, joined Eddie Condon's house band at Eddie Condon's Club, and really began to form a style of his own. In the '60s, Davison toured with his own band and in the mid-'60s and early '70s appeared with more than 100 bands and recorded 20 record albums. While touring England, he recorded with Alex Welsh, Lennie Hastings, and Fred Hunt before moving to Denmark. By 1985, Davison remained active, playing at jazz festivals and touring England. The Japanese government named him "Living National Treasure of Japan." "Wild Bill" Davison died on November 14, 1989, at the age of 83.

ZACK WHYTE

(Zack Whyte and His Orchestra) Born in Richmond, Kentucky in 1898. Whyte was a banjo player who studied at Wilberforce College. While in school, he played banjo and wrote for a student band led by Horace Henderson. In 1923, he formed his own band and, by 1929, was leading the Chocolate Beau Brummels. The band was a big hit musically but made few recordings. One of its hit records was "Mandy," recorded in 1929 for Gennett Records. The sidemen for the Whyte Orchestra included Sy Oliver, Al Sears, Vic Dickenson, Roy Eldridge, Quentin Jackson, and Herman "Ivory" Chittison. The Zack Whyte band worked into the '30s. Zack Whyte died in Kentucky on March 10, 1967.

ARTHUR FIELDS

(Arthur Fields and His Assassinators) Born August 6, 1888 in Philadelphia, Pennsylvania. A vocalist and novelty performer, Fields was a child singer, professional by age 11. He participated in minstrel shows and vaudeville, and later on radio. In the late '20s, he sang with Fred "Sugar" Hall on a daily morning radio show. Fields wrote music and/or lyrics to many popular songs, including "There Shall Be No More Tears," "I Got a Code in My Dose," "Our Hometown Mountain Band," "Eleven More Months," and "Ten More Days," "Who Else But God?," "There's a Blue Sky Way Out Yonder," "Auntie Skinner's Chicken Dinner," "On the Mississippi," and "Abba Dabba Honeymoon." Fields died in Largo, Florida on March 29, 1953. See Fred "Sugar" Hall, on page 46.

FRED "SUGAR" HALL

(Fred "Sugar" Hall and His Sugar Babies) Born on April 10, 1898 in New York City. Hall was a pianist, composer, and song plugger. He and his partner, Arthur Fields, composed hundreds of songs. Together with George Wiest and lyricist Billy Rose, they wrote songs like "Big Rock Candy Mountain," "I Got a Code in My Dose," "Did I Do Wrong?," "Dry Bones," "Brother Bill's the Sheriff," "Every Jack Must Have a Jill," "Hang It in the Henhouse," "I Love a Ukulele," "Hinky Dinky Parlez-Vous," "How Dry I Am," "She Cost Two Dollars," "The Mule Song," "Starlight Bay," "Sweet Potato Song," "Yazoo Mississippi," "Your Folks and My Folks," "One Hundred Years Ago," "Starlight Boy," "The Lonesome Trail," and "Sweet Potato Song." The duo was cognizant of the public's interest in novelties and carefree songs and when Fred Hall formed his orchestra in the '20s he gave it to them. During the late '20s, Fred Hall and Arthur Fields broadcast on *The Sunday Driver* radio program. The instrumentation of the band varied from seven to nine pieces and was most active from 1925 until 1932. Hall and Fields recorded eight duets prior to breaking up in 1932. Some of the members of the Fred "Sugar" Hall band included Joseph Mayo, drums; Al Morse, tuba; Albert Russo, banjo; Eddie Grosso, clarinet and alto saxophone; Harry Blevins, trombone; Jack Mollick and Mike Mosiello, trumpets; Phillip D'Arcy, violin, harmonica, and piano; and Fred Hall, piano and leader. Hall died on October 8, 1964 in New York City. He was 66 years old.

AL GOODMAN

(Al Goodman and His Orchestra) Born in Nikopol, Russia on August 12, 1890. When Goodman was five years old his father smuggled him and his family out of Russia and came to the U.S., where they settled in Baltimore. The talented Goodman attended Peabody Conservatory of Music in Baltimore as a piano major on a scholarship. In 1916, he met and plugged songs for Earl Carroll, including a book for the Broadway show *So Long Letty*. He worked with Al Jolson in 1918, when they produced Jolson's Sinbad, the show that produced Jolson's trademark, "Mammy." In 1927, Goodman founded the band that played in the Al Jolson movie *The Jazz Singer*, later forming a jazz group for nightclub engagements. He then worked with Irving Berlin, the Ziegfeld Follies, and Fred Allen before forming a new band and recording frequently. Tunes such as "I'm Just a Vagabond Lover," "Or What Have You?," and "When I Grow to Old to

Dream" met with great success. When the '50s came and LP recording became available, Goodman recorded hits from *My Fair Lady*, *South Pacific*, and an album featuring the music of Irving Berlin. He retired in 1971 and died in New York City on January 10, 1972.

HORACE HENDERSON

(Horace Henderson and His Orchestra) Born in Cuthbert, Georgia on November 22, 1904. Horace Henderson was the younger brother of Fletcher Henderson and was a pianist. He attended Atlanta University and Wilberforce University and led a college band that included Rex Stewart and Benny Carter. His band-leading career spanned from the '20s through the '70s—a fifty-year tenure. His first recordings were made for Parlaphone Records in the '30s. His piano technique was greatly influenced by his brother Fletcher who is more championed as an arranger. Horace joined the Don Redman band in 1931 as a pianist and arranger and from 1933 to 1936 played in his brother's band. Horace wrote many arrangements for the Benny Goodman band in 1935 on tunes such as "I Found a New Baby," "Chicago," "Dear Old Southland," "Always," "Walk Jennie Walk," and "Japanese Sandman." He moved to Chicago where he worked in the late '30s and his band recorded for Okeh and Vocalion records. At that time he had a number of stars in his band, including Emmett Berry, Ray Nance, and Israel Crosby. One of the tunes, "Christopher Colombus," which he wrote for brother Fletcher Henderson's band, was later entitled "Sing, Sing, Sing" by the Benny Goodman band. In 1941, while leading his own band, Horace wrote for the Charlie Barnet band, tunes, including "Charleston Alley" and "Little John Ordinary." That year he also served as musical director and pianist for Lena Horne. In the mid '40s, he lived in Los Angeles and recorded with small groups for Capitol Records. Moving to Chicago in the late '40s, he got into R&B music, recording for Decca. In the late '50s, he moved to Minneapolis, Minnesota where he led a small combo. During his long career he also wrote for the bands of Jimmie Lunceford, Glen Gray, and Tommy Dorsey. Horace Henderson died in Denver, Colorado on August 29, 1988.

HOOSIER HOT SHOTS

In 1923, the Hot Shots were called Ezra Buzzington's Rube Band and the Rustic Revelers. They were later named the Hoosier Hot Shots. The original band, which played the Midwest vaudeville circuit, included Jon Shafer, Ken Trietsch, Paul Treitsch, Bessie Trietsch, Charles Trietsch, and Frank Trietsch. The Hoosier Hot Shots, which foreran Spike Jones and His City Slickers, included most of the Trietsches and added Gabe Ward, broadcast on *The National Barn Dance* radio program from Chicago. The group made more than 250 recordings on Gennett and Yazoo records and 20 films during their existence. In 1930, with the death of vaudeville and the beginning of the Great Depression, the group disbanded. Ken, Paul, and Bessie Trietsch, and Gabe Ward played for local affairs and did the radio show *The National Barn Dance* at station WOWO in Fort Wayne, Indiana, from the early '30s to the mid-'40s. They added singer Skip Farrell and recorded on Decca, Perfect, Circle, Conqueror, Columbia, and Okeh records. They moved to California in 1947 at which time the band was comprised of Gil Taylor, bass; Gabe Ward, clarinet; Ken Trietsch, guitar; and Paul Treitsch, slide whistle and washboard. They signed a movie contract with Columbia Pictures, and worked in clubs and on radio. Although their career in movies and recording was over, they continued working in various clubs well into the '70s. Paul Treitsch died in 1979, Ken in 1987, and Gabe in 1992.

BOB GARBER

(Bob Garber and His Orchestra) Born in Washington, D.C. on April 23, 1903. Garber studied piano with his father who was a pianist, and learned to read music as well as to play "by ear." In the '20s, Garber formed his own band but that group never had a full-time job. Through the '30s, Bob Garber continued to lead part-time bands in various venues in and around Washington, D.C. Between 1937 and 1939, he played solo on the *Normandie* cruise ship and on the French line *SS Champlain*. He also played occasionally on radio stations WMAL, WJSV, and WOL. Although he played during the early '40s with musicians who had not been drafted, he disbanded in the late '40s and began playing solo piano around Washington, D.C. Moving to Florida, he continued to play singles until he became ill in 1987. He is thought to have been one of the first users of the Solovox, an electric keyboard. In 1941 Jack Benny and Mary Livingston were among his many fans. Garber died on March 6, 1988 in Ormond-by-the-Sea, Florida.

RED McKENZIE

(Red McKenzie and His Mound City Blue Blowers) Born in St. Louis, Missouri on October 14, 1907. William "Red" McKenzie played kazoo and hot comb, while leading the Mound City Blue Blowers. He was a bellhop at the Claridge Hotel in St. Louis, Missouri across the street from a soda shop called Butler Brothers. While a phonograph was playing, a shoeshine boy played rhythm while shinning shoes, Dick Slevin played a kazoo, Jack Bland played banjo, and McKenzie played hot comb. Gene Rodemich, a famous bandleader at that time, heard the group, took them to Chicago in 1924, and recorded them with his band as a novelty. When they got to Chicago, Rodemich took them to the Friar's Inn where Elmer Schoebel, Volly De Foul and Isham Jones were. Jones set them up for a recording date at Brunswick Records and they recorded "Blue Blues" and "Arkansas Blues." The accompanying records sold more than a million copies. They then played the Beaux Arts in Atlantic City and the Palace in New York City. Traveling to Europe, they played at the Stork Club in London. When they returned to America, McKenzie became a jazz promoter and arranged for the first Okeh record date for Bix Beiderbecke, Frankie Trumbauer, and Eddie Lang. In 1927, he arranged for a group of Chicagoans to record Friar's Point Shuffle for Paramount Records. In 1928, McKenzie and Condon's Chicagoans recorded four sides for Okeh Records. Red McKenzie died on February 7, 1948 in New York City.

JASPER TAYLOR

(Jasper Taylor and the Original Washboard Band) Jasper Taylor formed a band on the South Side of Chicago in the '20s. Taylor played wood blocks and washboard. He also played in a band led by Freddie Keppard and was featured on a Keppard recording "Stockyard Strut." Under the title Original Washboard Band with Jasper Taylor, Taylor recorded an original tune entitled "Jasper Taylor's Blues" for Vocalion Records on June 29, 1928. Some of the featured players were Taylor, B.T. Wingfeild, Cassino Simpson, and R.Q. Dickerson. The band later featured pianist Eddie Heywood and trombonist Eddie Ellis.

BEASLEY SMITH

(Beasley Smith and His Orchestra) Born in McEwen, Tennessee on September 27, 1901. Beasely Smith studied at Peabody College and Vanderbuilt University. He organized and led his orchestra in vaudeville, nightclubs, and various hotels during the mid to late '20s and early '30s. He played piano on radio and was director of station WEM in Nashville for 20 years. For five years, he served as the A&R director of Dot Records and wrote songs, including "That Lucky Old Sun," "Beg Your Pardon," "I'd Rather Die Young," "Night Train to Memphis," "Down in Tennessee," and "The Old Master Painter" with collaborators Ralph Freed, Francis Craig, and Haven Gillespie. Beasley Smith died in Nashville, Tennessee on May 14, 1968.

JONES AND COLLINS

(Davey Jones and Lee Collins and Astoria Hot Eight) Lee Collins was born on October 17, 1901 in New Orleans, Lousiana. Davey Jones was born in Lutchen, Louisiana in 1888. Collins was a trumpet player who led a number of bands in New Orleans. He co-led bands with Jelly Roll Morton, Zutty Singleton, and Pops Foster. Collins was the trumpet player who replaced Louis Armstrong in the King Oliver Band in Chicago in 1924. The Jones and Collins band was said to be one of only six black bands to be recorded during the '20s in New Orleans. The other five were Fate Marable's Society Syncopators, Louis Dumaine's Jazzola Eight, Armand Iron's New Orleans Orchestra, Oscar "Papa" Celestin's Original Tuxedo Jazz Orchestra, and Sam Morgan's Jazz Band. In the 1930s, Collins played with Johnny Dodds and formed a band, which toured the country until the mid '40s. In the '50s, he continued touring, including a tour of Europe with Art Hodes. Davey Jones died in 1956 in Los Angeles. Lee Collins died in Chicago on July 3, 1960.

VIC MEYERS

(Vic Meyers and His Orchestra) Meyers began as a Seattle club owner at the Club Victor on Fourth Avenue. He was a drummer, emcee, and led a dance band. He played with his band often at the Hotel Butler and the Trianon Ballroom. In the mid- to late '20s, the band made several recordings for Columbia and Vocalion records. They held record sessions in New York, Seattle, and Los

Angeles. They recorded "Shake It and Brake It" in 1923, "Dearie, Nay" in 1924, and "Rose Room" and "Congratulations" in 1929. The band primarily played music for dancing. Meyers had great charm and a wonderful sense of humor. In 1932, he ran for mayor of Seattle but lost the election. Driving to Olympia, he intended to file as the Democratic candidate for governor but in order to file for the governorship a $60 deposit was necessary. Since the lieutenant governorship only called for a $12 deposit, he filed, was elected, and served several terms as lieutenant governor. He later served as secretary of state. The Vic Meyers Band can be heard on the CBC Timeless Historical CD collection.

MISSOURIANS ORCHESTRA, THE

(The Missourians Orchestra) This band was greatly influenced by the Benny Moten Orchestra. Some of the sidemen included Leroy Maxey, drums; R.Q. Dickerson, trumpet; Priest Wheeler, trombone; and Andy Brown, saxophone. Cab Calloway took over the band in 1930 and made it his own.

LEE MORSE

(Lee Morse and Her Blue Grass Boys) Born in 1900. Lee Morse was active during the '20s and '30s and her bands included many well-known musicians from time to time. Carl Kress, Benny Goodman, Irving Brodsky, Manny Klein, Frank Signorelli, Rube Bloom, Charlie Butterfield, and Tommy and Jimmy Dorsey were members of the Lee Morse band at one time or another. She recorded her own song, "Golden Dream Girl," and tunes like "When I Dream of the Last Waltz with You" and "Mailman Blues" on Edison Golden Discs. The Rodgers and Hart show *Simple Simon* was to star Morse, but she became ill and Ruth Etting replaced her. The Rodgers and Hart tune "Ten Cents a Dance" was to have starred Morse, but Etting stole the show. Lee Morse recovered from her illness and was very active during the '30s. Her records of "I'm an Unemployed Sweetheart" and "I've Got Five Dollars" became big hits. She later authored a folio, *Comic Songs for the Ukulele*, which became a big seller in the late '20s. Other hit records from the '30s associated with Lee Morse are "'Tain't No Sin to Take Off Your Skin" and "Dance Around in Your Bones," "Ukulele Lady," "Yes Sir, That's My Baby," and "Let's Get Friendly," all on the Parlourphone PA Act, Columbia, Brunswick, Harmony, Okeh, and Gennett record labels. Morse died in 1954.

SIG MYER

(Sig Myer and His Orchestra) Myer led a Chicago-based band in the '20s. In the early '20s the Myer and Louis Armstrong bands had musical battles at the Columbia Hall Dancing School, a rough-and-tumble club in Chicago. The New Orleans Rhythm Kings had played there often. In 1922, the Myer band played at White City, a Chicago dance hall in the amusement park area. The featured cornetist on the band was Muggsy Spanier, the saxophonist, Mezz Mezzrow, and the drummer, George Wettling. Other musicians included Volly De Foul, clarinet; Myer, violin and leader; George Petrone, drums; Floyd Town, saxophone; Bob Picilli, trombone; Arnold Loyocano, bass; and Marvin Saxbe, banjo/guitar. After White City, the band reformed and played at Midway Garden and the Triangle Club.

RUBY NEWMAN

(Ruby Newman and His Orchestra) Born in Boston, Massachusetts in 1902. Newman led Boston's favorite society band in the '30s playing primarily at the Ritz-Carlton Hotel. Violinist Newman's band utilized a violin section but no trumpet section. Ruby frequently played violin solos with the band. Newman led various bands from the '20s through the '40s and played a short stint at the Rainbow Grill in New York City. The band was said to be a very "musical and pleasant" group and played at the White House in Washington, D.C. on several occasions. Newman led an orchestra during WWII and accompanied Danny O'Neil on CBS.

REDJACKETS, THE

The Redjackets was considered one of the most prominent bands playing in North Dakota in the late '20s. The leader was pianist Bob Carroll. The Redjackets played within a 200-mile radius of Fargo, North Dakota and in Minnesota. They did regular broadcasting over radio station WDAT from the Crystal Ballroom in Fargo and were heard in Canada as well as in the U.S. Bob Carroll later played with the Red Fio Rito Orchestra.

HARRY RESER

(Harry Reser and His Clicquot Club Eskimos) Born on January 17, 1896 in Piqua, Ohio. Reser was a banjo player who played around Ohio as a sideman in various groups when he was very young. He was working in Buffalo, New York in 1920. The following year, he was appointed the musical head of Brunswick Records and Gus Haenschen brought him to New York City to record. In 1922, a number of recordings of Reser were released, featuring him playing solo banjo. He also recorded several sides under the name Harry Reser's Jazz Pilots. Among other pieces they recorded were "The Monkey Doodle Doooo," "The Coconuts," and "I've Never Seen a Big Banana." All three tunes were recorded with drummer Tom Stacks. The instrumentation for the Jazz Pilots was cornet, sax, bass, drums, and three or four banjos. In 1925, the Clicquot Club Soda Company agreed to sponsor his group in a weekly half-hour radio program and they became the Chicquot Club Eskimos. At that time Reser was using a small drummer named Tom Stacks, who did most of the singing. The band also recorded under the name Tom Stacks and His Jumping Jacks. They remained under the sponsorship of the Chicquot Club Soda Company for ten years until 1935. During the band's active years, they recorded under many different names, including Harry F. Reser's Novelty Trio, The Blue Kittens, Harry Reser Trio, The Blue Jays, Harry Reser's Banjo Boys, Harry Reser and His Eskimos, Night Club Orchestra, the Volunteer Firemen, Monach Orchestra, and many, many others. Reser was active throughout his life playing in Broadway orchestras, leading television studio orchestras, writing banjo and guitar method books, and recording. Harry Reser died in New York in 1965.

ADRIAN ROLLINI

(Adrian Rollini and His Orchestra) Born in New York City June 28, 1904. Rollini was considered a child prodigy pianist. He was the brother of Arthur Rollini who played saxophone and clarinet with the bands of Will Bradley and Benny Goodman. Adrian and his brother, Arthur, both played with the California Ramblers; Adrian from 1921 to 1926. The manager of the band, Ed Kirkeby (né: Wallace Theodore Kirkeby) later became the manager for Fats Waller. Kirkeby suggested that Rollini play the bass saxophone and Rollini became one of the finest bass saxophonist in the country. The California Ramblers was considered the most prolifically recorded dance band of the '20s and, from time to time, included such future stars as Glenn Miller, the Dorsey Brothers, and singers Smith Bellew and Vernon Dalhart. After leaving the Ramblers, Adrian joined Fred Elizalde's orchestra in London, England, and worked with them from 1927 to 1929. He then freelanced through the late '20s and early '30s. In 1933, he formed his own band, Adrian Rollini and His Orchestra, which included sidemen Bud Freeman, Charlie Barnet, Bunny Berigan, Jack Teagarden, and Adrian's brother, Arthur. In 1935, Rollini opened Adrian's Tap Room at the President Hotel in New York. Adrian and his Tap Room Gang included Wingy Manone. Later, his 1938 band featured Buddy Rich and Bobby Hackett. He recorded on Sunbeam Records and the Swedish record company TAX. In the late '30s, Rollini played xylophone; it is said that he played with four mallets. In the early '50s, Rollini ran an inn in Florida. He died in Homestead, Florida on May 15, 1956.

JESSE STAFFORD

(Jesse Stafford and His Orchestra) The Stafford band was active and did recordings in the '20s. Jesse Stafford had been a sideman in the Herb Wiedoft Orchestra. Orchestra leader Clyde Lucas had also played in the Wiedoft Orchestra.

FRANKIE TRUMBAUER

(Frankie Trumbauer and His Orchestra) Born in Carbondale, Illinois on May 30, 1901. In the '20s and early '30s, Trumbauer led several bands that were not commercially viable but musically successful. Frankie Trumbauer and Bix Beiderbecke played together in Trumbauer's band in St. Louis, then with Jean Goldkette, and in the late '20s in Paul Whiteman's Orchestra. They made a normal living playing in commercial dance bands but played jazz on their own time. Many of the finest musicians of that era played in Trumbauer's band, including Bix Beiderbecke, cornet; Jack Teagarden, trombone; Pee Wee Russell, clarinet; Eddie Lang, guitar; and Joe Venuti, violin. Venuti and Lang inspired the Quintet of the Hot Club of France. With friends from the bands led by Whiteman and Goldkette, Beiderbecke and Tram (Trumbauer's nickname) made many jazz records. Trumbauer played the C-melody saxophone (an instrument almost totally discarded in the late '30s and replaced by the B-flat tenor). In the late '20s, Tram and Bix played in the Adrian Rollini band for a short time. After the beginning of WWII, Trumbauer virtually quit music and worked as a test pilot. When the war ended in 1945 he worked for the CAA (Civil Aeronautics Authority) and played with NBC's studio orchestra. During his busy tenure as a musician, he recorded many tunes, including "For No Reason at All in C," "Wringin' and Twistin'," and "Singing the Blues." It is believed that Trumbauer's easy, intelligent, style may have been the forerunner of the cool jazz period developed by musicians such as Gerry Mulligan, Miles Davis, and Chet Baker in the early '50s. Trumbauer died in Kansas City, Missouri on June 11, 1956.

BIX BEIDERBECKE

(Bix Beiderbecke and His Orchestra, Bix Beiderbecke and His Gang) Born in Davenport, Iowa on March 10, 1903. Beiderbecke is considered one of the major musicians of his era. His family members were all considered to be very musical. The music reporter Arnold Shaw said, "Handing him the instrument [cornet] was like giving a paintbrush to Picasso." Beiderbecke was never able to read music very well but played the "Second Hungarian Rhapsody" when he was three years old. He played the cornet left-handed (for eight years) and had a magnificent tone. In 1921, while attending the Lake Forest Academy, he and drummer Walter "Cy" Welge formed the Cy-Bix Orchestra. Bix was expelled from the school in 1922. During Bix's career he played with the great bands of his era, including those led by Paul Whiteman, Hoagy Charmichael, Jean Goldkette, Frankie Trumbauer, and The Wolverines. For a brief time he led a group called Bix Beiderbecke and His Gang. Bix Beiderbecke died in August 1931 at the age of 28.

ACE BRIGODE

(Ace Brigode and His Fourteen Virginians) Brigode formed his band in Charleston in 1921 and used the theme song "Carry Me Back to Old Virginny." During the 25-year tenure of the band, the instrumentation ranged from 10 to 19 members. They featured tunes such as "Goin' Home," "Yes Sir, That's My Baby," " Alabamy Bound," and "Wait 'Til It's Moonlight." For several years they played on the radio program *White Rose Gasoline Show* and toured throughout the United States. For four years they played at the Monte Carlo in

New York City. Although the band had a featured vocalist, the band members formed a vocal choir, which often sang. When Brigode retired from the music business in 1945, he became the manager for promotions at Chippews Lake Park in Cleveland, Ohio. It is said that after Brigode died on February 3, 1960, President Dwight D. Eisenhower played a recording of the Brigode band rendition of "Sleeping Beauty's Wedding," as he sat alone in the White House Oval Office. Brigode died on February 3, 1960.

DON BESTOR (BENSON)

(Don Bestor [Benson] and the Benson Orchestra of Chicago) Born in Langford, South Dakota on September 23, 1889. Bestor studied piano as a young child and by the age of 16 toured with the vaudeville circuit. In 1921, he began playing with the Benson band and, by the mid-'20s, he assumed the leadership and secured a Victor Record contract. Some of the tunes they recorded included "In a Covered Wagon with You" and "Copenhagen." Bestor formed his own band in the mid-'30s, which recorded for the Brunswick label and was featured on the *Walter O'Keefe Show*. The new band's theme songs were "I'm Not Forgetting" and "Teach Me to Smile." A new comedian named Jack Benny was signed to a radio program in 1934 and contracted the Bestor Orchestra. The program became an instant hit and Benny often was quoted as saying, "Play, Don, play!" Bestor wrote the commercial for the sponsor Jello. Although the Bestor band toured until 1943, his fame was beginning to wane. Two of the tunes associated with the band were "Forty-Second Street" and "Animal Crackers in My Soup." Bestor died on January 13, 1970.

EUBIE BLAKE

(Eubie Blake and His Orchestra) Born on February 7, 1883 in Baltimore, Maryland. By 1915, Blake teamed with Noble Sissle in vaudeville and they produced one of the top acts of the time. They continued their relationship for many years creating musical reviews, acts, and bands. Pianist and composer Blake is considered one of the giants in jazz history and popular music of the 20th century. He composed songs such as "Memories of You" and "I'm Just Wild About Harry" and produced the first black musical comedy on Broadway in 1921, *Shuffle Along*. Sophie Tucker used one of his songs, "It's All Your

Fault," as her theme song and hired the Blake-Sissle band to accompany her. The personnel of that band included Eubie Blake, leader; Hall Johnson, viola; William Grant Still, oboe; George Regues, drums; Russell "Pop" Smith, trumpet; Carrol Jones, trombone; and John Ricks, bass. During the years, Blake led several bands. His 1936 band recorded "It Looks Like Love" and "Bandanna Days." In 1950, 20th Century Fox released his *The Wizard of the Ragtime Piano*. He appeared at the White House on several occasions, on television, on college campuses, and the Marian McPartland radio program *Piano Jazz*. In 1995, the U.S. Postal Service issued a stamp honoring Eubie Blake, among several other jazz legends. Blake died in Brooklyn, New York on February 13, 1983 at the age of 100.

DAVID CARROLL

(David Carroll and His Orchestra) Carroll was an arranger and instrumentalist with many dance bands. He was a hi-fi fanatic and lived in Plum Grove Estates in Palantine, Illinois. He made an album for Mercury Records entitled *Let's Dance Again*, which became popular at the beginning of the stereo recording period.

CATO'S VAGABONDS

(Cato Mann and Lester Rhode and Cato's Vagabonds) This was an unusual organization in which Cato Mann managed the band and Lester Rhode was the front man, directing the orchestra. The band began in 1921 in Des Moines, Iowa and was a territory band playing mostly in the Minneapolis–St. Paul area. For several summers, they played in Fairmont, Minnesota at Interlaken Park. They played at the Kelpine Ballroom in Omaha, Nebraska in 1926 and were broadcast by radio station WOAW. The band grew from six to ten pieces and featured a girl singer, Nedra Gordonier. They branched our doing dates in Georgia and Florida. Lawrence Welk deemed Cato's Vagabonds his "greatest competition." In 1928, the band played at the Roseland Ballroom in New York City; in 1931, at the Syracuse Hotel; and in 1932, at the Marigold Restaurant in Rochester, New York. Cato's Vagabonds disbanded in 1936 and Cato Mann retired in Des Moines, Iowa.

BILLY COTTON

(Billy Cotton and His Orchestra) Born in Westminster, England in 1899. Cotton began his career as a drummer in the British army band. As a civilian, he formed his own band and played at the Astoria Ballroom in 1921. During the '30s, he played a number of radio broadcasts and, as a result, was invited to bring his band to the U.S. Cotton was a large man with a thin mustache and a broad smile who inspired cartoon figures. His showmanship and jokes were extremely popular in England. The band became famous due to their novelty hits such as "Ev'ry Single Little Tingle of My Heart," "Oh Monah," "The Tattooed Lady," "Oh Nicholas! Don't Be So Ridiculous," and "Two Cigarettes in the Dark." Lawrence Welk greatly admired the talents of Billy Cotton. Cotton died on March 25, 1969.

JOHNNY HAMP

(Johnny Hamp and His Kentucky Serenaders) Hamp's career began in the mid-'20s when he formed his dance band, which played through the mid-'30s. The Kentucky Serenaders were said to be a good band with outstanding arrangements and a full, pretty sound. In 1930, the band traveled to England and played some of the top venues in London and surroundings. The outstanding singers were Jayne Whitney and Johnny McAfee. The theme song of the Johnny Hamp Orchestra was "My Old Kentucky Home." The band recorded for Victor, Bluebird, and Melotone Records.

BERT LOWN

(Bert Lown and His Hotel Biltmore Music) Born in White Plains, New York on June 6, 1903. Prior to leading a band, Lown operated his own booking service beginning in 1926, booking bands for house parties, clubs, and private functions. He started his own band in 1928 but continued booking other groups at hotels in Brazil, Uruguay, and Argentina. Later, he started another band by picking up musicians at the AF of M union hall in New York for an engagement at the Biltmore Hotel, commencing on December 3, 1919 and ending in 1932. The personnel at that time included Smith Ballew, vocals; Stan King, drums; Adrian Rollini, bass saxophone and vibes; Ward Lay, bass; Tommy Felline, guitar; Chauncey Gray, piano; Lou Bode, clarinet and alto saxophone; Paul Mason, clarinet and tenor saxophone; Bert Lown and Al Philburn, trombones;

and Frank Cush and Ed Farley, trumpets. The band recorded such tunes as "Hello Baby," "Through" and their theme song, "Bye Bye Blues" (written by Bert Lown), for Fox Trot Records. Eventually Lown disbanded, booked other bands, and worked with radio and television stations. During WWII, he worked in various war relief organizations. He joined Muzak in 1946. In addition to "Bye Bye Blues," he wrote "By My Side," "My Heart and I," and "Tired." Lown died in Portland, Oregon on November 20, 1962 at the age of 59.

BERT AMBROSE

(Bert Ambrose and His Orchestra) Born in 1897 in London, England. Ambrose studied violin in New York City before returning to his home in England where he started his band in the early '20s. He opened at Luigi's Embassy Club where he played for five years. The following six years he played at the New Mayfair Hotel. During this period he led a commercial hotel band but commissioned new "swing" arrangements during the '30s and patterned his band's sound after that of Glenn Miller. He appeared in the British motion picture *Soft Lights and Sweet Music*. He continued to work through the '40s and '50s in various clubs, in theaters, and on radio. Bert Ambrose died in 1973.

PAUL ASH

(Paul Ash and His Orchestra) Born in Germany on February 11, 1891. The Ash family moved from Germany to Milwaukee, Wisconsin in 1910 and Paul Ash organized his first band there. Ash played piano and violin. During WWI, Ash served in the U.S. Army and, after his release, appeared in several silent movies. The Paul Ash Orchestra played in movie palaces in the Chicago area. The band made its first records in 1923. Various sidemen appeared in the band, including Red Norvo, Glenn Miller and Benny Goodman. Martha Raye was the band's vocalist. She later appeared with the Louis Prima band. For a number of years after the band disbanded, Paul Ash conducted the house band at the Paramount Theater in New York and Brooklyn. Singer Helen Kane appeared with that studio orchestra. Ash wrote the lyrics to "That's Why I Love You So" and Kay Kyser's theme song "Thinking of You." He also wrote "Who's Your Sweetheart," "Just Once Again," "That's Why I Love You," and "What Do We Care If It's One O'Clock." Paul Ash retired from the music business and died in New York City on July 13, 1958.

AL KATZ

(Al Katz and His Kittens) Al Katz (né: Al Katzenberger) was a bandleader in the Chicago area for many years. They played a lot of novelty tunes and were popular in the late '20s and early '30s. The band was originally formed in Kentucky but toured the Midwest and even traveled to New York City for some recording dates. They recorded for Gennett, Columbia, and RCA Victor Records. Some of the sideman on the Katz band were Jess Stacy, Fred Rollinson, Lewis Storey, George Schechtman, Joe Magliatti, Jerry Bump, Ray Kleemeyer, Joe Bishop, and Greg Brown. The Music Corporation of America (MCA) did most of the band's bookings. The band disbanded in the late '40s.

JOE KAYSER

(Joe Kayser and His Orchestra) Born in St. Louis, Missouri on September 14, 1891. Drummer Joe Kayser led a Navy band during WWI, a band that included a violinist named Benny Kubelsky (Jack Benny). When the war ended, he fronted a band for Meyer Davis in the Carolinas. In St. Louis in 1921, he organized and started his own band, which toured the Midwest for three years. From 1924 to 1936, he based his band in Chicago. Some of the outstanding sidemen in the Kayser band were Gene Krupa, drums; Muggsy Spanier, cornet; and Jess Stacy, piano. The various Chicago ballrooms, such as the Arcadia, Trianon, and Arargon were venues for the Kayser Orchestra and they also played for Sally Rand at the Chicago World's Fair, 1933 to 1934. The band recorded for the Brunswick and Gennett labels. In 1936, Kayser disbanded and worked for a booking agent handling bands and radio programming. Joe Kayser died in Evanston, Illinois on October 3, 1981.

TONY PARENTI

(Tony Parenti and His Orchestra) Born August 6, 1900 in New Orleans. Parenti began his music career at age 15 playing his first engagements with bands led by Jimmy Detroit, Nick LaRocca, and Papa Jack Laine. In 1921, he formed his own band and played at the Bienville Roof until 1922, when he played at the Vida Club until 1924. In the late '20s, he moved to New York City and played with bands led by Meyer Davis, Paul Ash, Arnold Johnson, Ross Gorman, Henry Busse, and Mike Markel. He also served on staff at CBS. For a time he was on radio with Ed Wynn on the show *The Palmolive Hour*. From 1930 to 1931, he played with the B.A. Rolfe band on the *Lucky Strike Hit Parade Radio Show*. While playing with the Fred Rich and Nat Brusiloff bands on various radio shows he also appeared on the Kate Smith radio program. For several years he played with Erno Rapee at Radio City Music Hall and toured with the Ted Lewis Orchestra from 1938 to 1944. Returning to New York in 1945, he played with various Dixieland groups and, from 1947 to 1949, he played in Chicago with Miff Mole and Muggsy Spanier. Various sidemen who played in bands led by Tony Parenti included Pops Foster, bass; Baby Dodds and Mark Hazel, drums; Wild Bill Davison, cornet; and James Ardhey, trombone. Parenti returned to New York in the early '50s and played at various places until he died on April 17, 1972.

LEO REISMAN

(Leo Reisman and His Orchestra) Born in Boston, Massachusetts in 1897. Leo Reisman began studying violin at age ten and had his first public performance at age 12. He played in various student symphony orchestras and hotel bands while in his teens. Reisman began his professional career as a violinist with the Baltimore Symphony Orchestra prior to forming his own dance band in the early '20s. It was a "high society" commercial band, which played good dance music and show tunes. In the late '20s, the band played in New York City at the Brunswick Hotel for ten years and the Central Park Casino. Songwriter Jerome Kern titled the Reisman Orchestra "The String Quartet of Dance Bands." Reisman added the two-piano team of Nat Brandwynne and Eddy Duchin in 1928 and brought in Lee Wiley to serve as the band's vocalist. By 1932, members of the band included dancer Fred Astaire, composer Harold Arlen, trumpeters Max Kaminsky and Bubba Miley, and Johnny Dunn. In 1937, the Reisman Orchestra played the International Exposition Paris, France, and in 1939, the band played at the Strand Theater in New York City and featured vocalist Dinah Shore. The band's theme song through the years was "What Is This Thing Called Love?" The band recorded for Decca, Vocalion, Victor, Brunswick, and Columbia Records. By 1941, the band's "corny" arrangements were no longer in style, as the swing era had begun, and the band dissolved. Reisman died in Miami, Florida on December 18, 1961.

DANNY RUSSO

(Danny Russo and His Oriole Orchestra) In the early '20s, violinist Danny Russo and Ted Fio Rito joined together to form the Russo-Fio Rito Orchestra and were booked into the Oriole Terrace in Detroit where the band became very popular. In 1927, Russo and Rito parted company and Russo formed his own band, the Oriole Orchestra, which played in Chicago and throughout the Midwest. Some of the featured sidemen included Jim Jackson, Don Hughes, Paul Wittenmeyer, Ralph Barnhart, Hector Herbert, Fritz Holtz, Roy Johnson, George Welsheipi, Ralph Pierce, and Max Williams. By the end of the '30s, Russo retired from the music business. He died on December 15, 1944.

NAT SHILKRET

(Nat Shilkret and His Orchestra) Born December 25, 1899 in Queens, New York. Nat Shilkret (né: Naftule Schuldkraut) began studying violin and clarinet at age four with George Gershwin's teacher, Charles Hambitzer. Shilkret called himself "just another Jew born on Christmas day." Two of Shilkret's brothers were also musicians—Harry played cornet and Jack led some bands. Nat Shilkret received a degree in civil engineering at Kansas's Bethany College and, in 1935, received a doctoral degree in music from the same institution. When he was 12 years old, he played with the Russian Symphony and the Arnold Volpe Orchestra. A few years later, he played with the New York Symphony Orchestra (later renamed the New York Philharmonic), conducted by Mahler and Safranov, and the Metropolitan Opera Orchestra, conducted by Walter Damrosch. He worked for the Victor Talking Machine Company (RCA) as director of light music in 1924. The first orchestra directed by Shilkret was the Victor Salon Orchestra, an operetta-playing studio band featuring jazz and popular music. He eventually also conducted the Hilo Hawaiian Orchestra, the Troubadours, the All-Star Orchestra, the Victor Orchestra, the International Novelty Orchestra, and Shilkret's Rhyth-Melodistes. In the early '20s, Shilkret and his brothers, with drummer Eddie King, recorded "When the Sun Goes Down" and "Bring Back My Blushing Rose" for Victor Records. During the period of 1924 to 1929, he recorded big hits, such as "The Sidewalks of New York," "Dancing with Tears in My Eyes," "Hallelujah," "All Alone Monday," and "Diane, I'm in Heaven When I See You Smile." During his studio days, he backed singers such as Lewis James, Franklyn Baur, and Gene Austin. Nat

Shilkret was always considered a rival of Paul Whiteman and it is said that Shilkret ended up conducting Gershwin's "Rhapsody in Blue" when Whiteman failed to show up for the recording session. When the record came out, Paul Whiteman was listed as the conductor. Eventually, Whiteman left Victor Records with the claim that Shilkret was receiving better treatment than he. Shilkret continued working for Victor until 1945. Nat Shilkret was the composer of "The Lonesome Road," a tune which became world famous. Shilkret died in Long Island, New York on February 18, 1982.

SMITH BALLEW

(Smith Ballew and His Orchestra) Born in Palestine, Texas on January 21, 1902. Ballew was a singer (baritone) who led a band in the Dallas–Fort Worth area in Texas in the early '20s. He attended the University of Texas and gained a reputation for his high baritone sound and wide vocal range. He made a number of recordings and, in the late '20s and early '30s, was heard on radio. He replaced Al Jolson on the radio program *Shell Château*. Great trumpet player Bunny Berigan played with the Smith Ballew Orchestra in 1932. From 1928 to 1937, Ballew sang in the New York area and recorded with a number of popular bands. In the late '20s, he made a number of records for Okeh, Banner, Crown, Columbia, and Paramount, including "Painting the Clouds with Sunshine," "Out Where the Blues Began," and "Just You, Just Me." Some of the sidemen who worked with the Smith Ballew Orchestra included Tommy and Jimmy Dorsey, Glenn Miller, Ray McKinley, Joe Venuti, Ellie Lang, Babe Russin, Jack Teagarden, and Bunny Berigan. Kay Weber was the female vocalist. The band's theme song was "Tonight, There is Music in the Air." They signed off with "Home." Ballew played a role in the Hollywood movie *Palm Springs* with Frances Langford. Ben Selvin took over the conductorship of band while he was gone. Ballew did not return and Tommy Dorsey started his own band using most of Ballew's sidemen so the Ballew band disbanded. Ballew remained in Hollywood and with his good looks and tall figure (six feet, five inches) became one of the original Singing Cowboys. After leaving the movie business, he became a manager in the missile division of an aircraft company. He retired to Fort Worth, Texas and died there on March 12, 1984.

BEN BERNIE

(Ben Bernie and All the Lads) Born May 30, 1894 in Bayonne, New Jersey. Ben Bernie (né: Bernard Anzelevitz) showed brilliance as a violin student at an early age and, at 15, taught violin in a local music school. After high school, he enrolled in a technical college and began producing college shows. When he left the technical college, he did violin playing and monologues in vaudeville in the Midwestern and Eastern states. He was not an instant hit  and returned to New York, where he served as an emcee at Reisenweber's Restaurant. Although he was grateful for this job, he longed to return to vaudeville to perform. Around this time, he met gagster Phil Baker and they teamed up and became successful, making some recordings prior to WWI. After the war Bernie decided that band leading would become his professional career patterning his band after Paul Whiteman's "symphonic" approach. To accomplish this, he took over a band formerly led by Don Juelee. He was quickly signed to open at a new hotel, New York's Roosevelt Hotel, and played there from 1923 until 1929. He had many live radio broadcasts from the hotel, and it was there that he developed, "This is Ben Bernie, the ol' maestro, yowsah," a trademark greeting familiar to all who lived during that period. He would typically close his broadcasts with, "Yowsah, yowsah, yowsah. And au revoir, chil'en... This is your ol' maestro, Ben Bernie, and All the Lads, sayin' God bless you and pleasant dreams." The Pabst Brewing Company sponsored the popular Bernie radio show from 1933 until 1937. At that time, the band recorded many popular songs and appeared in films (one, costarring with famous news reporter Walter Winchell). Some of the songs recorded by the band for Decca Records were "Out Where the Moonbeams Are Born," "Following You Around," "I'm Bringing a Red, Red Rose," "A Little Bit Bad," "There's a Lull in My Life," and "Sleepy Time Gal." Some of the band's personnel included singer Dinah Shore, saxophonist Dick Stabile, and trombonist Lou McGarity. The band's theme song was "Lonesome Old Town." They closed each evening with "Au Revoir." It was said that Ben Bernie was the one of most generous, thoughtful, and nicest bandleaders of his era. The band remained popular into the '40s. Bernie died in Beverly Hills, Calfornia on October 20, 1943.

BRADY'S CLARINET ORCHESTRA

(Brady's Clarinet Orchestra and Vicksburg Blowers) King Brady was a Chicago musician who played alto saxophone and clarinet. He originally came to Chicago from New Orleans. Brady's Clarinet Orchestra consisted of King Brady, Johnny St. Cyr, or Ikey Robinson, banjo; Tiny Parham, piano; Leroy Pickett, violin; and Ernest "Mike" Michall, clarinet. During the '20s, the orchestra made several records for the Champion record label and others. Brady also led a South Side Chicago band called the Vicksburg Blowers, a small band consisting of Brady, Ferman Tapp, banjo; Tony Snapp, piano; Sterling Payne, alto saxophone; and Ernest Michall, trumpet.

EARL BURTNETT

(Earl Burtnett and His La Biltmore Orchestra) Born in Harrisburg, Illinois on February 7, 1896. Burtnett began his professional music career in 1918 with the Art Hickman band in San Franscisco. The great promoter, Florenz Ziegfeld, moved the orchestra to New York City and featured them in the *Ziegfeld Follies* in 1929. In 1930, the Hickman band opened at the Coconut Grove in the Ambassador Hotel in Los Angeles. Hickman then retired and turned the band over to the leadership of Earl Burtnett. After making a success of the old Hickman band, Burtnett gained financial backing and started his own band, which, for many years, was the featured band at the Biltmore Hotel in San Franscisco. His band later backed the platinum blonde singer Ruth Lee at the Drake Hotel in Chicago. The band moved to Houston, Texas in 1933 and played at the Rice Hotel for a year and a half, after which they returned to Chicago and played at the Drake Hotel in the Gold Coast Room, broadcasting nightly on radio station WGN. Earl Burtnett retired and disbanded in 1936 but reorganized again in 1937. In 1941, he again left the music business to operate a restaurant in Bremerton, Washington with Catherine, his wife. Burtnett died in Chicago, Illinois on January 20, 1946.

FRANK DAILEY

(Frank Dailey and His Stop-and-Go Music) Born in 1901. Frank Dailey is primarily remembered for his club Frank Dailey's Meadowbrook in New York City. Dailey led several bands; one was called the Stop-and-Go Orchestra. Joe Mooney wrote the arrangements for another of Dailey's bands that included Louise Wallace as the girl singer. Sidemen with the Dailey band were Arnold Ross, Phil Baird, Curly Barron, Birt Apikian, George Odell, Louis Alpert, Gene Hammond, Harry Berman, Frank Hope, Cliff Cailey, Michael Treetino, Charles Amsterdam, Michael Jay, Jack Shilkret, Al Fish, Fred Eckert, Al Weber, Jack Margolin, Henry Muller, William Wachsman, Louis Martin, William Burger, and Phil Baird. The theme song of the Frank Dailey band was "Gypsy Violin." The band recorded for Vocalion, Embassy, Variety, and Bluebird records. Frank Dailey died on February 27, 1956 in Montclair, New Jersey.

CLYDE DOERR

(Clyde Doerr and His Orchestra) Born in Coldwater, Michigan. Doerr learned to play alto saxophone while attending high school at his hometown. He received his B.M. from the King Conservatory in San Jose, California, where he studied the violin. Art Hickman heard Doerr playing alto saxophone at the Techau Tavern in San Francisco in 1916 and hired him to play in the Art Hickman Orchestra. Doerr, Bert Ralton, and Frank Ellis recorded several records as the Hickman Trio. By 1919, Doerr had migrated to New York City and the show producer Florenz Ziegfeld hired the Doerr band to play in his show. In 1921, the Doerr group was playing at Club Royale and making records. By 1923, the band had moved to Chicago and were playing at the Congress Hotel. In 1927, Clyde Doerr published a folio of easy saxophone solos.

FRANCIS GRINNELL

(Francis Grinnell and the Eight Melody Boys; Francis Grinnell Orchestra) Born in Bay City, Michigan on April 17, 1905. Grinnell was the son of the president of the Grinnell Brothers Music Company, Jay Grinnell from Detroit. Francis Grinnell played banjo and guitar and led his own band in 1922 while still a high school student. Leaving high school, he played at the Detroit Athletic Club, The Greystone Ballroom, and at several theaters in the area. He went bankrupt when he took the vaudeville-style band on the road and, in 1927, joined the Orange Blossoms (later called the Casa Loma Orchestra). The personnel at that time included Howard "Howdy" Hall, piano; Knox Pugh, drums and vocals; Mike Kelly, bass; Francis Grinnell, banjo and vocals; Clem Johnson and Ken Ferguson, trumpets; Red Ginsler, trombone; Spike Knoblauch (Glen Gray), Ray Eberle, and Larry Teal, saxophones; Phil Levinson, violin; and Hank Biagini, leader. Eventually, Grinnell became a consultant to the Gibson Corporation for guitars and banjos. Francis married in 1926 and remarried in 1981. He died in Green Valley, Arizona on September 1991.

FRANK GUARENTE

(Frank Guarente and the Georgians) Born in Montemiletto, Italy in 1893. Guarente's parents moved to Allentown, Pennsylvania in 1910, and then to New Orleans four years later. It was in New Orleans that Frank began studying music, taking trumpet lessons from Joe "King" Oliver. He joined the U.S. Army in WWI and led a band in Europe exposing American jazz to many Europeans. Returning to the states after the war, Gurente joined Phil Specht's Dance band and formed a combo, the Georgians, within the larger Specht congregation. Each evening when the ballroom of the hotel in which the Specht Band was working closed, the smaller group, the Georgians, would entertain the guests in the hotel lounge. The Georgians were most active until 1923. After which, Frank Guarente joined the trumpet section in the Dorsey Brothers band. Guarente died in 1942.

GEORGE HALL

(George Hall and His Orchestra) Hall played violin and led a band that played stock arrangements and recorded for the ARC record label. The band was most active in the '20s. The first George Hall band was called the Arcaians. During the period of 1927 to 1929 his recording singers included Irving Kaufman Leroy Montesanto, Fred Wilson, and Scrapy Lambert. The Hall Orchestra's theme songs were "Every Minute of the Hour" and "Love Letters in the Sand," the latter being most closely associated with the band. While playing an extended engagement at the Taft Hotel in New York City the band had nightly radio coverage and signed a recording contract with the RCA Bluebird label.

The band later recorded for Pathe, Cameo, Banner, Variety, Okeh, and Vocalion records. In 1933, singer Loretta Lee was featured with the band and was considered one of the top big band singers at that time. She married and retired from the music business in 1935 and was replaced by Dolly Dawn. By 1937, the vocal group later known as the Modernaries with the Glenn Miller Orchestra joined the Hall Orchestra recording on Variety Records. In 1941, in a ceremony held in the Roseland Ballroom in New York, George Hall turned over his band to singer Dolly Dawn and retired. Soon after that Dolly changed the name of the orchestra to Dolly Dawn and Her Dawn Patrol Orchestra.

HENRY HALSTEAD

(Henry Halstead Orchestra) Henry Halstead formed his band in 1922 and played at the St. Francis Hotel in San Francisco. The exposure of hour-long radio broadcasts on station KGO brought fame to the band from Hawaii and the West Coast. The job lasted for three years. He then traveled to Los Angeles where he assumed the leadership of an organized band that had lost its leader. Returning to his hometown of Seattle, Washington, he leased a ballroom and went into business for himself. At that time, the band's roster included Harold Peppie, Ernie Reed, Ted Schilling, Chuck Moll, Hal Chanslor, Phil Harris, Don Hopkins, Zebe Mann, Abe Maule, Ross Dugat, Dick Hart, Glen Hopkins, Craig Leach, and Red Nichols. The band left Seattle and traveled to Spokane, Tacoma, and San Franscisco, where they played at Tait's Pompelian Room. In 1926, they opened at Los Angeles's Lafayette Hotel and the Edgewater Beach Club in Santa Monica followed by an extended job at the Plantation Ballroom. It is believed that the Henry Halstead Orchestra was the first band to make a movie short. The Halstead Orchestra short was shot in 1927 by Warner Brothers and was called *Carnival Nights in Paris*. The Halstead band recorded for Victor Records. Halstead disbanded his orchestra and retired in the early '30s in Phoenix, Arizona.

JOHNNY JOHNSON

(Johnny Johnson and His Hotel Statler Orchestra) Born in Washington, Indiana in 1902. Johnny Johnson (né: Malcolm Johnson) played piano and organ in various nightclubs while a student at Indiana University during his teens. He played piano in the Harry Yerkes Orchestra for a short while before forming his own band in 1922. Although he had talented sidemen in his band, including Red Nichols, Jack Teagarden and singers Harry McDaniel, Sam Browne, Franklyn Bauer, Bob Teaster, Walter Batsford, and Lee Johnson, the group was not too successful. By 1926, he disbanded and played piano with a band led by Ben Bernie. In 1929, he formed another band, which was also met without much success. At the beginning of the '30s, he changed the style of his group, from swing to commercial and the band worked more often. His theme songs were "If I Could Be with You" and "After All." By 1936, the band was broadcasting on radio regularly, including a series on the *Tasty-Yeast* radio program. The band did a series of recordings, which included tunes like "Sunbeams," "Thou Swell," and "Lullaby of Broadway." By the early '40s, Johnny Johnson disbanded, moved to New Jersey, and opened a piano-teaching studio, playing occasionally in local clubs.

ROGER WOLFE KAHN

(Roger Wolfe Kahn and His Orchestra) Born in Morristown, New Jersey on October 19, 1907. When Kahn was seven years old, he began to study the violin ultimately learning to play 18 instruments. Heir to a fortune, he considered music and his band a hobby. Kahn began to compose music when he was 12 and formed his first band by age 15, playing in and around New York City. During the course of his leadership, he hired the best musicians money could buy, including Jack Teagarden, Miff Mole, and Gene Krupa. By age 20, his band included Joe Venuti on violin and Eddie Lang on guitar. The Kahn Orchestra recorded for Brunswick, Columbia, and Victor records. By the mid '20s, Kahn owned his own nightclub and ran his own booking office. By the mid '30s, he got out of music and became interested in aviation and, by 1941, became a test pilot for an aircraft manufacturer. Kahn died at the age of 54 in July 12, 1962.

BENNY KRUEGER

(Benny Krueger and His Orchestra) Born on June 17, 1899. The management of RCA Victor Records felt that a jazz band should have a saxophone player and Ben Krueger was its choice. This was the reason that Krueger was placed in the Original Dixieland Jazz Band. It is thought that this was the first jazz band ever to include a saxophone. Prior to that appointment Krueger had recorded for

Brunswick and Gennett Records. When Krueger joined the ODJB in New York they recorded "Palesteena," a Conrad-Robinson tune. At that time, the personnel included J. Russel Robinson, piano; Benny Krueger, alto saxophone; Tony Sbarbaro, drums; Larry Shields, clarinet, Eddie Edwards, trombone; and Nick LaRocca, cornet. During the '30s, Krueger's band played behind a number of singers, including Bing Crosby, and during his career worked with Bill Rank, George Thow, Eddie Land, Woody Herman, J. Russel Robinson, Saxie Mansfield, Hank Stern, Tommy Dorsey, Henry Ragas, Jimmy Dorsey, Bunny Berigan, Will Bradley, and Larry Gomar. Krueger died on April 21, 1967.

ABE LYMAN

(Abe Lyman and His Californians) Born in Chicago, Illinois in 1897. Abe Lyman (né: Abraham Simon) began in music as a drummer and, during the Roaring '20s, Lyman and Gus Arnheim began their careers as co-leaders of a band called the Syncopated Five. At that time, they co-wrote the tune "I Cried for You." Lyman later wrote "After I Say I'm Sorry," "Mandalay," and "Mary Lou." When Lyman and Arnheim split up, Lyman formed his own band and opened at the Coconut Grove in Los Angeles. At various times, composer Teddy Powell played with the Lyman band, as did harpist Caspar Reardon. Lyman formed a new band in 1943, which included Ray Heath and Si Zenter, trombones; Marty Gold, violin; Wolfie Tannenbaum, saxophone; Billy Bauer, guitar; and his wife, Rose Blaine. Other sidemen included Yank Lawson, Carmen Cavallaro, Al Newman, Ray Lopez, and Gus Arnheim. The Lyman band was featured on the radio show *Waltz Time* in NBC. The band's theme songs were "Moon Over America" and "California, Here I Come." They recorded for Bluebird, Decca, and Brunswick records. Abe Lyman died in Beverly Hills, California in 1957.

MARION McKAY

(Marion McKay and His Orchestra) McKay was a banjo player who started his first band in the early '20s. McKay's band was a territory band and it is said that his was the first band to record on the new electrical system in Richmond, Indiana at Gennett Records. The McKay band played primarily in Cincinnati, Detroit and Cleveland with an occasional booking in New York City. The band's theme song was "Dreamy Melody," and the singers with the group included Fred Stuart and Jack Tillson. Instrumental sidemen were Eddie Page, Ernie Weaver, Marlin Skiles, Clem Johnson, Red Ginslar, Jack Tillson, Roger Beals, Skinny Budd, Harry Bason, Paul Weirick, Izzy George, Terry George, Russell Mock, Henry Lang, George Agonost, Ambrose Barringer, Leroy Morris, Doc Marshall, and Ernie McKay.

BENNIE MOTEN

(Bennie Moten and His Orchestra) Born in Kansas City, Missouri on November 13, 1894. Moten formed a trio in 1922 known as Bennie, Bailey & Dude sometimes referred to as Big, Black & Dirty which grew into a big band. With blues singer Ada Brown, the band made its first recording in 1923 and, by 1926, the band known as Bennie Moten's Kansas City Orchestra was recording for RCA Victor Records. Throughout the '20s, Moten also booked other bands that toured under his name. To improve the quality of his group, Moten began recruiting players from other bands to play in his band, musicians such as Ben Webster, saxophone; "Hot Lips" Page, trumpet; Jimmy Rushing, singer; and William "Count" Basie, piano and arranger. All of those men were taken from the Blue Devils Orchestra headed by Walter Page. In December 1932, the Moten group became known officially as Bennie Moten's Kansas City Orchestra and the instrumentation was Willie McWashington, drums; Walter Page, bass; Leroy Berry, guitar; Count Basie, piano and arranger; Ben Webster, tenor saxophone; Jack Washington, alto and baritone saxophones; Eddie Barefield, clarinet and alto saxophone; Eddie Durham, trombone and guitar; Dan Minor, trombone; Dee Stewart, Joe Keyes and Oran "Hot Lips" Page, trumpets; and Bennie Moten, leader and piano. In 1935, Bennie Moten had a botched tonsillectomy and died. William "Count" Basie took over the Moten Orchestra.

NEW ORLEANS OWLS

The New Orleans Owls were comprised of Lester Smith and Pinky Vidacovich, clarinets and saxophones; Benjie White, clarinet, saxophone and leader; Bill Pardon, cornet; Frank Netto, trombone; Dan LeBlanc, tuba; Nappy Lamare, banjo and vocals; Rene Gelpi, banjo and guitar; Moses Farrar and Sigfre Christensen, piano; Earl Crumb, drums; and Red Bowman, cornet and vocals.

The Owls played at hotels and clubs in New Orleans between 1922 and 1929, and were one of the few bands recorded in New Orleans in the '20s. The band was originally The Invincibles String band that played in New Orleans beginning in 1912. The New Orleans Owls often played for the society set in New Orleans.

RED NICHOLS

(Red Nichols and His Five Pennies) Born in Ogden, Utah on May 8, 1905. Red Nichols (né: Ernest Loring Nichols) developed his music abilities as a child as he studied cornet with his father who was a college music teacher. He was influenced by Bix Beiderbecke and used interesting harmonies in a polished, unemotional style. In 1923, he joined the Johnny Johnson Orchestra and traveled to New York City. From 1925 until 1932, he led a Broadway show pit orchestra playing for two George Gershwin productions, *Strike Up the Band* and *Girl Crazy*. He also organized a band for Cliff "Ukelele Ike" Edwards and it opened in 1925 at the Hotel Pennsylvania in New York City. By 1931, he was fronting a band in Cleveland, Ohio at the Golden Pheasant Restaurant. During that period, he also played part-time in bands led by Ross Gorman, Sam Lanin, Paul Whiteman, and Roger Wolfe Kahn. He recorded often, using names such as Charleston Chasers, the Louisiana Rhythm Kings, and the Red Heads. By 1934, Nichols was conducting a band for the radio series *Kellogg College Prom*. This band, previously organized by Gil Rodin, recorded under the name of Clark Randall and His Orchestra. At this time, Nichols was doing a series of records for the Brunswick Record Company under the name of Red Nichols and His Five Pennies. The band included sidemen such as Jimmy Dorsey, Benny Goodman, Glenn Miller, Arthur Shutt, Vic Berton, Miff Mole, Fud Livingston, Eddie Lang, and Joe Venuti. During the '30s, Nichols toured with his own big band and fronted several studio orchestras, including the *Bob Hope Show*. In the late '30s, he played around the Metroplex in Los Angeles. In 1940, he took a band, including Bill Darnell, singer; Harry Jaeger, drums and singer; Henie Beau, clarinet; and Bill Maxted, piano, into New York's Famous Door Club. In 1942, he joined Glen Gray and the Casa Loma Orchestra for a brief time before he moved to Hollywood. By 1959, the movie *The Five Pennies*, reflecting the life of Red Nichols with Danny Kaye playing Red, was released. During his lifetime, Red Nichols recorded often and many of his albums were released by

Capitol Records, including *Hot Pennies, Dixieland Dinner Dance, In Love with Red, Red Nichols at Marineland, Parade of the Pennies, Blues and Old-Time Rags, Meet the Five Pennies, The All-Time Hits of Red Nichols,* and *The Five Pennies and Dixieland Supper Club.* He also recorded for many independent record companies, such as Audiophile Records, Take Two Records, Broadway Intermission, and EMI Electrola. Many biographies have been written about Red Nichols who died in Las Vegas, Nevada on June 28, 1965.

BARNEY RAPP

(Barney Rapp and His New Englanders) Barney Rapp (né: Barney Rappaport) was a Midwest attraction, having formed his first orchestra in Connecticut during the early '20s. He built a reputation through a nightly radio broadcast from a club in Cincinnati after settling down in Cleveland, Ohio. Their recordings on the Bluebird and RCA Victor labels furthered the reputation of the band. One of the first singers with the Rapp band was Doris Day. Barney Rapp recommended two young singers from Cincinnati to Tony Pastor in 1947, Rosemary and Betty Clooney. At that time, Rosemary was 17 and Betty was 15 years old. Barney Rapp's younger brother, Barry Wood, was also a singer and was contracted for the radio show *Lucky Strike Hit Parade,* and eventually became a television producer. Rapp eventually went to California and appeared in a motion picture. He died in Cincinnati in the early '70s.

FREDDIE RICH

(Freddie Rich and His Orchestra) Born in Warsaw, Poland on January 31, 1898. Rich was a pianist who fronted a big band in the '20s. He toured Europe from 1925 to 1928, returned to the U.S. and played for many months at the Waldorf-Astoria in New York City. He then led many studio bands, which featured jazz musicians such as Tony Parentini, the Dorsey Brothers (Tommy and Jimmy), Benny Goodman, Joe Venuti, and Bunny Berigan. Elmer Feldkamp was one of his singers in the early '30s. The Rich Orchestra was featured on several radio shows, including *The Family Hotel, The Abbott and Costello Show,* and *Penthouse Party.* The theme songs of the Rich band were "So Beats My Heart for You" and "I'm Always Chasing Rainbows." The band recorded for Camden, Vocalion, Paramount, Columbia Harmony, Banner, Gennett, and Okeh records. In the late '30s, Rich was music director of several radio stations. In the early '40s, he moved to Hollywood and took a staff position with United Artists Studios. He was badly injured from a fall in 1945 and suffered partial paralysis. Freddie Rich died in Beverly Hills, California on September 8, 1956 at the age of 58.

VINCENT ROSE

(Vincent Rose and His Montemartre Café Orchestra) Born in Palermo, Italy on June 13, 1880. The Vincent Rose Orchestra began in the early '20s in Hollywood, California. The Montemartre Café was the hangout of many movie stars of the day, many of whom played instruments and sat in with the band. Stars like Fatty Arbuckle and Tom Mix were regulars. Harry Owens was the featured trumpet player. The band later played at the Ritz-Carlton in New York and at the College Inn in Chicago. During the early '30s, the band toured often and recorded for Banner, Victor, Columbia, Perfect, and Gennett Records. In addition to Owens, sidemen included Jack Van Cott, Albert Jaeger, Jackie Taylor, Bobby Burns, and Buster Johnson. Singers were Smith Ballew, Dorothy Brent, Scrappy Lambert, Joe Prince, Irving Kaufman, Dick Robertson, and Chick Bullock. In the mid-'30s, Rose disbanded. Rose died in Rockville Center, New York on May 20, 1944.

VIRGINIANS, THE

(The Virginians Orchestra) A group of musicians who performed under different leaders, The Virginians recorded in the early '30s led by Ross Gorman. [See Ace Brigode and His Fourteen Virginians.]

CHARLIE DAVIS

(Charlie Davis and His band) The Davis band began in Indianapolis, Indiana during the early '20s and toured through the '20s and '30s. During their travels they starred at the Paramount Theater in New York City in 1930. The singer at that time was Dick Powell who later became a headliner in motion pictures. Charlie Davis and Bix Beiderbecke composed the famous tune "Copenhagen." Davis wrote a book, which was published in 1982, entitled *That Band from Indiana.*

DUKE ELLINGTON

(Duke Ellington and His Orchestra) Born on April 29, 1899 in Washington, D.C. Edward Kennedy (Duke) Ellington was born of moderately well-to-do parents and began to take piano lessons when he was eight. When in high school, he attended some black neighborhood "rent parties" and heard many of the great pianists of the day, including James P. Johnson and Jimmy Yancey. While working in an ice cream parlor, the Poodle Dog Café, he wrote his first composition. In 1919, he played in a group led by Elmer Snowden and met the drummer Sonny Greer, with whom he would have a 31-year relationship. He began with a small group in D.C. and eventually took over a band called the Washingtonians. The band played at the Hollywood Club in New York City in

1923. His band became known for its "jungle style" and even some of the early recordings of the Duke Ellington Orchestra labeled him Duke Ellington and the Jungle band. During the '30s and '40s, the band evolved into a definite jazz role with great soloists and an increasing number of original compositions by the Duke. A number of outstanding soloists joined the band, including Johnny Hodges, alto saxophone; "Tricky" Sam Nanton, trombone; Harry Carney, baritone saxophone; and Bubber Miley and Cootie Williams, trumpets. Some of the band members remained with the Duke for 20 and 30 years. Ellington's theme songs were "Take the A Train," "Solitude," and "East St. Louis Toodle-oo." He collaborated with composer-arranger Billy Stayhorn on a number of successful pieces and the two of them created some enduring compositions. Some of those works are "Black-and-Tan Fantasy," "Sophisticated Lady," and "Harlem Airshaft." Of the more than 1,000 songs written by Ellington, "I Let a Song Go Out of My Heart," "Satin Doll," "Just Squeeze Me," "Sentimental Lady," "Creole Love Call," "Sentimental Mood," and "Sophisticated Lady" are just a few. The Ellington band recorded for Musicraft, Columbia, Regal, Victor, Okeh, Gennett, Brunswick, Harmony, and Vocalion records. Ellington died in New York City on May 24, 1974.

LANI McINTIRE

(Lani McIntire and His Orchestra) Born in Honolulu, Hawaii on December 15, 1904. McIntire was educated at the College of Hawaii and was a member of a U.S. Navy band. In the '20s, he appeared as a singer with his own orchestra. In the early '30s, he scored the music for early sound films in Hollywood and appeared in hotels, on radio, and in various nightclubs. McIntire also appeared in the movie *Waikiki Wedding*. George McConnell and Dick Sanford were his chief collaborators in songwriting. They wrote "Hearts Are Never Blue in Blue Kalua," "Next Door to Heaven," "Sailing Away from the Islands," "My Little Red Rose," "The One Rose That's Left in my Heart," "Sweet Hawaiian Chimes," "I Picked a Flower in Hawaii," "Aloha," and others. McIntire died in New York City on June 17, 1951.

SCOTT (BUD) FISHER

(Bud Fisher and His Commodores, Scott Fisher and His Orchestra) Born in the Bronx, New York on June 16, 1905. Fisher's family moved to Bogota, New Jersey when Scott was 13 years old. His younger brother, William Hardy "Billy" Fisher, started a group known as the Musical Fishers in 1923 and played at the Sphinx Club in the Waldorf-Astoria Hotel in New York City on the bill with Will Rogers. At that time, saxophonist Scott was 17 years old and pianist-brother Billy was nine. Scott's first band was known as Bud Fisher and His Commodores. Scott's orchestra became well known in New York and New Jersey during the early '30s, being heard on radio stations WADA, WJZ, WAAT, WEAF, and WABC on a regular basis. The group played at the Rustic Cabin in New Jersey for two years among other engagements. They also played with some regularity on the Cunard cruise line, sailed as far as Cuba, and played a winter engagement in Bermuda at the Bermudiana Hotel. They returned to New York to play an extended engagement at the Park Central Hotel. Some of the prominent sidemen to play with Fisher included Hal Mooney, Gordon Griffin, and Toots Camarata. After a brief tour, the band split up and Fisher became a music copyist for Ray Bloch and for Broadway shows such as *My Fair Lady*, *The Music Man*, *The Apple Tree*, *Golden Boy*, and *How to Succeed in Business Without Really Trying*. Fisher died on August 2, 1972 in Flemington, New Jersey. His brother Billy, although younger, preceded him in death, passing away on April 24, 1972.

GEORGIA MELODIANS

Violinist Charles Boulanger, who fronted the band, is generally listed as the leader but it was thought that Hill Hudchins and Ernie Intelhouse really co-led the Melodians. The group was most active from 1923 to 1927, but the original band actually broke up in December of 1924. The Edison Recording Company continued to use the name through 1926. The original band included Oscar Young, piano; George Troupe, trombone; George Troupe, trombone; Elmer Merry, banjo; Carl Gerrold, drums; and Charles Boulanger, violin. The band played in Lynchburg, North Carolina in 1923 and traveled to New York City in 1924 where they played at the Cinderella Ballroom opposite the Paul Van Logan Orchestra. The band which made the 1924–1925 recordings for Edison was made up of original musicians Boulanger, Young, Merry, and Gerrold, with

Vernon Dalhart, vocals; Ernie Intelhouse, cornet; Herb Winfield, trombone; Merritt Kenworthy, clarinet and alto and baritone saxophones; and Clarence Hutchins, clarinet and alto and tenor saxophones. Abe Lincoln, trombone; Mickey Bloom, trumpet; and Charlie Butterfield, trombone, played on some of the Edison record dates. The Melodians left the Cinderella Ballroom to play at the Strand Roof opposite the Henri Gendron Orchestra. They played a New Year's Eve job at the Hotel Almac in New York and disbanded. Some great tunes were recorded by the band for Edison Records, including "I Can't Get the One I Want," "Red Hot Mamma," "Everybody Loves My Baby," "Doo Wac a Doo," "I'm Bound for Tennessee," "Give Us the Charleston," "Red Hot Henry Brown," "Spanish Shawl," "Hangin' Around," "Rhythm of the Day," "Why Did You Do It?" "Charley, My Boy," "San," "I'm Satisfied," "My Mammy's Blues," "Yes Sir," "That's My Baby," "She's Drivin' Me Wild," "Charleston Ball," "I Found a New Baby," and "Everybody's Charleston Crazy."

MAL HALLETT

(Mal Hallett and His Orchestra) Born in Roxbury, Massachusetts in 1893. Hallett was a handsome, six-and-one-half-feet-tall, waxed-moustache, wavy-haired bandleader. He graduated from the New England Conservatory of Music and, during WWI, toured France, playing with the Al Moore band. In the '30s, the Mal Hallett Orchestra did one-nighters throughout the New England states and was considered one of the early "swing" bands. The Hallett theme song was "The Boston Tea Party." Many of his sidemen became legends, including Gene Krupa, drums; Frankie Carle, piano; Clark Yocum, singer; Buddy Welcome, saxophone; Buddy Wise, saxophone; Dick Taylor, trombone; Toota Mondello, saxophone; Jack Teagarden, trombone; and Mickey McMickle, trumpet. The Hallett Orchestra recorded for Okeh, Vocalion, Decca, Percfect, Columbia, Harmony, and Paramount records. Mal Hallett died in Boston on November 20, 1952.

CASS HAGAN

(Cass Hagan and His Orchestra) Born in Edgwater, New Jersey in 1904. Hagan, a pianist and arranger, attended Manhattan College where he formed a combo that included Lennie Hayton. They played clubs and resorts in the Eastern part of the U.S. In 1926, Hagan expanded the band and worked at the Hotel Manger in New York City (it later became the Taft Hotel). The band opened at the Park Central Hotel with personnel that included Al Philburn, Pee Wee Russell, Don Murray, and Red Nichols. Hagan disbanded temporarily in early 1928 but reorganized with new personnel and toured the Midwest. In the late '20s, Hagan and Nichols formed a combo and toured the West Coast. In the '30s, Hagan became a nightclub owner and retired from the music business. The Hagan band recorded for Columbia and Edison records.

ART LANDRY

(Art Landry and His Call of the North Orchestra) Landry organized his band in the early '20s, playing clarinet and fronting the band, and they toured throughout the U.S. The famous host of the *Major Bowes Amateur Hour* radio program, Ted Mack, was a sideman in the Landry Orchestra. The Landry group recorded for RCA Victor and Gennett Records prior to the beginning of the big band era.

RAY MILLER

(Ray Miller and His Orchestra) Ray Miller led an obscure band in the early '20s. Some very important musicians played on the Miller band from time to time, including Wingy Manone, Frankie Trumbauer, Miff Mole, Rube Bloom and Muggsy Spanier. Some of the records they cut for Sunbeam Records include *That's Plenty*, *Angry*, *Weary Blues*, and *Stomp Your Stuff*. In addition to Sunbeam Records, the band also made recordings for Brunswick from 1924 to 1930. In 1939, the Ray Miller Orchestra played for the *Sunny Meadows* radio program and recorded for Brunswick, Okeh, Columbia, and Vocalion records.

BOYD SENTER

(Boyd Senter and His Senterpedes) Born on November 30, 1899 in Lyons, Nebraska. Senter was primarily a clarinetist but played many other instruments as well. By age 17, he was playing in various theater bands and from 1921 to 1922 led his own band in Atlantic City, New Jersey. He played in the Chicago Deluxe Orchestra in 1923 and, during the remainder of the '20s, led various-sized groups. During the early '30s he directed the orchestra at the Colonial Theater in Detroit. The band's theme song was "Bad Habits." All during WWII, he did defense work for the U.S. and, in the late '40s, led a band in the Detroit area, continuing through the '50s and '60s when he operated Boyds's Sport Senter in Mio, Michigan. The Senter band recorded for Okeh, Victor, and Paramount records.

BEN SELVIN

(Ben Selvin and His Orchestra) Born in 1900. Selvin began his career in the early '20s as a music contractor, an agent. He booked bands for one-nighters, dances, and record dates. At that time, many other band leaders, e.g., Edgar Benson, Meyer Davis, Sam Lanin, etc. also acted as contractors. As a band-leader, he recorded for nine record companies, under nine different names. It is said that he recorded more than 9,000 different tunes, more than Bing Crosby who was said to have recorded 2,700. Famous sidemen such as Tommy and Jimmy Dorsey, Benny Goodman, Joe Venuti, Manny Klein, Miff Mole, Eddie Lang, and Red Nichols recorded with the Ben Selvin Orchestra. The Selvin Orchestra recorded for Harmony, Velvetone, Clarion, and Diva Records. In the early '40s, Selvin worked for the head of the Musicians Union, James Petrillo. His principal job was to take a survey of the recording industry and how it affected musicians, but before he could begin the survey Petrillo called a musi-cians' strike, which lasted for two years. During his career, Selvin held positions in charge of Majestic Records and RCA Victor Records. He spent many days as consultant to various corporations and founded the Associated Transcription Company, which eventually gave birth to Muzak. He invested heavily in real estate prior to his retirement.

AUSTIN WYLIE

(Austin Wylie and His Orchestra) Born in Cleveland, Ohio in 1893. A Cleveland, Ohio band in the '20s and '30s that played regularly at the Golden Pheasant. In the '20s, Artie was the clarinetist and arranger and Claude Thornhill, the pianist. Other sidemen included Vaughn Monroe, Bill Stegmeyer, Billy Butterfield, Joe Bishop, Tony Pastor, and Spud Murphy. Clarence Hutchenrider replaced Artie Shaw in the '30s. The Wylie Orchestra recorded for Vocalion and Beltoba Records. Wylie disbanded in the early '40s to manage the Artie Shaw Orchestra. He then briefly reorganized for a short period before retiring from leading a band to other business ventures in Cleveland.

HORACE HEIDT

(Horace Heidt and His Orchestra) Born in Alameda, California on May 21, 1901. Heidt played in vaudeville during the '20s and at Oakland's Lake Theater from 1929 to 1930 before doing a U.S. tour. In 1931, the band played the Palace Theater in New York City and toured Europe. The band disbanded for a year and, in 1932, Heidt, formed a new orchestra and played the Golden Gate Theater in San Franscisco. By 1936, the band had moved to Chicago, playing at the Drake Theater and broadcasting nationally. At that time, the Horace Heidt Orchestra was featuring guitarist Alvino Rey and The Triple-Tonguing Trumpeteers. By 1937, the band was called the Brigadiers and was using 16 singers, featuring The King Sisters and 14 instrumentalists. In 1939 he added a violin section—Virginia Drane, Mary Drane, and Beatrice Perron. In 1941, the Heidt Orchestra became the house band for the Biltmore Hotel, a position they held for more than eight years. During WWII, the band toured military bases and in 1945 Horace Heidt disbanded and went into real estate. By 1948, he again formed a band and played on the *Youth Opportunity* radio show for three years. He was also featured on *Family Night* with Horace Heidt, *Treasure Chest*, and *Welcome Home*. By 1953, he was hosting *Horace Heidt for Lucky Strike* and, in 1954, *The Swift Show Wagon* and the television program *Pot of Gold*. In 1956, he developed the Horace Heidt Country Club Estates in the San Fernando Valley. During his career, Heidt received two stars on Hollywood's Walk of Fame. A few of the outstanding musicians and singers appearing with the Horace Heidt Orchestra over the years were Gordon MacRae, Art Carney, Frank Devol, Frankie Carle, Bill Finegan, Irving Fazola, Pete Fountain, Al Hirt, Shorty Sherock, Ralph Edwards, Dick Contino, Ronnie Kemper, Larry Cotton, Jean Farney, Bob McCoy, Charles Goodman, Donna Wood, Ruth Davies, Gene Walsh, Frank Lowerey, Henry Russell, and Warren Covington. At this writing Horace Heidt's son Horace Heidt Jr. leads the Heidt band under the Musical Knights banner. During Heidt's leadership the band recorded for Victor, Columbia, and Brunswick records. The theme song was "I'll Love You in My Dreams." By the late '50s, he retired from music. Heidt died on December 1, 1986. He was 85 years old.

FLETCHER HENDERSON

(Fletcher "Smack" Henderson and His Orchestra) Born in Cuthbert, Georgia on December 18, 1898. Henderson organized his first band in 1921, the Black Swan Troubadours, and toured with the singer Ethel Waters while attending Atlanta University, where he majored in chemistry. Moving to New York City, he was hired as a song plugger by the W.C. Handy music publishing company. Leaving Handy, Henderson went into business with his friend Harry Pace. Together, they formed the Black Swan Record Company, where Henderson became the music director and hired Ethel Waters to make her first recording, "St. Louis Blues." In 1924, the Black Swan Record Company was absorbed by Black Patti Records, which went under in a year. Fletcher Henderson then formed a band and, in 1922, opened at the Club Alabam with sidemen that included Coleman Hawkins and Don Redman, saxophones; Charlie "Big" Green, trombone; Howard Scott and Elmer Chambers, trumpets; Bob Escudero, tuba; Kaiser Marshall, drums; Charlie Dixon, banjo; and Henderson, piano and leader. By 1926, Buster Bailey was playing clarinet, and Louis Armstrong, Elmer Chambers, Howard Scott, and Charlie Green made up the trumpet section. The band continued to grow in size and, by 1927, was comprised of Benny Morton and Jimmy Harrison, trombones; Russell Smith, Joe Smith, and Tommy Ladnier, trumpets; June Cole, tuba; and Coleman Hawkins, Buster Bailey, and Don Pasquall, saxophones. The rhythm section remained the same. By the early '30s, the personnel had changed somewhat with Billie Holiday's father Clarence on guitar, Walter Johnson, drums, and, of course, Fletcher as pianist and leader. Joining Coleman Hawkins in the saxophone section were Edgar Sampson and Russell Procope; trombonists Sandy Williams and J.C. Higginbotham joined Rex Stewart, Russell Smith, and Bobby Stark, trumpets, in the brass section. The Henderson band's theme song was "Christopher Columbus." In late 1934 and early 1935, Henderson joined the Benny Goodman band, bringing his great library written by him and Don Redman, and disbanded his own organization. He had written a few arrangements for the Goodman band, like "King Porter Stomp," prior to joining them. Historians credit Fletcher "Smack" Henderson with being one of the "inventors" of swing and swing bands. Henderson died in New York City on December 29, 1952.

GUY LOMBARDO

(Guy Lombardo and the Royal Canadians) Born in London, Ontario, Canada on June 19, 1902. The four Lombardo brothers— Carmen, Liebert, Victor, and Guy— started the Royal Canadians band in the early '20s. Liebert and Carmen actually owned the band when it first started in London, Ontario, Canada, but Guy quickly took charge and became the group's undisputed head. The band started with the "whiney" saxophone sound and kept that imprimatur throughout its existence. By the mid '20s, the band was recording for the Gennett Record

Company in Cleveland, Ohio. The Lombardo band is thought to be the first band to use the "medley" in programming as previous bands, particularly in jazz, had not used that form of arrangement. By 1927, the Royal Canadians were playing at the Grenada Cafe in Chicago and after several weeks Guy was able to convince the owners to broadcast each evening on WBBM radio. This started as a 15-minute shot and by midnight the program had picked up two sponsors and became the talk of Chicago. In 1929, the founder of MCA, Jules Stein, brought the band to New York City where they opened at the Roosevelt Grill, a job that lasted for 33 years! The shows were broadcast on station WABC, and every New Year's Eve the Royal Canadians welcomed the New Year over the NBC network. In 1933, the band traveled to Hollywood and opened at the Coconut Grove, playing for the movie stars and celebrities. They also played that year for the inauguration of President Franklin D. Roosevelt and every president since. In 1934, the band appeared in the movie *Many Happy Returns*. By 1941, all of the Lombardos had moved to Long Island, New York and, by 1954, Guy began to produce summer shows for the Long Island State Park Commission at the Jones Beach Marine Theater and produced *Hit the Deck*, *Song of Norway*, *Showboat*, *Paradise Islands*, *Mardi Gras*, *Around the World in Eighty Days*, *Arabian Nights*,

The King and I, South Pacific, Fiddler on the Roof, Showboat, Finian's Rainbow, and *Oklahoma*. By 1963, the band had sold over 200 million records and more than 6 million people had danced to their music. It is thought that the band recorded more hit records than any other band; more than 500 hit songs. During the band's heyday, Carmen Lombardo wrote "Boo-Hoo," "Coquette," "Sweethearts on Parade," "Seems Like Old Times," "You're Driving Me Crazy," "Little White Lies," "Annie Doesn't Live Here Anymore," "Little Girl," "September in the Rain," and "Everywhere You Go," among others. On November 5, 1977, Guy Lombardo died.

JIMMY NOONE

(Jimmy Noone and His Apex Club Orchestra) Born on April 25, 1895 in New Orleans, Louisiana. Noone studied clarinet with Sidney Bechet when he was very young. Noone, Bechet, and Johnny Dodds are considered the top three Dixieland clarinetists in the New Orleans tradition. Noone played with the Freddie Keppard band and the Young Olympia band in New Orleans, from 1913 to 1914. He moved to Chicago in 1917 and played with Keppard's Creole band until it dissolved in 1918, when he moved to King Oliver's band. He played for a brief period with the Ollie Powell band in 1923 and had his own group at the Nest later that year. He remained at the Nest (renamed the Apex Club) and, by 1928, Earl Hines joined the band and they began recording for Vocalion Records. The band, known as the Apex Club Orchestra, recorded "Sweet Lorraine" (their theme song) and "Four or Five Times" for Vocalion. Although the Apex Club closed in 1929, the Noone band continued working, using the same name. In 1931, Noone turned down an offer to work with the Cab Calloway band at the Cotton Club in New York, continued to live in Chicago, and toured in New Orleans, Memphis, and St. Louis through 1938. In 1943, he moved to Hollywood, played at the Streets of Paris Club and recorded with the Capitol Jazzmen. In 1944, Noone joined a Dixieland band, the New Orleans All-Stars, formed by Orson Welles for his radio show, which eventually became Kid Ory's Creole Jazz Band. Jimmy Noone died in Los Angeles, California on April 19, 1944.

CECIL SCOTT

(Cecil Scott and His Orchestra) Born in Springfield, Ohio on November 22, 1905. Scott, a clarinetist and tenor saxophonist, formed his first band in 1923 called Scott's Symphonic Syncopators. The Syncopators—comprised of Cecil Scott, saxophone and leader; brother Lloyd Scott, drums; and Don Frye, piano—moved to New York City and played in various clubs. In 1928, they worked at the Savoy Ballroom with John Williams and Harold McFeeran, saxophones; Frankie Newton and Bill Coleman, trumpets; Dicky Wells, trombone; Don Frye, piano; Lloyd Scott, drums; and Cecil Scott, saxophone and leader. Scott's injury from a fall forced his inactivity for a while during the early '30s and caused his leg to be amputated. He filled in with the Fletcher Henderson band for a short time and led the band at the Ubangi Club in 1942. By the mid '40s he played with Hot Lips Page in Chicago and Art Hodes in New York City. Scott freelanced in New York during the '40s and '50s and led a band with Jimmy McPartland and Chick Morrison in the early '50s. Cecil Scott died in New York City on January 5, 1964.

TED WEEMS

(Ted Weems and His Orchestra) Born in Pitcairn, Pennsylvania on September 26, 1901. Weems studied enginéring at the University of Pennsylvania and became so fascinated with the trombone that he began to play in various local college bands. In 1923, Weems formed an orchestra, which was a favorite in the Midwest during the '20s, '30s, and '40s. The song "Piccolo Pete" brought the band national recognition. They featured vocalists Red Ingle, Art Jarrett, Perry Como, and Marilyn Maxwell. The band began in vaudeville and various ballroom venues leading to affiliation with a number of radio programs, e.g., Jack Benny, James Melton, and Fibber McGee and Molly. The band was based in Chicago and began to record in 1933 when they featured the song "Heartaches." The tune failed to make a hit until 1947 when a programmer in North Carolina began to plug it. The band's theme song was "Out of the Night." Other singers identified with the Ted Weems Orchestra were Mary Lee, Country Washburn and Parker Gibbs. The Ted Weems Orchestra recorded for Decca, Bluebird, Columbia, and Victor records. All of the Weems band members served in the U.S. Merchant Marines during WW II. Weems died in Tulsa, Oklahoma on May 6, 1963 at the age of 61.

HERB WIEDOFT

(Herb Wiedoft and His Orchestra) In the early '20s, Wiedoft, while playing trumpet at the Cinderella Roof in Los Angeles, California, formed a band and recorded for Brunswick Records. The band was comprised of three brother teams; three Wiedoft brothers, Herb, Guy and Rudy; two Rose brothers, Gene and Vincent; and the Lucas brothers, Clyde and Leon. Other members of the band included Larry Abbot, Fred Bibesheimer, Dub Kirkpatrik, Joe Memoli, Gene Secrest, Jess Stafford, Jose Sucedo, and Art Winters. Rudy Wiedoft eventually became a well-known New York saxophonist and Claude Lucas eventually left to form his own band. The band recorded for Brunswick Records in the middle to late '20s. The band's theme song was "Cinderella Blues." Herb Wiedoft died in an automobile accident near Klamath Falls, Oregon in May 1928.

ALPHONSO TRENT

(Alphonso Trent and His Orchestra) Born in Fort Smith, Arkansas on August 24, 1905. Trent studied music at Shorter College in Little Rock, Arkansas. In 1923, he led a territory band in the Midwest. From 1925 to 1935, his band played in Dallas, Texas at the Adolphus Hotel (it is believed to have been the first all-Black band to have done so). The band had a number of very talented sidemen, including Sy Oliver, Snub Mosley, Harry "Sweets" Edison, Stuff Smith, and Peanuts Holland. The Trent Orchestra made a number of records for Gennett Records, including tunes like "Gilded Kisses," "Louder and Funnier," "St. James Infirmary," and "After You've Gone." Although Alphonso Trent left the band in 1932, the band continued to use his name until 1935, when Trent formed a sextet that included guitarist Charlie Christian and Alex Hill. By the '40s, Trent had gotten out of the music business and was selling real estate. Alphonso Trent died on October 14, 1959 at age 54.

BERNARD ADDISON

(Bernard Addison and His Orchestra) Born in Annapolis, Maryland on April 15, 1905. Addison's family moved to Washington, D.C. when he was very young and his next-door neighbor played the banjo. Addison soon learned to play banjo and guitar and, as a teenager, played with various local bands in D.C. He and one of his friends, Claude Hopkins, formed a band, which played on the outskirts of New York City in 1924. While in New York, he met Louis Armstrong and played guitar in the Armstrong band. There he had the opportunity to play with Eubie Blake, Art Tatum, Fats Waller, and Jelly Roll Morton. Addison then played with Fletcher Henderson until the mid-'30s when he formed his own band. In the mid-'30s, his band accompanied the Mills Brothers for several years and played at the Cotton Club and the Apollo Theater in New York. When he retired, Addison had led at least ten bands. He recorded in Canada with the Ink Spots and in the U.S. with the Chocolate Dandies, Billie Holiday, and Sidney Bachet. When he died on December 22, 1990 Bernard Addison was 85 years old.

CHARLIE AGNEW

(Charlie Agnew and His Orchestra) Born on June 22, 1901. Agnew, who played several reed instruments, began playing with commercial bands, including Dell Lamper, in the Chicago area in the early '20s. In 1924, he formed his own band and quickly earned a good reputation for leading one of the best hotel bands. His band traveled the country playing in some of the best hotel ballrooms in hotels like the Trianon and the Peabody. Live radio broadcasts, including the *Lucky Strike Magic Carpet* and *The Armandes Face Cream Program*, quickly brought a positive national reputation to the band. Agnew also wrote tunes like his theme song "Slow But Sure," "Fools in Love," and "Too Many on My Mind." The Charlie Agnew Orchestra recorded for Columbia and RCA Victor and singer Jeanne Carroll was featured on many of the recordings. Agnew died in Chicago, Illinois on October 22, 1978.

WALTER BARNES

(Walter Barnes and His Royal Creolians) Born in 1907 in Vicksburg, Mississippi. He attended high school in Chicago, studied music, and played clarinet in small groups in the early '20s. After high school, he went to the American Conservatory of Music and Chicago Musical College. Barnes formed Walter Barnes and His Royal Creolains in Detroit in 1924. After touring the South, the band played for two years in Cicero, Illinois at the Cotton Club. Nightly radio programs helped spread the band's reputation and they became a popular attraction in New York and throughout the Southern states. In 1938, the

16-piece band toured Kentucky and all through the Midwest before playing in Chicago at the Savoy Ballroom in 1939. The Barnes Royal Creolians recorded for Brunswick Records. Some of the sidemen in the Barnes band were Otis Williams, Don Pullen, Bud Washington, Wally Mercer, and Oscar Brown. On April 23, 1940 they played in Natchez, Mississippi and were at the Rhythm Club there when a fire demolished the entire building. Walter Barnes, his vocalist, and eight sidemen perished in the fire. Barnes was 34 years old.

SIDNEY BECHET •

(Sidney Bechet and His Orchestra) Born in New Orleans, Louisiana on May 14, 1897. Bechet borrowed his older brother's clarinet at age six and within two years became a protégé of clarinetist George Baquet, a member of John Robichaux's Orchestra. He also studied with "Big Eye" Louis Nelson from the Imperial Jazz Band. When Bechet was still very young, he played with the Silver Bell Band. Bechet's brother Leonard led the band. Bechet continued learning and playing through his teens and one of his fellow musicians, Bunk Johnson, introduced him to the Eagle Band in 1912. Bechet never learned to read music. He joined the Will Marion Cook Orchestra in 1912 and traveled to Europe. He suffered an arrest with the police and was forced to return to the U.S., where he joined a show that featured Bessie Smith and started playing soprano saxophone. In 1924, Bechet formed his own band, left it briefly to play with Duke Ellington in 1925, and toured Europe, once again, with the Black Revue. In 1927, he toured Russia with the Tommy Ladnier band and, in 1928, played in Paris with the Noble Sissle Orchestra. In Paris, he got into a "shooting scrape" and spent a year in jail. During the period of 1928 to 1938, he played with the Sissle Orchestra and Duke Ellington's Orchestra. In 1938, he opened a tailor shop in New York City, and during 1939 and 1940, he played at Nick's in New York City, leading a trio, and at Town Hall with Eddie Condon. Louis Armstrong said, "Bechet's tone was pure and deep rooted like a jug of golden honey." Duke Ellington wrote: "Sidney Bechet was one of the truly great originals. I shall never forget the first time I heard him play at the Howard Theater in Washington around 1921. I had never heard anything like it. It was a completely new sound and conception to me." Bechet died on his birthday, May 14, 1959 in Paris, France.

CALIFORNIA RAMBLERS

over
pub
othe
pla
Bil
Cl
Fa
M

Many think the band was misnamed as most of the players we
original Ramblers were first organized by band agent Ed
become Fats Waller's manager) who found them a job playing
Shirley. The Ramblers first leader was Ray Kitchenman who pl.
original band broke up and was reorganized by violinist Arthur
led a band whose sidemen included the Dorsey Brothers, Adria
Loring "Red" Nichols. Kitchenman led the band in Shanley's L
Broadway in New York and at the Post Lodge in Pelham Bay Park ir
County, which they renamed the California Ramblers's Inn. The gr
an instant hit and they played there for more than ten years, re
Columbia and other record companies under names like Ted Walla
Orchestra, Goldie's Syncopators, the Palace Gardens Orchestra, and t
Gate Orchestra. By 1924, the manager, Kirkeby, formed a small group
orchestra to play novelty tunes and jazz. The personnel were Stan Kin
and kazoo; Ray Kitchenman, banjo; Irvin Brodsky, piano; Adrian Roll
saxophone and goofus; and Bill Moore, trumpet. The band recorded un
name the Little Ramblers for Columbia; as the Goofus Five for Okeh Re
and the Five Birmingham Babies for Pathe Records. At various times, othe
members played in the group, including Abe Lincoln, trombone; Ch
Quealey, trumpet; Bobby Davis, alto saxophone; and Red Nichols, cornet.
California Ramblers are rated alongside Fletcher Henderson and Paul Whiter
as one of the top bands of that era. It is said that they influenced many, ma
bands in the United States and England.

JEAN (GENE) GOLDKETTE

(Jean Goldkette and His Orchestra) Born in Valenciennes, France on March 18,
1899. Goldkette was educated in Russia. His family was a traveling theatrical
troupe and Jean studied classical piano, preparing to be a concert pianist, at the
Moscow Conservatory of Music. In 1910, the family immigrated to the U.S. and
Jean attended the American Conservatory of Music and the Lewis Institute in
Chicago. He played in the Imperial Player Roll Company as the International
Dance Sensation, playing "La Seduccion" making the princely sum of 50 cents.
Recognizing that he could make money playing commercial music, he became
the music director for the Detroit Athletic Club in 1921 and, by 1924, had taken

the Graystone Ballroom, formed the Victor Recording Orchestra and
ished the *Graystone Topics*, a newspaper promoting his schedule. He booked
r groups under his name and had a number of bands traveling though the U.S.
ing under the title the Jean Goldkette Orchestra. His band included sidemen
Rank, Bix Beiderbecke, Don Murray, Howdy Quicksell, Ray Ludwig,
auncey Morehouse, Irving Riskin, Frank Trumbauer, Spiegle Wilcox, Fred
rrar, Steve Brown, Bill Challis, Joe Venuti, Pee Wee Russell, Eddie Lang, Russ
organ, Danny Polo, and the Dorsey Brothers. The Goldkette theme songs were
he Old Refrain," "I Know That You Know," and "Sweetheart Time." In 1938,
oldkette formed the American Symphony Orchestra, and during a concert in
939, he conducted the orchestra featuring the compositions by George Gershwin
nd Edward MacDowell. The classical concert also featured the Goldkette Swing
Ensemble and the Charioteers. He continued with his commercial orchestra in the
'40s but toured as a concert pianist in the '50s. Jean Goldkette died in Santa
Barbara, California on March 24, 1962.

EARL HINES

(Earl "Fatha" Hines and His Orchestra)
Born in Duquesne, Pennsylvania on
December 28, 1905. Earl Hines became a
professional musician at age 13 and
formed his own band in 1928. He always
claimed that he invented jazz and was
known among fellow musicians as
"Fatha." The pianist played with Louis
Armstrong's Hot Fives and Hot Sevens.
His trademark was sitting at the piano
smoking a cigar. During the '30s, the
singers with the band included such nota-
bles as Herb Jeffries and Walter Fuller and
featured well-known instrumentalists like trombonist Trummy Young. By 1940,
the band was featuring outstanding soloists like Dizzy Gillespie, Budd Johnson,
and Charlie Parker. Singer Billy Eckstein brought female singer Sarah Vaughan
on the band. Hines wrote many famous songs, including "You Can Depend on
Me," "Rosetta," "Jelly, Jelly," "Piano Man," and "A Monday Date." The band's

theme songs were "Deep Forest" and "Cavernism." "Fatha" Hines recorded for Fantasy, Capitol Vocalion, Brunswick, Victor, and Columbia Records. In 1947, Hines broke up his band and rejoined the Louis Armstrong band, which, by the mid '60s was touring Japan, Russia, and the U.S. Hines died on April 22, 1983.

FREDDY JOHNSON

(Freddy Johnson and His Orchestra) Born on March 12, 1904. By the age of 20, Freddy Johnson was leading his own band playing piano and, by 21, had disbanded and joined the Elmer Snowden band. In 1926, he was working with Billy Fowler and, by 1927, with Henry Sapard. In the late 1920s, he played with bands led by Noble Sissle and Sam Wooding. He went on a European tour in 1929 and settled at the Bricktop's Club in Paris. Between 1930 and 1932, he fronted another band and worked with the Arthur Briggs Orchestra. In 1933, he joined the Freddy Taylor Orchestra. During Johnson's career he recorded for Decca Records. Johnson died in New York City on March 24, 1961.

ART KASSEL

(Art Kassel and His Castles in the Air Orchestra) Born in Chicago, Illinois on January 18, 1896. Art Kassel led a territory band that played regularly at the Bismark Hotel and the Aragon Ballroom in Chicago. One of the sidemen in his early bands was Benny Goodman. Former members of the Austin High Gang, Bud Freeman, Frankie Teschmacher, Jim Lannigan, and Jimmy and Dick McPartland played in the Art Kassel Orchestra when the Austin High Gang disbanded. The Art Kassel Orchestra recorded on Bluebird, Columbia, and Victor Records. The theme songs of Art Kassel and His Castles in the Air Orchestra were "Hell's Bells" and "Doodle Doo Doo." In the early '60s, the band played at the Hollywood Palladium during the weekends, the Golden West Ballroom in Norwalk and Myron's Ballroom. Kassel died on February 3, 1965 in Van Nuys, California.

PHIL OHMAN

(Phil Ohman and His Orchestra) Born in New Brittian, Connecticut on October 7, 1896. Phil Ohman (né: Philmore Wellington Ohman) studied piano with Edward Laubin while in high school and 2 more years of organ study with

Alexander Russel. His original teacher, Edward Laubin, encouraged Ohman's family to send him to Europe for advanced study but the family finances were not sufficient to support that venture. Phil Ohman began his career as a piano salesman for Wannamakers' New York store in 1915 and, by 1919, worked for QRS, recording "Player Piano Rolls." He soon developed a friendship with fellow QRS arranger Victor Arden, and they began a two-piano team. From 1922 and 1923, Ohman was accompanist for singers and piano player for the Paul Whiteman band. The two-piano team of Ohman and Arden continued to work until 1934, when they split up. Ohman moved to California and worked for the studios, recording for stars who needed to simulate playing the piano in movies. He also scored and wrote some songs for various movies and did radio work until his death on August 8, 1969.

WILL OSBORNE

(Will Osborne and His Orchestra) Born in Canada on November 25, 1905. Osborne was the heir to the Barony of Gask, Scotland, as the son of Lord Oliphant. Osborne was a drummer and singer and led his first band in 1924. In 1929, the band left the Heigh-Ho Club in New York to play in a motion picture in Hollywood. In the early '30s, he lead a swing band but, by the mid '30s, his band featured novelty tunes with cardboard megaphones, glissing trombones, and slide trumpets. In the later part of the '30s, he lead a more serious dance band, which featured Dick "Stinky" Rogers on vocals. This band was called Will Osborne and His Slide Music. When Osborne left the band, Rogers took it over. Osborne formed another band, which featured the singer Marianne, and was primarily a dance band. Those previous bands were pretty much based in New York. In the '40s, Osborne moved to California and led a band, which was the feature on the *Abbot and Costello* radio program. They also played on the *Camel Cigarette Show*, the *Corn Products Show*, and *The Blue White Diamond Show* in New York City. The band gradually dwindled to seven pieces. Osborne got out of the music business in 1957 and became the entertainment director at Harvey's Casino in Las Vegas. Osborne had a soft singing style. Several girl singers appeared with the Osborne bands. Among them were Eileen Wilson, Dorothy Rogers, Joan Whitney, and Lynn Davis. The band had two theme songs, "The Gentleman Awaits" and "Beside an Open Fireplace." Over the years the band recorded for Varsity, Decca, Columbia, Oriole, Banner, Perfect and Melotone, and ARC record companies. Osborne wrote a number of tunes, including "On a Blue and Moonless Night," "Wouldst Could I But Kiss Thy Hand," "Oh Babe," "Pompton Turnpike," and "Between 18th and 19th on Chestnut Street." Osborne died in Newport Beach, California on October 22, 1981.

RED PERKINS

(Red Perkins and His Dixie Ramblers) Red formed his first band in 1925 in Omaha, Nebraska. A small band of six pieces with many players doubling on several instruments, it quickly grew into a medium-sized territory band. Perkins played trumpet and sang. The band's agent, the National Orchestra Service, booked the Dixie Ramblers into hotels, ballrooms, and theaters in Nebraska, Kansas, Iowa, and the Dakotas. During the '20s and '30s, the band recorded for Gennett Records. Some of the sidemen in the Perkins Ramblers were Charlie Watkins, Harry Fooks, Clarence Gray, Bill Osboen, Jabbo Smith, Jim Alexander, and Jay Green. By the mid-'40s, Red disbanded and became a professional photographer in Minneapolis, Minnesota.

ANSON WEEKS

(Anson Weeks and His Orchestra) Born in Oakland, California on February 14, 1896. Weeks formed his first "hotel" band in Oakland, California in 1924, quickly gained national recognition, and appeared on the weekly radio show the *Lucky Strike Magic Carpet Show*. He attended the University of California at Berkeley and was considered a pioneering bandleader. For several years the Weeks Orchestra played at the Top of the Mark's Peacock Room in San Francisco, California. In the early '30s, the band employed singers, such as Carl Ravazza, Bob Crosby, Dale Evans, and Tony Martin, and future bandleaders like Griff Williams and Xavier Cougat. The band's theme songs were "I'm Writing You This Little Melody" and "I'm Sorry, Dear." Weeks was also a song-writer who contributed tunes like "We'll Get a Bang Out of Life," "That Same Old Dream," and "I'm Sorry, Dear." The band recorded for Brunswick, Decca, Fantasy, and Columbia records. Their identification phrase was "Let's go dancin' with Anson." In the mid-'30s, Weeks was badly injured when the bus he was riding had a serious accident; he eventually recovered and again toured with the band until 1946, when he retired and went into the real estate business in Santa Rosa, California. By 1956 he had formed another band and began touring again. Weeks died in Sacramento, California on February 7, 1969.

WOVERINES, THE

(The Woverines) The Woverines was organized in the early '20s. Famous cornetist Bix Beiederbecke dropped out of school in 1923 and became the star of this exciting band. The personnel at that time included Bob Gillette, banjo; Dick Voynow, piano; Vic Moore, drums; Min Leibrook, tuba; George Johnson, saxophone; Jimmy Hartwell, clarinet; Al Gande, trombone; and Bix Beiderbecke, cornet. They first played in Chicago in 1923, followed by a long date in New York at the Cinderella Ballroom, and made their first record for Gennett Records in 1924. Al Gande, trombonist, dropped out of the band shortly after the record date. In early '25, Bix left the band and was replaced by another famous cornetist, Jimmy McPartland.

SAM WOODING

(Sam Wooding and His Orchestra) Born in Philadelphia, Pennsylvania on June 17, 1895. Sam Wooding (né: Samuel David Wooding) formed his orchestra in the mid-teens and made several records for Vocalion Records. While in Germany in 1925, the band recorded "Alabamy Bound" and "By the Waters of the Minnetonka." At that time the personnel included Wooding, piano and leader; Johnny Mitchell, banjo; George Howe, drums; John Warren, tuba; Herbert Flemings, trombone; Bobby Martin, Maceo Edwards, and Tommy Ladnier, trumpets; Garvin Bushnell, Gene Sedric, and Willie Lewis, saxophones. Wooding died on August 1, 1985 in New York City.

IRVING AARONSON

(Irving Aaronson and the Commanders) Born in New York on February 7, 1895. By age 11, Aaronson was already playing piano for silent movies. In 1926, he joined a band, the Crusaders, which he took over and changed the name to the Commanders within a few months. By 1928, the band had personnel, including stars such as Mickey Bloom, Gene Krupa, Claude Thornhill, Phil Saxe, Artie Shaw, Tony Pastor and Chummy MacGregor. The singers were Lois Still and Betty Cannon. In 1928, the band played the Broadway show *Paris* by Cole

Porter, which included the star Irene Bordoni. As a result, the Aaronson's backed up Bordoni on four Victor records: *Two Little Babes in the Woods*, *Let's Misbehave*, *The Land of Going-to-Be*, and *Don't Look at Me That Way*. Irving Aaronson and the Commanders also accompanied Bing Crosby in several songs he recorded, including "Love in Bloom" and "She Loves Me Not." Three other singers sang with the Aaronson band, Betty Cannon, Belle Mann, and Lois Still. During the band's existence, it recorded on the Columbia, Vocalion, Brunswick, Victor, and Edison labels. The band's theme song was "Commanderism." When Aaronson disbanded the Commanders, he became a musical supervisor for MGM Motion Picture Studios. Aaronson died in Hollywood on May 10, 1963.

ARDEN AND OHMAN

(The Arden and Ohman Orchestra) Right after WWI, Victor Arden (born 1903 in Winona, Illinois) traveled to New York to record piano rolls. He soon met pianist Phil Ohman (born October 7, 1896 in Santa Monica, California) and they joined together and formed a piano duo to make piano rolls and to play in clubs in New York. Some of the piano rolls they recorded were "Canadian Capers," "Raga Muffin," and "Dance of the Demon." They played for the Gershwin Broadway musical *Lady Be Good* in 1924 and for a number of other shows. Soon after, Arden and Ohman formed an orchestra. The Arden and Ohman Orchestra became the pit orchestra for many Broadway shows from the mid-'20s to the mid-'30s. In 1926, they played for the show *Tip Toes* and, in 1929, *Spring Is Here*. The orchestra also played background music for news reports and commercials, soon pioneering their own radio programs. They eventually fronted their own bands for a few years but joined together and recorded for Brunswick Records by the mid-'30s, and for RCA Victor thereafter. The band featured several numbers like "Ooh! That Kiss," "Funny Face," "Fine and Dandy," "That Certain Feeling," and "Dance of the Paper Doll." By the '50s, Ohman had retired and Arden fronted the band, which accompanied the Dick Powell recordings of "Outside of You" and "Lone Gondolier." Victor Arden died on August 8, 1962; Phil Ohman in 1954.

BILLY BUTLER

(Billy Butler and His Orchestra) The Butler Orchestra formed the nucleus for the band that became the Savoy Bearcats in 1926. The personnel for the Butler group included Jimmy Green, banjo; Leroy Tibbs, piano; Willie Lynch, drums, Ramon Hernandez and Englemar Crummel, saxophones; Gilbert Paris and Demas Dean, trumpets; James Revey, trombone; Chink Johnson, tuba; and Billy Butler, violin, saxophone, and leader.

THOMAS "MUTT" CAREY

(Thomas "Mutt" Carey and His band) Born in New Orleans, Louisiana on March 8, 1891. Thomas "Mutt" Carey, aka "Papa Mutt" Carey, began his career in New Orleans with his brother, Jack. They both led old-style brass bands in parades, for the B.P.O. Elks or similar organizations, up and down Canal Street. Carey began playing with Kid Ory in 1914 and assumed the leadership of the band when Ory left in 1925. It is said that Carey was the first Black trumpet player in New Orleans to be recorded. The record session took place in 1921 while Carey was playing in Kid Ory's Sunshine Orchestra. They played "Society Blues" and "Ory's Creole Trombone." Carey and Ory split up when Ory left in 1925 but were reunited for several years in the mid-'30s before Carey moved to New York to form Mutt Carey and His New Yorkers. That band recorded several songs, including "Cake Walking Babies" in 1948. Prior to that, in 1944, Nesushi Eertegun organized a band of New Orleans players that included Kid Ory, Mutt Cary, and Jimmie Noone for his newly found record company Crescent Records. Most of Carey's recordings have been compiled on the Crescent Record label. Thomas "Mutt" Carey died in San Francisco in 1948 at age 57.

GENE COY

(Gene Coy and His Harlem Swing Band) Although the Coy band was heard often on various radio shots, the band never recorded. The Gene Coy and His Harlem Swing Band began in Amarillo, Texas, toured throughout the Midwestern and Southern states from the '20s until the late '50s, and featured jazz tunes and ballads. This 14-piece aggregation traveled in an old bus and featured Tyree Johnson, Alson Moore, and Gene's wife, Ann. Other members of the Coy band included Andre Duryea, Charlie Lewis, Henry Powell, Otto

Sampson, Junior Raglin, Lester Taylor, Eddie Walker, Dick Wilson, Oscar Cobb, Ishiah Young, Allen Durham, Ben Webster, Clyde Durham, Ted Manning, Alton Moore, and Red Thompson. When Gene retired, he sold his library for $1,000. He died in California in 1966.

AL DONAHUE

(Al Donahue and His Orchestra) Born in Boston, Massachussetts on June 12, 1904. Donahue was a violinist who graduated from the Boston Law School. Donahue led a commercial band at the Rainbow Room in New York City in the late '20s and '30s. In the '40s, he built a swing orchestra featuring singer Paula Kelly. Other vocalists were Dee Keating, Snooky Lanson, Phil Brito, and Lynne Stevens. The band's theme song was "Lowdown Rhythm in a Top Hat." The Donahue Orchestra recorded for Vocalion Records. The band never achieved great success and Al Donahue never became a "name." Al Donahue died on February 20, 1983.

JIMMY JOY

(Jimmy Joy and His Band) Born in Texas in 1912. Jimmy Joy (né: James Monte Maloney) led a jazz band during the '20s in the Southwest and recorded for the Okeh Records. By the '30s, he had changed his style to a sweet music dance band and become popular in the Midwest. Some of the instrumentalists were Al King, Oscar Reed, Oscar Miller, Elmer Nordgren, Ernie Mathias, Orville Andrews, Matty Matlock, Norman Smith, Amos Ayalla, Dick Hammell, Johnny Cole, Lynn Harrell, Rex Preis, Jack Brown Clyde Austin, Jack Brown, Hollis Bradt, and Gilbert O'Shaughnesy. The band's theme song was "Shine On, Harvest Moon." They recorded for Decca, Brunswick, and Okeh records. As an instrumentalist, he is remembered to have been able to play two clarinets simultaneously. Joy died in Dallas, Texas in March 1962.

HAL KEMP

(Hal Kemp and His Orchestra) Born in Marion, Alabama on March 27, 1905. While a student at the University of North Carolina, Hal Kemp formed his first orchestra called His Merrymakers. This band featured Jack Pettis and Bunny Berigan on trumpets. At that time, bandleader Fred Waring was so impressed with the Kemp Orchestra that he gave it musical advice and financial support. The band's reputation quickly grew and arrangers Lou Busch, Hal Mooney, and John Scott Trotter wrote for the band. By the '30s, the band had added singers like Maxine Gray and Bob Allen. The drummer, Skinnay Ennis, also sang and made hits like "Got a Date with an Angel" (the band's theme song), "It's Easy to Remember," "The Touch of Your Lips," "Lamplight," "You're the Top," "It's Easy to Remember," and "Heart of St. Francisco." In the late '30s and early '40s, the band's singer was Janet Lafferty, who later, as a Hollywood actress, she had changed her name to Janet Blair. Kemp died on December 21, 1940 in a head-on automobile collision while driving from Los Angeles to San Francisco.

JOE "WINGY" MANONE

(Joe "Wingy" Manone and his Club Royale Orchestra) Born in New Orleans, Louisiana on February 13, 1904. "Wingy" Manone (né: Joseph Manone) lost an arm in a streetcar accident when he was a child and was given the nickname "Wingy." When he played the trumpet, he always wore a prosthetic arm. Manone began studying trumpet when he was a child and, by age 17, in 1921, began playing on Mississippi riverboats and with the Crescent City Jazzers, who later became the Arcadian Serenaders. In 1922, Manone played at the Valentine Inn in Chicago and, by 1924, "Wingy" made his first recording with the Serenaders. By 1925, he had moved to San Antonio, Texas, where he led his own band. He played in Houston briefly with pianist Peck Kelley and a band led by Ham Crawford. In 1926, he joined the Doc Ross Orchestra and they traveled through Texas, California, and Mexico. He soon left the Ross band and started his own band in Biloxi, Mississippi. In the later part of 1927, "Wingy" moved to New York to make some records and then to Chicago, where he led his band, Joe Manone's Harmony Kings, while occasionally sitting in with bands like Charlie Straight and Ray Miller. In 1929, he recorded with Benny Goodman and His Boys in New York, played for a short time with Speed Webb, and then led his own band in Ohio. By 1930, Manone was leading his band at My Cellar in Chicago and, by 1933, had moved to the Brewery Club. In 1934, he played for a while in Milwaukee prior to returning to New York's 52nd St. and playing at the Famous Door, Maria's, and the Hickory House. By 1939, and after recording "Isle of Capri," "Wingy" moved to Florida where he remained until 1940, when he moved to Hollywood and appeared in several motion pictures, including *Sarge Goes to College*, *Hi-Ya Sailor*, and *Rhythm on the River*. He remained in California, doing scheduled broadcasts with Bing Crosby until 1954, when he took a job in Las Vegas, Nevada and settled there. During the '50s and '60s, he led his own band, touring Europe, Canada, and the U.S. He wrote many songs, including "Hello Out There Hello," "Early Morning Blues," "Downright Disgusted," "Deep Jungle, Clarinet Ramble," "Can't Get You Off My Mind," "Box Car Blues," "Bouncin in Rhythm," "The Big Parade," "Awful Waffle Man," "Annie Laurie," "Where's the Waiter," "Up the Country Blues," "Tuscaloosa Bus," "Trumpet on the Wing," "There'll Come a Time," "Tailgate Ramble," "Swing Out Swinging'" "At the Hickory House," "Strangeblues," "Stop the War," "The Cats Are Killing Each Other," "San Sue Strut," "The Round Square Dance," "Real Gone," and "Pawn Shop Blues." Manone died in Las Vegas, Nevada on July 9, 1982.

BENNY MEROFF

(Benny Meroff and His Orchestra) Born in 1901. Meroff began as a vaudevillian playing saxophone, clarinet, and violin. He formed his first band in the mid-'20s playing jazz. He featured himself playing a straight-baritone saxophone (about six-feet long). His sidemen were some of the best musicians of the '20s: Al D'Artega, Wild Bill Davidson, and Santo Pecora. The band toured between Chicago and New York City and played theaters, clubs, and hotels. Later important sidemen were Don Ellis and Bill Hughes. The theme song of the Meroff Orchestra was "Diane." Meroff wrote "Wherever You To" and "What's the Use of Cryin' the Blues?" The band recorded for Columbia, Victor, and Okeh records. Meroff was considered a top-notch emcee as well as a fine musician. In the '40s, Benny Meroff disbanded and retired. He died in 1973 at age 72.

McKINNEY'S COTTON PICKERS

(McKinney's Cotton Pickers Orchestra) The band started as a quartet led by drummer William McKinney (born in 1894 in Paducah, Kentucky) in the early '20s. It gradually became the Sinco Septet, which grew into a ten-piece band called the Cotton Pickers, which played at the Arcadia Ballroom in Detroit, Michigan. By the late '20s, the members of the band were William McKinney's, drums and leader; Joe Smith, Langston Curl, and John Nesbit, trumpets; Todd

Rhodes, piano; Dave Wilborn, banjo; George Thomas, tenor saxophone; and Cuba Austin, drums. This group played most often at the Greystone Ballroom while, at the same time, the Fletcher Henderson band was playing at Jean Goldkettes featuring arrangements by Don Redman. McKinney's made Redman the official leader of the Cotton Pickers band and the band began to swing. The two copyists for the band were Bob Zurke and Glen Gray. At that time, Prince Robinson and George Thomas were the saxophonists; Sidney Deparis and Joe Smith were on trumpets; and Dave Wilborn, Redman, and Thomas shared the vocals. During the late '20s, the band also had such sidemen as Coleman Hawkins and Fats Waller. The band recorded for RCA Victor and had hits such as "Baby, Won't You Please Come Home" and "If I Could Be with You One Hour Tonight." Don Redman left the band in 1931, Benny Carter led the band briefly in 1934.

HUSK O'HARE

(Husk O'Hare's Red Dragons) One of the first radio bands, the O'Hare band played in the Midwest for a number of years under the name the Blue Friars. When Husk O'Hare took over the band, he named it the Red Dragons. The Dragons eventually became Husk O'Hare's Wolverines and included in its personnel Franklyn Marsh, Arnold Sweatman, Harry O'Connor, Dave North, Floyd O'Brien, Bix Beiderbecke, Frank Teschemacher, Jimmy Lannigan, Bud Freeman, and Jimmy McPartland. The band's theme song was "The One I Love." They recorded for Gennett and Decca records. The Wolverines toured through the Midwest in Baltimore, Philadelphia, Pittsburg, Cleveland, and Atlantic City. O'Hare retired from music and began to manufacture novelties in Chicago in the early '40s.

WALTER PAGE

(Walter Page and His Orchestra) Born in Gallatin, Missouri on February 9, 1900. Page studied music in Kansas City concentrating on bass, violin, piano, woodwinds, arranging, and composition. He played with the Bennie Moten band from 1918 to 1923, when he left Kansas City to tour with Billy King's Road Show. When the show closed in Oklahoma City in 1925, Page took over the band and named it Walter Page's Original Blue Devils. At that time, the personnel included Jimmy Rushing, Bill Baise, Buster Smith, and Hot Lips Page. In 1931, Page freelanced for a while and rejoined Bennie Moten with whom he worked until 1934. In the mid-'30s, he played with the Jeter-Pillars band and joined the Count Basie Orchestra in late 1935 and remained with them until 1942. After jobbing with Jesse Price in Joplin, Missouri, Page rejoined the Basie band from 1946 to 1948. After playing several years with Hot Lips Page, Walter Page freelanced through the '50s in New York City, playing with Jimmy McPartland, Wild Bill Davison, Eddie Condon, Jimmy Rushing, and Roy Eldridge. Page died of pneumonia in New York City on December 20, 1957.

TINY PARHAM

(Tiny Parham and His Orchestra) Born in Kansas City, Missouri on February 25, 1900. Tiny Parham (né: Hartzell Strathdene Parham) started in vaudeville when he was in his teens and in 1925 moved to Chicago where he worked as an organist and piano player in theaters, as a talent scout for Paramount Records, and arranger for various bands in the area. In the late '20s, RCA Victor Records recorded Tiny Parham and His Musicians a number of times. Other names that Tiny used during his career were Dodds and Parham Orchestra, Tiny Parham's Four Aces, Parham's Black Patti Band, and Tiny Parham and His Forty-Five. The band was very active during the '30s and played in the Chicago area. From 1933 to 1939, Parham wrote and arranged for floorshows in Dennis Cooney's Royal Frolics Club. Tiny disbanded in the late '30s and played organ in a Chicago roller-skating rink. He died in Milwaukee, Wisconsin on April 4, 1943, in his dressing room during a show.

BEN POLLACK

(Ben Pollack and His Orchestra) Born in Chicago, Illinois on June 22, 1903. Pollack was a drummer and singer who played with the New Orleans Rhythm Kings in the early '20s. In 1925, he formed his own band that was hailed as one of the finest big bands of the '20s, with such sidemen as Benny Goodman, Glenn Miller, Charlie Spivak, Bud Freeman, Jack and Charlie Teagarden, Jimmy McPartland, and Fud Livingstone; the nucleus of the forthcoming band was led by Bob Crosby like Matty Mattlock, Dean Kincaide, Eddie Miller, Nappy Lamare, Yank Lawson, Ray Baduc, and Gil Rodin. When Pollack disbanded in 1934 Bob Crosby formed his band which many referred to as "The Ben Pollack Alumni Association." Pollack often used the expression "May it please you," when introducing or ending a tune. The Pollack Orchestra recorded such hits as "Cryin' for the Carolines" and "I'm Following You." When he disbanded in 1934, he wanted to devote time to furthering the career of his wife, Doris Robbins. By 1936, Pollack had started a new band featuring sidemen like Harry James, Shorty Sherock, brass; Dave Matthews, saxophone; and Irving Fazola, clarinet. The theme song of the Ben Pollack Orchestra was "Song of the Islands." They recorded for Decca, Victor, Variety, and Columbia records. After 1938, he led small Dixieland groups playing drums part-time and ran a small record company and his own nightclub. He died in 1971, hanging himself in Palm Springs, California.

BLUE STEELE

(Blue Steele and His Orchestra) Blue Steele (né: Gene Staples) led a band in the mid '20s primarily through Florida and the Midwest. He began in Atlanta, Georgia and featured sweet and semi-hot arrangements. When he was quite young, he sang with Watson's Bell Hops traveling through the South. In addition to his vocals, other singers with the Blue Steele band included Bob Nolan, Kay Austin, Mabel Batson, Clyde Davis, and George Marks. Instrumental sidemen were Arnell Schwartz, Ollie Warner, Ben Saxon, Tookie Tranthgm, Galen Grubb, Red Roundtree, Jack Echols, B. English, Ernie Winburn, Jesse James, Frank Myers, Irving Verette, Moe Goodman, George Marks, Bob Nolan, Clyde Davis, Pat Davis, Henry Cody, Ted Delmarter, Marvin Long, Sol Lewis, Kenny Sergent, Pete Schmidt, John Langley, Frank Krishner, Frank Martinez, G. Morrison, Ole Hoel, and Sam Goble. The band's theme song was "Coronado Memories." The Steele band recorded for Victor Records. Blue Steele was noted for his quick and violent temper and many sidemen were afraid to give their notice for fear of being beaten up by Steele. Dancers were hesitant to give requests. In the early '40s, Steele moved to Mexico City, where he led a small combo.

LAWRENCE WELK

(Lawrence Welk and His Champagne Music) Born in Strasburg, North Dakota on March 11, 1903. Lawrence Welk played accordion and led one of the most successful, extremely commercial bands in the U.S. His parents were farmers who had immigrated to the U.S. from Russia, originally from Alsace-Lorraine, and he was one of eight children. Welk had to leave school while still in the elementary grades to work on his parent's farm, and did not learn to speak English until he was in his 20s. His father taught him to play accordion and he earned extra money for the family by entertaining at church dances and weddings. When he was 17, he formed his first band, a two-piece (accordion and drum) unit known as the Biggest Little band in America. The duo played regularly on radio station KNAX in Yankton, South Dakota. At age 21, Welk left home and, by 1927, he formed the Hotsy-Totsy Boys band. He later formed the Lawrence Welk's Fruit Gum Orchestra. He gave away a free stick of gum to anyone who attended a performance of his band and this made him so popular he toured Minnesota and the Dakotas. By 1938, the band was playing at the William Penn Hotel in Pittsburg and a fan commented that "Listening to Lawrence Welk's music was like sipping champagne," which gave birth to the moniker Lawrence Welk and His Champagne Music. By the late '40s, Welk had settled in Los Angeles and, by 1951, was working at the Aragon Ballroom, where KLTA television began broadcasting his shows. After four years, the band was hired by Chrysler to do a weekly show on ABC. This show ran from 1955 to 1971, when the show went into syndication for 11 years. In 1959, he fired the Champagne Lady, Alice Lon, as he felt her dress was too short. Since 1987, reruns of the Welk show have run on public TV. The theme song of the Welk band was "Bubbles in the Wine." Various sidemen in the Welk bands included Myron Floren, Pete Fountain, Joann Castle, and Bob Ralston. Singers were Ava Barber, Joe Feeney, the Lennon Sisters, Guy & Ralna, Norma Zimmer, Larry Hopper, Alice Lon, Roberta Linn, Jayne Walton, Mildred Stanley, Lois Best, and Walter Bloom. The band's biggest record sellers were "Calcutta," "Baby Elephant Walk," and "Last Date." The Welk empire continues with the Lawrence Welk Champagne Theater in Branson, Missouri; Lawrence Welk Village, a 1,000-acre resort-retirement complex in Escondido, California; and Ramwood Productions, a music publishing firm that owns the rights to more than 20,000 songs, including the complete catalog of Jerome Kern's music. During the life of Lawrence Welk and His Champagne Music, the band recorded for Ranwood, Decca, Coral, Dot, Okeh, Gennett, and Vocalion records. Welk died in Santa Monica, California on May 17, 1992.

GUS ARNHEIM

(Gus Arnheim and His Coconut Grove Orchestra) Born on September 11, 1897. Arnheim led a band that was described as well rehearsed and hard-driving. Many sidemen who eventually became leaders and personalities in their own right included bandleaders Jimmy Grier and Stan Kenton (who played piano and wrote arrangements for Arnheim); singers Bing Crosby, Shirley Ross, Joy Hodges, and Russ Columbo; tenor saxophonist Fred McMurray; and drummer Art Fleming (future game show host). Arnheim died in January 1955.

PHIL BAXTER

(Phil Baxter and His Band) Born in Navarro, Texas on September 5, 1896. The six-piece Phil Baxter band and made its first record in October 1925 in St. Louis, Missouri. He recorded again in Dallas, Texas in October 1929. Baxter fronted a band from the mid '20s through the mid '30s, when he fell ill with a severe arthritic condition. One of the tunes the Baxter band recorded was "I Ain't Got No Gal Now" and one of the known players in that band was trumpeter Ray Noone. Baxter died on November 21, 1972 in Dallas, Texas.

DOC CHEATHAM

(Doc Cheatham and His Orchestra) Born in Nashville, Tennessee on June 13, 1905. Adolphus Anthony "Doc" Cheatham began playing trumpet profession- ally when he was 13 years old. He toured with Albert Wynn in the mid-'20s, led his own band, and recorded with Ma Rainey. In 1929, he went to Europe with Sam Wooding, where they recorded "Downcast Blues." In 1932, he joined McKinndey's Cotton Pickers and then Cab Calloway, with whom he played until 1938. In the early '40s, he played with Teddy Wilson, led his own band, and played on Billie Holiday's recording "Come Back to Me." In the '50s, he played with Perez Prado and toured with his own band in the '60s and with Benny Goodman in the '70s. Doc completed another successful European tour in the '80s. While playing at the Bern Jazz Festival, some of his performances were recorded, including "Swing That Music" and "Limehouse Blues." He also recorded a disc for Columbia Records in the '90s entitled *Legendary Pioneers of Jazz*. In the '90s, Cheatham was quoted as having said: "People keep trying to find my place in history. I say, if you close your eyes and enjoy what you hear, then this is all the history I need to a part of." Cheatham died in Washington, D.C. on June 2, 1997.

CHARLIE COOK

(Charlie "Doc" Cook and His Dreamland Orchestra) Born in Louisville, Kentucky on September 3, 1891. Charlie Cook (né: Charles L. Cooke) began writing music when he was eight years old and organized his first band, an eight-piece combo at age 15. When he was 18, his parents moved to Detroit, where Cook played with the Fred Stone Orchestra and with a band led by Ben Shook. He led a Chicago-based band in the '20s that featured some of the town's leading musicians, including Clifford King, Johnny St. Cyr, Robert Shelby, Joe Poston, Jimmie Noone, Don Pasquall, Kenneth Anderson, Zutty Renaud, Freddie Keppard, Elwood Graham, Andy Hillaire, Fred Garland, and Bert W. Green. Cook died in Wurtsboro, New York on December 25, 1958.

JELLY ROLL MORTON

(Jelly Roll Morton and His Orchestra) Born in Gulfport, Mississippi on September 20, 1885. Jelly Roll Morton (né: Ferdinand Joseph Morton) played piano, in an advanced style for the era (the early 1900s) in New Orleans sporting houses. He toured through Mississippi and Louisiana in a minstrel show from 1909 to 1911, jobbed in Chicago, Kansas City, and St. Louis from 1911 to 1917, and published his famous *Jelly Roll Blues* in Chicago in 1917. He then moved to California where he worked for five years. In 1923, he went to work for the Melrose Brothers Music Company in Chicago, who also published more Morton's jazz compositions. By 1923, he was recording extensively and, during the period from 1926 to 1930, recorded for Victor Records. In 1928, he moved to New York City and played at the Rose Danceland. In 1935, he led a band and settled in Washington, D.C. By 1938, he had semi-retired and managed a jazz club. During the late '30s and early '40s, Morton did more recording and a few public appearances. He wrote "The Pearls," "Kansas City

Stomp," "King Porter Stomp," "Milenberg Joys," "Shoe Shiner's Drug," "The Crave," and many more. In addition to Victor Records, Morton recorded for Gennett, Bluebird, Biltmore, and Paramount Records. Jelly Roll Morton died in Los Angeles, California on July 10, 1941.

JACK EVERETTE

(Jack Everette and His Orchestra) Born in Cedar Rapids, Iowa. Jack Everrette (né: John Everette Jackson) started his first band in Cedar Rapids, Iowa in 1926 and dropped his last name as another band led by a Jack Jackson had been playing in that town for several years. Everette's theme song was "Dance Awhile." Many feel that the term "territory band" began with the Jack Everette Orchestra because it played in that area most of its existence. The band gained popularity due to weekly radio broadcasts over station KWCR. For many years, Everette played all of the major ballrooms in the area, Plamor, Mayfair, etc. and opened his own ballroom in Springfield, Missouri. Some of the Everette sidemen were Al Knorr, Kelly Christensen, Skeets Evans, George Mull, Eddie Rommers, Bill Williams, Vern Scollon, Earl Hulen, and Lock Lohman. The band disbanded at the start of WWII, but by the end of the war, it reorganized and continued to travel until 1956, when Everette's son, David Owens Everette, founded his own dance band. By 1962, Jack Everette and son David opened the Jackson Artist Corporation, a music booking office in Kansas City. Jack Everette died on Father's Day in 1972.

DEWEY JACKSON

(Dewey Jackson and His Peacock Orchestra) Born in St. Louis, Missouri in 1900. Jackson played with the Odd Fellows band when he was 12 years old and eventually played on the riverboats with Fate Marable and Charlie Creath. In the mid-'20s, he formed his own six-piece band, which grew to 11 pieces, and recorded briefly for Vocalion Records. Harry Dial was the drummer in the Peacock Orchestra.

AL KING

(Al King and his band) Born in 1905. As a young man, Al King played trumpet with the California Ramblers, the New Orleans Jazz Band, and the Original Dixieland Jazz Band. He started his own band in New York City in the mid-'20s and fulfilled a long engagement at the New Yorker Hotel. Some of the sidemen in the King band were Nappy Lamare, Nat Farber, Sterling Bose, Matty Mattlock, Doe Rando, Eddie Miller, Jack Teagarden, Charlie Spivak, Eddie Yederman, Elmer Ronka, Herman Drewes, Billy Wolfe, John Turner, Tony Spargo, and Dick Wilson. The theme song of King's band was "It's No Fun Dancing if the band Don't Swing." King was a prolific songwriter and wrote "Hop, Skip and Jump," "Kiss Me, My Darling," "Pasta Fazoola," and the band's theme song. King died in 1989. He was 84 years old.

KAY KYSER

(Kay Kyser and His College of Musical Knowledge) Born in Rocky Mount, North Carolina in 1906. Kyser was attending Law School at the University of North Carolina when Hal Kemp, leader of the Carolina Club Orchestra, approached Kyser, then a cheerleader, to serve as a replacement conductor. Kyser was so hesitant that he asked his friend Johnny Mercer to conduct the band. By the the time classes resumed in the fall 1927, he advertised for people to join the band. Sol "Sully" Mason was the first to join the saxophone section. The assistant bandleader was George Duning, the band's arranger for its entire lifetime. The idea of the College of Musical Knowledge was developed with the band and its early gimmick was to play a few measures of a song and ask the audience to name the song. When he graduated in 1928, Victor Talking Machine Records recorded the band and promoted it as Kay Kyser and His Victor Recording Orchestra. In 1930, while the Kay Kyser and his College of Musical Knowledge Orchestra was playing in New York, the *Times* called him "a genius of jazz." In 1932, while doing 15-minute spots on radio, Kyser implemented the "singing song title" idea to eliminate the need for spoken announcements between tunes. In 1934, he subbed for Hal Kemp at the Blackhawk in Chicago. While playing at the Blackhawk, Kyser developed the musical quiz show *Kay Kyser's Kampus Klass* and, by 1939, began starring in movies, making seven films in five years. He soon hired a trumpet player, Merewyn Bogue (and renamed him Ish Kabibble) and three vocalists—Harry Babbit, Ginny Simms, and Sully Mason. By 1944, Kyser fell in love and married his then singer, Georgia Carroll. When the U.S. entered WWII, he was the top-grossing band with 50 records on the charts, ten records in the Top Ten, and spent his time working for the war effort helping to start the Hollywood Canteen, selling war bonds, and playing for the troops. In 1945, he discovered a new singer, Michael Dowd, and gave him the stage name of Mike Douglas. In 1948, Kyser developed arthritis, and the big band era was waning, so he disbanded and retired in North Carolina. Kyser died in North Carolina on July 23, 1985.

HARRY OWENS

(Harry Owens and His Royal Hawaiians) Born on April 18, 1902 in O'Neil, Nebraska. He started his first band in 1926 and played the Lafayette Cafe in Los Angeles, California. Ted Mack, later the host of *Major Bowes Amateur Hour* when Bowes died, was a member of the Harry Owens congregation. In 1934, Owens traveled to Honolulu, Hawaii, and became the music director at the Royal Hawaiian Hotel. He earned his fame by writing and playing Hawaiian music. His theme song was "Sweet Leilani." Owens wrote a number of songs, including "Linger Awhile," "Voice of the Trade Winds," "Hawaii Calls," "Hawaiian Paradise," "To You Sweetheart Aloha," "Princess Poo Pooly," and the theme song. Beginning in 1949, Owens had his own TV show, which ran for nine years. During the tenure of Harry Owens and His Royal Hawaiians, the band recorded for Columbia, Hamilton, Capitol, and Decca records. Owens died in Eugene, Oregon on December 11, 1986 of a heart attack.

CHICK WEBB

(Chick Webb and His Orchestra) Born in Baltimore, Maryland on February 10, 1902. William "Chick" Webb studied drums as a youngster. Webb was a four-foot-tall, hunchback dwarf, and led his swinging band from the drummer's throne. He learned to play drums in order to exercise his nearly paralyzed body. He moved to New York City in 1924 and played with a small Harlem band led by Edward Dowell. In the mid-'20s, he organized a band that featured Louis Bacon and Taft Jordan, trumpets; Sandy Williams, trombone; and Edgar Sampson, alto saxophone and arranger. From 1931 to 1935, the Webb Orchestra was the "house" band at the Savoy Ballroom in New York City and his manager, Moe Gale, owned the Savoy. Other big bands would often engage in "musical cutting" contests with the Chick Webb Orchestra but the swinging Webb outfit would always conquer. Chick discovered Ella Fitzgerald at the Harlem Opera House and hired her in 1934. Ella scored big with her hit "A-Tisket, A-Tasket," arranged for her by Van Alexander (then Al Feldman). When Chick Webb died from tuberculosis of the spine on June 16, 1939, in Baltimore, Maryland, his mother was at his bedside. Chick said, "I'm sorry, I gotta go"; then, he closed his eyes and died. He was 30 years old. Ella Fitzgerald sang "My Buddy" at his funeral.

EDGAR HAYES

(Edgar Hayes and His Orchestra) Born in Lexington, Kentucky on May 23, 1904. Hayes attended Wilberforce University and Fisk University and organized his first band in the late '20s that played at the Alhambra Theater in Harlem. In the early to mid-'20s, he played piano and wrote for Lois Deppe and Fess Williams. In the mid-'20s, he made piano rolls. From 1930 to 1936, he worked as the pianist and arranger for Mills Blue Rhythm Band and, in 1937, formed another band that worked until 1941. His recording of "Star Dust" in 1938 was a big hit. In 1942, he moved to California, where he worked as a soloist and with various combos at the Somerset House in Riverside and other clubs. In 1946, he co-led a group with Teddy Bunn in Los Angeles at Billy Berg's Club. In the '50s, he worked as a single in the Diamond Lounge in San Bernadino and, during the '60s, in various Reuben's Restaurants. Hayes continued playing through the '70s. He wrote "The Growl," "Someone Stole Gabriel's Horn," "Love's Serenade," "Out of a Dream," and "African Lullaby." Edgar Hayes recorded for Exclusive, Decca, V-Disc, and Varsity records.

HENRY BIAGINI

(Henry Biagini and His Orchestra) In 1927 Biagini was the first leader of the Casa Loma Orchestra. When it became incorporated in 1928, Mel Jenssen led that orchestra. Biagini then formed his own orchestra, which worked through the '30s and '40s. In the early stages of the Biagini Orchestra, Charlie Barnet was a member of the saxophone section. Biagini died in an automobile accident in 1944.

SUNNY CLAPP

(Sunny Clapp and His Band O' Sunshine) Sunny Clapp wrote the music and lyrics to "Girl of My Dreams" in 1927. He made his first record for the Okeh Record Company in San Antonio, Texas on June 11, 1929. Clapp played alto saxophone, clarinet, and trombone. His 1931 band was made up of singers Hoagy Carmichael, George Marks, Arthur Keller, Jeanne Geddes, Tom Howell, Bob Hutchingson, and Lew Bray; Tom Howell and Bob Hutchingson, trumpets; Lee Howell, trombone; Sunny Clapp, trombone and leader; Mac Mccracken and Disney Arodin, saxophones; George Marks, piano; Roy Smeck, guitar; Francis Palmer, tuba; and Joe Hudson, drums. Sunny Clapp and His band O' Sunshine recorded more than 20 albums from 1929 through 1931.

EDDIE CONDON

(Eddie Condon and His Orchsetra) Born in Goodland, Indiana on November 16. 1905. Eddie Condon's original instrument was banjo, which he played at age 17 with the Hollis Peavey Jazz Bandits and the Austin High Gang. In 1927, he co-lead the McKenzie-Condon Chicagoans on a record date. In 1929, he switched instruments and began playing the guitar and moved to New York City, where he played with Red Nichol's and His Five Pennies and Red McKenzie's Mound City Blue Blowers. That same year he played with Louis Armstrong and His Savoy Ballroom Five. In 1930, his friend from Chicago, Joe Marsala, was playing at John Popkin's Hickory House and asked Condon to join his band, which he did for nearly ten years. Between 1937 and 1944, he played at Nick's in Greenwich Village in New York. By 1938 he was recording for the Commodore Record Company, owned by Milt Gabler, and from 1944 through 1945, he did a series of weekly broadcasts from Town Hall. In 1945. Pete Pesci, manager of Julius's Bar, and Condon opened a club, Eddie Condon's in the Village. Some of the sidemen who played with him at the club included Wild Bill Davison, Bobby Hacket, and Muggsy Spanier, trumpets; Big Sid Catlett, drums; Gene Schroeder, piano; and Pee Wee Russell, clarinet. Condon's biography, *We Called It Music: Generation of Jazz*, was published by the Henry Holt Company in 1947. In 1950, he recorded for Columbia Records. His club moved to the Hotel Sutton in 1961 and closed in 1967. The club's policy was "We don't throw anybody in, and we don't throw anybody out." Condon died on August 4, 1973 at the age of 68.

CLAUDE HOPKINS

(Claude Hopkins and His Orchestra) Born in Alexandria, Virginia on August 24, 1903. Claude Hopkins (né: Claude Driskett Hopkins) was a pianist who graduated from Howard University. In 1924, he played piano with the Wilbur Sweatman Orchestra. Hopkins was the intermission piano player at Jimmy Ryan's on 52nd Street in New York City. He lead a well-established band in the mid '30s that included stars like Vic Dickenson, trombone; Ed Hall, clarinet; and Shirley Clay and Jabbo Smith, trumpets. Other sidemen were Floyd Brady, Ben Smith, Arville Harris, Lincoln Mills, Henry Turner, Bobby Sands, Eugene Jackson, Pete Jacobs, Walter Jones, Fred Norman, Sylvester Lewis, and Fernando Arbello. Additionally he had singers Orlando Robeson and Ovie Alston who also played trumpet. In the '40s, Claude Hopkins led a combo in New York. Hopkins died in New York City on February 18, 1984.

WAYNE KING

(Wayne King, The Waltz King) Born on February 16, 1901 in Savannah, Illinois. King attended Valparaiso University, played alto saxophone and sang with the Benson Orchestra at the Morrison Hotel in Chicago, commuting by train from Savannah. During 1921, he worked for a Chicago insurance company and as a garage and railroad mechanic. He played in a pit band at the Riviera Theater prior to playing with a band directed by Del Lampe from 1925 to 1927. When the Aragon Ballroom opened in 1927 Lampe organized another band to play there and appointed King the bandleader. By the early '30s, the band had gained a lot of popularity at the Aragon and began to record. The theme song was "The Waltz You Saved for Me." Among the band's early record hits were "Star Dust," "Goofus," and "Blue Hours." The band was heard on radio in 1931 on the *Lady Esther Serenade Show* and, in the mid-'30s, made its first extended tour. Its biggest hit, "Josephine," was recorded in 1937 and, by the early '40s, when singer Buddy Clark joined, the band was considered to be at its best. After WWII, King formed a new band and was heard on another radio series. From 1949 to 1952, the Waltz King was seen on a television show and, during the remainder of the '50s and into the '70s, on various tours, and recordings were plentiful. King wrote many songs, including "I'd Give My Kingdom for a Smile," "That Little Boy of Mine," "The Waltz You Saved for Me," "Goofus," "So Close to Me," "Blue Hours," "With You Beside Me," "Josephine," and

"Annabelle and Baby Shoes." The band recorded for Victor Records. King died on July 16, 1985.

JIMMIE LUNCEFORD

(Jimmie Lunceford and His Orchestra) Born in Fulton, Missouri on June 6, 1902. Jimmie Lunceford studied trombone, clarinet, flute, guitar, and saxophone with Wilberforce Whiteman (father of Paul Whiteman) in Denver, Colorado. Whiteman also taught bandleader Andy Kirk. Lunceford played alto saxophone in a local Denver theater in 1922. He then attended and graduated from Fisk University in Nashville and traveled to New York where he took graduate courses at the City College of New York. After teaching music and serving as the athletic director at Manassas High School in Memphis, Tennessee, he started his first big band in 1927. By the mid '30s, the band really hit its stride with arrangements by Sy Oliver (who later wrote for Tommy Dorsey), the composer of "T'aint What You Do, It's the Way Thatcha You Do It." In 1933, the band signed on at the Cotton Club. The Lunceford Orchestra had some of the biggest names in the music business associated with it: singers like the Lunceford Glee Club; Trummy Young, trombone; Willie Smith, alto saxophone; and Sy Oliver, arranger and composer. The Lunceford Orchestra recorded for Decca, Victor, Columbia, and Vocalion records. Lunceford died in Seaside, Oregon on July 13, 1947.

LUIS RUSSELL

(Luis Russell and His Orchestra) Born in Careening Clay, Boca Del Toro, Panama on August 6, 1902. In Panama, Luis Russell played many instruments. He traveled to New Orleans in 1919 and played piano in various brothels and saloons. By the early '20s, he was leading small groups as well as playing with various local bands, including one led by Albert Nicholas. He joined the King Oliver band in Chicago in 1925 and, by 1927, had formed his own band, touring out of New York City. The Luis Russell Orchestra at one time or another had players, such as J.C. Higginbotham, trombone; Big Sid Catlett, drums; and Henry "Red" Allen and Louis Armstrong, trumpets. The band's theme song was "New Call of the Freaks." In 1935, Louis Armstrong led the band, which Luis Russell left in 1940 to form a new band. After a few tours, Russell disbanded and went into business. He died in New York City on December 11, 1963.

THELMA TERRY

(Thelma Terry and her Playboys) Thelma Terry was a double bass (string bass) player and led a Chicago-based band from 1927 to 1929. It is said that she led her band from the double bass position. By 1928, she had hired drummer Gene Krupa and featured Bob Zurke, who led his own famous band later. During 1928, the Terry band made its only recordings in Chicago and New York. Her records were mainly instrumental but highlighted her bass playing, which was equal to any of the great bassists of her day.

HARRY ARCHER

(Harry Archer and His Orchestra) Born in Creston, Iowa on February 21, 1888. Archer studied the trumpet and all of the other brass instruments prior to attending Knox College, the Michigan Military Academy, and Princeton University. He met Paul Whiteman in 1912 and wrote the score for *The Pearl Maiden*, a Broadway musical. Archer continued composing and arranging writing for shows like *Little Jessie James* (1923), *My Girl* (1924), and *Just a Minute* (1928). Archer was also a prolific songwriter, writing tunes like "The Sweetest Girl This Side of Heaven," "Alone in My Dreams," "Heigh-Ho Cheerio," "A Girl Like You," and "I Love You." When Archer left the Broadway scene he moved to Chicago and formed a dance band, which played in various ballrooms and did a series of remote radio shows. During its active period, the band recorded for Brunswick Records doing tunes such as "When Day Is Done," "My Heart Stood Still," "Thinking of You," "It Must Be Love," "Sunny," and the band's theme song, "I'll Always Remember You." Archer died in New York on April 23, 1960.

LUIS ARCARAZ

(Luis Arcaraz and His Orchestra) Born in Mexico City, Mexico on December 5, 1910. Luis Arcaraz (né: Luis Arcaraz Torras). Arcaraz's parents had backgrounds in music. Luis was interested in bullfighting and music, but his father recognized his music talent and encouraged him to pursue it. For a time, Luis Arcaraz studied music and engineering in Spain but he returned to Mexico City and got a job with radio station XEW singing and accompanying himself on the piano. He was payed 36 cents per hour. He gained recognition and success in

Tampico in 1928, when he made his music debut and began doing arranging and composition for motion pictures. He soon formed his own band, which, by 1949, was considered to be the finest aggregation in Mexico. The band always finished fourth in the polls of the best dance bands following Duke Ellington, Tommy Dorsey, and Glenn Miller. During the '50s, the Arcaraz Orchestra toured throughout Mexico with the finest musicians in the country. The great Conrad Gozzo was his lead trumpet player. The band quickly signed a recording contract with RCA Victor Records. By 1951, he was given Mexico's Gold Record Award (a Mexican Grammy) for "Quinto Patio," one of his compositions and, in 1952, his band received the Best Orchestra of the Year award. He had composed the music for 24 films by 1963. It is said that the band did not feature Latin-American music but relied on North American standards and popular tunes. In the '50s, the Arcaraz Orchestra often toured the U.S. and was one of the most popular bands to play at the Paladium in Los Angeles, California. By the '60s, Arcaraz had moved to Monterrey, Mexico and died in a tragic car accident near San Luis Potosí on December 15, 1963.

LEON BELASCO

(Leon Belasco and His Orchestra) Born in Odessa, Russia in 1902. Leon Belasco (né: Leonid Simeonovich Berladsky) is best remembered as a Hollywood star who played "butler" roles. His family moved to California and he began doing odd jobs in and around Hollywood. He first acted in a silent movie film, *The Best People* (1926), and he played violin between movies to sustain himself. He gradually formed a big band and toured the West and then the East Coasts. Moving to New York in 1936, he hired the Andrew Sisters as vocalists and played in various hotels in New York City. The band's theme song was "When Romance Calls." His love of acting continued to draw him back to the stage and he returned to Hollywood to do a bit movie part. He disbanded his orchestra, never to return to music, and appeared in the Crosby-Astaire film *Holiday Inn*, as well as *Topper Takes a Trip*, and *Casablanca*. In 1966, after making the film *The Russians Are Coming, The Russians Are Coming*, he retired from acting. Leon Belasco died on June 1, 1988 at age of 85.

VIC BERTON

(Vic Berton and His Orchestra) Born in Chicago, Illinois on May 7, 1896. Berton was something of a child genius, playing drums in a Milwaukee pit orchestra at seven years old. During WWI, he played in a Navy band under the direction of John Philip Sousa. When the war was over, he played in Chicago with various jazz bands and was highly regarded by his fellow musicians. He designed a bass pedal that was called the "Charleston Pedal" and attached bicycle pedals to his timpani drums to allow for a free bass line that was applauded by bands with which he worked like Eddie Lang, Joe Venuti, and Red Nichols. With Nichols, he recorded "Alabama Stomp" and "Washboard Blues"; with Charlie Charleston, "Red Hot Henry Brown; and he recorded "Feelin' No Pain," "Hurricane," and "Alexander's Band" with Miff Mole. In 1922, he managed the Wolverines band and wrote "Sobbin' Blues" that featured the young Bix Beiderbecke. In the late '20s, he moved to California and formed his own band, which recorded "Dardanella" and "Taboo." Berton died in Hollywood, California on December 26, 1951.

TOM GERUN

(Tom Gerun and His Orchestra) Tom Gerun (né: Thomas Gerunovitch) formed his jazz band in the late '20s. By the '30s, his sidemen included Tony Martin and Woody Herman. His singer was Ginny Simms. In the mid '30s, Gerun ran his own venue on the West Coast, the Bal Taharin. The Tom Gerun Orchestra recorded for Brunswick Records.

CAB CALLOWAY

(Cab Calloway and His Orchestra) Born December 25, 1907 in Rochester, New York. Calloway was raised in Baltimore, Maryland and studied piano in his early childhood and attended Crane College. In the early '20s, he worked with his sister, Blanche, and made his first stage appearance at the Loop Theater in Chicago, Illinois. In 1928, while acting as the emcee on Chicago's South Side in the Sunset Café, he did a number with the co-op band Marion Hardy's Alabamians. The band members were so impressed they asked Calloway to be their leader and he accepted their offer. The band traveled to New York in 1929 and when the band returned to Chicago, Calloway stayed in New York and took over the Missourians band for a short time. By spring 1929, he returned to Chicago and became emcee and singer with the Alabamians, leading them once again. In 1930, he returned to New York to do a stage appearance with the Hot Chocolate Revue and rejoined the Alabamians at the Savoy Ballroom. The Missourians asked him to lead them once again and he accepted. They opened at the Cotton Club and he changed the name of the group to Cab Calloway and His Orchestra. They did the first broadcast of *Minnie the Moocher* from the Cotton Club. The story goes that one evening he forgot the words to a tune and began to scat, "Hi-dee-hi-dee-ho." In 1932, Calloway appeared in several films in Hollywood, including *Stormy Weather* with Lena Horne and *The Singing Kid* with Al Jolson. By 1938, the personnel of the band included Leroy Maxie, drums; Milton Hinton, bass; Danny Barker, guitar; Bennie Payne, piano; Wheeler De Priest, Keg Johnson, and Claude Jones, trombones; Doc Cheatham, Lammar Wright, Irving Randolph, and Shad Collins, trumpets; Chu Berry, Walter Thomas, Andrew Brown, and Chauncey Raughton, clarinets and saxophones. By the '40s, a few of the top musicians in the Calloway band were drummer Cozy Cole, trumpet players Jonah Jones and Dizzy Gillespie, and saxophone players Hilton Jefferson and Ben Webster. In the late '40s and early '50s, Calloway led small combos, but in 1951, he took a big band to Montevideo and from 1952 to 1954 played the role of Sportin' Life with the touring company of George Gereshwin's opera, *Porgy and Bess*, in the U.S. and Europe. He did a solo act from 1954 until retirement. He died in Hockessin, Delaware on November 19, 1994.

CANNON'S JUG STOMPERS

(Cannon's Jug Stompers) This band recorded for RCA Victor Records in the late '20s and was considered the best blues oriented of all the Memphis jug bands recording for Victor at that time. Even though the band was only a trio, all of the jug bands at that time were trios and all were called "bands." The Jug Stompers were comprised of Noah Lewis, harmonica; Gus Cannon, banjo and leader; and Ashley Thompson, Elijah Avery, and Hosea Woods, each of whom played guitar at one time or another. Cannon's Jug Stompers played deep emotional blues and ragtime pieces. Cannon and Lewis served as vocalists. Woods died in the '30s and Thompson died in the '70s. Little is known of the other members of the group.

VICTOR SCHERTZINGER

(Victor Schertzinger and the Tunesmiths) Born in Mahanoy City, Pennsylvania on April 8, 1890. Schertzinger was considered a child prodigy as a young violinist and, at eight years old, was soloist with the Victor Herbert Orchestra. He toured the U.S. as a teenager and played concerts abroad as well. He studied at the University of Brussels School of Music and moved to Los Angeles, where he conducted pit bands, and to New York to conduct Broadway shows. He settled in Hollywood in the late '20s to compose for movies. He wrote the music for the first full-length silent movie with original background music, *Civilization*. By 1942, just after his death, his score for the movie *The Fleet's In* was heard. Schertzinger wrote several songs, including "Kiss the Boys Goodbye," "Tangerine," "Marcheta," "Dream Lover," and "One Night of Love." Schertzinger wrote the music for the following movies: *Marcheta* (1913), *The Love Parade* (1929), *Heads Up* (1930), *One Night of Love* (1934), *Love Me Forever* (1935), *Follow Your Heart* (1936), *Something to Sing About* (1937), *Road to Singapore* (1940), *Kiss the Boys Goodbye* (1941), and *The Fleet's In* (1942). Victor Schertzinger died in Hollywood, California on October 26, 1941.

CHOCOLATE DANDIES ORCHESTRA

The Chocolate Dandies Orchestra was active from the late '20s to the '30s and rehearsed by stellar musicians like Benny Carter and Don Redman. The Dandies were considered a smaller version of the McKinney Cotton Pickers band and at one time or another featured players like Chu Berry and Teddy Wilson. In July 1928, the McKinney Cotton Pickers recorded 25 tunes. As several members of that band took a break, the remaining group recorded nine more songs and those songs were released under the name the Chocolate Dandies Orchestra. Chocolate Dandies had been the name of the 1924 Broadway show written by Noble Sissle and Eubie Blake. By 1928, the Dandies recorded four additional songs. Although the leader of the orchestra was Don Redman, his name was not included on the record labels.

LEW DAVIES

(Lew Davies and His Orchestra) Born in Ashland, Kentucky on September 25, 1911. Lew Davies attended the Cincinnati Conservatory of Music and studied composition at a later date with Tibor Serly. By 1928, he was arranging for dance bands and working as a musician in radio studios. He played with various groups in various places until the late '50s, when he went to Command Records to work for Enoch Light. He became the top composer and arranger for Command and was wooed away by Columbia Records, where he was credited for having produced one album. With Command Records, he did arrangements for Lawrence Welk, Lena Horne, and Perry Como. It is said that he wrote arrangements that had a "stereo" quality, which, at the start of stereo recording, made his writing very much in demand. Some of his albums include *A Cheerful Earful*, *The Kissing Cousins Sing*, *Two Pianos and Twenty Voices*, *Strange Interlude*, and *Delicado*. Davies died in New York City on December 11, 1968.

CARROLL DICKERSON

(Carroll Dickerson and the Savoyagers) Born in 1895. Louis Armstrong or Earl "Fatha" Hines usually led the Carroll Dickerson band. Carroll Dickerson was a violinist who led a band in Chicago around 1928 and at times had excellent sidemen like Earl Hines, Natty Dominique, Honroe Dutrey, Louis Armstrong, and other musicians from New Orleans. The band was the resident organization at the Savoy Ballroom in Chicago. The band also toured on the Pantages Vaudeville circuit and recorded under Dickerson's name. The 1928 personnel were Carroll Dickerson, violin and leader; Zutty Singleton, drums and vocals; Fred Robinson, trombone; Homer Hobson and Louis Armstrong, trumpets; Bert Curry and Crawford Wethington, alto saxophones; Jimmy Strong, clarinet and tenor saxophone; Mancy Carr, banjo; Pete Briggs, tuba; and Earl Hines, piano. Dickerson died in Chicago, Illinois in October 1957.

TED FIO RITO

(Ted Fio Rito and His Orchestra) Born in Newark, New Jersey on December 20, 1900. Pianist Ted Fio Rito began as co-leader with Dan Russo of the Oriole Terrace Orchestra. Russo left the orchestra in the '20s, and for many years, Fio Rito continued to write songs in addition to leading the band. The Ted Fio Rito

Orchestra played the Skelly Gasoline show. Some of the sidemen in the orchestra were Dusty Rhodes, Frank Flynn, Al King, Candy Candido, Charlie Price, Bill Ross, Ray Hendricks, and Woody Taylor. Singers were June Haver, Bob Carroll, Del Casino, Maureen O'Connor, Stanley Hickman and Muzzy Marcellino. He wrote tunes like "Toot Toot Tootsie," "I Never Knew," "Laugh Clown, Laugh," "When Lights Are Low," and "Sometime." The theme song for the Ted Fio Rito Orchestra was "Rio Rita." He had a number of famous personalities in his band, including bass player Candy Candido, and singers Kay Swingle and Her Brothers, Leif Ericson, and Betty Grable. The Ted Fio Rito Orchestra recorded for Decca, Brunswick, and Victor Records. Ted Fio Rito died in Scottsdale, Arizona on July 22, 1971.

HERBIE KAY

(Herbie Kay and His Orchestra) Born in 1904. Herbie Kay (né: Herbert Kaumeyer) studied music and played with various bands during the '20s. He formed his band in Chicago in the early '30s and played at the Drake Hotel and the Blackhawk restaurant. They traveled throughout the country playing at the Lakeside in Dencer, the Santa Catalina Casino, Sebastian's Cotton Club in Los Angeles, and the Mural Room of the St. Francis Hotel in San Francisco. In 1937, they made a musical short for Paramount Pictures. Kay married one of his singers, Dorothy Lamour, in 1935 but they divorced in 1939. Other female singers who appeared with the Herbie Kay Orchestra were Wynne Fair and Ellen Conner. Some of the sidemen who appeared with the Kay band were Bill Epple, drums; King Harvey, guitar; Jim Bishop, bass; Claude Kennedy, piano; Ralph Destefano and Ray Winegar, trumpets; Ken Skersick, Bill Lower, and Charles Probert, trombones; Fuzzy Combs, Norm Weldon, Dick Herschleder, and Jim Williams, saxophones. The theme song of the Herbie Kay Orchestra was "Violets." Herbie Kay died on May 11, 1944 in Dallas, Texas.¯

ENOCH LIGHT

(Enoch Light and the Light Brigade) Born in Canton, Ohio on August 18, 1905. Light graduated from Johns Hopkins University and studied at the Mozarteum in Salzburg, Austria. During the '30s, he remained in Europe leading various orchestras and recorded for Columbia and RCA Victor records. In 1940, he returned to the U.S. and formed a new dance band, which played throughout the Northeast. The Light Brigade recorded for Vocalion, RCA Victor, and Bluebird records. The theme song of the Light Orchestra was "You Are My Lucky Star." In 1948, he disbanded, completed his master's degree at NYU, and worked for various record companies. Light became president of Waldorf Music Hall Records in 1954, and by 1956, he formed his own record company, Grand Award, which produced such hits as a Dixieland record by the Charleston City All-Stars and the solo piano album *Knuckles O'Toole Plays the Greatest All-Time Ragtime Hits* by Dick Hyman. Enoch Light wrote a number of songs, including "Carribe," "Daniel Boone," "Private Eye Suite," "Via Veneto," "Cinderella," "The Daddy of Them All," "Big Band Bossa," and "Rio Junction." From 1959 to 1965, he taught at New York University; he formed his second company, Command Records, and still another company, Project Three Records, several years later. During his career, Light initiated many new innovations, including stereo recordings, 35mm magnetic film recording, four-channel recording, and multi-microphone recording. He died in Redding, Connecticut on July 31, 1978 at age 73.

FRANKIE MASTERS

(Frankie Masters and His Orchestra) Born in St. Mary's, West Virginia on April 12, 1904. Masters first band was organized in the '20s and was based in Chicago, where they played at the Hotel Sherman's College Inn. By 1939, the Frankie Masters Orchestra had a hit record, "Scatterbrain," which was also his theme song. The band toured throughout the country and settled in New York, where they played at the Essex House. Singer Phyllis Miles joined the band in 1941 and eventually became Mrs. Frankie Masters. During WWII, the Masters band played a number of radio programs entitled *Victory Parade of Spotlight Bands* and toured extensively. His record company in 1945 was Vogue Records. In addition, the band recorded for Mercury, Columbia, Victor, Vocalion, and Okeh Records. In the late '40s, the band played the West Coast and spent some time in residence at the Boulevard Room of the Stevens Hotel (now the Conrad Hilton). It played for Vickie Carr, Mel Torme, Helen O'Connell, Jim Nabors, Milton Berle, Bob Hope, Margaret Whiting, Myron Cohen, Phyllis Diller, Phil Harris, Jonathan Winters, George Gobel, Dennis Day, the Harmonicats, Sally Rand, Cab Calloway, the Smothers Brothers, Victor Borge, and many others.

Masters died on January 29, 1991 at the age of 87.

RAY NOBLE

(Ray Noble and His Orchestra, the New Mayfair Dance Orchestra) Born in Brighton, England on December 17, 1903. At age 19, he was already a fine musician, composer, and arranger; he won the Melody Maker (England's *Down Beat*) award. From 1929 until 1934, he was the director for light music for the English arm of RCA Victor Records and HMV. The New Mayfair Orchestra was the RCA recording orchestra. He came to the U.S. in 1935; he became the musical director for Radio City in New York City and brought with him his drummer, Bill Harty, and his singer, Al Bowlly. While in New York, Glenn Miller organized a band for Noble, which played the Rainbow Room. That band had outstanding personnel and included Johnny Mince, clarinet; Charlie Spivak and George "Pee Wee" Irwin, trumpets; George Van Eps, guitar; Will Bradley, trombone; Bud Freeman, tenor saxophone; Delmar Kaplan, bass; and Claude Thornhill, piano. Other personnel included Will Bradley, Milt Yaner, Jim Cannon, Danny D'Andrea, Delmar Kaplan, Milt Bernhart, and others. He and Miller had a disagreement and Noble moved to Hollywood, California, where he took a position working on a number of films as well as the Burns and Allen and Edgar Bergen–Charlie McCarthy radio shows. The theme song for Noble was "The Very Thought of You," which was among the many songs that he wrote, including "Love Locked Out," "By the Fireside," "Love Is the Sweetest Thing," "The Touch of Your Lips," "Cherokee," and "The Very Thought of You." After Hollywood, Noble returned to New Jersey, where he lived until 1970. He died in Santa Barbara, California on April 3, 1978.

JOE REICHMAN

(Joe Reichman and His Orchestra) Born in St. Louis, Missouri in 1898. Joe Reichman played piano and formed a band that played in the late '20s and through the '30s. His bandsmen called him "The Old Piano Pounder." Reichman recorded more than 80 records for RCA Victor and ARC records. The band, which played hotels, featured vocals by Siggy Lane, Chester Leroy, Jane Fulton, Gege Schill, Larry Neill, Janette, Marionn Shaw, Paul Small, Joe Martin, Chick Bullock, Chris Fletcher, Mildred Monson, and Joe Sudy. In 1941, the personnel of the band included Carroll Consitt, drums; Joe Reichman, piano and leader; Jim Bishop, bass; Ed Gregory, guitar; Fred Fellensby, Ed Mihas, James Williamson and Clem Zuzenak, saxophones; Art Lewis, trombone; and Bert Lamar and Chuck Grifford, trumpets. The Reichman Orchestra themes were "Little Thoughts" and "Paliacci Variations in G." The band recorded for Victor, Arc, and Perfect records. Reichman died in Dallas, Texas on April 14, 1970.

BUDDY ROGERS

(Buddy Rogers and His California Cavaliers) Born in Olathe, Kansas in 1904. Rogers (né: Charles Rogers) played trumpet and trombone and eventually learned to play every orchestral instrument with some dexterity. He also aspired to be an actor and, in 1925, as his band played at the Pennsylvania Hotel in New York City, he appeared in his first film. At that time, the sidemen were Ben Freeman, Tommy Reo, George Macy, Andrew McKinney, Corkey Cornelius, Johnny Mince, Ward Silloway, Mike Doty, Ray Biondi, Barry Wood, and Gene Krupa. The band was billed as "The Newest Thing in Swing" and the theme song was "My Buddy." Rogers' female singers were Marvel Maxwell and Liz Tilton. In the late '30s, the Rogers band toured the Eastern U.S. and Canada and opened at the Palomar Ballroom in Los Angeles. The Rogers band recorded for Vocalion and Victor Records. Rogers married Mary Pickford on May 18, 1938 and during the West Coast tour, the band appeared at the Avalon Ballroom in Catalina. When Rogers disbanded he continued to act in motion pictures and to handle business investments.

PAUL TREMAINE

(Paul Tremaine and the Band from Lonely Acres) Tremaine started his first dance band in New York City in the late '20s. Some of the sidemen included Cliff Harkness, Jay Wade, Arnold Lehner, Archie Newman, Bob Tremaine, and Sonny Dunham who also sang. The Tremaine Orchestra was considered a good commercial dance band. The band was based out of Yoeng's Chinese-American Restaurant in New York City in the early '30s where they produced shows for the restaurant's patrons and for various radio broadcasts. The theme song of the band was "Lonely Acres" and they recorded for Columbia and RCA Victor records. Paul Tremaine took a temporary retirement in the middle '30s but reorganized his band a year later and continued performing well into the '40s.

TOMMY TUCKER

(Tommy Tucker and His Orchestra) Born in Souris, North Dakota on May 18, 1908. Tommy Tucker (né: Gerald Duppler) received a degree in music from the University of North Dakota in 1929 and formed his first band that year. His first recordings listed the group as Tommy Tucker and His Californians; Tucker sang all the vocals. By 1935, he had formed another band, which set his style for the next 25 years. The Tucker Orchestra featured music for slow, romantic dancing and played in ballrooms and hotels throughout the U.S. "I Love You" and "Oh How I Love You" were the theme songs of the Tommy Tucker Orchestra. From 1936 to 1937, the orchestra played on the *Fibber McGee and Molly* radio program and, in 1938, the *George Jessell Show*. In 1941, the Tucker Orchestra made its biggest recording, "I Don't Want to Set the World on Fire," featuring singer Amy Arnell. It was that year that Tommy Tucker met his future wife, Virginia Dare, whom he married later that year. Tucker continued to lead his band and also run a furnishing store. He simultaneously owned a songwriting company and founded the Tommy Tucker School of Music. Tucker was a successful songwriter, penning songs like "Cool, Calm, and Collected," "The Man Who Comes Around," and his theme song, "I Love You." During the mid-'40s, Tucker lead a swing band for a short time, returning to the dance band format within a year. In the early '50s, the personnel included singer Eydie Gorme and baritone saxophonist Gerry Mulligan. Tucker retired from the band business in 1959, taught English in a local high school, and joined the faculty of the department of music at Monmouth College in New Jersey as an assisstant professor. He remained at the college for 18 years and eventually became the dean. In 1978, he retired and moved to Florida. Tucker died in Sarasota, Florida on July 13, 1989.

RUDY VALLÉE

(Rudy Vallée and his Connecticut Yankees) Born at Island Point, Vermont on July 28, 1901. Hubert Prior "Rudy" Vallée grew up in Westbrook, Maine. His father was a pharmacist and ran a drugstore. A drummer in his high school band, he left school to join the Navy in 1917 but was dismissed for being underage. Returning home he worked as a movie projectionist and studied clarinet and saxophone. He also reenrolled and finished high school as he practiced and wrote to saxophonist Rudy Wiedoeft. Wiedoeft finally responded when he had received eight letters from Vallée. In 1921, Vallée enrolled at the University of Maine and joined the Sigma Alpha Epsilon fraternity. Being aware of Vallée's admiration for Rudy Wiedoeft's saxophone playing, Vallée's fraternity brothers nicknamed him Rudy. In 1922, he transferred to Yale University (in Connecticut), hence, the name Connecticut Yankees. At Yale, he played saxophone at various social events (e.g., dances, social functions, country clubs, etc.) and used a megaphone to enhance his voice (there were no microphones yet in use). In 1924, he left school and took a job playing saxophone at the Savoy Hotel with the eight-piece Savoy Havana band. He remained with that band for a year, made some recordings, and was heard via radio broadcasts. In 1925 he returned to Yale, eventually graduating. In New York City, he met bandleader Bert Lown, and he and Lown formed a band, Connecticut Yankees, and played at the Heigh-Ho Club; Vallée would introduce the show with "Heigh-ho, everybody." The band broadcasted 25 times per week and chalked up big box office successes and also played at the Paramount Theater and the Palace. Vallée's theme song was "My Time Is Your Time" and his band recorded for Arc, Bluebird, Victor, Columbia, and Harmony records. In 1929, the band appeared in the movie *Vagabond Lover* before returning to New York to play at the Villa Vallée. The band did early broadcasts and featured guests like Edgar Bergen, Ezra Stone, Gloria Swanson, Bob Hope, Cole Porter, Beatrice Lillie, George Gershwin, Boris Karloff, Kate Smith, and a host of others. In 1931, Vallée was one of the stars of the *George White Scandals* and played a series of Paramount Theaters for $12,500 per week. After ten years of popularity, in 1939, Vallée ended his radio show. During the early part of WWII, Vallée joined the U.S. Coast Guard and toured with a 40-piece band. He returned to radio in 1944 with co-star Monti Wooley prior to retirement. Vallée died in Hollywood, California on July 8, 1986.

JACK HYLTON

(Jack Hylton and His Orchestra) Born in Lancashire, England in 1892. Hylton played the organ in various theaters when he was a young man. During WWI, he served in the British millitary. After the war he served in the band at the Queen's Langham Place. After a year, he became the leader of the band and he began recording and playing the best venues throughout England. In 1926, the band became a favorite being heard nationally on radio. Ted Health joined the Hylton band in 1925 and, by 1930, the band was featuring singer Ella Logan. During the late '20s, the band toured Belgium and France and, in the early '30s, Germany. In the early '30s, some of the Hylton's recordings were released in the U.S. on Victor Records. One of the records featured American tenor saxophonist Coleman Hawkins soloing on "Dancing on the Ceiling." In late 1935, Hylton came to America and led a band composed of U.S. musicians, including Dave Rose, Murray Mceachern, and George Wettling. Hylton was heard on U.S. radio with Alec Templeton in 1935 performing "She Shall Have Music." In 1936, Jack Hylton returned to England and in his later years became a theatrical producer. Hylton recorded on His Master's Voice, Decca, Victor, and Brunswick records. Hylton died on January 29, 1965.

HERMAN WALDMAN

(Herman Waldman and His Orchestra) Waldman was a Texan who started his first band in Dallas and played at the Adolphus and Baker hotels there. In the late '20s, the band toured throughout the Southwest and Western U.S. In the '30s, the Herman Waldman Orchestra played the Peabody Hotel in Memphis, Tennessee and the Muehlebach Hotel in Kansas City, Missouri. Trumpeter Harry James first played with the Waldman band. Other Waldman sidemen from time to time were Bill Clemens, Rex Pries, Tink Natural, Bob Harris, Jim Segars, Ken Sweitzer, Arnold Wadsworth, Tom Blake, Vernon Mills, Barney Dodd, Reggie Kaughlin, and Jimmie Mann. The band recorded for Bluebird and Brunswick records.

DON AZPIAZU

(Don Azpiazu and His Casino Orchestra) Azpiazu formed his first band in 1928 and gained early fame from a song adapted from El Manisero called "The Peanut Vendor." The Azpiazu Orchestra recorded the tune in November 1930 on RCA Victor Records and it became a huge hit for two months. The band also played the song in the movie *Cuban Love Song* in 1931. Also in 1931, the Azpiazu Orchestra made the first recording of the tune "Green Eyes" (recorded many years later by the Jimmy Dorsey Orchestra).

TED BLACK

(Ted Black and His Orchestra) Ted Black formed his first band in 1929. The band's theme songs were "Pagan Moon" and "On the Beach with You." It was noted for having top-rated arrangements on the sweet-commercial side. The band played on Broadway appearing in the musical *Ballyhoo* in 1931. Victor Records released the "Love Letters in the Sand" with vocal by Ted Black, which brought great interest in the band. In 1932, the Black Orchestra recorded "Banking on the Weather," "Masquerade," and "Pagan Moon."

DICK COY

(Dick Coy and His Racketeers) The Coy band made their only record in Richmond, Indiana in 1930 recording "Eleven-Thirty Saturday Night" and "Barnacle Bill the Sailor." Many noted sidemen played with the Coy band, including vocalist Jimmy McPoland, Jud Foster, Larry Kenyon, Jimmy Hayes, and Dick Coy, pianist and bandleader.

JACK CRAWFORD

(Jack Crawford and His Orchestra) Jack Crawford played the "C" melody saxophone and organized his first band in the Midwest in the later '20s. At that time, his sidemen were Manny Stein, Paul McKnight, Joe Bueher, Earl Center, Carroll Willis, Harry Sosnick, Ted Willis, Joe Snyder, Jerry Miller, and Bob Huffl. It was said that Crawford looked just like Paul Whiteman. He was crowned "The Clown Prince of Jazz" due to his comedic actions. He became a big favorite in the Midwest by the mid-'30s, playing ballrooms and touring from coast to coast, and was broadcast frequently on radio. In 1942, he disbanded his big band and formed a four-piece cocktail lounge group. The Crawford theme songs were "Larger" and "Dance 'Till Three." Jack Crawford and His Orchestra recorded for RCA Victor and Gennett Records.

CHARLIE JOHNSON

(Charlie Johnson and His Orchestra) Born in Philadelphia, Pennsylvania on November 21, 1891. Pianist Charlie Johnson was raised in Lowell, Massachusetts and played in Atlantic City during the late teens and early '20s. In 1925, he organized his first band and opened at Small's Paradise Club in Harlem where he remained until the late '30s. He also toured during that time and played in Atlantic City occasionally. He had an excellent band that featured trumpets Frankie Newton, Sidney Deparis, Jabo Smith, and Roy Elridge, saxophonists Benny Carter and Edgar Sampson, and trombonist Dickie Wells. In 1938, he disbanded and jobbed around in New York City until an illness caused his retirement. Johnson wrote "Fat and Greasy" and "Viper's Dream." The Charlie Johnson band recorded for Victor, Bluebird, and Embassy records. Johnson died in New York City on December 13, 1959.

SHEP FIELDS

(Shep Fields and His Rippling Rhythm) Born in Brooklyn, New York on September 12, 1910. Shep Fields was a saxophone player who first played with the Jack Denny Orchestra in New York City at the Hotel Pierre while attending St. Johns University in Brooklyn. For a brief time he left the Denny Orchestra to go on the road with the dance team of Veloz and Yolanda. The billing read, "The Veloz and Yolanda Orchestra Under the Direction of Shep Fields."When he returned to New York, he rejoined the Denny Orchestra at the Hotel Pierre where he remained for a while. When he formed his own band he played at Jenny Grossinger's Catskill Resort Hotel many times. The Fields band played the *Woodbury Show* on radio for several seasons. Bluebird and Decca were the band's record labels. The theme songs of the Shep Fields Orchestra were "Rippling Rhythm" and "Ritual Fire Dance." Among the "stars" that played in the Fields band were Ralph Young, Ken "Fustus" Curtis, and Sid Caesar who was a saxophone player. Fields moved to Houston, Texas and played at the Shamrock Hotel frequently until he disbanded to go into the personal management business. Shep Fields died in Houston, Texas of a heart attack on February 23, 1981.

GLEN GRAY

(Glen Gray and the Casa Loma Orchestra) Born on June 7, 1906 in Roanoke, Illinois, Glen Gray was born "Spike" Knoblaugh. The Casa Loma Orchestra was the first cooperative orchestra in the U.S. Some musicians, who were managed by Jean Goldkette, originally formed it in the mid-'20s in Detroit. At that time, the band was named the Orange Blossoms, a name they used until 1929. In 1925, the band's personnel were Ed Murray, piano; Al Cox, banjo; Irish Henry, tuba; Tommy Gargano, drums; Reggie Comben, tenor saxophone; Ray Eberle and Gene Prendergast, alto saxophones; Ed Arnold, trombone; and Henry Biagini, trumpet and leader. In 1926, the band played at Lake Orion in Pontiac, Michigan and in 1927 at the Graystone Ballroom in Detroit. At that time, the personnel included Francis Grinnel, banjo; Bill Maitland, tuba; Marlen Skiles, piano; Know Pugh, drums; Doc Snyder and Larry Teal, alto saxophones; Walter "Pee Wee" Hunt, trombone; Clem Johnson and Henry Biagini, trumpets; and Gene Prendergast, tenor saxophone and leader. When the prince of Wales visited Canada in 1927, a new club called Casa Loma was built for his visit. The Orange Blossoms were booked for that opening but for various reasons, the club never opened. Nevertheless, by 1929, the Blossoms decided to rename themselves the Casa Loma Orchestra and formed a corporation issuing stock to all members of the band. By 1935, a number of personnel changes had taken place, including the addition of Larry Clinton, arranger (who wrote "Smoke Rings," the band's theme song); Danny Andrea, saxophone; Murray McEachern, trombone; Dick Jones, arranger; Art Ralston, brass horns; Jacques Blanchette, guitar and fiddle; and Fritz Hummel, trombone and fiddle. In 1937, Gray was appointed to front the  orchestra and Larry Wagner joined the band as songwriter. The band had grown to include Dan D'Andrea, Kenny Sargent, C. Hutchenrider, Pat Davis, Art Ralston, saxes; and Glen Gray, saxophone and leader; Sonny Dunham, Grady Watts, and Frank Zullo, trumpets; Murray MacEachern, Pee Wee Hunt, and Bill Rausch, trombones; Tony Briglia, drums; Jacques Blanchette, guitar; Stan Dennis, bass; and Howard Hall, piano. Other players and arrangers who participated in the Casa Loma Orchestra were Tutti Camarata, Henry Rogers, the Lebrun Sisters, Corky Cornelius, Don Boyd, Lon Doty, Red Nichols, Herb Ellis, and Bobby Hackett. The band recorded for Decca, Brunswick, and Okeh records and played until 1945. Gray died at Plymouth, Massachusetts on August 23, 1963.

MARION HARDY

(Marion Hardy and His Alabamians) Hardy led the band that became the first Cab Calloway Orchestra. Formed in the late '20s, the personnel consisted of Ralph Anderson, piano; Leslie Corley, banjo; Jimmy McHendricks, drums; Hardy and Artie Starks, saxophones; Henry Clark, trombone; Charlie Turner, tuba; and Eddie Mallory and Elisha Herbert, trumpets.

JACQUES RENARD

(Jacques Renard and His Orchestra) Renard led a commercial band on radio and records during the late '20s and '30s. In 1931, the Renard band recorded "As Time Goes By" that became a big hit. In the mid-'30s, he was heard on the radio show *Manhattan Merry-Go-Round, Burns & Allen* (1935), and *Eddie Cantor*

(1936–1938). In 1937, the Renard Orchestra played the *Texaco Town Show* and the *Joe Penner Show* in the late '30s. During the early '40s, the Renard Orchestra was heard on the summer show featuring Igor Gorin and Ella Logan. The Jacques Renard Orchestra recorded for Vocalion, Brunswick, and Victor records.

ANDY KIRK

(Andy Kirk and His Twelve Clouds of Joy Orchestra) Born in Newport, Kentucky on May 28, 1898. Andy Kirk (né: Dewey Andrew Kirk) was raised in Denver, Colorado and was taught by Wilberforce Whiteman, the father of Paul Whiteman. By 1921, Kirk was playing tuba in the George Morrison Orchestra in Denver. In Kansas City in 1928 Andy Kirk took over the Cloud of Joy Orchestra led by Terrence "T" Holder. At that time, Andy was playing bass saxophone and the pianist and arranger was Mary Lou Williams. The band became known as Andy Kirk and His Twelve Clouds of Joy Orchestra. The band had such sidemen as Fats Navarro, Don Byas, Howard McGhee, Dick Wilson, Floyd Brady, Claude Williams, Earl Miller, and Jim Lawson. One of the band's big hits was "Until the Real Thing Comes Along," which was one of the band's theme songs; the other was "Clouds." The Kirk band recorded for Decca and Brunswick Records, was one of the earliest bands to use the amplified guitar, and was always considered among the great Kansas City bands. Kirk retired in the late '40s but returned as a music booker in the early '60s. Kirk died in New York City on December 11, 1992.

GEORGE E. LEE

(George E. Lee and the Novelty Singing Orchestra) Born in Booneville, Missouri in October 1908. George Ewing Lee led a ten-piece band that featured singer-pianist Julia Lee in the late '20s. The Lee Orchestra recorded for Brunswick Records and was often booked as a smaller band out of Kansas City. The band traveled widely in the Southwest and played occasionally in New York as well. Some of the featured players were Sam Auderbach, trumpet; Abe Price, drums; Chester Clark, tuba; Julia Lee, voice and piano; and George E. Lee, tenor saxophone. Lee died in San Diego, California in October 1958.

SPEED WEBB

(Speed Webb and His Orchestra) Born in Peru, Indiana on July 18, 1911. Speed Webb (né: S. Lawrence Webb) Studied violin and drums when he was a child. He played in local bands prior to forming a cooperative group, the Hoosier Melody Lads, in the mid-'20s. Taking the band to California, they appeared in various silent movies, including *Sins of the Father*, *Riley the Cop*, and an Ethel Waters's short subject, *On with the Show*. During the '30s, Webb led bands with the names the Dixie Rhythm Kings, Jack Jackson's Pullman Porters, the Brown Buddies, and the Hollywood Blue Devils. Some of the noted sidemen participating in these orchestras were Wingy Manone, Teddy Buckner, Vic Dickenson, Henderson Chambers, Art Tatum, Teddy Wilson, and Roy and Joe Eldridge. In 1938, Webb gave up music to obtain a degree in embalming. He moved to South Bend, Indiana, ran his own mortuary and wrote for the *Indiana Herald*.

ENRIC MADRIGUERA

(Enric Madriguera and His Orchestra) Born on February 17, 1904 in Barcelona, Spain. Enric Madriguera studied arranging, composition, and violin at the Barcelona Music Conservatory and concertized throughout Spain and immigrated to South America, where he became the music director for Columbia Records. He traveled to New York in the late '20s and started his first band. His was considered the first "Latin" band in the U.S. and many groups that followed emulated his style. After playing various club dates, hotel rooms, and theater circuits during the '30s and '40s, the band disbanded in the early '50s. Madriguera was the composer of many songs, including "The Language of Love," "Take It Away," "Minute Samba," "Forbidden Love," "Flowers of Spain," and "Adios." Many sidemen worked with the Enric Madriguera Orchestra; among them were Ernie Warren, James Pasquerelli, Tito Rodriguez, Jim Migliore, William Mikulas, Bernard Lazaroff, Bill Michails, Leon Kellner, Alfredo Jamesworth, Rocky Jordan, Pete Ippillito, Alfredo Jamesworth, Rocky "Rocco" Galgano, John Fisher, Art Foster, Fred Dombach, Miguel Duchene, James Cuarana, Tony de Simone, Jimmy Carroll, James Cuarana, Sol Amato, Joe Brittain, and Harry Bloom. The Madriguera Orchestra recorded many tunes on Vogue, Victor, Decca, Columbia, and Brunswick records, including "A Man, a Moon, and a Maid," "Vem Vem (The Cuban Kissing Game)," "Mujercita," "So

It Goes," and "The Spanish in My Eyes." The band's theme song was "Adios." Enric Madriguera disbanded the orchestra in the early '50s. Madriguera died on September 7, 1973 in Danbury, Connecticut.

JOE SANDERS

(Joe Sanders and His Orchestra) Born in Thayer, Kansas on October 15, 1896. Joe Sanders ("the Old Lefthander") grew up playing baseball; hence his nickname. He was the singer and co-leader of the Coon-Sanders Orchestra during the '20s and early '30s. When Carleton Coon died in May 1932, Sanders led his own band playing hotels throughout the Midwest. Moving to the West Coast, the Sanders band played the Trianon Ballroom in Los Angeles. The theme songs of the Sanders Orchestra were "I'll Never Forget I Love You" and "Do You Miss Me?" By 1950, Sanders disbanded and worked with the Kansas City Opera Company. Joe Sanders wrote a number of tunes, including "I Found a Rose in the Snow," "Nighty Night Dear," "The Wail," "Sluefoot," "High Fever, Blazin'," "Tennessee Annie," "What a Girl," and many others. Sanders died in Kansas City, Missouri on May 15, 1965.

BORAH MINNEVITCH

(Borah Minnevitch and Harmonica Rascals) The oldest and most well-known harmonica band was formed in the late '20s. The members were Borah Minnevitch (leader), Leo Diamond, Johnny Puleo, Jerry Murad, Richard Hayman, and Al Fiore. Although the group played until the early '50s, Leo Diamond left in the early '40s and formed his own trio. In 1944, Al Fiore and Jerry Murad left the Rascals and formed the Harmonicats. The Rascals played in vaudeville and on various concert stages and appeared in several Hollywood musicals. Richard Hayman eventually appeared with various big bands, arranging and performing. Johnny Puleo, who was a midget, provided comedy routines for the group until he left to do solo work.

JACK RUSSELL

(Jack Russell and His Orchestra) Russell began his music career as a sideman in The Kentuckians prior to forming his first band in 1929 in Waukegan, Illinois. Their first job was at the Valencia Ballroom followed by the Drake Hotel, the

Vanity Fair, and the Granada Cafe. The orchestra's theme song was "Into My Heart." The band worked in the greater Chicago area and was featured at the World's Fair in 1933 playing on the same stage as Texas Guinan. After the fair, the Russell Orchestra played the Congress Hotel, the Merry Garden Ballroom, the Canton Tea Gardens, and the Morrison Hotel Terrace Gardens in Chicago. During the summer 1934, they played at the Grand Beach Hotel in Michigan and returned to Chicago where they worked at the Melody Mill Ballroom from 1935 to 1937. The Russell Orchestra played the Dodge Program on radio CBS. Remaining in Chicago, the Russell Orchestra was featured at the Triabnon and Aragon Ballrooms, the Panther Room of the Sherman Hotel, the Boulevard Room of the Stevens Hotel, and the Marine Dining Room of the Edgewater Beach Hotel. In 1938 Jack Russell disbanded and became a talent scout.

LOUIS ARMSTRONG

(Louis Armstrong and His Orchestra) Born in New Orleans, Louisiana on August 4, 1901. Louis Armstrong (né: Daniel Louis "Satchmo" "Satchelmouth" Armstrong) was raised without a father. His mother was 15 years old when Louis was born and was rarely around. Satchmo hung out and learned a lot of bad tricks from other children in the "red light" district of New Orleans. Louis and some of his friends would often sing in the streets for pocket change. When he was 13, he was arrested for shooting a gun in the street on New Year's Eve and sent to the Colored Waifs Home for Boys. There he became interested in the cornet, played in the Waifs' band and later said, "Me and music got married at the home." When he got out of the home, he played with bands led by Fate Marable and Kid Ory and most of the best black bands in New Orleans. In 1922, Satchmo went to join the Joe "King" Oliver band in Chicago and made his first recording with the Oliver band. Louis always felt that Oliver was his real mentor. When he was still in his 20s, he wrote "I Wish I Could Shimmy Like My Sister Kate." When he left Oliver, he played with the Fletcher Henderson Orchestra all the while recording with Oliver, Henderson, Clarence Williams, and Bessie Smith, the blues singer. From 1925 to 1929, he recorded with his own groups, the Hot Five and the Hot Seven. From 1929 to 1941, he fronted bands originally led by Carroll Dickerson, Luis Russell, Les Hite, and the Blue Rhythm Band. He recorded with many groups through those years, including the bands of Andy Iona and His Islanders, the Casa Loma Orchestra, and the Dorsey Brothers Band. His 1965 recording of "Hello Dolly" took over first place from the Beatles. "Mack the Knife" recording Louis completed also became an instant hit worldwide. The U.S. State Department sent Louis and his orchestra on official tours around the world several times as representatives from America. He is thought to have had an influence on every jazz musician from Billie Holiday to Dizzy Gillespie. When Satchmo died in on July 7, 1971, the *New York Times* stated, "Armstrong was more than a great jazz virtuoso. He was the root source that moved jazz onto the path along which it has developed for more than 45 years."

NOBLE SISSLE

(Noble Sissle and His Orchestra) Born on July 10, 1889 in Indianapolis, Indiana. After completing high school Noble Sissle toured for two years with the Thomas Jubilee Singers. He then attended Butler College in Indianapolis, Indiana for two years before moving to New York where he assisted Jim Europe, a club impresario. He served in WWI as a drum major in Jim Europe's service band. After the war, the team of Sissle and Europe played vaudeville as a vocal-piano duo. Sissle then composed the score for the Broadway show *Shuffle Along* in 1921, *Elsie* in 1923, and *Chocolate Dandies*, 1924. The team split up and Sissle played in London and Paris from 1928 to 1930. On his return to the U.S., Sissle formed his band. Sissle was considered a well-schooled musician who had excellent sidemen in his orchestra. Some of the sidemen were Charlie Parker, Buster Bailey,

Tommy Ladnier, and Sidney Bechet. Lena Horne sang with the Noble Sissle Orchestra. The Sissle Orchestra played at Billy Rose's Diamond Horseshoe in New York for a four-year stint. Sissle wrote many songs and Broadway show tunes like "I Was Meant for You," "Characteristic Blues," "Low Down Blues," "Hello, Sweetheart, Hello," and "Gypsy Blues." The band recorded for Victor and Okeh Records. The Noble Sissle Orchestra was one of the first black bands to play white clubs. Sissle died in Tampa, Floria on December 17, 1975.

EDMUNDO ROS

(Edmundo Ros and His Orchestra) Born in Venezuela in 1910. The Ros Orchestra had a fine percussion section, due to Ros's expertise as a drummer, and was considered a very good dance band. The band, which was popular in England as well as in the U.S., was active for more than 30 years. One of the band's popular numbers was "Everybody Loves Saturday Night."

Bands directed by the following were known to have existed but there was insufficient historical information to include them: Leon Abbey, Jack Albin, Jack Davies, Jack Pettis, Eli Rice, Gene Rodemich, and David Silverman.

CHAPTER

THE DEPRESSION YEARS
(1930–1939)

The great Southern Drought, the Great Depression begins and caused 26,000 American businesses to collapse; 3,500 banks went under; 12 million people were unemployed (25% of the workforce); crop prices plummeted; land was selling for as little as 30 cents an acre. Adolph Hitler gained power in Germany (Nazi party membership grew from 17,000 in 1926 to one million in 1931). Joseph Stalin gained control of Russia; Benito Mussolini of Italy. In Germany, the Nuremberg Race Laws were enacted and Jews were persecuted. In 1936, Jesse Owens won four gold medals and dominated the track and field competition in the Berlin Olympics. The most popular radio show in the mid-'30s was the *Chase and Sanborn Radio Hour*, which featured Edgar Bergan and Charlie McCarthy. On October 30, 1936, Mercury Theater presented Orsen Welles's *The War of the Worlds*; Franklin Delano Roosevelt was reelected in a landslide vote. In 1937, Disney's first full-length cartoon, *Snow White and the Seven Dwarfs*, was produced for the movie theater. *Life* magazine was started by Henry Luce (who also founded Time magazine). In 1939, Mussolini seized Albania, and Hitler marched into Prague taking over Czechoslovakia.

1930: Penicillin was discovered. Various electronic instruments, including the Emicon, Hellertion, Ondium Pechadre, Radiotone, Sonar, and Trautonium were developed.

1931: The Empire State Building was completed. The Hawaiian steel guitar was designed. The first electronic percussion instrument, the Rhythmicon, was designed.

1932: Franklin Delano Roosevelt was elected (he garnered 22.8 million votes to Hoover's 15.7 million votes). The first electronic piano was developed.

1933: Prohibition was repealed. Roosevelt's NRA (National Recovery Administration) called upon industry to cooperate on pricing and wages). Hitler was made chancellor of Germany. A photoelectric keyboard instrument, the Polytone, was developed.

1934: Hitler became the Führer of Germany. The electronic guitar, designed by the Gibson Company, was manufactured. The Hammond organ was invented. The FCC was established by the Federal Communications Act (remote wires were set up for live broadcasts of music).

1935: George Gershwin wrote *Porgy and Bess*. First record albums appeared. Dealers sold record players near cost to encourage record sales. The Photona, a photoelectric keyboard instrument, was developed

1936: Sulfa drugs were introduced in U.S. Margaret Mitchell wrote *Gone with the Wind*. The Pianotron, an electric piano, was manufactured. An electronic device, the Vocoder, was developed.

1937: Amelia Earhart disappeared in the Pacific Ocean. Electronic pianos, Electone, and Variachord were designed. A keyboard-operated speaking machine, Voder, was developed.

1938: Neville Chamberlain promises "peace in our time." Irving Berlin wrote "God Bless America." A portable electric piano, Pianotron, was manufactured. Chromatic electronic timpani was built. The Melodium, a monophonic electronic keyboard instrument, was developed.

1939: Hitler invaded Poland, marking the beginning of World War II. The American Allen Organ was marketed. BMI (Broadcast Music Incorporated) was established by the National Association of Broadcasters. The NovaChord, an electronic music instrument, was developed. Jukebox operators were buying 13 million records annually to serve their machines. And 440 vibrations per second was unanimously adopted as the standard pitch by the International Conference on Pitch held in London, England.

BANDS FIRST ORGANIZED DURING
1930–1939

PERRY BRADFORD

(Perry Bradford and His Jazz Phools) Born in Montgomery, Alabama on February 14, 1893. Bradford studied music as he grew up in Montgomery, Alabama. As a piano player and songwriter, he joined a band led by Jimmy Johnson. By 1920, singer Mamie Smith recorded songs written by Bradford, "That Thing Called Love" and "Crazy Blues." During his career, Bradford wrote more than 1,000 songs, including "Keep a-Knockin'," "It's Right Here for You," "I'll Be Ready When the Great Day Comes," "Lonesome Blues," "Fade Away," "Hoola Boola Dance," "Lucy Long," and "I Don't Want It All." Many contemporary musicians, including Little Richard, recognize Bradford with laying the groundwork for what would later become rock 'n' roll. Bradford died in New York City on April 22, 1970.

GEORGE CORLEY

(George Corley and His Royal Aces Orchestra) Born in Austin, Texas in 1912. In 1930, George Corley formed a band with two of his brothers: Wilford, a saxophone player, and Reginald, a trumpet player. By 1931, Gene Ramey was the band's sousaphone player. When Ramey was in Kansas City, after leaving the Corley Orchestra, Walter Page taught him to play upright string bass.

ANN DUPONT

(Ann Dupont and Her Twelve Men of Music) Born on January 2, 1915 in Universal, Pennsylvania. Ann Dupont (né: Ann Bata) grew up in Florida and studied clarinet and violin. She began to front a band during the '30s and was often called the female Artie Shaw. During a gig at Cape May, New Jersey in 1945, she met and married George Maki, a U.S. Navy lieutenant. In addition to her prowess as a musician, she was a successful real estate salesperson and built two different homes with her own two hands. She and her husband retired and moved to Fairport Harbor, Ohio.

LES HITE

(Les Hite and His Orchestra) Born in Duquoin, Illinois on March 13, 1903. Hite graduated from local schools in Urbana, Illinois and attended the University of Illinois where he played saxophone. He played in his family's band throughout his youth and toured with the *Helen Dewey Show* until 1925. He then joined the Spikes Brothers Orchestra before spending time on the road with Mutt Carey, Curtis Mosby, Paul Howard, Vernon Elkins, and Henry "Tin Can" Allen. In 1930, he assumed the leadership of Paul Howard's Quality Serenaders Orchestra in Los Angeles and played at the Soloman Penny's Dance Palace. During his tenure as leader, his sidemen included Lawrence Brown, Britt Woodman, Al Morgan, Marshall Royal, Joe Wilder, T-Bone Walker, Lionel Hampton, "Snookie" Young, and Dizzy Gillespie. While playing at New York's new Cotton Club, he featured guest stars like Fats Waller and Louis Armstrong. The Hite band did a number of recordings for records and film soundtracks. The theme song of the Les Hite Orchestra was "It Must Have Been a Dream." When Hite retired from leading a band, he managed a talent-booking agency for five years. Hite died in Santa Monica, Calfornia on February 6, 1962 at the age of 59.

MILLS BLUE RHYTHM

(Mills Blue Rhythm Orchestra) In 1930, drummer Willie Lynch organized the Blue Rhythm Orchestra, and in 1931, Irving Mills, band agent, took over as manager and owner and changed the name to Mills Blue Rhythm Orchestra. The band ultimately recorded for Melotone, Vocalion, Brunswick, Victor, Perfect, and Banner records. Willie Lynch left the organization and it then appeared under the leadership of Baron Lee. In 1934, Lucky Millinder took over the band and it often appeared at the Cotton Club in New York City. During its lifetime the band had other names as well, including King Carter and his Royal Orchestra (directed by Benny Carter), the Blue Rhythm band, the Mills Rhythm Orchestra, and the Mills Hotsy Totsy Gang. Personnel in the band included Harry "Sweets" Edison, Henry "Red" Allen, and Charlie Shavers, trumpet; Tab Smith and Charlie Holmes, alto saxophones; Edgar Hayes and Billy Kyle, piano; Joe Garland, tenor saxophone; Spencer O'Neil, drums; and Benny "Buster" Bailey, clarinet. When the band disbanded in 1938, Millinder formed his orchestra.

OZZIE NELSON

(Ozzie Nelson and His Orchestra) Born in Jersey City, New Jersey on March 20, 1906. Ozzie Nelson (né: Oswald George Nelson) organized his first band while a student at Rutgers College. He had previously played in several college groups. The Nelson Orchestra first recorded for Brunswick Records in 1930 and later recorded for Bluebird and Vocalion as well. Through the years, Ozzie sang on many of his bands records. Other singers included his wife Harriet Hilliard and Rose Ann Stevens. Some of the important sidemen on the Nelson band included trumpet and arranger Billy May and alto saxophonist Buff Estes. The theme song of the Ozzie Nelson Orchestra was "Loyal Sons of Rutgers." Ozzie Nelson wrote a number of songs, including "I'm Looking for a Girl Who Plays Alto and Baritone," "Doubles on Clarinet, and Wears a Size 37 Suit," "And Then Your Lips Met Mine," "Baby Boy," "Swinging on the Golden Gate," and "Mary." Nelson disbanded his orchestra in the early 1940s. During the '50s, Ozzie and Harriet and their two sons, Ricky and David, and starred on their own sitcom TV show. Nelson died on June 3, 1975.

STUFF SMITH

(Stuff Smith and His Orchestra) Born in Portsmouth, Ohio on August 14, 1909. Stuff Smith (né: Hezekish Leroy Smith) was studying the violin by age six. His father was a violinist and his mother played piano. He attended Johnson C. Smith University on a music scholarship when he was 15 and, while in college, heard Louis Armstrong for the first time. He immediately gave up the idea of becoming a classical musician and turned to jazz. While touring with a show, he was given the name "Stuff" and, from 1926 to 1928, worked with the Trent Alphonso Orchestra and then briefly with Jelly Roll Morton. When he returned to Buffalo, New York in 1930, he led his own band for several years and relocated to New York City in 1938, where he worked on 52nd Street and formed a sextet with drummer Cozy Cole and Johah Jones. During that period, he recorded for Vocalion Records, singing and playing amplified violin. He composed and recorded "I'se a Muggin'" and "You'se a Viper." He continued to record through the early '40s, and when Fats Waller died in 1943, Smith took over Fats' band. In the '50s, Stuff Smith worked as a sideman with Dizzy Gillespie and Sun Ra. By 1957, Smith was featured on several of Norman Grantz's Verve recordings with the Oscar Peterson Trio, Dizzy Gillespie, Carl

Perkins, and with the French violinist Stephane Grappelli. During the '60s, he continued to record and travel in Europe and the U.S. and, in 1965, moved to Copenhagen, Denmark. Smith died in Chicago, Illinois on November 25, 1967.

HARRY TURNER

(Harry Turner and His Orchestra) In the early '30s, the Harry Turner Orchestra was often heard on a daily radio broadcast station KFY in Bismarck, North Dakota, which aired in Canada as well as the U.S. Primarily a territory band, the Turner Orchestra played various dances in ballrooms, hotels, and halls in the Bismark area. Many of Turner's sidemen left occasionally to play with the Ted Weems Orchestra in Chicago.

MARIO BRAGGIOTTI

(Mario Braggiotti and His Orchestra) Born in Florence, Italy on November 29, 1909. Mario Braggiotti attended the New England Conservatory of Music, where he studied with Converse and Adamowsky. He later attended the Paris Conservatory of Music and Fontainebleu, France, where he studied with Nadia Boulanger. He debuted at the Salle Pleyel in Paris and Carnegie Hall in New York City in a piano team with Jacques Fray. Braggiotti and Fray established their own radio series, in which Braggiotti conducted the orchestra. They later toured and presented a program called *From Bach to Boogie Woogie*. During WWII, Braggiotti conducted for the U.S. Occupational Army in Italy and Africa. Returning to the states, he toured as a soloist with various symphony orchestras. He also wrote "Variations on Yankee Doodle" and "Lincoln's Gettysburg Address" for orchestra and the score to the ballet *The Princess*.

DON VORHEES

(Don Vorhees and His Orchestra) The Vorhees Orchestra was first heard on a *Hit of the Week* paper disc in 1930. The tune was "Tiptoe Through the Tulips with Me" and featured sidemen Joe Tarto, tuba; Charlie Butterfield, trombone; Bill Trone, mellophone and trombone; and Fred "Fuzzy" Farrar and Red Nichols, trumpets. The "paper disc" was made of Durium. It was guaranteed to last longer than any existing record and was invented by a Columbia University professor. *The Hit of the Week* jury was Vincent Lopez, Eddie Cantor, and Florenz Ziegfeld.

BILLY BISHOP

(Billy Bishop and His Mayfair Music Orchestra) Billy Bishop (né: Billy Bisset) was the pianist for the Bissett-McLean Orchestra in 1930, prior to organizing his own band in 1931 in Toronto, Canada. The band was very musical and its reputation was highly respected in the U.S. Leaders like Guy Lombardo and Tommy Dorsey offered Bishop the piano chair in their orchestras but Bishop declined in order to travel with his band throughout the world. Many of the recordings the band did in London are just now available in the U.S. on CDs. The band's singers included Dennis Day and Bishop's wife, Alice Mann. Bishop disbanded in 1953 to become a stockbroker for Merrill Lynch in Beverly Hills, California. The theme song of the Billy Bishop orchestra was "Billy." Bishop wrote the song "Hoping." When he retired, he moved to Poway, California, played piano, and wrote music for St. Michael's Church. Bishop died in Poway, California on July 11, 1995.

FRANK LaMARR

(Frank LaMarr and His Orchestra) Born in New York City on January 24, 1904. Frank LaMarr (né: Frank Joseph LaMotta) attended private schools and studied saxophone and clarinet. He served as the assistant conductor in the Isham Jones and Ferde Grofe orchestras until the late '20s. In 1930, LaMarr started his first band that worked through the '30s at venues, including Young's Restaurant and Roseland Ballroom. In 1939, the Frank LaMarr Orchestra toured South America and Europe. LaMarr collaborated with Johnny Graham, Babe Hart, Jose Melis, and Carmen Cavallaro in writing songs like "A Lover's Lullaby," "Dolores," "When You Saw Him Last," "Dancing with a Dream," "At Twlight Time," "You Are the One in My Heart," "Shame-Shame-Shame on You," "My Own," and "While the Night Wind Sings."

WILLIE BRYANT

(Willie Bryant and His Orchestra) Born in New Orleans, Louisiana on August 30, 1908. Willie Bryant (né: Wiliam Steven Bryant), known as "the unofficial mayor of Harlem," was a well-known bandleader who led a band at the Savoy Ballroom in New York City for several years. The band's theme song was "It's Over Because We're Through." The band played riffs like "Steak and Potatoes" and "Viper's Moan." Several of the famous sidemen included drummer Cozy Cole, piano player Teddy Wilson, Lionel Hampton, vibist, and trumpeter Benny Carter. Bryant died in Los Angeles, California on February 9, 1964.

HENRY BUSSE

(Henry Busse and His Orchestra) Born in Magdeburg, Germany on May 19, 1894. When Henry Busse was a teenager, his family immigrated to the United States from Germany and settled in Ohio. After studying music as a teenager, Busse moved to San Francisco and soon formed a band with Paul Whiteman. Because Henry Busse was not yet fluent in English, Whiteman became the leader of the band. While he was with Whiteman, Busse wrote his famous "Hot Lips," which became his trademark song during his entire career in music. In 1928, Busse left Paul Whiteman and formed his own band that, by the early '30s, was playing at the Chez Paree in Chicago. There, his band developed the shuffle rhythm beat, which made him so famous. In 1938, he was playing at the Hotel New Yorker and was heard on frequent broadcasts. The theme songs for the Busse band were "Hots Lips" and "When Day Is Done." The band appeared in a number of movie shorts, including *Hit Tune Serenade* and Busse Rhythm. During WWII, Henry Busse and His Orchestra appeared on the weekly radio shows *Coca-Cola Spotlight* and *The Fitch Bandwagon*. Singers that appeared with the band included the King Sisters, Phil Gray, Carl Grayson, Bob Hannon, Roberta Lee, Skip Moor, Elaine Bauer, and Billy Sherman. Some of the outstanding sidemen were Sandy Runyon, Phil Gray, Ted Tillman, Bob Baker, and Ted Kennedy. The band recorded for Coral, Cosmo, Columbia, Decca, and Victor Records. Busse died in Memphis, Tennessee on April 23, 1955.

BUDDY CAMPBELL

(Buddy Campbell and His Orchestra) The Campell Orchestra existed only on paper. See Ray Carroll and His Orchestra.

RUSS COLUMBO

(Russ Columbo and His Orchestra) Born in Philadelphia, Pennsylvania on January 14, 1908. Columbo was a violinist who began playing professionally for silent movies. In 1928, he played with Gus Arnheim along with Bing

Crosby. That same year Columbo appeared in a movie with the Arnheim Orchestra. In the late '20s, Columbo organized his own band and recruited a number of outstanding sidemen, including drummer, Gene Krupa. An excellent crooner, he recorded a number of hit tunes, including "Prisoner of Love," "You Call It Madness" (his theme song), "Time on My Hands," "Sweet and Lovely," "All of Me," "Goodnight Sweetheart," "You're My Everything," and "I See Two Lovers and Paradise." Columbo would have been a major motion picture star except for the fact that he was accidentally shot by a friend playing with a gun. Columbo died in Hollywood, California on September 2, 1934.

EDDIE DUCHIN

(Eddie Duchin and His Orchestra) Born in Cambridge, Massachusetts on April 10, 1910. Eddie Duchin began with the Leo Reisman Orchestra in the late '20s as one of the pair in the two-piano team with Nat Brandwynne. In the early '30s, Eddie Duchin lived New York and assumed the leadership of the Reisman Orchestra at the Central Park Casino. Through nightly radio broadcasts, the band quickly built a national reputation. The piano player in the "relief" band at the casino was Carmen Cavallaro. The band also worked at the Ambassador Hotel in Los Angeles and back in New York City at the Persian Room at the Hotel Plaza. The Duchin Orchestra was featured on various radio shows, including *The George Burns & Gracie Allen Show*, *Texaco's Ed Wynn Show*, and *Going Places*, a radio talent hunt show. The Eddie Duchin band recorded for Columbia and Brunswick Records. The singer on the band through 1936 was Lew Sherwood. Some of the sidemen were Buddy Morrow, Al Carroll, Stew McKay, Fred Morrow, Milt Shaw, Lester Morris, and Lew Sherwood. The band's theme song was "My Twlight Dream." Duchin died on February 9, 1951.

BARON ELLIOT

(Baron Elliot and His Orchestra) Born in Pittsburgh, Pennsylvania on December 3, 1914. Baron Elliot (né: Charles Craft) was a clarinet and alto saxophone player who played with the Herbert Fristche Orchestra in Pittsburgh while still in high school at Alleghany High. During his senior year in school, he formed his own dance band and took on the name of Baron Elliot. A year after he graduated from high school, he signed a contract with MCA and was booked throughout Pennsylvania, Ohio, and West Virginia. In 1936, Pittsburgh radio station WJAS invited the band to become the staff band for the station, and through regular broadcasts, the Baron Orchestra became known throughout Illinois and Indiana. The Elliot Orchestra became the staff band for the Mutual Network station (WACE) in Pittsburgh in 1940, where Baron remained until he was drafted into the U.S. Army in 1943. While in the Army, he fronted a band with personnel, including sidemen who had played in top bands in civilian life: Charlie Mandra (from the Charlie Spivak Orchestra), Bobby Sims and Joe Susi (from the Bobbie Sherwood band), and Larry Triguero (from Louis Prima band). After the war, Elliot returned to WCAE in Pittsburgh, reorganized his band, and played throughout the Midwest. In the mid '50s, the Elliot band appeared on television on KDKA in Pittsburgh and played in the area until 1981 when Elliot disbanded and moved to Florida. The band recorded for National, Musicraft, and Decca records and its theme song was "Stardust."

SEGER ELLIS

(Seger Ellis and His Choir Of Brass Orchestra) Born in Houston, Texas on July 4, 1904. Seger Ellis's career in music as a professional began when he was 21 years old. At that time, he was employed by radio station KPRC in his hometown to do a weekly solo piano broadcast. In 1925, Victor Records recorded two new tunes with Ellis and his band, "You'll Want Me Back Someday" and "Mama." The management of Victor Records was impressed with the quality of Ellis's Orchestra and recorded 14 additional songs in Camden, New Jersey, the home of Victor Records. Two of the songs—"Sentimental Blues"and "Prairie Blues"—became hit records. These were the first two songs ever recorded using an electric microphone. The band went on to record for Okeh and Columbia records and had as sidemen Louis Armstrong, Joe Venuti, Mannie Klein, Eddie Lang, Muggsy Spanier, and Tommy Dorsey. In 1930, Ellis, by this time a full-time singer, did a nightly program in Cincinnati on radio station WLW, where he discovered the Mills Brothers and became their first manager. In 1934, Ellis made several movie shorts in Hollywood and guested on Paul Whiteman's radio show. In 1935, he formed a big band, using only one clarinet and eight brass, becoming the Seger Ellis and His Choir of Brass Orchestra. At that time the band recorded for Decca Records with arrangements by Spud Murphy. In 1941, he disbanded and joined the Army Airforce. When he was released, he became a full-time songwriter penning such hits as "December" (Count Basie), "You're All I Want for Christmas," "Little Jack Frost," "Get Lost" (Bing Crosby), "Gene's Boogie" (Gene Krupa), "My Beloved Is Rugged," and "11:60 p.m." (Harry James). Ellis died in Houson, Texas on September 29, 1995.

RICHARD HIMBER

(Richard Himber and His Orchestra) Born in Newark, New Jersey on February 20, 1907. The Richard Himber Orchestra, with arrangements by Bill Challis was considered one of the best during its time. In the early '30s, Himber was leading studio orchestras, and by 1934, he was leading his band, Righard Himber and His Essex House Orchestra in New York City. The singer was Joey Nash and the theme song was "It Isn't Fair." Many famous musicians played with the Himber Orchestra, including Bunny Berigan, Artie Shaw, Adrian Rollini, Hank d'Amico, Charlie Margulis, Jerry Colonna, and Jack Lacy. Himber, also a songwriter, penned "Day After Day," "Moments in the Moonlight," "Time Will Tell," "Am I Asking Too Much?," "I'm Getting Nowhere Fast with You," and "It Isn't Fair." The band continued playing in New York, primarily in the Central Park South area, and would imitate any band called upon by the audience. They called the act the Parade of the Bands. Recording affiliates were Decca, Vocalion, Victor, and Bluebird records. Himber's Orchestra won the best band contest in 1939. Himber died on December 11, 1966.

JETER-PILLARS

(The Jeter-Pillars Orchestra) The Jeter-Pillars Orchestra evolved out of the Alphonso Trent Orchestra and was primarily a St. Louis–territory band playing floorshows in the area. James Jeter played alto saxophone and Hayes Pillars tenor saxophone. Some of the outstanding sidemen in the band were Carl Pruitt, Jimmy Forrest, Floyd Smith, Big Sid Catlett, Walter Page, and Kenny Clarke. The Jeter-Pillars Orchestra toured the South Pacific during WWII for the U.S.O and was disbanded after ten years.

GENE KARDOS

(Gene Kardos and His Orchestra) Born in New York City on June 12, 1899. Kardos fronted a territory band in the New York area from 1931 to 1938 that performed often at the Roseland Ballroom. The band was considered a good swing orchestra with the theme song "Business in F." In 1940, he married his childhood sweetheart, and they had two sons, Jimmy and Charles. The Kardos band recorded for Victor Records in 1931. The bands singers were Dick Robertson, Cecil Bridge, Don Carrol, Pat Henry, Chick Bullock, Bea Wayne, and Jackie Gale. The band's arrangers included Vic Schoen and Bernie Green. Among the bands personnel were Smith Howard, drums; Max Goodman, bass; Joel Shaw, piano; Sal Sussman, guitar; Pete Salemi, trombone; Red Hymie and Sam Caspin, trumpets; Nat Brown, Joe Slone, Moe Cohen, and Gage Galinas, saxophones. In addition to Victor, the band also recorded for the American Record Company. Kardos died on August 27, 1980.

MART KENNEY

(Mart Kenney and His Western Gentlemen) Kenny organized his first band in Vancouver, British Columbia in 1931 when he was still a teenager. The group toured Alberta and British Columbia during the early '30s and, by the mid-'30s, was heard regularly on various radio networks. At that time, they worked at the Pealey's Academy, Chestermere Lake, Hotel Saskatchewan in Regina, and Lake Louise. Later in the '30s, the band played the Banff Springs Hotel and he Royal York Hotel and did extensive touring. The band recorded for Camden and Victor Records.

WILLY LEWIS

(Willy Lewis and His Entertainers) Born in Cleburne, Texas on June 10, 1905. Willy Lewis (né: William T. Lewis) studied music at the New England Conservatory of Music after playing in several variety theaters. He played the saxophones, clarinet, and sang. After leaving the conservatory, he played with Sam Wooding in New York City at the Nest Club before touring with the Will Marion Cook Orchestra. He toured North Africa, South America, and Europe with Wooding's Symphonic Syncopators in 1925, and formed his own band in 1931, when the Syncopators disbanded. Throughout the '30s, he toured Europe with a number of prominent musicians, including Bill Coleman, George

Johnson, Herman "Ivory" Chittison, Frank "Big Boy" Goudie, and Benny Carter. He disbanded in the early '40s because of WWII and took a job in New York City as a waiter and cook. Two of his recorded hits are "Swinging for a Swiss Miss" and "Christopher Columbus." Lewis died on January 13, 1971 in New York City.

CLYDE LUCAS

(Clyde Lucas and His California Dons) Born in 1901, Clycde Lucas was raised in Los Angeles, California, and in the early '20s, he played trombone with Herb Wiedorff. Lucas's brother, Leon Lucas, also played in the Wiedorff band. In the early '30s, Lucas formed his own band which became known as the "doublers band," each sideman playing several instruments. The vocal group was known as Four Men Only. The band recorded for Columbia and Vocalion records. Clyde Lucas and His California Dons played background music in some of the early "talkies" films but was best known for its work in hotels and theaters. The band's theme song was "Dance Mood." Lucas disbanded the group in the late '40s, following WWII.

FREDDY MARTIN

(Freddy Martin and His Orchestra) Born in Cleveland, Ohio on December 9, 1906. Freddy Martin was raised in a Springfield, Ohio orphanage, attended high school in Cleveland and began as a high school band director, who also worked for a music instrument manufacturer. When the Guy Lombardo Orchestra was playing in Cleveland, Martin attempted to sell them some new saxophones, which he failed to do. Lombardo heard Martin's Orchestra in 1931 and recommended that the Martin band substitute for the  Lombardo Orchestra on occasion. This marked the beginning of success for

Freddy Martin. Throughout his career, Martin had a number of important sidemen, including singers Buddy Clark, Merv Griffin, Helen Ward, and Stuart Wade; and instrumentalists Jack Fina and Claude Thornhill, piano; Bunny Berigan, trumpet; and Eddie Stone, violin. Freddy martin recorded a number of hits for Capitol, Victor, Columbia, Brunswick, and Bluebird Records, including "Why Don't We Do This More Often" and "Tonight We Love." The band's theme songs were "Bye Lo Bye Lullaby" and "Tonight We Love." Martin died in Newport Beach, California on October 1, 1983.

PAUL PENDARVIS

(Paul Pendarvis and His Dixie Ramblers) Born in Enid, Oklahoma in 1907. Pendarvis attended the University of California at Los Angeles, played violin, and appeared in motion pictures in minor roles. After leaving UCLA he moved to Kansas City where he formed his first band playing in local hotels, clubs, and on various radio shows. Following successful appearances in the Kansay City area, the Paul Pendarvis Orchestra played the Congress Hotel in Chicago. Some sidemen in the Pendarvis band were Charlie Watkins, Ernie Redd, Bill Osborn, Bob Hall, Herb Wiggins, and Willie Parr. The band recorded for Columbia and Gennett records. Pendarvis did the singing and played trumpet in the band. When Pendarvis disbanded in the early '40s, he became a radio station musical director.

DON REDMAN

(Don Redman and His Orchestra) Born in Piedmont, West Virginia on July 29, 1900. Redman learned to play every instrument at a young age and, in 1920, worked with Charlie Johnson's Paradise Club Orchestra. In 1923, he played with Billy Paige's Broadway Syncopators and, in 1924, joined the Fletcher Henderson Orchestra where he remained until 1927. He then became the music director for the McKinney's Cotton Pickers. During the '30s, Redman fronted his own band, did radio broadcasts for Chipso, performed in a Hollywood film short subject, and arranged for Paul Whiteman's band. In 1940, he disbanded and toured for a short while with the Snookum Russell band. He then freelanced, doing arrangements for several bands, including Jimmy Dorsey, Harry James, Count Basie, and the NBC Studio Orchestra. In 1946, he formed a new band and did an overseas tour. He disbanded in 1949, did a TV series for CBS, and became music director for

Pearl Bailey. In the '50s, Redman did some recording and had an acting role with Pearl Bailey in her Broadway show, House of Flowers. Redman's theme song was his own composition, "Chant of the Weed." Redman also wrote "Cherry" and "How'm I Doin'?" Don Redman died in New York City on November 30, 1964.

DON ALBERT
(Don Albert and His Orchestra) Born in New Orleans, Louisiana in 1909. Don Albert (né: Albert Dominique) played in bands in the New Orleans area prior to moving to Texas and playing with the Troy Floyd band in 1926. In 1929, he returned to New Orleans and formed a touring band that ended up in Texas. The band did a few recordings for the Okeh, Vocalion, and Southland Records and eventually disbanded in the late '30s. Albert spent the '40s living in New York City and booking bands. In the '50s and '60s, he lived in San Antonio, Texas where he freelanced as a musician. Albert died in San Antonio, Texas in 1980.

FRANK BLACK
(Frank Black and His Orchestra) Born in Philadelphia, Pennsylvania on November 29, 1894. Black worked at the Century Theater in New York City as music director prior to fronting bands during radio broadcasts in the '20s. He established a vocal group, the Revelers, which performed on NBC radio and made a few records, including "Beside a Lazy Stream," "The Varsity Drag," and "It's a Million to One." Black's bands played classical and semi-classical music at the time. The Frank Black band played the *Jack Benny Show* in 1934 and, during the '30s, *The Bell Hour*, *Harvest of Stars*, *Music America Loves Best*, *The String Symphony Program*, *Coca-Cola Show*, and *The Contented Hour*. Black wrote a number of tunes, such as "Bells at Eventide," "A Sea Tale," and Starlight." In his later years, he played in Hollywood and Broadway musicals and light operas. Black died in Atlanta, Georgia on January 29, 1968.

NAT BRANDWYNNE
(Nat Brandwynne and His Orchestra) Born In New York City on July 23, 1910. In the '30s, the Leo Reisman Orchestra featured the two-piano team of Nat Brandwynne and Eddy Duchin. Brandwynne formed his own band and played for various social affairs in New York City, featuring singers Dick Stone, Diane

Courtney, Art Gentry, Jerry Wayne, Lois Wynne, Buddy Clark, and Bernice Parks. The band never became well known outside the city but was heard on the *Kate Smith Radio Show*. Brandwynne's theme song was "If Stars Could Talk." The Brandwynne band recorded for Decca, Brunswick, and Arc records. Nat Brandwynne wrote "If Stars Could Talk," "Stars Over Bahia," "Peacock Alley," and "Little Rock Rag." He died in New York City in 1978.

BOB WILLS

(Bob Wills and His Texas Playboys) Born in Limestone, Texas on March 6, 1905. Wills studied violin as a child and got a job in the early '30s as a violinist on a Fort Worth, Texas radio station. He eventually played with the W. Lee O'Daniel Light Crust Doughboys. In the mid-'30s, he formed his own band, Bob Wills and His Texas Playboys, which was heard on radio from Tulsa, Oklahoma, and toured the Southwest. By the late '30s, he had added a brass section and a woodwind section to the band and got a large ensemble sound, approaching the sound the Bob Crosby band was getting at that time. He featured singers Tommy Duncan and Leon MacAuliffe, the latter of whom also played steel guitar. The band's theme song was "Steel Guitar Rag." The Wills band was extremely popular in the Southwest during the '30s and '40s, recorded often and were heard on radio and seen in several movies. The band's most famous tune was "New San Antonio Rose." Wills spent some time in the military during WWII. When he was discharged he built a new band and continued to play throughout the '40s and '50s. The Bob Wills band recorded for Vocalion, MGM, Okeh, and Columbia Records. Wills wrote "Big Beaver," "Let's Ride with Bob," "Stay a Little Longer," "Wills Breakdown," "Betty's Waltz," "My Confession," "Take Me Back to Tulsa," "Texas Playboy Rag," "Lone Star Rag," and many others.

GUS HAENSCHEN

(Gus Haenschen and His Orchestra) Born in St. Louis, Missouri. Gus Haenschen (né: Walter Gustave Haenschen) attended Washington University in St. Louis and served as an executive for Brunswick Records before the 1920s. He organized Ernie Hare and Billy Jones into a team that became popular in the '20s. By the mid-'30s, Haenschen was conducting on radio for the top shows of the day, including the *Maxwell House Show Boat, Lavender and Old Lace, Bayer Musical Review, Coca-Cola Song Shop,* and *Saturday Night Serenade.* In the '40s, he composed "Manhattan Marry-Go-Round," "Silver Star," "Rosita," "Easy Melody," "Lullaby of Love," "Silver Star," and "Underneath the Japanese Moon." In 1945, Haenschen received an honorary degree—doctor of music—from Ithaca College. He continued to conduct and record into the '60s, when he also produced the Metropolitan Opera Broadcasts. The Gus Haenschen Orchestra was also known as the Carl Fenton Orchestra. Haenschen died in Stamford, Connecticut.

RAY CARROLL

(Ray Carroll and His Sands Point Orchestra) The same sidemen played in the Ray Carroll, Chester Leighton, Lloyd Keating, and Buddy Campbell Orchestras, playing at the Roof Garden and Golden Terrace. They formed pick-up bands during the '30s and '40s that allowed for one band to be salaried by a number of several recording companies, specifically, Clarion and Okeh records. Several well-known artists played with the bands, including Mannie Klein, Benny Goodman, Tommy Dorsey, and singer Dick Robertson. Some of the tunes recorded included "Love Is Like That," "There Ought to Be a Moonlight Savings Time," "Let's Get Friendly," "I Want to Sing Again," and "Wrap Your Troubles in Dreams."

LOU DANDRIDGE

(Lou Dandridge and His Orchestra) Born in Richmond, Virginia on January 13, 1902. Lou Dandridge (né: Louis Dandridge) was a singer-pianist who formed his first orchestra in 1932 in Cleveland, Ohio, and moved to New York in 1934. During 1935, he joined the Adrian Rollini band and appeared at the Tap Room in the President Hotel in New York. During the late '30s, he formed a group made up of New York studio musicians and worked at the Hickory House on 52nd Street while recording for various labels. Dandridge died in Wall Township, New Jersey on February 15, 1946.

PUTNEY DANDRIDGE

(Putney Dandridge and His Orchestra) See Lou Dandridge, previous entry.

HAL GRAYSON

(Hal Grayson and His Orchestra) Grayson formed his first band in the early '30s and played many ballrooms on the West Coast. He featured several singers who became movie stars, including Betty Grable, Martha Tilton, and Shirley Ross. Stan Kenton played piano with the Grayson Orchestra in the '30s. Although he remained active in the music business, Grayson disbanded in the mid '40s. Grayson died in Hollywood, California in 1959.

JIMMIE GRIER

(Jimmie Grier and His Orchestra) Born in Pittsburgh, Pennsylvania. A clarinet and saxophone player, Jimmie Grier organized his orchestra in the early '30s after arranging for the Coconut Grove Orchestra led by Gus Arnheim. His theme song was "Music in the Moonlight," although the band was best known for its recording of "The Object of My Affection." Some of the singers appearing with the band were Loyce Whitman, Donald Novis, Dick Webster, Harry Barris, Pinky Tomlin, and Larry Cotton. The sidemen included Bill Hamilton, Jack Mootz, Paul King, Stanley Green, and Wally Roth. The band boosted the tagline "The musical host of the coast." Radio shows included *The Joe Penner Show* and *The Jack Benny Show*. The band recorded for Victor, Decca, Columbia, and Brunswick records. By the '50s, Grier had disbanded and sold real estate. Grier died in California on June 4, 1959.

PHIL HARRIS

(Phil Harris and His Orchestra) Born in Linton, Indiana on January 16, 1904. Harris played drums in the Henry Halstead and Francis Craig bands in the early to mid '20s. In the late '20s, he co-led the Lofner-Harris band in California. In the early '30s, Harris assumed leadership of the band and, by 1936, became the band for *The Jack Benny Radio Show*. The female vocalist was Leah Ray, who later became the wife of the owner of the New York Jets, Sonny Werblin. It is said that Phil Harris brought Guy Lombardo and His Orchestra to Hollywood from Canada in the '30s. During that same period, he married the actress Alice

Faye. The featured sidemen in the Harris band were Nappy Lamare, Nick Fatool, and Bill Fletcher. The Phil Harris Orchestra recorded for ARA, Victor, Decca, Columbia, and Vocalion records. Harris's biggest hit was "That's What I Like About the South." His theme song was "Rose Room." Harris died on August 11, 1995 in Rancho Mirage, California.

JOE HAYMES

(Joe Haymes Orchestra) Born in Marchfield, Missouri in 1908. Haymes organized his first band in the early '30s. He was an outstanding arranger and composer, but lacked the kind of business acumen necessary to sell a big band. The original band had notable sidemen, including Pee Wee Erwin, Toots Mondello, and Bud Freeman. When that group disbanded, he formed a 14-piece orchestra that toured until 1936. At that time, Tommy Dorsey left the Dorsey Brothers Orchestra and recruited 12 members of the Haymes band to start his own group. After Haymes built up another band, Ray Noble repeated the Tommy Dorsey deed by taking most of the great players from the Haymes Orchestra. Although Haymes built still another great band—which included sidemen like trumpet players Zeke Zarchy and Chris Griffin and pianist Bill Miller—the group never received the public support that it deserved. The singers were the Headliners, Rose Blane, Jane Dover, Phil Dooley, and Skeeter Palmer. The theme song for the Haymes Orchestra was "Midnight." The band recorded for many labels, including Columbia, Victor, Banner, Bluebird, and American Records. When Haymes disbanded, he moved to Dallas, Texas and arranged for various bands.

HENRY JEROME

(Henry Jerome and His Orchestra) Born in New York City in 1917. Henry Jerome began leading a band in high school and continued after graduation in the mid '30s. The Jerome Orchestra was a commercial group and worked at hotels and ballrooms, on steamships, etc. At that time, the band's title was Henry Jerome and His Stepping Tones. The singer was Kay Carlton and the guitarist was Billy Bauer. After WWII, Jerome reformed his band into a modern unit featuring the music of the day, bebop, and musicians like sax players Lenny

Garment and Al Cohn, drummer Tiny Kahn, and arranger Johnny Mandel. Jerome wrote a number of tunes, including "I Love My Mama," "Until Six," "Oh, How I Need You," "Theme from Brazen Brass," "Nice People," "Night Is Gone," "Homing Pigeon," and "Joe." The theme songs of the Henry Jerome Orchestra were "Nice People" and "Night Is Gone." The Henry Jerome band was heard on several radio shows, including *Dinner at the Green Room*. Jerome disbanded in the '50s and became the music director for Decca Records producing a series of records entitled Brazen Brass. In the late '50s, he left Decca to become the A&R director for Coral Records.

DICK JURGENS

(Dick Jurgens and His Orchestra) Born in Sacramento, California on November 9, 1911. Jurgens was considered a good trumpet player by age 14. He and his brother, Will, formed their first band while at Lake Tahoe in summer camp. When the band was inactive, they worked as garbage men. In the late '20s, the Jurgens band was playing in many major hotels on the West Coast and, by 1934, was in residence at the St. Francis Hotel in San Francisco. At that time, the vocalists were Buddy Moreno, Harry Cool, and Eddy Howard. In the late '30s and early '40s, the Jurgens Orchestra played at the Elitch Gardens in Denver, Colorado, and the Avalon Ballroom in Catalina Island, California. As they traveled the Midwest, they played at the Aragon Ballroom in Chicago. Jurgens and his brother joined the U.S. Marines during WWII and entertained the troops in the South Pacific war areas. When the war ended, the Jurgens brothers returned to Chicago, where they reformed a band and played at the Aragon Ballroom once again, and at the Trianon Ballroom. In 1956, they disbanded. In 1969, Dick Jurgens formed a band and played at the Willowbook Club near Chicago. The theme song of the Jurgens Orchestra was "Day Dreams Come True at Night," which was one of the songs written by Jurgens; another was "Elmer's Tune." The Dick Jurgens Orchestra recorded for Columbia, Vocalion, Okeh, and Decca records. Jurgens died in Sacramento, California on October 5, 1995.

SAMMY KAYE

(Sammy Kaye and His Orchestra) Born in Lakewood, Ohio on March 31, 1910. Sammy Kaye played clarinet at Ohio University, where he majored in civil engineering and organized his first band in the '30s at the Statler Hotel in Cleveland, Ohio. He immediately used the slogan, "Swing and Sway with Sammy Kaye." The Kaye band was a big hit and recorded tunes like "Daddy," "It Isn't Fair," and "Harbor Lights." His singer was Don Cornell. Kaye established a routine he called "So You Want to Lead a Band," where he invited people in the audience to come onstage. Kaye would hand the baton over and the new "director" would "lead the band." It was said that Sammy Kaye was so dictatorial that his entire band walked out on him one time. The Kaye Orchestra played on the following radio shows: *So You Want to Lead a Band*, *The Chesterfield Supper Club*, *The Old Gold Cigarette Program*, and *Sammy Kaye's Sunday Serenade*. They recorded for Victor, Columbia, and Vocalion. Andy Russell and Ralph Flanagan were sidemen on the Sammy Kaye Orchestra. When Kaye retired and moved to California, his first trumpet player, Roger Thorpe, took over the band. Kaye invested in various publishing enterprises and bowling rinks during his retirement. He died in New York, City on June 2, 1987.

JAY McSHANN

(Jay McShann and His Orchestra) Born in Muskogee, Oklahoma on January 2, 1909. McShan moved to Kansas City while in his teens and formed his first band in Kansas City, Kansas in 1936, which played until 1942. Among the many stars in that band were Walter Brown, singer, and the incomparable Charlie "Bird" Parker. In 1942, McShann served in the U.S. Army. When he was discharged in 1944, he played in Kansas City as a sideman for various groups. In 1948, he traveled to Los Angeles, California, where he worked with several groups and formed a small band. McShann recorded for Capitol and Decca Records. By 1958, McShann had returned to his hometown, where he continued to front his own band, play various club dates, and travel though the U.S. doing concerts. McShann was still active through the '90s.

LUCKY MILLINDER

(Lucky Millinder and His Orchestra) Born in Anniston, Alabama on August 8, 1900. Lucky Millinder (né: Lucius Millinder) moved with his family to Chicago, Illinois when he was very young. While a teenager, he began his career as an emcee, having never studied music nor playied an instrument. In the early '30s, he assumed leadership of the Mills Blue Rhythm Orchestra. By 1938, he worked with the Bill Doggett band. Millinder had a sense of what was great in music and what the people liked and hired great musicians like Henry "Red" Allen, Dizzy Gillespie, Harry "Sweets" Edison, Charlie Shavers, Bull Moose Jackson, Freddie Webster, Ellis Larkins, Billy Kyle, Bill Doggett, and Sister Rosetta Tharpe. By 1940, he formed the Lucky Millinder Orchestra, signed with Decca Records, and recorded hits like "When the Lights Go On Again." He also recorded for Victor Records. Millinder died in New York City on September 28, 1966.

ORRIN TUCKER

(Orrin Tucker and His Orchestra) Born in St. Louis, Missouri on February 17, 1911. Orrin Tucker (né: Evelyn Nelson) studied to be a medical doctor but led a commercial band. He hired singer Wee Bonnie Baker, who brought identification and positive notoriety to the band after recording a WWI tune, "Oh Johnny." Ultimately, several singers appeared with the band, including Scotty Marsh, Lorraine Benson, Jack Bartell, Eddie Rice, the Bodyguards, and Gil Mershon. The band recorded for Columbia and Vocalion. George Liberace, Dick Robinson, Doc Morrison, Elmo Hinson, Doc Essick, Joe Strassburger, Will Flanders, Phil Patton, Arnold Jensen, Lorry Lee, George Sontag, Roy Cohan, Morton Wells, Norgert Swtammer, and Everett Ralston were also members of the Tucker organization from time to time. Tucker bought Hollywood ballroom on Sunset Boulevard, the Stardust Ballroom, in 1975 and fronted his band there.

JOE VENUTI

(Joe Venuti and His Orchestra) Born in Philadelphia, Pennsylvania on September 16, 1904. Joe Venuti (né: Giuseppe Venuti) was born on an ocean liner as his family immigrated to America. He studied violin in Philadelphia where he grew up. At age 21, he met the jazz violinist Eddie South, who played with the the Hot Club of France quintet, which included the violinist Stephane Grappelli and guitarist Django Reinhardt. Venuti and South became friends and worked together for eight years, recording with many major groups, including those headed by Jean Goldkette, Red Nichols, Phil Napoleon, Hoagy Carmichael, Adrian Rollini, Red Mckenzie, Frank Trumbauer, Roger Wolfe Kahn, and the Dorsey Brothers. In 1926, Venuti recorded under his own name and used famous sidemen like Jimmy Dorsey, Bud Freeman, Benny Goodman, Adrian Rollini, Don Murray, Jerry Colonna, Louis Prima, Glenn Miller, Tommy Dorsey, and Jack and Charlie Teagarden. In 1929, Paul Whiteman contracted Venuti and guitarist Eddie Lang to appear in movies and they appeared in the technicolor movie *The King of Jazz*. In 1934, Venuti toured England. During the '40s, Venuti's singer was Kay Starr and, by 1945, he used two singers, Johnny Prophet and Ruth Robbin. In 1950, he appeared as a soloist in a small group on the *Bing Crosby* and *Duffy's Tavern* radio programs and, by the '60s and '70s, he was considered a legend as he played at the festivals sponsored by Newport and Concord. He also played at the Montreux Jazz Festival and on the *Dick Cavett Show*; he recorded in France, the Netherlands, the U.S., and Italy with many outstanding musicians such as Stephane Grapelli, Ross Tompkins, Dave McKenna, Earl Hines, Scott Hamilton, Dick Hyman, George Barnes, Urbie Green, Benny Goodman, and Jimmy McPartland. Joe Venuti's theme song was "Last Night." He recorded on Decca, Columbia, Okeh, and Bluebird records. Venuti died in Seattle, Washington on August 14, 1978.

FATS WALLER

(Fats Waller and His Orchestra) Born in New York City on May 21, 1904. Fats Waller (né: Thomas Waller) studied classical piano prior to becoming a professional at age 15. By the early '20s, he was playing for various blues singers, including Bessie Smith, in theaters and cabarets as well as piano and organ solos. In 1925, he played in Chicago with the Erskine Tate band and, in the late '20s, co-wrote the music (with Andy Razaf) for the Broadway show *Connie's Hot Chocolates*. In 1929, Waller recorded with McKinney's Cotton Pickers and, by the early '30s, he was heard on radio station WLW in Cincinnati, Ohio. In 1931, he recorded with the Ted Lewis Orchestra and, by 1932, Waller played in Paris, France and recorded with the Blue Rhythm Orchestra. In 1934, Fats Waller and His Rhythm recorded several songs for Victor Records, including "Blue Turning Gray Over You," "Ain't Misbehavin'," and "Your Feets Too Big." Some of the sidemen who appeared with Waller at that time were drummer Slick Jones, clarinetist Gene Sedric, guitarist Al Casey, bassist Cedric Wallace, and trumpet players John Hamilton and Herman Autry. Many of Waller's original songs were sold in the Brill Building in New York City. In the early '40s, Waller fronted a 13-piece band that played primarily in New York. His theme song was "Ain't Misbehavin'." Waller recorded for Victor, Columbia, and Bluebird records. Waller died on December 15, 1943 on a train returning to New York City from Hollywood, where he had made some movies.

LEW STONE

(Lew Stone and His Orchestra) Born in England in 1899. Lew Stone died in England on February 13, 1969. Stone was the arranger for the Ambrose band in the late '20s. By the early '30s, he was working for Roy Fox who was featured at the Monseigneur Restaurant. Stone specialized in writing arrangements for good singers, including Al Bowlly and Nat Gonella. Stone immigrated to the U.S. in 1935–1936 and joined Ray Noble. He formed his own band and was often heard on radio and seen on television. He returned to England and conducted for English movies remaining active into the '60s. Stone recorded for Decca, Columbia, and Rezono records.

HENRY KING

(Henry King and His Orchestra) The Henry King Orchestra was first organized in New York City in the early '30s and was most popular in the mid-'30s and played for society dances. King was a pianist who had begun his career as a concert artist, but switched to popular music. The King band played many venues, including the Mark Hopkins in San Francisco, the Cosmopolitan in Denver, the Peabody and Claridge in Memphis, the Shamrock in Houston, and the Biltmore in Los Angeles. They also played on the *Burns & Allen Show.* There were many singers on the band from time to time, including Bob Carroll, Phil Hanna, Don Taymond, Carmina Calhoun, Eugenie Marvin, Sonny Schuyler, Sidney Sudy, Don Reid, Ray Hunkel, and Dick Robertson. The theme song of the Henry King Orchestra was "A Blues Serenade." King died in Houston, Texas in August 1974.

JOHNNY LONG

(Johnny Long and His Orchestra) Born in Newell, North Carolina on August 2, 1915. Long began studying violin when he was six. A farm accident injured his right hand so badly that he learned to play the violin left-handed. He attended Duke University, where he formed his first band, the Duke Collegians, which succeeded the college band, begun by Les Brown. After graduation, the band became the Johnny Long Orchestra and played throughout the Midwest and the East Coast in various ballrooms and hotels. The original singers were Helen Young and Bob Houston. These singers were identified on recordings as the Glee Club as the band recorded for Decca Records. The theme song was "The White Star of Sigma Nu." Several hits were recorded by the band, including "No Love," "No Nothin'," "Time Waits for No One," "In a Shanty in Old Shanty Town," and "My Dreams Are Getting Better All the Time." By 1943, the band had appeared in two movies—*Follie's Girl* and *Hit the Ice*—and was heard on the *Teen-Timers* and *Judy, Joe, and Johnny* radio shows. It is said that the Johnny Long band epitomized the hotel bands of the '40s. Long featured a song he had written entitled "Just Like That." Various personages in the Long Orchestra included singers Janet Brace, Francie Laine, George Haywood, Phyllis Rogers, Jojean Rogers, George Richmond, and sidemen Kirby Campbell, King Walker, Irv Neilson, Ed Butner, Walter Benson, Carl Pool, Ed Fennell, Allen Mays, Floyd Sullivan, Bill Utting, H.L. Shockey, and Ray Couch. Long died in Parkersburg, West Virginia on October 31, 1972.

RUSS CASE

(Russ Case and His Orchestra) Born in Hamburg, Iowa on March 19, 1912. Russ Case studied the trumpet when he was a teenager and joined the radio staff at WOC in Davenport, Ohio as trumpet player and staff arranger. In the '20s, he went to Chicago and joined the Frankie Trumbauer band. In the '30s and after a stint with the Paul Whiteman Orchestra in New York, where he played, arranged, and composed, he joined Benny Goodman. He then became the music director for Rondo Records in New Jersey, where he orchestrated, composed, and conducted studio orchestras for a number of radio and television programs, record dates, transcriptions, and film shorts. Case died in Miami, Florida on October 10, 1964.

LOUIS PRIMA

(Louis Prima and His Orchestra) Born in New Orleans, Louisiana on December 12, 1912. Louis Prima studied violin for a number of years before switching to trumpet. At age 17, he was playing in a theater in New Orleans. In the early '30s, Prima formed a band, Louis Prima and His New Orleans Gang, with sidemen Sidney Arodin, Eddie Miller, Nappy Lamare, George Brunis, and Ray Baduc. During the swing era, Prima began playing popular music, as opposed to jazz, and added singer Lily Ann Carol. Besides his competency as a trumpet player, Prima wrote several songs, including the one that helped to make Benny Goodman famous—"Sing, Sing, Sing"—which became Prima's theme song along with "Way Down Yonder in New Orleans." The Prima band recorded for Columbia, Brunswick, Mercury, Majestism, and Victor records. In the '50s,

Louis' wife, Keely Smith, became the singer with his group. During the '60s and '70s, the Prima band became a small lounge combo. Louis Prima died in New Orleans on August 24, 1977.

REGGIE CHILDS

(Reggie Childs and His Orchestra) Born in England. Reggie Childs organized his band in the '30s and patterned his band after the Hal Kemp Orchestra. Jimmy Palmer (then known as Jimmy Dipalma) was the male singer and Gloria Gale, the female. Gale later became Miriam Shaw when she sang with Les Brown. By the early '40s, the singers were Lucille Doran and a vocal group called the 3 Cs. The band's personnel during various periods included Paul Von Tayre, Herman Paul, Roy Shaefer, Ernie Geiger, Huck Rounds, Bill Stumpf, Woody Fay, and Eddie Rhodes, trumpets; Jack Parker, Joe Anderus, Mal Little, John Hayers, Bill Kroll, and Tay Olson, saxophones; Don Girard, Anton Russe, and Bill Page, piano; Harvey Poulin, Ken Fye, and Ange Liotta, bass; Fred Roberts, guitar; Ernie Wolff and Arnold Lehman, drums. The band's theme songs were "Just a Little Love Song" and "I Love You." The Childs Orchestra recorded for Varsity and Decca records.

GAY CLARIDGE

(Gay Claridge and His Orchestra) The Claridge Orchestra was a popular orchestra in the Chicago area during the '30s. The band's theme songs were "When Summer Is Gone" and "This Is Love." Gay Claridge and His Orchestra played for many stage shows in theaters in Chicago and made many transcriptions for various radio broadcasts. Claridge sang and played saxophone and trumpet. No commercial recordings were made of the Claridge Orchestra.

ERNIE FIELDS

(Ernie Fields and the Territory Big Band) Born in 1905. Ernie Fields led a Territory Big band during the '30s and '40s, first fronting the band in Kansas City in 1938. The band was "discovered" by record producer John Hammond who brought the band to New York City for a tour and performances at the Apollo Theater. Fields managed to adopt all of the music styles through the '40s, '50s, and into the '60s, and was highly touted by many critics and authors. He died in Tulsa, Oklahoma on May 11, 1997. He was 92 years old.

EDDIE STONE

(Eddie Stone and His Orchestra) Born in Bicknell, Indiana in 1907. Eddie Stone (né: Eddie Marblestone) attended Bicknell High School and was the star quarterback on the football team. He enrolled in Purdue University, played football, but was injured during his freshman year. He sang on various dance bands throughout Indiana until he joined the Isham Jones Orchestra—singing and playing violin—and traveled extensively from 1929 to 1936. He then formed his own band, recorded, and played a swing style. In 1937, he disbanded and rejoined the Jones band momentarily until he formed a new band in 1938. In 1939, he again disbanded and joined the Freddy Martin Orchestra. In 1943, he again formed a new hotel band that he led into the '50s. Eddie Stone recorded for Bluebird, Perfect, and Vocalion records.

TERRY SHAND

(Terry Shand and His Orchestra) Born in Uvalde, Texas on October 1, 1904. Shand was a pianist and singer who began playing piano in silent movies during the '20s. He toured with pianist Peck Kelley, playing drums in the greater Houston, Texas area from 1921 to 1922. Trombonist Jack Teagarden also played with Kelley at that time. In 1933, Shand sang and played piano with Freddy Martin and, by 1938, formed his own big band that specialized in playing hotels. Shand wrote many songs, including "My Extrordinary Gal," "Why Doesn't Somebody Tell Me These Things?," "Cry, Baby, Cry," "I'm Gonna Lock My Heart," "What's the Matter With Me?," "I Wanna Wrap You Up," "Dance with a Dolly," "If You're Ever Down in Texas Look Me Up," and "Bye-Lo-Bye Lullaby." Shand recorded for Decca and Vocalion records.

CECIL GOLLY

(Cecil Golly and His Orchestra) Born on May 9, 1911. Golly started his band while attending the University of Iowa in the '20s. He established residence in Minnesota and played a steady gig at Lake Minnetonka, the Radisson Inn at Christmas Lake. The band's publicity line was "Dance and be jolly with music by golly." They then played for several years at the Raison Hotel in Minneapolis. The band then toured for several months ending up in Memphis, where Golly met and married Mildred Stanley, who later became one of

Lawrence Welks's Champagne Ladies. Golly continued to travel, appearing at Donahue's in New Jersey and featuring sidemen Hal Pfeiffere, guitar; Clyde Koch, piano; Don Kelsey, drums; Johnny Woods, bass; Ray Carroll and Jimmy Engler, violins; Ray Shaffer, Hal Collyer, and Jimmy Stewart, trumpets; Gene Eyeman, Harry Green, Bob Boydston, and Joe Baldwin, saxophones; and Snooky Lanson, vocals. In the early '40s, Golly was drafted and served in the U.S. Navy. When he was discharged in 1946, he reorganized his band and played various society jobs until he became ill. Golly died on August 17, 1987 in Minneapolis, Minnesota.

JOE GUMIN

(Joe Gumin and His Orchestra) Gumin fronted a territory band in the early '30s that played in the Wisconsin/Illinois area. The band recorded for Broadway and Columbia records and included tunes "Jingle Bells" and "I'll Think of You." A specialty of the orchestra was to record in many languages, including English, Yiddish, Italian, Polish, German, Chinese, and Pig Latin.

MILT ROSENSTOCK

(Milt Rosenstock and His Orchestra) Born in New Haven, Connecticut on June 9, 1917. Milt Rosenstock (né: Milton Max Rosenstock) studied at the Institute of Musical Art and the Juilliard School of Music on a clarinet scholarship. He also studied composition and conducting with Simeon Bellison, Vittorio Giannini, Bernard Wagenaar, and Albert Stoesse. He began to conduct on Broadway and directed the following shows in the '30s and '40s: *This Is the Army*, *On the Town*, *Billion Dollar Baby*, *Finian's Rainbow*, *High Button Shoes*, *Gentlemen Prefer Blondes*, *Make a Wish*, *Can-Can*, *Belles Are Ringing*, *Gypsy*, *Stop the World*, *Funny Girl*, and revivals of *The King and I*, *Fiddler on the Roof*, *Gypsy*, and *A Funny Thing Happened to Me on the Way to the Forum*. Rosenstock wrote several songs and instrumental works.

DEAN HUDSON

(Dean Hudson and His Florida Clubmen) Born in 1906. Dean Hudson formed his band while attending the University of Florida in the '30s. The theme song of the Hudson band was "Moon Over Miami." A couple of the sidemen were

Ray Teal and Blue Steele. It is said that a number of people fronted the Hudson Orchestra from time to time, including Eli Katz, Marion Brown, Banzai Currie, and Leon Robbins. The band was booked by the Music Corporation of America (MCA) and recorded extensively through the '40s. When WWII ended, Hudson assumed the leadership of the Bobby Byrne band. The arrangers were Sy Oliver and Les and Larry Elgart. In the early '50s, Lennie Love wrote arrangements for the band, which featured a trombone choir and a vocal choir. At that time, the theme songs were "Miami Dreams" and "Moon Over Miami." The Hudson band recorded for Okeh, Musicraft, Bullett, and Brunswick records.

LEON KELNER

(Leon Kelner and His Orchestra) Leon Kelner's Orchestra played for many years at the Roosevelt Hotel in New Orleans and played on many radio shows on CBS and the Armed Services Network broadcasts during the '30s and '40s. The band played variations of tunes, including rags, rambles, cha-chas, waltzes, and fox-trots. They recorded for Decca Records and did tunes like "Yours," "More," and "Fascination." Kelner died on March 7, 2000.

FRANK "PEE WEE" KING

(Pee Wee King and His Orchestra) Born in Abrams, Wisconsin on February 18, 1914. Frank "Pee Wee" King (né: Julius Frank Anthony Kuczynski) first appeared on local radio shows in Milwaukee in 1933. From 1935 to 1936, he was heard on Louisville radio with the Log Cabin Boys. In 1936 he formed the Golden West Cowboys and appeared with regularity at the Grand Ole Opry in Nashville, Tennessee from 1937 to 1947 and had his own radio show on Knoxville radio. The featured singer and fiddler was Redd Stewart. Eddy Arnold appeared with the King band for a time. The band was heard on radio and seen on television in Louisville from 1947 to 1957 and in Cleveland and Chicago in the late '50s. King was a prolific composer and wrote "Tennessee Waltz," "You Belong to Me," "Bonaparte's Retreat," "Slow Poke," "Tennessee Tango," "Silver and Gold," and "River Road Two-Step." He continued to be active into the '60s. The Pee Wee King band recorded for Victor Records.

ELMO MACK

(Elmo Mack and the Purple Derby Orchestra) This band at the Purple Derby Club featured Joe Sullivan, piano; George Wettling, drums; and Gray Gordon, saxophone and clarinet in the early '30s. Gordon later led his own band called Gray Gordon and His Tick-Tock Rhythm.

TED STRAETER

(Ted Straeter and His Orchestra) Born in St. Louis, Missouri in 1914. Straeter played piano in vaudeville and radio during the '20s. He moved to New York City in 1935 where he arranged for various radio programs and served as pianist for the Broadway show *Jumbo*. During 1938 to 1943, he arranged and led his own band and chorus on the *Kate Smith* show. In '42 he conducted the band on the *Jerry Wayne* radio program and began booking the band on New York society dates. He later played on the West Coast for various radio programs. His theme was "The Most Beautiful Girl in the World." During the '50s and '60s, he led bands in New York, mostly at the Persian Room of the Plaza Hotel. Straeter recorded for MGM, Columbia, Vocalion, Capitol, Lion, and Liberty Music Shop records.

BILLY MILLS

(Billy Mills and His Orchestra) Born in Flint, Michigan on September 8, 1894. Billy Mills studied in Michigan and worked in a theater as a pianist and conductor. During WWI, Mills served in the military as a conductor with Seymour Simons, Victor Young, Ted Fio Rito, Isham Jones, and Frank Westphal. He formed his first band in Chicago in 1922 and was heard on Flint radio in 1925. He served as music supervisor on CBS radio in Chicago in 1933. Mills led a novelty-type band during the '30s and '40s and did more than 10,000 radio broadcasts. The Billy Mills Orchestra was featured on the *Fibber McGree and Molly* radio show and recorded a number of records. On the radio show, announcer Harlow Wilcox called Billy Mills "Rico" and would often say, "Take it away, Rico." By the '40s, Mills added singer Martha Tilton and vocal quartet, the King's Men, to the show and appeared in the movie *Biding My Time*. Billy Mills wrote several hit tunes, including "We Two," "Mister Rainbow," "One Magic Hour," "I Sang a Song," and "Wing to Wing." Mills died in Glendale, California on October 21, 1971.

HENRI RENE

(Henri Rene and His Orchestra) Born in Germany. Rene studied music at the Royal Academy of Music in Berlin, Germany and played the Musette accordion. In the mid '20s, he immigrated to the U.S., played with several bands, and returned to Germany, where he became the music arranger for a record company in Berlin. In the mid-'30s, he returned to the U.S. to become the music director for Victor Records. After a short stint in Hollywood, he returned to New York and led his own radio show, *The Musette Music Box*, which featured his instrument. In the early '40s, he enlisted in the U.S. Army Special Services Division and entertained the troops. When he was released, he returned to his job with Victor Records and produced a great number of albums on Victor, Decca, Camden, and Imperial records, including *White Heat, The Swinging 59, They're Playing Our Song, Riot in Rhythm, Paris Loves Lovers, Passion in Paint, Music for the Weaker Sex, In Love Again, Music for Bachelors, Compulsion to Swing,* and *Dynamic Dimensions.*

RITA RIO

(Rita Rio and Her All-Girl Orchestra) Born on November 15, 1914 in Miami, Florida. Rita Rio (né: Rita Novella) was a leading lady who started her all-girl band and singing group, the Girl Friends, in the '30s and appeared in many films during the '40s and 50s. Throughout her career she appeared using a number of different names, including Dona Drake, Rita Shaw, and Una Velon. Rio died on June 20, 1989 in Los Angeles, California

WARNEY RUHL

(Warney Ruhl and His Orchestra) Warney Ruhl lead an orchestra in the Chicago area that primarily toured the Midwest. Ruhl organized his first band in the '30s and was heard on various radio shows as he appeared at the Rice Hotel in Houston, Texas, the Club Casino in Quincy, Illinois, the Cleveland Hotel in Cleveland, Ohio and the Riviera Ballroom in Lake Geneva, Wisconsin. By the 1960s, he was traveling out of Detroit, Michigan. Some of the sidemen in the Ruhl Orchestra included Ruhl's wife, Vinah Ruhl, piano; Ed (Luke) Lucas, bass; Fex Mueller, saxophone; Dale Jones, trumpet; and Adda May Lang, singer. Ruhl died in the '70s in Detroit, Michigan.

HENRY RUSSELL

(Henry Russell and His Romancers) Russell began as a singer in Horace Heidt's band. He organized his own orchestra in the late '30s and recorded for Vocalion Records. The Russell band was originally called Henry Russell and His Mystic Music but was later changed to Henry Russell and His Romancers.

LEITH STEVENS

(Leith Stevens and His Orchestra) Born in Mount Moriah, Missouri on September 13, 1909. Stevens studied music as a child in Kansas City and graduated from the Juilliard School of Music in New York City during the early '30s. After serving as pianist for the Chicago Opera Company he had a show on CBS. In the late '30s, he conducted on the radio series *Big Town*, which starred Edward G. Robinson. He began scoring for films while in Hollywood, but during WWII, he worked as a civilian employee of the U.S. Office of War Information. Through the late '40s, he worked as musical director for several radio shows and scored the music for several movies, including *The Five Pennies*, *A New Kind of Love*, and *The Gene Krupa Story*. During the '50s, he conducted and wrote music for the television series Lost in Space and Mission Impossible. During his career, Stevens recorded for Decca, Capitol, Dor, Warwick, Colpix, Coral, and Omega records. He died in Hollywood, California on July 23, 1970.

SAMMY WATKINS

(Sammy Watkins and His Orchestra) Sammy Watkins led a popular band during the '30s and '40s. The orchestra enjoyed a long tenure in Cleveland at the Hotel Hollendon's Vogue Room. Among the sidemen were singer Dino Crocetti (Dean Martin) and drummer Fred Borgerhoff.

MIDGE WILLIAMS

(Midge Williams and Her Jesters) Born in California in 1908. During the late '20s, Midge Williams sang in the family quartet, which toured the Far East. In the early '30s, she sang in China in various jazz clubs and recorded with the Tommy Missman Orchestra on Columbia-Japan Records in 1934. In the mid-'30s, she toured with Fats Waller and worked in radio in Los Angeles. She was featured on Rudy Vallée's radio program in 1936 and made a number of records for Vocalion and Variety Records under the name Midge Williams and Her Jesters during the late '30s, which featured Charlie Shavers, Buster Bailey, Frankie Newton, and Raymond Scott. During that period, she also recorded with Lil Hardin Armstrong, Frank Froeba, and Bunny Berigan. From 1938 to 1940, she toured with Louis Armstrong. Williams died in the 1940s.

MEREDITH WILLSON

(Meredith Willson and His Orchestra) Born in Mason City, Iowa on May 18, 1902. Wilson was a talented musician, arranger, and composer who attended the Damrosch Institute of Music in New York and played flute and piccolo in the John Phillip Sousa Concert Band in the early '20s. In the mid-'20s, he played in the New York Philharmonic. During the early '30s, he formed his first band playing various theater dates and radio shows. His theme song on the radio was "You and I" and, during live performances, "Thoughts While Strolling," songs that he had written. He also wrote "It's Beginning to Look a Lot Like Christmas," "Two in Love," and "May the Good Lord Bless and Keep You." During his career he played on various radio programs with personalities such as Fanny Brice, Tallulah Bankhead, and John Nesbitt. He was associated with Maxwell House Coffee for many years and during the summer of 1942 he had his own radio program. As an arranger and composer he wrote several hit Broadway musicals, including *The Unsinkable Molly Brown* and *The Music Man*, the latter won him a Grammy Award in 1958, the first ever presented. Willson died on June 15, 1984.

VICTOR YOUNG

(Victor Young and His Orchestra) Born in Chicago, Illinois on August 8, 1900. Victor Young's parents had emigrated from Russia to Chicago, where Young was born. In 1910, he was orphaned and went to live with his grandfather in Warsaw, Poland. Young studied violin, attended the conservatory, and eventually played in the Warsaw Philharmonic Orchestra. During that period, a wealthy patron presented Young with a 1730 Guarnerius violin, an instrument that remained with him throughout his music career. After WWI, in which Young was imprisoned by the Germans, he traveled to America and, by the late

'20s, was playing and writing popular music as a member of the Ted Fio Rito Orchestra. In the '30s, he played with the Isham Jones Orchestra, conducted theater orchestras, and wrote arrangements and compositions for radio, movies, and his own orchestra. During that period, he was music director for Decca and Brunswick records and worked for Paramount Pictures. He was a prolific song-writer, penning tunes such as "When I Fall in Love," "Stella by Starlight," "A Ghost of a Chance," "Street of Dreams," "Sweet Sue (Just You)" "Beautiful Love," "The Old Man of the Mountain," and "Around the World." Young received an Academy Award for his score for the movie *Around the World in 80 Days* and was a member of the Songwriters' Hall of Fame. Young died in Palm Springs, California on November 11, 1956.

CHARLIE BARNET

(Charlie Barnet and His Orchestra) Born in New York City on October 26, 1913. Barnet grew up in a wealthy family atmosphere. His father was the first vice president of the New York Central Railroad. At age 12, Barnet was given a C-melody saxophone by his family but, after hearing Coleman Hawkins a few years later, switched to tenor sax. Prior to enrolling at Yale University, he attended Blair Academy and Rumsy Hall boarding schools. He left Yale in the middle of his freshman year to go on the road with various bands before forming his own band in 1933 that included sidemen such as Eddie Sauter, Tuttie Camarata, Chris Griffin, and singer Harry Von Zell. In a review by *Metronome* magazine of that band, the reviewer stated that it was "the Blackest White band around." In 1934, the band included clarinet player Artie Shaw, pianist Teddy Wilson, and trom-bonist Jack Jenny. In 1936, the vocal group the Modernaires joined the band and, by 1937, Frank Newton and John Kirby were in the Barnet band. In 1939, the band recorded "Cherokee," which became a big hit and a trademark of the group. By 1941, the band included singer Lena Horne and the 1942 band featured outstanding modern players such as Al Killian, Dodo Marmarosa, Neil Hefti, and Buddy DeFranco. The singer was Frances Wayne. In later years, the band included trumpeters Jimmy Nottinham, Clark Terry, and Doc Severinson; Oscar Pettiford, bass; Trummy Young, trombone; Barney Kessel, guitar; and arranger and pianist Ralph Burns. The singers were Buddy Stewart, Dave Lambert, Judy Ellington, Harriet Clark, Jean Louise, Bunny Briggs, Fran Warren, and Kay Starr. Charlie Barnet and His Orchestra recorded for Mercury, Clef, Verve, Everest, Columbia, Capitol, Victor, Decca, and Bluebird records. The theme songs of the Barnet bands were "Redskin Rhumba" and "I Lost Another Sweetheart." Barnet wrote "Skyliner," "In a Mizz," "Redskin Rhumba," "Tappin' at the Tappa," "Myna and Knockin' at the Famous Door." During the '50s, Barnet disbanded, moved to Palm Springs, California and fronted various small groups. Barnett died in San Diego, California on September 4, 1991.

BENNY CARTER

(Benny Carter and His Swing Orchestra) Born in New York, New York on August 9, 1907. Benny Carter began as an alto saxophone player in his youth, attended Wilberforce College studying theology, and quit college to become a member of a band led by classmate Horace Henderson, named Horace Henderson's Wilberforce Collegians Orchestra. After he left, the Collegians he played with Fletcher Henderson, McKinney's Cotton Pickers, Chick Webb, and Duke Ellington. In 1928, he made his first recording with Charlie Johnson's Paradise Club Hot Ten. In the early '30s, Carter organized his own band with sidemen that included Big Sid Catlett, Wilbur DeParis, Chu Berry, and Teddy Wilson. In 1934, he worked as a sideman, playing trumpet with the Willie Bryant Orchestra. In 1935, he spent three months in Europe and was the staff arranger for the BBC house band, the Henry Hall Orchestra. By 1937, Carter led a band in the Netherlands and worked in France and Sweden and returned to New York in 1938, where he worked with Lionel Hampton on some recordings for Victor Records and formed another band. This group opened at the Savoy Ballroom in 1939 and included sidemen Tyree Glenn, Eddie Heywood, Johah Jones, and Vic Dickenson. After a year and half, he disbanded and formed another band that played at the Famous Door on 52nd Street. During 1940,

Carter wrote arrangements for the radio show the *Lucky Strike Hit Parade* and, by 1941, had formed a sextet, cut several records with the Artie Shaw band, which had a string section and included sidemen J.C. Higginbotham and Henry "Red" Allen. In '42, Carter formed still another band to accompany singer Billie Holiday. By 1943 Benny Carter had moved to Los Angeles where he formed a new band and opened at the Swing Club. The new group included singer Savannah Churchill and instrumentalists Max Roach, Henry Coker, J.J. Johnson, Joe Albany, Buddy Rich, Hal Schaefer, and Jerry Wiggins. The Carter band recorded for Verve, Capitol, Deluxe, Decca, Vocalion, Okeh, Bluebird, and Columbia records. Benny Carter wrote the music for the films "The Five Pennies," "The View from Pompey's Head," "The Snows of Kilimanjaro," and "The Gene Krupa Story." After 1946 Carter disbanded his big bands and continued to play in small band settings at various venues.

BOB CAUSER

(Bob Causer and his Cornellians Orchestra) Causer began managing a hotel in Ithaca, New York and hired a few musicians from Cornell University to play in the hotel's ballroom. This was the beginning of his band-leading career and led to a recording contract with Mercury Records and extensive touring during the '30s. It is said that the band's singer was Russ Morgan. The Causer Orchestra recorded "Seein' Is Believin'" and "Flowers for Madame" among other hits of the day.

JOLLY COBURN

(Jolly Coburn and His Orchestra) Jolly Coburn (né: Frank J. Coburn) was a trumpet player who fronted a band that played primarily in the New York City area. Coburn graduated from Columbia University and the U.S. Naval Academy, formed a band, and from 1934 to 1937, the Coburn Orchestra recorded for Bluebird and Victor Records. Among the various singers appearing with the band were Joan Brooks, Marilyn Duke, Harold Kolb, Bill Hawky, Harold Richards, Roy Strom, and Harold Van Emburgh. The instrumental sidemen included Roy Johnson and Coburn, trumpets; Art Foster, trombone; Cecil Armitage, Buddy Saffer, Harold Kolb, and Larry Tice, saxophones; Max Tanfield, violin; King Johnson, drums; Nick Fisher, bass; Benny Mortell, guitar;

and Bert Stevens, piano. The band played many venues, including the Rainbow Room atop the RCA Building in Rockefeller Center, New York City.

DEL COURTNEY

(Del Courtney and His Orchestra) Born in Oakland, California in 1910. After graduating from the University of California, Del Courtney formed his first band that played at the Claremont Hotel in San Francisco in 1933. He recorded for various record companies and did a number of radio shows, including the *Kodak Camera Show*, which was said to be quite lucrative. During the mid-'30s, the Del Courtney Orchestra toured the West Coast playing various ballrooms in hotels and clubs and gained quite a bit of popularity. The band featured tunes like "The Singing Hill," "Monstro the Whale," "Hawaiian War Chant," and "An Apple for the Teacher." The featured singer on the band was Joe Martin. In 1940, the band played in New York City at the Ambassador and New Yorker hotels, the Blackhawk Restaurant in Chicago, and the Royal Hawaiian Hotel. The theme songs of the Del Courtney Orchestra were "The Old Smoothie," "Good Evening," and "Three Shades of Blue." The Courtney band recorded for Okeh, Brunswick, Capitol, and Columbia. Disbanding, Del Courtney worked as a radio disc jockey and opened a television dealership in Oakland. By the '70s, Courtney had organized another band and was playing for the Oakland Raiders football team.

XAVIER CUGAT

(Xavier Cugat and His Orchestra) Born in Spain on January 1, 1900. When Cugat was very young his family moved to Havana, Cuba, where Xavier studied violin. By the age of 12, he became the first violinist with the National Theater Orchestra in Havana. He traveled to Berlin, Germany where he continued his music studies before Enrico Caruso brought him to America where he served as Caruso's accompanist. After playing in bands led by Phil Harris and Vincent Lopez he formed his first Latin-American band, which played for the opening of the Coconut Grove in Los Angeles, California. In the early '30s, Cugat recorded the hit tune "El Manicero," which helped to start a rumba boom. During the '40s, Cugat's band served as the house band at the Waldorf-Astoria Hotel in New York City and recorded for Columbia Records. The Cugat band was heard on many coast-to-coast radio shows, including *Spotlight Bands*, *The Drene Show*, and *The Camel Cigarette Show*. The band's theme song was "My Shawl" and the singers were Carmen Castillo, Lorraine Allen, Abbe Lane, and Charo Baeza. Cugat was also a well-known caricaturist and King Features syndicated his drawings.

BASIL FOMEEN

(Basil Fomeen and His Orchestra) Basil Fomeen (né: Wasily Fomin) was an accordionist who worked with bands led by Meyer Davis and Joe Moss prior to organizing his first band. In 1933, the Basil Fomeen band opened at the Savoy Plaza in New York City for a two-year stint. After another two years spent at the St. Moritz, he opened at the Waldorf-Astoria where he became a perennial musician. The band also played often in Washington, D.C. prior to traveling to the West Coast, where they became very popular at Ciro's in Hollywood. During WWII, the Basil Fomeen Orchestra played in China, Europe, Africa, and India as a U.S.O group. After the war, the band played in Rio de Janeiro at the Copacabana Casino for a long tenure. The Fomeen Orchestra recorded for Decca, Brunswick, Victor, and Columbia records. The theme song was "Manhattan Gypsy."

JOHNNY GREEN

(Johnny Green and His Orchestra) Born in New York City on October 10, 1908. Johnny Green began arranging and composing while attending Harvard University. After college he worked on Wall Street for a brief time but began devoting full time to music in the late '20s. He wrote "Coquette" for Guy Lombardo, which became a big hit, and "Body and Soul" for the Broadway show *Three's a Crowd*. Johnny Green formed a short-lived orchestra in the '30s, which played *The Ruth Etting Show* and, in 1934, played *The Jack Benny Show*. By 1936, his band was featured on *The Fred Astaire Show*. During the late '30s and early '40s, he played *The Phillip Morris Show* prior to moving to the West Coast and writing for motion pictures. By the late '40s, he was music director for MGM and subsequently wrote music for many theater and television productions. His theme song was "Hello, My Lover, Goodbye." He is best remembered as a prolific songwriter penning such tunes as "Body and Soul," "I'm Yours," "I Cover the Waterfront," "Hello, My Lover, Goodbye," and "Coquette." Green died in 1989.

TEDDY HILL

(Teddy Hill and His Orchestra) Born in Birmingham, Alabama on December 7, 1909. Teddy Hill (né: Theodore Hill) began as a saxophone player in the Luis Russell band. In 1934 he left Russell and formed his own band. By 1937, the band toured France and England and made frequent appearances at the Savoy Ballroom in Harlem. Many famous sidemen played in bands led by Teddy Hill. Among them, Chu Berry, Roy Eldridge, Bill Coleman, Bill Dillard, Frankie Newton, and Dizzy Gillespie were great soloists. Although he was inactive as a bandleader in the '40s, he was well known as the owner of Minton's Playhouse in Harlem, the club that is associated with the beginning of bebop. Hill died in Cleveland, Ohio on May 19, 1978.

AL KAVELIN

(Al Kavelin and His Orchestra) Kavelin was a graduate of the Royal Verdi Conservatory in Milan, Italy. He organized his band in the '30s and featured pianist Carmen Cavallaro. MCA signed Kavelin to a long-term contract and he toured coast-to-coast playing at the Waldorf, Biltmore, and Essex House in New York City, the Blackstone in Chicago, Peabody in Memphis, Baker in Dallas, and the Roosevelt in New Orleans, among other venues. The theme song of the Kavelin Orchestra was "Love Has Gone." He co-composed the tune "I Give You My Word," which became the number-one song on the *Lucky Strike Hit Parade* Show. The Kavelin Orchestra recorded for Okeh, Vocalion, and Decca records. Kavelin led a band through the late '40s, when he moved to California and became a music publisher.

BOYD RAEBURN

(Boyd Raeburn and His Orchestra) Born in Faith, South Dakota on October 27, 1913. Boyd Raeburn studied medicine at the University of Chicago and won a college band contest held at the Hotel Sherman in Chicago that led to a job for the band, playing at the World's Fair. Raeburn, a saxophone player, played with various bands during the '30s and formed a commercial, society-type orchestra in the late '30s. His true love was jazz and pioneered a great experimental jazz band in the '40s with arrangers George Handy, Ralph Flanagan, Johnny Richards, and Eddie Finckel. The sidemen included Buddy Defranco, clarinet;

177

Johnny Bothwell and Hal McKusick, alto saxophones; Dizzy Gillespie and Benny Harris, trumpets; Trummy Young and Earl Swope, trombones; Don Lamond, drums; Oscar Pettiford, bass; Ike Carpenter and Dodo Marmarosa, piano. The singers were Ginnie Powell (Mrs. Boyd Raeburn), David Allyn, and Don Darcy. The band recorded a number of interesting tunes, including "There Is No You," "Dalvatore Sally," "Toncilectomy," "Summertime," and "Boyd Meets Stravinsky." His theme song was "Moonlight on Melody Hill." The Raeburn band recorded for Guild, Grand, and Jewel records. Raeburn retired in the Bahamas in the '50s. He died in Lafayette, Louisiana on August 2, 1966.

AL TRACE

(Al Trace and His Orchestra) Born in Chicago, Illinois on December 25, 1900. Trace began playing drums and singing with small combos in Chicago in the late '20s and early '30s. In 1933, Al Trace formed his first band that worked at France's Streets of Paris at Chicago World's Fair. After the fair, the Trace Orchestra played at the Blackrock Restaurant and the Sherman Hotel for about three years. The singers were Bob Vincent and Toni Arden. Later the band played for the radio show *It Pays to Be Ignorant* and recorded for Columbia, MGM, Mercury, and Damon records. Trace was a prolific songwriter, penning such hits as "You Call Everybody Darling," "Wishing," "Brush Those Tears from Your Eyes," and "If I'd Known You Were Comin', I'd Have Baked a Cake." Trace's theme songs were "Maizy Doats," "Sweet Words," and "Music." In the late '50s, Trace retired to Scottsdale, Arizona, where he joined Tommy Reed in establishing the Southwest Booking Agency.

GRIFF WILLIAMS

(Griff Williams and His Orchestra) Born in La Grande, Oregon in 1911. Williams attended Stanford University and led the college dance band. In the early '30s, he played with the Anson Weeks Orchestra and formed his own band in 1933. The band played the Edgewater Beach Hotel in San Francisco prior to moving to Chicago in the late '30s. Griff Williams played for four years at the Stevens Hotel during WW II. The theme of the Griff Williams Orchestra was "Dream Music." When the war was over the band worked most of the time in Chicago and San Francisco. The singers were Buddy Moreno, Walter King,

Lois Lee and the Williams Trio. Featured sidemen included Bob Kirk, Don Mulford, Bob Logan, Paul Hare, and Buddy Moreno. They recorded for Varsity, Columbia, and Okeh records. Williams disbanded in 1953 and went to work for a magazine publishing company in Chicago. In 1956, he put together a band for a local television program. He died in Chicago, Illinois in February 1959.

HARRY AKST

(Harry Akst and His Orchestra) Born in New York on August 15, 1894. Harry Akst was secretary to Irving Berlin when he was a teenager, assisting Berlin to notate Berlin's songs since Berlin did not read nor write music. When he left Berlin, he began to write songs and book bands for various occasions. By 1921, he had written "Home Again Blues," which became a bit hit, and in the middle and late '20s, he wrote such hits as "Dinah," "It's a Million to One You're in Love," "Am I Blue," and "Baby Face." Although he led a band during those years, he was always a bigger hit as a songwriter than as a bandleader. He also wrote the music for several Broadway musicals and movies. In the mid '30s, he played for Martha Raye in a Broadway revue entitled *Calling All Stars*. After WWII, he wrote "All My Love" and "Where Were You Last Night?" and, in the mid '50s, "Anema E Core." Akst died in Hollywood, California on March 31, 1963.

DANNY ALVIN

(Danny Alvin and His Orchestra) Born in New York on November 29, 1902. Drummer Danny Alvin played for singer Sophie Tucker in New York City while a teenager. During the '20s, he worked with Aunt Jemima in New York City and Arnold Johnson and other small bands in Chicago and Florida. For a short while, he played with Wayne King but formed his own band in 1934, where he had a chance to play jazz, the music he loved. Musicians working with him included Muzz Mezzrow, Wingy Manone, and Art Hodes. By the late '40s, Alvin was playing with the George Zack band on the East Coast. Throughout the '40s and '50s, Alvin continued to lead a band in Chicago, where he eventually bought his own nightclub. Alvin died in Chicago, Illinois on December 5, 1958.

ARCHIE BLEYER

(Archie Bleyer and His Orchestra) Bleyer got into music as an arranger in the early '30s, prior to forming his own band in Hollywood where he played at Earl Carroll's Nightclub. He eventually became the music director for the radio program *Arthur Godfrey Show*. When he disbanded, he became the president of Cadence Records.

TINY BRADSHAW

(Tiny Bradshaw and His Orchestra) Born in Youngstown, Ohio in 1905. Tiny Bradshaw (né: Myron Bradshaw) graduated from Wilberforce University in Ohio with a degree in psychology. He was a singer who moved to New York City and got a job working with the Savoy Bearcats. Subsequently he sang with the Mills Blue Rhythm Band in 1932, Marion Hardy's Alabamians, and the Luis Russell Orchestra in Harlem. The theme song of the Tiny Bradshaw Orchestra was "Fascination." Bradshaw formed his own band in 1934, recorded for Decca Records, and played a long engagement at the Renaissance Ballroom in New York City. He then toured, playing in Philadelphia, New York's Savoy Ballroom, and ending in Chicago. The Bradshaw band had many famous sidemen. Among them, Russell Procope, Clarence Johnson, Billy Kyle, Charlie Shavers, Charlie Fowlkes, Gil Fuller, and Sonny Stitt. In 1945, the Tiny Bradshaw Orchestra toured Japan for the U.S.O. He continued working until a stroke forced his retirement. Bradshaw died in Cincinnati, Ohio on November 26, 1958.

BOB CROSBY

(Bob Crosby and His Bobcats) Born in Spokane, Washington on August 23, 1913. Bob Crosby (né: George Robert Crosby) was the younger brother of singer Bing Crosby. After Ben Pollack's band was stranded in New York City, Bob Crosby and the saxophonist Gil Rodin took over as co-leaders and Crosby was elected the front man. The orchestra became a corporation and was owned by Gil Rodin, the Rockwell O'Keefe Booking Agency, and Crosby. It was considered a large Dixieland band and for a time played as the Red Nichols band on the radio show *Kellogg's College* and briefly as Clark Randall and His Orchestra. The original sidemen on the band included Deane Kincaide, saxophone and arranger; Eddie Miller, saxophone; Nappy Lamare, guitar; Yank

Lawson, trumpet; Bob Haggart, bass; and Ray Baduc, drums. As time went on, various sidemen who played in the Bobcats band included Billy Butterfield and Charlie Spivak, trumpets; Ward Silloway, trombone; and Jess Stacy, piano. Joe Sullivan and Bob Zurke also were alumni of the Crosby Bobcats. A number of other instrumentalists, arrangers, and singers appeared with the band, including Kay Starr, Gloria Dehaven, Doris Day, The Bob-o-Links, Paul Weston, Nelson Riddle, Henry Mancini, Ray Coniff, Jimmy Mundy, Mugsy Spanier, Eddie Wade, Bob Peck, Sterling Boze, Billy Graham, Shorty Sherock, Sonny Dunham, Zeke Zarchy, Johnny Mercer, and Helen Ward. The theme song of Bob Croby and His Bobcats was "Summertime." The Bob Crosby Bobcats recorded for Coral, Dot, and Decca records. Crosby died on March 9, 1993.

DORSEY BROTHERS

(The Dorsey Brothers Orchestra) Beginning in 1934 the Dorsey Brothers, Jimmy and Tommy, led an all-star band, including sidemen Ray McKinley and Glenn Miller. The brothers were part of the famous Chicago musicians, which included Jimmy McPartland, Eddie Condon, Max Kaminsky, Pee Wee Russell, Benny Goodman, and other Dixieland musicians. In 1935, while the band was working at the Glen Island Casino, in New Rochelle, New York, the brothers had a blowup and disbanded, each brother forming his own orchestra. Jimmy Dorsey continued on with the sidemen from the Dorsey Brothers Orchestra and Tommy Dorsey took over the Joe Haymes Orchestra, which was playing at the McAlpin Hotel in New York City. During the late '50s, the brothers joined together once again to form the Dorsey Brothers Orchestra.

FREDDIE FISHER

(Freddie Fisher and the Schnicklefritzers) Born in Lourdes, Iowa in 1904. A pre–Spike Jones–styled band, the Schnicklefritzers began in Winona, Minnesota in 1934 while playing at the Sugarloaf Tavern and broadcasting over radio station KWNO. The band's theme song was "Colonel Corn." Clarinetist Freddie Fisher's band was playing in St. Paul, Minnesota in 1937, when Rudy Vallée heard the band and hired them to be guest stars on his network radio show. The Schnicklefritzers were featured in *The Gold Diggers in Paris*, a Warner Brothers film starring Rosemary Lane and Rudy Vallée in 1938. The trombonist, Stan Fritts, left the band in 1939 and started his own group, the Korn Kobblers. The Schnicklefritzers starred in movies *Make Mine Laughs* and *The Sultan's Daughter* in the '40s and recorded for Decca Records. Fisher led a Dixieland band in the '50s.

BENNY GOODMAN

(Benny Goodman and His Orchestra; a.k.a "The King of Swing") Born in Chicago, Illinois on May 30, 1909. Benny Goodman (né: Benjamin David Goodman) studied music as a child at the Hull House in Chicago. He appeared with the Benny Meroff Orchestra when he was 13 years old, imitating Ted Lewis. Shortly after that appearance, he joined the Ben Pollack band in Los Angeles at the Venice Ballroom. In 1929, he left Pollack, moved to New York, and became a studio musician. In 1934, Goodman formed his first band and was heard on the NBC radio network in a program called *Let's Dance*. At the same time, he was playing at Billy Rose's Music Hall and the Roosevelt Hotel. After six months, the Goodman band did a coast-to-coast tour ending at the Palomar Ballroom in Los Angeles, California. Returning to New York, the band appeared at the Paramount Theater and had the "bobbysoxers" dancing in the aisles. It was the beginning of the "big band swing sound" credited to arrangers, including Fletcher and Horace Henderson, Spud Murphy, Jimmy Mundy, Edgar Sampson, Benny Carter, and, later, Deane Kincaide and Eddie Sauter. From time to time, the Goodman Orchestra was comprised of great sidemen, including "Slam" Stewart, Charlie Christian, Cootie Williams, Lionel Hampton, Teddy Wilson, Harry James, Gene Krupa, Ziggy Elman, Terry Gibbs, Red Norvo, Louie Bellson, Milt Bernhart, Roy Eldridge, Billy Butterfield, Dave Barbour, and singers Ella Fitzgerald, Jimmy Rushing, Helen Ward, Martha Tilton, Peggy Lee, and Louise Tobin. The Goodman

Orchestra recorded for Capitol, Decca, Columbia, and RCA Victor records. The band's theme songs were "Let's Dance" and "Good-Bye." Goodman died in New York City on June 13, 1986.

INA RAE HUTTON

(Ina Rae Hutton and her Melodears) Born in Chicago, Illinois on March 13, 1916. Ina Rae Hutton (née: Odessa Cowan) was dancing on Broadway in the George White Scandals and the Ziegfeld Follies before she was 18 years old and after tap dancing as a child in vaudeville shows with Gus Edwards. Irving Mills hired her to front an all-girl band, which he had formed in 1934, and the band was an instant hit and featured personnel like pianist Betty Rouderbush, saxophonist Betty Sattley, and multi-instrumentalist Alyse Wells. In 1936, Eddie Durham handled the bands repertoire as they recorded and appeared in movies. In 1938, Hutton and Mills parted professional company, Hutton disbanded and formed an all-male orchestra that included Randy Brooks, trumpet; Jack Purcell, guitar; singer Stuart Foster; and Hal Schaefer, piano. In 1943, she added the Kim Loo Vocal Trio. By 1944, Ina Rae and Randy Rooks married and Hutton formed a new all-girl band and appeared in another movie. The pianist Ruth Lowe wrote two great hits for Frank Sinatra—"Put Your Dreams Away" and "I'll Never Smile Again." The Hutton Melodears recorded for Okeh, Vocalion, and Victor records. Their theme song was "Gotta Have Your Love." Hutton died in Ventura, California on February 19, 1984.

ORVILLE KNAPP

(Orville Knapp and His Orchestra) Born in Kansas City, Missouri on January 1, 1904. Orville Knapp played saxophone while attending Central High School in Kansas City. When he graduated, he moved to New York City, where he and his sister, Pauline, performed in vaudeville as a dance act. While in New York, he played saxophone with orchestras led by Vincent Lopez and Leo Reisman. In 1923, he played in Kansas City with the Coon Sanders Nighthawks Band. Knapp traveled to Hollywood to visit with Pauline, who had signed with Warner Brothers in 1933. She eventually played in Perils of Pauline and Sinner's Holiday. Knapp played briefly with a jazz group at the Café de Paree, formed a big band, and played at the Silver Palm Room of the Grand Hotel in Santa

Monica, California. With that band were singers Don Raymond and Virginia Verrill. In August 1934, the Knapp Orchestra recorded for Decca Records. In 1936, the band played at the Waldorf-Astoria Hotel in New York City and recorded for Brunswick and Decca Records. The band's theme songs were "Indigo" and "A New Style in Melody." The band was taken over by George Olsen in 1936 and prior to disbanding in 1938 the Orville Knapp Orchestra played at the William Penn Hotel in Pittsburgh and the Gibson Hotel in Cincinnati. Knapp died in Beverly, Massachusetts on July 16, 1936.

HARLAN LEONARD

(Harlan Leonard and His Rockets) Born in Kansas City, Missouri on July 2, 1904. Saxophonist Leonard began playing with the George E. Lee band in 1923. Shortly after, he joined the Bennie Moten Orchestra where he remained for eight years. In the early '30s, Leonard played with Thamon Hayes's Kansas City Sky Rockets. In 1934, Harlan Leonard formed Harlan Leonard's Rockets when the Kansas City Sky Rockets disbanded. Leonard's band toured in and around Kansas City and, by 1940, was playing in Los Angeles at the Club Alabam and in New York City. The Harlan Leonard Rockets had outstanding sidemen, including Buster Smith, guitar and alto saxophone; Eddie Durham, guitar; Tadd Dameron, piano and arranger; Fred Beckett, trombone; and Henry Bridges, tenor saxophone. In 1943, Leonard disbanded and moved to Los Angeles, where he built another orchestra with singers Darwin Jones, Ernie Williams, Myra Taylor, and James Ross; and instrumentalists Jessie Price, drums; William Smith, piano; Stan Morgan, bass; Effergee Ware; guitar; Jimmy Keith, Hank Bridges, and Darwin Jones, saxophones; Richmond Henderson, trombone; and James Ross, Bill Smith, and Ed Johnson, trumpets. In 1946, he became an IRS Agent for the U.S. Government. While active Harlan Leonard and his Rockets recorded for Bluebird and Victor records. The theme song was "Rockin' with the Rockets." Leonard died in Los Angeles, California in 1983.

PAUL MARTELL

(Paul Martell and His Orchestra) Born in Brooklyn, New York on January 6, 1905. Paul Martell attended high school and led his own band in various ballrooms, hotels, and on radio beginning in 1936. He played piano, accordion, and conducted. As a songwriter, he collaborated with Ervin Drake and Milton Berle in writing "Suspense Tango" and "I Wuv a Wabbit."

MIKE RILEY (RILEY-FARLEY)

(The Riley and Farley Onyx Club Boys) Mike Riley was born in Fall River, Massachusetts on January 5, 1904. Eddie Farley was born in Newark, New Jersey on July 16, 1905. In the middle '30s, Mike Riley and Eddie Farley were playing at the Onyx Club in New York City when, together with Red Hodgson, they wrote *The Music Goes Round and Round*, for which they became nationally famous overnight. The band subsequently recorded under the names the Top Hatters, the Rhythm Kings, and Ted Russell's Orchestra. Some of the sidemen appearing with the Riley and Farley Onyx Club Boys were Pops Darrow, Arthur Enz, Frank Froeba, George Tookey, and Bill Flanagan. The only hit the Riley and Farley Onyx Club Boys ever produced was their theme song, "The Music Goes Round and Round," but it sustained them throughout their careers. They recorded for Decca and Champion Records. Mike Riley died in September 1985.

PHIL SPITALNY

(Phil Spitalny and His Hour of Charm Orchestra) Born in Odessa, Russia on November 7, 1890. Spitalny led an all-girl orchestra, which featured the concert-mistress Evelyn and Her Magic Violin. The radio show of the orchestra was *The Hour of Charm*, and Arlene Francis was the mistress of ceremonies. Phil Spitalny eventually married Evelyn and they moved to Miami Beach, where Phil served as the music critic for the *Miani Beach Sun* newspaper until his death, when Evelyn took over the critic's column. The theme song of the Phil Spitalny Orchestra was "My Isle of Golden Dreams." Spitalny died in Miami Beach, Florida on October 11, 1970.

J. FRANK TERRY

(J. Frank Terry and His Chicago Nightingales) The Terry Orchestra was primarily a touring orchestra that traveled more than 50,000 miles a year. Little is know about Terry other than that he fronted the band and played trombone. The personnel of the band in the mid-'30s comprised of Francis Williams, Willie

Lewis, Dick Vance, and James Willis, trumpets; Terry and John McConnell, trombones; Alfred Gibson and Bill Crump, clarinets and saxophones; Howard Fields, bass; Phil Keeble, drums; and Howard Watson, piano. Terry's theme song was "In the Garden of the Sun."

FESS WHATLEY

(Fess Whatley and His Vibra Cathedral Band) The Fess Whatley band played in and around Birmingham, Alabama during the '30s and, while there were no recordings made, a number of talented young musicians developed their talent in the Whatley band. In the late '30s, the instrumentalists Mary Alice Clarke, piano, vocals, and vibes; Albert Jones, vibes; Alton Davenport, drums; James Swyne, bass; John Reed, J.L. Lowe, Wilton Robertson, and Amos Gordon, saxophones; Paul Coman, trombone; and Arthur Miller, Fess Whatley, and Johnny Grimes, trumpets.

MITCHELL AYRES

(Mitchell Ayres and His Fashions in Music Orchestra) Born in Milwaukee, Wisconsin on December 24, 1910. Mitchell Ayres (né: Mitchell Agress) first played with the Little Jack Little Orchestra in the early '30s. In the mid '30s, he and other members of the Little band left the group to form a co-op band and named Ayres as the leader. Singers on the band included Tommy Taylor, Maryann Mercer, and Meridith Blake. Some of the sidemen were Warren Covington, Dean Kincaid, Dick Dale, Milt Laufer, and Babe Russin. The Ayres band recorded for Bluebird and Vocalion records. The theme song was "You Go to My Head." In the mid-'40s, the band disbanded and Ayres became the musical director for the *Perry Como* program and Columbia Records. Ayres died on September 5, 1969 in Las Vegas, Nevada.

KENNY BAKER

(Kenny Baker and His Orchestra) Born in Monrovia, California on September 30, 1912. Baker studied music at Long Beach Junior College and won the Texaco Radio Open singing contest. He was awarded an appearance at the Coconut Grove in Los Angeles and appeared there for a long engagement. In 1935, he appeared on the *Jack Benny Show* and was featured there throughout the '30s. In the late '30s, he was featured on the *Texaco Star Theater* program and, in the early '40s, starred on the *Fred Allen Show*. He had a singing role in several movies and starred on Broadway in the musical *One Touch of Venus*. Little is known about the Kenny Baker Orchestra other than it played on the West Coast in the '30s, and many of the sidemen formed the nucleus for the Stan Kenton band when it was formed in 1941. The Baker Orchestra's singer was Liz Tilton, the sister of Martha Tilton.

WILLIAM "COUNT" BASIE

(Count Basie and His Orchestra) Born in Red Bank, New Jersey on August 21, 1904. Basie played in and around Kansas City, Missouri with the Benny Moton band for several years prior to 1935. When Moton died, Basie became the band's leader. On a broadcast at the Reno Club on radio station WXBY, the announcer commented that were a pair of well-known bandleaders named "Duke" and "Earl" and suggested that Bill Basie's name be changed to "Count" Basie. Basie's band was noted for its rhythm section with Jo Jones on drums and Freddie Green on guitar. Other famous musicians like tenor saxophonists Lester Young and Herschel Evans and trumpeter Buck Clayton were responsible for the early reputation of the Basie band. Many famous sidemen played with the Basie Orchestra throughout the years, including Marshall Royal, Frank Foster, Frank Wess, Thad Jones, Wardell Gray, Clark Terry, Buddy De Franco, J.J.

Johnson, Vic Dickenson, Joe Newman, Al Killian, Emmett Berry, Paul Gonsalves, Illinois Jacquet, Lucky Thompson, Buddy Tate, Don Byas, and Harry Edison. Featured singers were Joe Williams, Helen Humes, Billie Holiday, Earl Warren, and Jimmy Rushing. The band's theme songs were "One O'Clock Jump" and "The Red Bank Flash." Count Basie and His Orchestra recorded for Reprise, Roulette, Verve, Victor, Decca, Okeh, Vocalion, and Columbia records. Basie died on April 26. 1984.

LOU BRING

(Lou Bring and His Orchestra) Singer and pianist Lou Bring played piano in the Vincent Lopez Orchestra prior to forming his band in the mid-'30s. The band, considered a "society" orchestra, played primarily in the New York City area. The featured vocalist was Frances Hunt, who joined the Benny Goodman band after leaving the Bring organization. She later returned to the Lou Bring Orchestra and married Lou.

CHICK BULLOCK

(Chick Bullock and His Orchestra) Born in 1906. Chick Bullock (né: Charles Bullock) was said to be the most recorded singer in the '30s. His name was listed as the leader on many recordings even though he simply sang with a number of organizations. Bullock was heard on radio and recorded with a lot of bands doing numbers like "I'm One of God's Children" with Nat Shilkret, "Somewhere in Your Heart" with Joe Reichman, "It's You I Adore" with Russ Morgan, "Keep a Song in Your Soul" with Duke Ellington, "Jealous" with Vic Berton, and "Swing Mister Charlie" with Bunny Berigan. He recorded for Vocalion, Columbia, Mercury, Victor, and Brunswick records. Bullock retired from the music business in 1942 and, in 1946, moved to California and opened a real estate firm. Bullock died in California on September 15, 1981.

BOB CHESTER

(Bod Chester and His Orchestra) Born on March 20, 1908. Chester grew up in Detroit, attended universities there, and played saxophone with Paul Specht, Irving Aaronson, Ben Pollack, Arnold Johnson, Ben Bernie, and Russ Morgan. In the mid-'30s, he led the band at the Detroit Athletic Club. In 1939, when the band was unable to survive financially, he moved to New York and moved in with Tommy Dorsey who financed a new band for Chester. The new band's singers were Bob Haymes, Betty Bradley, Gene Howard, Kathleen Lane, Lou Gardner, and Dolores "Dodie" O'Neil. The featured trumpet player was Alec Fila. Other top sidemen included Herbie Steward and John LaPorta, alto saxophones; and Bill Harris and Joe Harris, trombones. The Bob Chester Orchestra recorded for Bluebird Records. The band's theme songs were "Slumber" and "Sunburst." After a number of successful years, Chester disbanded and moved back to Detroit where he entered the automotive business.

FRANCIS CRAIG

(Francis Craig and His Orchestra) Born in Dickson, Tennessee on September 10, 1900. Pianist Francis Craig organized his first band in Nashville, Tennessee in the mid-'20s and played at the Hermitage for several years, being heard on radio in that area. The band toured the Midwest and South and had a number of prominent sidemen, including George Thomas, Newton Richards, Clarence Morrison, Ray McNeary, Herb Hill, Phil Harris, Malcolm Crain, Ken Binford, Cecil Bailey, and Powell Adams. The singers included James Melton and Kenny Sargent. In the late '40s, Craig's tune "Near You" catapulted the band into national prominence. Craig later wrote the songs "Foolin'," "Do Me a Favor," "A Broken Heart Must Cry," "Tennessee Tango," and "I Beg Your Pardon." The band recorded for MGM, Columbia, Decca, and Bullet records. The theme songs were "Near You" and "Red Rose." Craig died in Sewanee, Tennessee in 1966.

JOHNNY "SCAT" DAVIS

(Johnny "Scat" Davis and His Orchestra) Born in Brazil, Indiana on May 11, 1910. Johnny "Scat" Davis (né: John Gustave Davis) played trumpet, sang, and was a comedian with Fred Waring and His Pennsylvanians in the early '30s. After making records with his Trio and a few big bands he appeared in more than a dozen movies starting in *Varsity Show* (1937), *The Cowboy from Brooklyn* (1938), *Slapsie Maxie* (1939), *Sarong Girl* (1942), and ending with *Knickerbocker Holiday* (1944). In the later film, he sang "September Song." In 1937, Davis and Johnny Mercer wrote the music for the movie Hollywood Hotel and Mercer's song "Hooray for Hollywood" was sung by Johnny "Scat"

Davis. Many famous musicians worked with Davis, including Buddy DeFranco. The band recorded for Decca Records. In the mid-'40s, the Davis band accompanied a striptease show, which was headed by Ann Corio and played at San Diego, California at the Fox West Coast Theater. Davis died in Pecos, Texas on November 28, 1983.

SAM DONAHUE

(Sam Donahue and His Orchestra) Born in Detroit, Michigan on March 8, 1918. Sam Donahue was a saxophonist who played with various bands during the '30s and formed his first orchestra in 1942. After disbanding, he played with Gene Krupa until he enlisted in the U.S. Naval Reserve and played with Artie Shaw. When Shaw was discharged from the service, Donahue assumed control of the band and recorded many V-discs during the war. When WWII was over, Sam formed a new civilian band that encountered a mild success and disbanded when the big band era ended. Some of the Donahue sidemen were Doc Severinsen, Clyde Reasinger, Bill Turner, Bob Burgess, O.B. Masingill, Ed Fromm, Dick Clay, Ronny Bedford, and many others. Donahue had many good singers, including Frances Wayne, Shirley Lloyd, Bill Lockwood, Bob Matthews, and Irene Day. When the Dorsey Brothers died, the estate chose Donahue to lead the Dorsey band, which he did until his retirement. The theme songs of the Sam Donahue Orchestra were "I Never Knew," "Lonesome," and "Minor Deluxe." Donahue died in Reno, Nevada on March 22, 1974.

JIMMY DORSEY

(Jimmy Dorsey and His Orchestra) Born in Shenandoah, Pennsylvania on February 29, 1904. Jimmy Dorsey and his brother Tommy were taught music by their father, who was the leader of the Elmore band in Shenandoah, Pennsylvania. When Jimmy was nine years old, he played for two days in the J. Carson McGee's King Trumpeters vaudeville act in a New York theater. Jimmy played cornet until 1915, when he took up

the alto saxophone. In 1917, he worked for a brief time in a coal mine, as had his father. Shortly after that he and his brother Tommy formed a band they first called Dorsey's Novelty Six, later changing the name to Dorsey's Wild Canaries. For a brief time, the band played for clubs and broadcasts in Baltimore, after which they disbanded and the brothers joined Billy Lustig's Scranton Sirens. With that band, they recorded "Fate" and "Three O'Clock in the Morning." Through the remainder of the '20s, Jimmy played with Jean Goldkette, Red Nichols, Vincent Lopez, Harry Thies, Paul Whiteman, and the California Ramblers, doing radio broadcasts and recordings. In the early '30s, Jimmy Dorsey played with Ted Lewis, Andre Kostelanetz, Jacques Renard, Rudy Valee, Fred Rich, Lennie Hayton, Victor Young, and Daniel Rubinoff. In 1934, Jimmy and Tommy Dorsey organized a band together, which made a formal debut in Long Island, New York at the Sands Point Beach Club. In 1935, the band played the Glen Island Casino in New Rochelle and disbanded. Jimmy kept the sidemen from the joint band and became very successful featuring sidemen such as Freddy Slack, piano; Ray McKinkey, drums; Roc Hilman, guitar; Jack Ryan, bass; Sonny Lee and Bobby Byrne, trombones; Don Mattison, Shorty Sherock, and Talph Muzzillo, trumpets; and Charles Frazier, Leonard Whitney, Herbie Hamyer, and Milt Yaner, saxophones. In 1943, singer Helen O'Connell was added to the band with Ray Eberly. The band recorded a string of hits, including "Maria Elena," "Green Eyes," "Amapola," "Besame Mucho," and "Tangerine." The Dorsey band appeared in many movies, including *The Fabulous Dorseys, Four Jacks and a Jeep, Lost in a Harem, I Dood It, The Fleet's In, Shall We Dance?*, and *That Girl from Paris*. The Jimmy Dorsey Orchestra recorded for Brunswick and Decca records. In 1953, Jimmy rejoined the Tommy Dorsey Orchestra, renamed the Fabulous Dorsey's Orchestra. Jimmy Dorsey died in New York City on June 12, 1957.

TOMMY DORSEY

(Tommy Dorsey and His Orchestra) Born in Shenendoah, Pennsylvania on November 19, 1905. By 1925, Tommy Dorsey was playing trombone with the California Ramblers. He joined the Paul Whiteman Orchestra in 1927 and 1928 formed the Dorsey Brothers Orchestra with brother Jimmy. The brothers split up at the Glen Island Casino in New Rochelle, New York in 1935 and Tommy formed his own band by assuming the leadership of the Joe Haymes Orchestra.

He immediately added arranger Axel Stordahl, singer Jack Leonard, trumpet player Joe Bauer, drummer Dave Tough, and saxophonist Bud Freeman. Stordahl, Leonard, and Bauer also constituted the vocal trio known as the Three Esquires. Dorsey became known as the "Sentimental Gentleman of Swing." By 1938, Dorsey had brought many new faces to the band, including singer Edythe Wright; Hymie Schertzer, Fred Stuice, Johnny Mince, and Babe Russin, saxophones; Lee Castaldo, Yank Lawson, and Charlie Spivak, trumpets; Elmer Smithers, Les Jenkins, and Moe Zudecoff, trombones; Howard Smith, piano; Gene Traxler, bass; Carmen Mastren, bass; and Maurice Purtill, drums. By the '40s, Dorsey added Sy Oliver to do arrangements, drummer Buddy Rich, singer Frank Sinatra, and the vocal group the Pied Pipers. Tommy Dorsey added a string section and arranger Bill Finegan to the band during WW II. The Tommy Dorsey band recorded on Bell, Capitol, Victor, and Decca records. The theme song was "I'm Getting Sentimental Over You." In 1953, brother Jimmy rejoined the Tommy Dorsey Orchestra and the name of the band was changed to the Fabulous Dorsey's Orchestra. Tommy Dorsey died in Greenwich, Connecticut on November 26, 1956.

ERSKINE HAWKINS

(Erskine Hawkins and His Orchestra) Born in Birmingham, Alabama on July 26, 1914. Erskine Hawkins attended State Teachers College in Alabama and replaced J.B. Sims as leader of the school band. Prior to his leadership, the band had traveled extensively in the South and recorded for Vocalion Records. When Hawkins took over the band, they took a trip to New York City with an appearance at the Harlem Opera House. On a follow-up trip, they participated in a two-band performance alongside Chick Webb's band at the Savoy Ballroom and were signed to a recording contract with Bluebird Records. The Hawkins band recorded many hits, among them were "Tippin' In," "Don't Cry Baby," "Whispering Grass," "Dolomite," and "Tuxedo Junction." Hawkins was an excellent trumpet player and wrote several hits, including "Tuxedo

Junction" and "Gin Mill Special." Singers on the band included Laura Washington, Carol Tucker, Jimmy Mitchelle, Delores Brown, Ida James, Merle Turner, and Billy Daniels. A few of the outstanding sidemen were Jimmy Mitchelle, alto saxophone; Avery Parrish, piano and arranger; Paul Bascomb, tenor saxophone; and Wilbur "Dud" Bascomb, trumpet. In addition to Bluebird, the Hawkins band recorded for Decca, King, Coral, and Victor records. Hawkins disbanded in the mid-'50s and led a quartet. He retired in the early '80s after playing in the Catskill Mountains at the Concord Hotel. Hawkins died in Willingbors, New Jersey on November 11, 1992.

ART JARRETT

(Art Jarrett and His Orchestra) Born in New York City in 1909. Art Jarrett was primarily a singer who also played guitar and trombone. He was with the Earl Burtnett Orchestra in 1926 and 1927, before joining the Ted Weems group in late 1927, where he was featured on several recordings. He remained with Weems until 1931, when he was heard on radio and recordings in New York and Chicago. In 1932, he succeeded Buddy Rogers in the Broadway musical *Hotcha*. By 1933, he was singing in the motion pictures *Dancing Lady*, *Sitting Pretty*, and *Let's Fall in Love*. In 1935, he formed a dance band in Chicago and featured arrangements by Jule Styne and, by 1936, included his future wife, singer Eleanor Holm. In the late '30s, Jarrett starred in the movie *My Lucky Star* and on Broadway in *Walk with Music*. In 1941, he took over the Hal Kemp Orchestra, when Kemp was killed which featured singer and future movie star, Gale Robbins. The band recorded often and played for a time at the Black Hawk in Chicago. Jarrett served in the U.S. Navy during WWII and formed a new band in 1946, when he was released from service. When he retired from the music business in the early '50s, he moved to Beverly Hills, California and became a salesman. The Jarrett band recorded for Columbia, Brunswick, and Victor records. The theme song of the Art Jarrett Orchestra was "Everything's Been Done Before."

LITTLE JACK LITTLE

(Little Jack Little and His Orchestra) Born in London, England on May 28, 1900. Little Jack Little came to the U.S. at an early age and eventually studied pre-medicine at the University of Iowa. While at the university, he led a dance band. In the mid-'20s, when he left the university, he appeared as a single and did many song-patter shows on radio, singing and playing piano. Little formed his first band in the early '30s. His string section was lead by violinist Mitchell Agres (Mitchell Ayres) and first hit record was Hold Me. By 1934, he was playing at the Ambassador Hotel in Atlantic City and the Lexington Hotel in New York City, where he received good radio coverage. He disbanded in the later '30s and appeared as a single in various venues. Ayres left the Little band and formed his own orchestra. The Little Jack Little Orchestra recorded for Brunswick, Vocalion, and Columbia records. After WWII, Little became a disc jockey in Washington, D.C. Little Jack Little wrote a number of songs, including "Jealous," "In a Shanty in Old Shanty Town," "Hold Me," "You Broke the Only Heart That Ever Loved You," and "Raindrops." The theme song of the Little Jack Little Orchestra was "Little by Little." Little died in Hollywood, Florida on April 9, 1956.

MATTY MALNECK

(Matty Malneck and His Octet) Born in Newark, New Jersey on December 10, 1904. When Matty Malneck was a young child, the family moved to Denver, Colorado and he studied violin. At 16, he began playing with bands, including the Paul Whiteman Orcestra with whom he played for 11 years. He formed his first band in the mid-'30s, which eventually included Milton Delugg, accordion, and Mannie Klein, trumpet. The band accompanied a number of outstanding Hollywood personalities in movies and on recordings. By the 1940s, Maleck was featured on the Duffy's Tavern and Joe E. Brown radio shows. Malneck was a prolific songwriter, penning tunes like "Hey, Good Lookin'," "Gypsy," "I'm Through with Love," "Goody, Goody," and "I'll Never Be the Same." Matty died in Hollywood, California on February 15, 1981.

JIMMY McPARTLAND

(Jimmy McPartland and his All-Stars) Born in Chicago, Illinois on March 15, 1907. Cornetist McPartland began playing with the Blue Friars in Chicago before joining the Austin High School Gang, which included Davey Tough, drums; Joe Sullivan, piano; James Lanigan, tuba and contrabass; Dick McPartland, banjo and guitar; Frank Teschemacher, clarinet; and Bud Freeman, tenor saxophone. When Bix Beiderbecke resigned from the Wolverines in 1924, he recommended that McPartland replace him and gave one of his cornets to McPartland that he would played throughout his career. Between 1926 and 1928, he played with Art Kassel, McKenzie, and Condon's Chicagoans, and the Ben Pollack Orchestra. McPartland went to New York in 1929 and played with Russ Columbo and the Harry Reser band; in 1936, he formed his own band, which he led until 1941, when he was drafted into the U.S. Army. The McPartland band recorded for Decca Records and featured sidemen Joe Rushton, Royce Brown, Rosie McHargue, Joe Harris, and George Wettling. During WWII, he participated in the Normandy invasion. When he was discharged in 1945, he remained in Europe and played at various U.S.O clubs and eventually marrying Marian Page (Marian McPartland), the British jazz pianist. The theme for the McPartland band was "The World Is Waiting for the Sunrise." McPartland died on November 30, 1957.

RUSS MORGAN

(Russ Morgan and His Orchestra) Born in Scranton, Pennsylvania on April 29, 1904. When Morgan was very young, he studied trombone, saxophone, piano, and vibes. At age 21, he had already arranged for bands led by John Phillip Sousa and Victor Herbert and, in a short time, became a trombonist and arranger for the Jean Goldkette Orchestra and the Detroit Symphony Orchestra. As he became more and more interested in commercial music, he became recording director of Brunswick Records and a studio musician. He worked as music director for the *Phillip Morris* and *Lifebouy* radio shows and as a staff conductor for NBC. Toward the mid-'30s, Morgan played with Jean Goldkette along with well-known musicians Charlie Spivak, Freddie Martin, and Artie Shaw. In 1935, Morgan was involved in a major automobile accident. When he recovered, he joined Freddie Martin's newly formed band as a piano player. He eventually switched back to trombone, and while playing with Martin at the

Roosevelt Hotel in New York City, Morgan developed his famous "wah-wah" sound. Later, when Martin refused a recording date, Morgan formed his own band, which included Flip Phillips, tenor saxophone, and Claude Thornhill, piano. The band's theme song was "Does Your Heart Beat for Me?" The tagline was "Music in the Morgan manner." In the late '40s, the Morgan band had three big hits, "Cruisin' Down the River," "Sunflower," and "For Ever and Ever." Morgan wrote a number of hit tunes, including "Somebody Else is Taking Your Place," "Does Your Heart Beat for Me?," "So Tired," and "You're Nobody 'til Somebody Loves You." Morgan recorded for Everest, Vocalion, Brunswick, and Decca records. Morgan died in Las Vegas, Nevada on August 8, 1969.

ADRIAN KNOX

(Adrian Knox and His Famous CBS Orchestra) Born in Plankinton, South Dakota on February 15, 1911. Knox organized his band in the '30s after playing with various territory groups. He was heard on many Midwest radio stations and played such venues as the Lake Lawn Hotel in Wisconsin, the Pavilion at Lake Delavan, and Guyon's Paradise in Chicago. It was said that the Knox Orchestra played for more than one million dancers. Knox eventually disbanded, returned to college, and became a professor of mathematics at the Illinois Institute of Technology in Chicago. After living in Anaheim, California, he retired to Florida and died in Clearwater, Florida on January 28, 1996.

FREDDY NAGEL

(Freddy Nagel and His Orchestra) Freddy Nagel organized his band in the early '30s and, by the mid-'30s, was touring the Northwest playing for various social dances, galas, and parties. The Nagel band was featured at Jantzen Beach in Portland, Oregon and at the Natatorium Park in Spokane, Washington. Many thought of the band as a "Kay Kyser Type" orchestra that used a lot of show-manship but was short of musicianship. The band eventually toured the Midwest appearing in Chicago at the Trianon and Aragon Ballrooms. Nagel featured singers and among them were Allen Overend, Bob Locken, Ken Jackson, and Lorraine Benson. The band's theme song was "Sophisticated Swing." After WWII, Nagel disbanded and retired in Susanville, California.

EDDIE PAUL

(Eddie Paul and His Paramount Orchestra) The Eddie Paul band was probably a studio orchestra with a number of records made on Vocalion, Melotone, Banner, Perfect, and Arc records, but there is no record of the band having traveled. The singers were Johnny Hauser, Tony Sacco, and Francis Stevens. Most of the recordings were made in the mid '30s and were of the popular-tune variety.

CARL RAVAZZA (RAVELL)

(Carl Ravazza and His Orchestra) Born in Alameda, California in 1912. Ravazza was orphaned at eight years old, raised by his grandmother, and studied violin. While a senior at Alameda High School, Ravazza organized his first dance band. He began singing in Tom Coakley's band, while attending St. Mary's College studying pre-medicine. In 1933, he joined the Anson Weeks band at the Mark Hopkins Hotel in San Francisco and played violin and singing in the section with Xavier Cugat. Bob Crosby was the banjo player. In 1934, he rejoined the Coakley band and, in 1936, took over the band when Coakley opened his law practice. The singer on that band was Carole Landis. The newly organized Ravazza Orchestra played at the Chase Hotel in St. Louis, the Aragon and Trianon Ballrooms in Chicago, the Blackhawk Hotel in New York, and the Lexington Hotel and the St. Francis Hotel in San Francisco. While playing in New Orleans at the Roosevelt Hotel, the owners changed his name to Carl Ravell. The band recorded "Gone with the Wind" under "Carl Ravell." By 1937 he returned to the St. Francis Hotel in San Francisco and reverted to his given surname, Ravazza. The band recorded for Bluebird, Melotone, and Hindsight records, and its theme song was "Vieni Su." The Ravazza Orchestra appeared at many war bond rallies in WWII and featured guests Bing Crosby and Dinah Shore. The bands singers were Dawn Meredith and Ravazza himself. In 1959, while appearing at the Hotel Nacional in Havana, Cuba, Fidel Castro's revolutionary army entered the city and disrupted the band's appearance. Ravazza retired in 1960 and died on July 29, 1968.

JAN SAVITT

(Jan Savitt and His Top Hatters Orchestra) Born in Petrograd, Russia on September 4, 1914. Jan Savitt's family immigrated to the U.S. when the violin prodigy was 15. He won a scholarship for playing and conducting at the Curtis Institute in Philadelphia and became the youngest musicians to play with the Philadelphia Orchestra under Leopold Stokowski. He later became a studio musician at radio station KYW and CBS. Forming a band, he hired singers Bon Bon, Carolotta Dale, and Gloria Dehaven. The Savitt Orchestra's theme song was "Quaker City Jazz" and was heard on the CBS radio show *Rhapsody in Rhythm*, sponsored by the P. Lorillard Company. The song "720 in the Books" became popular because of Savitt's recording; the band was given that name since that was the number of the tune in the library of the Savitt's orchestra. The Savitt band ultimately appeared in several movies, including *That's My Gal*, *Betty Coed*, and *High School Hero*. The band had outstanding arrangers, including Billy Moore, Johnny Watson, Abe Osser, Eddie Durham, and Savitt. Savitt died in California on October 4, 1948.

STERLING YOUNG

(Sterling Young and His Orchestra) Sterling Young was raised off the coast of Southern California on Catalina Island. When he was eight, he began to study violin and took weekly lessons from Calmon Lubovski in Los Angeles. He played with Ted Dahl in Hollywood on the radio at age 19. By the mid-'30s, he had formed his own band and played in Los Angeles at the Wilshire Bowl. The Music Corporation of America booked the band on an extended tour that took them to Pittsburg, Pennsylvania, where they played at Bill Green's Casino. The band's saxophone player, Max Walter, was also the arranger. During the late '30s, the band toured the West Coast and played at Santa Monica's Del Mar Club, the San Clemente Casino, the Wilshire Bowl, the California Grape Festival, and Jantzen Beach in Portland, Oregon. Many visitors would sit in and perform with the band: Mickey Rooney and Judy Garland were among the guests. The band's theme song was "Blue Is the Night." Sterling Young recorded for MacGregor and Mercury Records. Young served in the military during WWII and led a band on the West Coast during the late '40s and '50s.

RAY HERBECK

(Ray Herbeck and His Music with Romance Orchestra) Born in Los Angeles, California on November 27, 1910. While in high school, Ray Herbeck played saxophone and clarinet, studied pre-dentistry at the University of Southern California, and left school because of the Depression. In the mid-'30s, he formed a band with his friend Claude Bunzell and played initially in Los Angeles at the Café de Paris. The band did periodic radio broadcasts on CBS from the Café, which assisted them in getting a job playing at Lake Tahoe at the Tahoe Tavern where they were advertised as Ray Herbeck and His Music of Romance. The theme song of the Herbeck Orchestra was "Romance." In 1941, Herbeck formed a swing band and changed his tagline to Modern Music with Romance. In 1943, the group disbanded as most of the members went into the service due to WWII. When the war ended, Herbeck formed a new, sweet music band, featuring singer Lorraine Benson with arrangements by James Baker, who also played alto saxophone. Herbeck wrote the tune "Time Stood Still." The band recorded on Bullet, Fourstar, Columbia, Okeh, and Vocalion records. When he disbanded in the mid-'50s, Herbeck moved to Phoenix and sold real estate. He died in Phoenix, Arizona on January 17, 1989.

BUD BARCLAY

(Bud Barclay [Bubbles Becker] and His Orchestra) Little is known about Bud Barclay or "Bubbles Becker," but they seem to be one and the same. The band played at the New Kenmore Hotel in Albany, New York in the late '30s; at the Continental Gardens in Akron, Ohio in the early '40s; and in Huntsville, Alabama in the early '50s.

BLUE BARRON

(Blue Barron and His Orchestra) Born in Cleveland, Ohio on March 22, 1911. Blue Barron (né: Harry Friedland) played violin in the campus band at Ohio State University. He began his professional career as a theatrical agent booking bands, including Kay Kyser, Horace Heidt, Guy Lombardo, and Sammy Kaye in the greater Cleveland, Ohio area. In the mid-'30s, he organized his own band billing it, "The music of yesterday and today, styled in the Blue Barron way." The singers, from time to time, were Russ Carlyle, Clyde Burke, and Jimmy

Brown. In 1938, he performed successfully at the Taft Hotel Green Room, where he did three radio broadcasts each week. While serving in the airborne division in WWII, his band continued to work under the leadership of singer Tommy Ryan. After WWII, Barron recorded "Cruisin' Down the River" for MGM Records, which became the country's number one hit. The theme song for the Blue Barron Orchestra was "Sometimes I'm Happy." In the '50s, he disbanded but continued leading local bands. In addition to MGM, the Barron band also recorded for Victor on the Bluebird label.

BUNNY BERIGAN

(Bunny Berigan and His Orchestra) Born in Hilbert, Wisconsin on November 2, 1908. Bunny Berigan (né: Roland Bernard Berigan) first played in New York with the Frank Cornwall band. Hal Kemp heard him and hired Berigan for his band. After leaving the Kemp Orchestra, Berigan played as a studio musician on records and radio and had his own show called *Bunny's Blue Boys* on CBS. After a time, he played with the Benny Goodman band for about six months. Berigan organized his first band in 1936 and, in 1937, was playing at the Hotel Pennsylvania in New York City. The personnel included Georgie Auld, saxophone; Ruth Bradley, clarinet and vocals; Joe Buskin, piano; Ray Conniff, trombone; and Buddy Rich, drums. In 1938, he added Dick Morgan, bass; Hank Wayland, guitar; Nat Lebrousky, trombone; Harry Goodman and John Naptan, trumpets; Clyde Rounds, Gus Rivona, and Milton Schatz, saxophones; and Jayne Dover, singer. In 1940, Berigan disbanded and joined the Tommy Dorsey Orchestra. Because of various disagreements, he only stayed six months, leaving after an NBC radio broadcast. In 1941, Berigan formed another band, but by 1942, he developed cirrhosis of the liver, and Pee Wee Erwin took over the band. Berigan died in New York City on June 2, 1942.

SHARKEY BONANO

(Sharkey and His Sharks of Rhythm) Born in New Orleans, Louisiana on April 9, 1904. Sharkey Bonano grew up and learned to play the trumpet in New Orleans. During the '20s, he played with all of the stellar groups in New Orleans. In the early '30s, he formed his first band in New Orleans—a band that was short-lived. Moving to New York City in 1936, he formed a new band that was billed as Sharkey and His Sharks of Rhythm, which had radio exposure, played in various clubs, and recorded. The band was a big hit and lasted until 1941, when WWII began to effect the U.S. That band recorded several hits; among them were "The Missouri Waltz," "Swingin' On the Swané Shore," "If I Had You," "Old Fashioned Swing," and "Auf Wiedersehen, Sweetheart." Bonano returned to New Orleans after WWII and spent the remainder of his life playing the music he loved most, Dixieland. When Bonano died, more than 300 musicians attended his New Orleans jazz-style funereal. He died in New Orleans on April 5, 1972.

LOU BREESE

(Lou Breese and His Orchestra) Born on February 10, 1900. Trumpeter Lou Breese (né: Lou Calabreese) played in various theater bands during the '20s and performed in the greater Chicago area with bands like Paul Specht and Bert Lown. In 1936, he formed his first band that featured the woodwind section. After a couple of years, he disbanded and became the stage show producer for the *Chez Paree* in Chicago. In 1939, he took over Bob Baker's band, the house band for *Chez Paree*. The Baker band had originally been formed by Henry Busse in Chicago and retained that Busse sound. In the '40s, the Breese Orchestra played most of the major theaters in and around Chicago and recorded tunes such as "Wait for Me," "Chiquita and Sweetheart," "Humpty Dumpty Heart," and "Swamp Fire" for Decca Records. The theme song of the Breese Orchestra was "Breezing Along with the Breeze." One of the outstanding sidemen of the Breese band was clarinetist Paul Specht. Other musicians included Vince Micko, tenor saxophone, and Leon Ruby, trumpet. Breese died in January 1969.

TEDDY BUCKNER

(Teddy Buckner and His Orchestra) Born in Sherman, Texas on July 16, 1909. Teddy Buckner's (né: John Edward Buckner) family moved to Los Angeles, California when Teddy was a small child. As a teenager in the early '30s, he studied trumpet and worked with the Sonny Clay Orchestra. By 1934, he was playing with Buck Clayton who toured extensively, including an appearance in Shanghai, China. Returning to U.S., Buckner joined the Lionel Hampton band.

In 1936, Benny Goodman discovered Hampton, who was playing at the Paradise Club. Hampton left to join the Goodman band and Teddy Buckner took over the Hampton Orchestra. Buckner disbanded at the start of WWII and recorded with Benny Carter and Kid Ory. While playing with Ory, he was featured on the recording "Yaaka Hula Hickey Dula," which brought him much positive notoriety; he also appeared with the Ory band at the Club Hangover during the mid-'50s and was heard on various radio broadcasts from that venue. In 1954, Buckner formed a new band, recorded three Dixieland jubilee record albums, and toured the West Coast. In 1955, he recorded the trumpet track on "Pete Kelly's Blues." Buckner died in Los Angeles, California on October 4, 1994.

FRANK CHACKSFIELD

(Frank Chacksfield and His Orchestra) Born at Battle, Sussex, England on May 9, 1914. Chacksfield studied piano at age seven and gave his first solo recital at 14. When he was 22, he formed his first orchestra (1936), which traveled extensively until WWII. During the war, he joined the Royal Signals and just prior to being sent overseas he became ill. While recovering, he made a BBC broadcast that led to his being assigned to the Army's entertainment division in Salisbury. During the ensuing years, he broadcasted regularly and met Charlie Chester, with whom, after the war, he co-hosted studio bands before signing a record contract. In 1953, Frank Chacksfield formed a group known as the Tunesmiths and signed a contract with Parlophone Records. He recorded a hit, "Red Monkey," after assembling a large group with strings and it was remarked that the new group sounded like Mantovani's. Two other songs, "Ebb Tide" and "Limelight," were soon recorded and became hits. Throughout the '50s, other tunes like "Memories of You," "Flirtation Waltz," and "On the Beach" became hits and sold millions of records. Other albums followed, including *Donkey Cart* and *In Old Lisbon*, which were devoted to the music of the Beatles, Irving Berlin, Cole Porter, and others, and achieved gold records. Chacksfield died on June 9, 1995.

JUAN ESQUIVEL

(Juan Esquivel and His Orchestra) Born in Tampico, Parnaulipas, Mexico on January 20, 1918. Juan Esquivel (né: Juan Garcia Esquivel) moved with his family to Mexico City when he was ten years old. He had already shown talent at the piano and was a featured soloist on radio station XEW, when he arrived in Mexico City. By the time he was 18, he organized his own 22-piece band, for which he arranged, composed, and conducted. The band did eight radio broadcasts a week and appeared on many concert stages in the area. To keep control of his band, which had grown to 54 pieces, he had all members sign a document entitled "The Rules and Regulations of Belonging to the Esquivel Organization." During that period, bands led by Perez Prado and Louis Alcarez were also quite popular in Mexico. Herman Diaz Jr., the manager and producer for Victor Records, brought Esquivel to Hollywood in 1958, where he recorded albums *Other Worlds, Other Music, Four Corners of the World,* and *To Love Again* with a 26-piece orchestra. In 1959, two more albums were released— *Exploring New Sounds in Hi-Fi* and *Exploring New Sounds in Stereo.* In 1959, Esquivel went to New York, where he wrote arrangements for other artists and recorded another album for Victor, *The Merriest of Christmas Pops.* In 1960, with the Ames Brothers, he recorded "Hello, Amigos," "The Living Strings," and "In a Mellow Mood." After leaving Victor Records and signing a contract with Reprise Records, he moved to Las Vegas where he was involved in a stage show, *The Sights and Sounds of Esquivel* and organized a 26-piece orchestra, which played at the Stardust Hotel. At various times, the Esquivel band had such sidemen as Buddy Cole, organ; Jack Castanzo, bongos; Larry Bunker, drums; George Roberts, bass trombone; Frank Rosolino, trombone; Muzzy Marcelino and Pete Condoli, trumpets; Alvino Rey and Laurindo Almieda, guitars; and Stan Getz, tenor saxophone. Esquivel admired Pete Rugolo, Stan Kenton, Lalo Schifrin, Johnny Williams, and Henry Mancini. Esquivel retired in 1992 and died on January 3, 2002, in Mexico.

JOE & ADELE GIRARD-MARSALA

(Joe & Adele Girard-Marsala Orchestra) Adele Girard-Marsala was born in 1913. Joe Marsala was born in Chicago, Illinois on January 4, 1907. Girard was a harpist and had played with the Harry Sosnick Orchestra. Marsala initally studied the saxophone. His brother, Marty, played drums, and the two of them played in local Chicago bands in the '20s. In 1927, Joe was playing in a Dancing School Trio when he decided to join the Harold West Orchestra, an Ohio Territory band. During Prohibition, he played saxophone and clarinet in Chicago Speakeasies with Art Hodes and Floyd O'Brien. During the late '20s and early '30s, Marsala played with Wingy Manone. In 1935, Joe Marsala moved to New York City, where he played at Adrian Rollini's Tap Room and then at the Hickory House with Wingy Manone. In 1936, Manone moved to Chicago and Marsala formed his own band, which played at the Hickory House from 1937 to 1948. The original band featured Joe Buskin, Henry "Red" Allen, and Eddie Condon. It later featured Adele Girard, harp, and Bobby Hackett, guitar and trumpet. Girard and Marsala had married in 1937. Among other musicians who played in the Marsala band during that period were Shelly Manne, Dave Tough, Carmen Mastren, and Marty Marsala. In 1948, the Marsalas semi-retired and moved to Colorado, where they lived until moving back to New York in 1953. There they opened a music publishing office and wrote several big hits, including "And So to Sleep Again," "Little Sir Echo," and "Don't Cry Joe." Joe and Adele Girard-Marsala recorded for Decca and Brunswick Records during their active days. When Joe died in Santa Barbara, California on March 4, 1978, Adele Girard continued playing and recorded a CD on Arbors Records. She died in Denver, Colorado on September 7, 1993.

GRAY GORDON

(Gray Gordon and His Tic Toc Music) Born in Freeport, Illinois on May 4, 1904. Gray Gordon (né: Jerome Rohkar) was a saxophonist who organized his first band, the Pretzel Five, while attending high school. By the mid-'20s, Gordon had moved to Chicago, where he worked with the Elmo Mack's Purple Derby Orchestra and the Seattle Harmony Kings. By the mid-'30s, he moved to New York and formed his first orchestra; while playing at the Hotel Chase in St. Louis, he legally changed his name to Gray Gordon. In 1937, while playing in Chicago he developed the tic-toc style using the drummer's temple blocks. The tic-toc rhythm brought the band fame during a long-time engagement at the Hotel Edison Green Room in New York City. The band's biggest selling record was *Blue in the Black of Night*, which was produced by Bluebird Records. Cliff Grass was the band's vocalist. The band recorded for Bluebird and Victor records and the theme song was "One Minute to One." Some of the bands singers included Rita Ray, Art Perry, Meredith Blake, Betty Bradley, Betty Lane, Shirley Lane, Cliff Bruce, and Cliff Grass. The sidemen included Hal Tennyson, Chet Roble, Johnny Johnson, Alex Goldstein, Joe Dale, Glen Rolfing, Roy Mace, Bobby Blair, and Chet Bruce. In 1945, Gordon disbanded his orchestra and joined Guy Lombardo as second alto saxophone next to Carmen Lombardo. When he retired, he worked in Miami, Florida as a public relations director. Gordon died in New York City on July 18, 1976.

BOBBY HACKETT

(Bobby Hackett and His Orchestra) Born in Providence, Rhode Island on January 31, 1915. When he was very young, Bobby Hackett studied violin, banjo, guitar, and cornet, and played guitar with local bands as a teenager. By 1933, he was playing with Pee Wee Russell in Boston. In 1936, Hackett formed his own band, which played at the Theatrical Club in Boston. Moving to New York in 1937, he performed with Joe Marsala at the Hickory House on 52nd Street playing guitar and cornet. In 1938, Hackett led his own band at the Carnegie Hall concert that featured the Benny Goodman Orchestra. After leading his band at The Famous Door, Hackett disbanded and joined the Horace Heidt Orchestra, in which he played until 1940. From 1941 to 1942, he played in the Glenn Miller Orchestra. In 1944, he joined the Glen Gray band, where he played for two years. From 1946 until 1956, Hackett was a studio musician in New York before touring with Ray McKinley and Benny Goodman. Hackett was an active performer until his death, in Chatham, Massachusetts on June 7, 1976.

WOODY HERMAN

(Woody Herman and the Herman Herd) Born in Milwaukee, Wisconsin on May 16, 1913. At the age nine, Woody Herman was playing saxophone in vaudeville. After playing for a time with the Tommy Gerun Orchestra, which featured singers Herman, Al Morris (Tony Martin), and Virginia (Ginny) Simms, Herman played with the Harry Sosnick Orchestra, the Gus Arnheim band and Isham Jones.When the Isham Jones Orchestra disbanded in 1936, Herman formed his first orchestra, the band That Plays the Blues, and signed a recording contract with Decca Records. In 1945, the Woody Herman Orchestra became the First Herd and recorded for Columbia Records. In 1946, Woody Herman retired for a time prior to forming the Second Herd. In 1947, Woody disbanded and became a disc jockey on a radio station in Hollywood. Reorganizing, he took to the road once again with a modern band and switched record labels, going with Capitol Records. In the '50s, he disbanded his large band and organized a combo for a brief period. He quickly reorganized his big band and was on the road through the '60s, 70's, and into the '80s. Herman had some of the country's outstanding musicians in his various bands through the years, including Milt Bernhart, Bill Chase, Urbie Green, Red Mitchell, Al Cohn, Jake Hanna, Vince Guaraldi, Zoot Sims, Stan Getz, Milt Jackson, Terry Gibbs, Red Norvo, Dave Tough, Flip Phillips, Bill Harris, Deane Kincaide, Conti Candoli, Pete Candoli, Cappy Lewis, and many others. The theme songs of the Herman band were "Blue Flame" and "Blue Prelude." Herman died in Los Angeles, California on October 29, 1987.

HUDSON-DeLANGE

(The Hudson-DeLange Orchestra) Will Hudson was born in Barstow, California on March 8, 1908. Eddie DeLange (né: Edgar DeLange) was born in Long Island City, New York on January 12, 1904. In the mid-'30s, musician Hudson and lyricist DeLange formed a band, which DeLange, an extrovert, fronted. Hudson, who was considered more of an introvert, only traveled with the band on occasion. This difference in personalities caused a split-up in 1938, which was an unpleasant experience for both men; however, by 1943 the men once again joined forces but the new band failed to succeed. Eddie DeLange moved to Hollywood where he worked in films. Will Hudson became the arranger for the Glenn Miller Army Air Force Band. Their music, published by Irving Mills was very successful and included tunes like "Moonglow," "Sophisticated Swing," "Deep in a Dream," "Remember When," "Monopoly Swing," "Organ Grinder's Swing," "Love Song of a Half Wit," and "Sophisticated Swing." The theme song of the Hudson-Delange Orchestra was "Eight Bars in Search of a Melody" that they also wrote. Much of their music was recorded for Master Records. Will Hudson died in South Carolina in 1981. Eddie DeLange died in Los Angeles, California on July 13, 1949.

McFARLAND TWINS

(The McFarland Twins Orchestra) Twin brothers, both of whom played saxophone, led the McFarland Twins Orchestra. Their first orchestra was formed in the '30s and was said to be of inferior quality; the '40s orchestra was much better musically. The band featured pianist Geoff Clarkson and singers Dick Merrick and Betty Engels. There is no record of the band's existence after WWII.

JOHNNY MESSNER

(Johnny Messner and His Orchestra) Born in New York City on October 13, 1909. Johnny Messner and his four brothers all studied music in their youth. Messner studied violin and clarinet and performed with his brothers at various civic events and on local radio stations billing themselves as the Five Messner Brothers. When Johnny finished high school he was offered a scholarship to attend the Juilliard School of Music in New York. In 1933, the Messner Brothers formed a big band which was based in New York, featured at the Park Central Hotel, the Hotel Lincoln, and toured the East Coast. In 1935, the Dick Messner band recorded for Melotone Records, and in 1937, the band disbanded when the other brothers—Bill, Charlie, Fred, and Dick—decided to quit the music business. In May 1937, Johnny Messner formed a new band and played at the Hotel McAlpin in New York for six months. The band's biggest selling record, *She Had to Go and Lose It at the Astor*, was recorded on the Varsity Record label. They also recorded for Decca, Bluebird, Vocalion, and Brunswick. The band's theme was "Can't We Be Friends." The band was heard via radio on the Fitch bandwagon and Spotlight bands shows. During WWII, Messner led various service bands and made a V-disc in 1945. In 1946, as a civilian once again, Johnny Messner reformed his band and returned to the Hotel McAlpin. After several months, the band took to the road, playing various venues in the New York–New Jersey area until the early '50s. Johnny Messner then disbanded and joined the Vincent Lopez Orchestra as saxophonist, singer, and arranger. In the mid-'60s, he resigned from the Lopez Orchestra and began writing commercial jingles. Johnny Messner wrote a number of tunes, including "Sing for Joy," "Catching the 802 Local," "Toy Piano Minuet," "Piano Roll Rock," and "Toy Piano Jump." Messner died in Ridgefield Park, New Jersey in January 1986.

RED NORVO

(Red Norvo and His Orchestra) Born in Beardstown, Illinois on March 31, 1908. Norvo played with Paul Whiteman as soloist in the late '20s and, by 1935, formed a sextet, which played in New York City at the Famous Door. The following year Norvo fronted a ten-piece band in Syracuse, New York at the Syracuse Hotel. At that time, his singer was Nancy Flake after which Red's wife, Mildred Bailey, took over the vocal chores. After leaving Syracuse, the band took an extended gig at the Blackhawk Restaurant in Chicago. At that time the trumpet player and arranger was Eddie Sauter. In 1938, the Red Norvo band played in New York City at the Commodore Hotel and featured drummer George Wettling. By 1939, after completing a stay at the Famous Door, the band was disbanded. After a short period of reorganization and a job at Tuckahoe's Murray's, the band broke up due to finances. Red Norvo enrolled in the Juilliard School of Music for a short time but organized another band in 1940 that had a short life. Late in 1941, Norvo formed a 16-piece band, featuring arrangements by Johnny Thompson and the girl vocalist Linda Keene, which made two records prior to the AF of M band on recordings and the WWII draft of all eligible men, which caused the breakup of the band. The band had some top sidemen, including John Kirby, Russell Procope, Eddie Sauter, Ralph Burns, Clyde Lombardi, Dave Barbour, Hank D'Amico, George Wettling, and Charlie Shavers. The Norvo band's theme song was "I Surrender, Dear." They recorded for Vocalion and Brunswick. Red then joined the Benny Goodman band until 1942 when Woody Herman hired him away. After playing with Herman's Woodchoppers, Norvo settled in Los Angeles. Red Norvo died in Santa Monica, California on April 6, 1999.

ARTIE SHAW

(Artie Shaw and His Orchestra) Born in New York City on May 23, 1910. Shaw was raised in Connecticut and began playing alto saxophone when he was 12. In his early teens he played in local bands. At age 15 he left home for Kentucky, where he hoped to get a job. Finding none he played with the Joe Cantor and Merle Jacobs bands on tour in order to get back home. He joined the Don "Johnny" Cavallaro Orchestra in New Haven, Connecticut and traveled with them to Florida on tour. In 1926, Shaw switched to clarinet and arranging and worked as the music director of the Austin Wylie band. He then played clarinet and tenor saxophone with the Irving Aronson Commanders. By 1929, he had moved to New York City, played with Willie "the Lion" Smith in Harlem at Pod's and Jerry's and sat in at various jam sessions. He then played on various record dates with Billie Holiday, Teddy Wilson, and the more commercial bands of Paul Specht, Roger Wolfe Kahn, and Vincent Lopez. By 1931, he was playing in the Red Nicols band at the Park Central Hotel. From 1931 until 1934, Shaw played with Fred Rich, again with Roger Wolfe Kahn, and freelanced in clubs, studios, and on record dates in New York City. In 1936, Shaw organized a band with strings for a date at the Imperial Theater that turned out to be very successful, enabling him to form a standard-instrumentation group for a debut in Boston and to fulfill a record date. By 1937, he hired Jerry Gray as arranger and the band recorded the highly successful *Begin the Beguine* which featured great sidemen, including Buddy Rich, drums; Tony Pastor, tenor saxophone; Georgie Auld, tenor saxophone; Cliff Leeman, drums; and Johnny Best, trumpet. During 1938, Billie Holiday was his singer followed by Helen Forrest and Kitty Kallen in 1939. The 1938 sidemen were Ronny Perry, Hank Freeman, Les Robinson, and Tony Pastor, saxophones; Chuck Peterson, Claude Bowen, and Johnny Best, trumpets; Harry Rogers, George Arus, and Russell Brown, trombones; Cliff Leeman, drums; Sid Weiss, bass; Al Avola, guitar; and Les Burness, piano. In 1939, Shaw appeared in the movie *Second Chorus* and he added a string section to his band and renamed the band the Gramercy Five. The band recorded a number of hits, including "Frenesi," "Summit Ridge Drive," "Concerto for Clarinet," and "Special Delivery Stomp." In 1942, Artie Shaw served in the U.S. Navy and formed a band that toured the South Pacific. In 1944, he received a medical discharge and formed a new band which included stars Roy Eldridge and Stan Fishelson, trumpets; Chuck Gentry, reeds; Dodo Marmarosa, piano; Barney Kessel, guitar; along with other top players of the day. In the late '40s, Shaw appeared in Carnegie Hall with the National Symphony Orchestra and toured with a big band. He formed several small groups in the early '50s prior to retiring from music to spend more time as a writer. Artie Shaw died in California in 2005.

BILLY McDONALD

(Billy McDonald and His Royal Highlanders) McDonald sang with the Carol Lofner band and on staff at CBS radio in Hollywood where he formed a trio, Three Midshipmen, during the late '30s. He then formed his own band and played in various venues on the West Coast and through the Midwest. The Billy McDonald Orchestra played in Honolulu, Hawaii in 1941 and was playing when the Japanese attacked Pearl Harbor on December 7. The theme song of the McDonald band was "Loch Lomond." The band recorded for Decca and D&S records. In 1942, after he returned to the mainland, McDonald joined the service. After WWII, McDonald resumed his career as a bandleader until 1948 when he disbanded and began a career as a booking agent with the Fredericks Brothers Agency. He later worked for William Morris and then moved to the Hollywood office of the Associated Booking Corporation.

DICK STABILE

(Dick Stabile and His Orchestra) Born in Newark, New Jersey on May 29, 1909. Stabile first played in various Broadway theater bands, including pit bands for Sunny and Captain Jinks in 1925. He played with the Ben Bernie band from 1928 until 1935 and formed his own group, Dick Stabile & His Saxophones in 1936 that recorded for Panachord Records. His first big band in 1936 was Dick Stabile and His Orchestra and included sidemen Eddie Farley, Bunny Berigan and Mike Riley. The singers were Paula Kelly and Burt Shaw. The band played at the World's Fair 1939–1940, and in several major hotels in New York City. At this time, the band recorded for ARC, Decca, Bluebird, and Vocalion/Okeh records. The Stabile band was heard on the radio shows *The American Can Company Show* and *The Chesterfield Show*. Stabile served in the U.S. Army beginning in 1942 and the female vocalist at the time, who was also his wife, Grace Barrie, fronted the band while Dick was in the service. After his release from the service at the end of the war, Stabile moved to Los Angeles, where he worked at Ciro's, recorded and did TV appearances with Dean Martin and Jerry Lewis. During the '50s and '60s, Stabile played with Vincent Lopez and Jimmy Dorsey. By the '70s, he was playing at the Hotel Roosevelt in New Orleans. Dick Stabile died in New Orleans, Louisiana, on September 18, 1980.

GAREWOOD VAN
(Garewood Van and His Orchestra) In the late '20s and early '30s, Van played with bands led by Victor Young, Eddie Oliver, Lennie Hayton, and Hal Grayson. In 1936, Garewood Van formed his own hotel orchestra in Los Angeles, California that played at various hotels, casinos, and resorts in the area. Singers in the early band were Gail Storm and Maxine Conrad. During the remainder of the '30s, the band played at the Florentine Gardens, Ciro's, and the Trocadero. In San Francisco, they appeared at the Mark Hopkins and St. Francis hotels; at the Hotel Utah in Salt Lake City; at the Chase Hotel in St. Louis; and at the Muehlebach Hotel in Kansas City. As they traveled on the East Coast, they played the Statler hotels. Prior to WWII, in the early '40s, the Garewood Van band played various venues in Las Vegas and following the war and during the '50s played in Vegas many times, including a five-year tenure at the Frontier Hotel Casino. The Van Orchestra recorded for Modern Records. Garewood Van retired in Las Vegas in 1962.

CHARLES BAUM
(Charlie Baum and His Orchestra) Baum studied piano in his youth and fronted his band in the mid '30s. It was reported that Baum's piano playing was of much higher quality than his bands. He was a much sought after studio pianist. The band was said to be a fine ballad orchestra but couldn't swing. There were no recordings of the Charlie Baum Orchestra listed and information about Baum and his band is scarce.

JERRY BLAINE

(Jerry Blaine and His Orchestra) Blaine formed his first band in the early '30s. The Jerry Blaine Orchestra toured, was heard on radio, and recorded for Bluebird Records, including tunes "The Big Dipper" and "The Snake Charmer." In 1937, the band's personnel included Fred Train, Buddy Pottle and George Schmidt, trumpets; Irving Broucke, Harry Roberts, Abe Markowitz and Tony Antonelli, saxophones; Jack Mattias, piano; Joel Livingston, guitar; Carl Tandberg, bass; and Eddie Ross, drums. The singers were Jerry Blaine, Johnny McKeever, and Phyllis Kenny. When Blaine disbanded and retired he founded the Jubilee Record Company. Blaine died on March 14, 1973.

LARRY CLINTON

(Larry Clinton and His Orchestra) Born in Brooklyn, New York on August 17, 1909. Clinton was a sideman and arranger for Ferde Grofé in 1932. During the mid-'30s, he wrote for Isham Jones, Glen Gray, Claude Hopkins, Bunny Berigan, and the Dorsey Brothers. He composed a number of tunes at that time, including "Satan Takes a Holiday," "The Big Dipper," "Bolero in Blue," "Study in Surrealism," "Study in Green," "Boogie Woogie Blues," "Whoa Babe," "My Silent Mood," "An Empty Ballroom," "Calypso Melody," and many others. In 1937, Clinton formed his band and recorded for Victor Records. He featured singer Bea Wain and some great jazz players, including Toots Mondello, Skeets Herfurt, Wolfe Tannenbaum, Tony Zimmers, and Babe Russin. That same year several of his tunes were broadcast on the *Hit Parade Show*, including "The Dipsy Doodle," "My Reverie," "Our Love," and "It Took a Million Years." The Larry Clinton Orchestra met with great popularity from 1939 to 1941, but was disbanded when Clinton went into military service due to WWII. When Clinton was discharged in the late '40s, he established a record and publishing business and was appointed the A&R director for Kapp Records. Clinton died on May 2, 1985.

AL COOPER

(Al Cooper and the Savoy Sultans) Born in 1911. Al Cooper (né: Lofton Alfonso Cooper) formed a co-op band that was owned by all the players, none of whom had contracts. Al Cooper formed the band from sidemen who had played with trumpet player Pat Jenkins at Club 101 in New York and at a New

Jersey Club named Harlem-on-the-Hudson. Willie Bryant and John Hammond heard the band and recommended them to the manager of Harlem's Savoy Ballroom, Charles Buchanan. They opened at the Savoy in 1937 and were immediately loved by the dancers there. The sidemen in the Cooper Sultans included Sam Massenberg, trumpet; George Kelly, tenor saxophone; Rudy Williams, alto saxophone; Razz Mitchell, drums; Grachan Moncur, bass; Cyril Haynes, piano; and Al Cooper, saxophone/clarinet/leader. In 1974, David "Panama" Francis formed a band modeled after Al Cooper's Savoy Sultans and they worked through the '90s. Cooper died in Florida on October 5, 1981.

SONNY DUNHAM

(Sonny Dunham and His Orchestra) Born in Brockton, Massachusetts on November 16, 1914. Sonny Dunham (né: Elmer Lewis Dunham) organized his first band in 1937 and named it Sonny Lee and the New York Yankees. Prior to that time the trumpeter-trombonist worked with the Paul Tremaine and Casa Loma Orchestra. When his first band failed he rejoined the Casa Loma Orchestra, where he played until 1940. At that time the theme song of the Casa Loma Orchestra was "Memories of You," the tune that became the theme song of the Sonny Dunham band later. The second band was successful due to the financial support of a trumpet-mouthpiece manufacturer who supported the band as it toured the nation seeking talented young trumpet players. During this tour Pete Candoli was discovered. Arranger George Williams and tenor saxophonist Corky Corcoran shared the spotlight with male vocalist Ray Kellogg. The female vocalist was Harriet Clark. In 1942, the Dunham band appeared in the movies *Off the Beaten Track* and *Behind the Eight Ball*. The Dunham band recorded for Vogue, Hit, and Bluebird records. In the early '50s, Dunham disbanded and played with Tommy Dorsey and Bernie Mann for a time. In the '60s, he retired to Miami where he freelanced and fronted bands occasionally. Although musicians praised the band, it never made a big hit with the audience. Dunham died in Florida on June 18, 1990.

LENNIE HAYTON

(Lennie Hayton and His Orchestra) Born in New York City on February 13, 1908. Hayton began studying piano at age six, and by 1926, he and Spencer Clark joined the Little Ramblers. After a year with the Ramblers, Hayton became the pianist with the Cass Hagen Orchestra and during 1928 and 1929 played with Paul Whiteman's band. During this period, Hayton worked dates with many famous musicians, including Miff Mole, Red Nichols, Joe Venuti, Frankie Trumbauer, Eddie Lang, and Bix Beiderbecke. Hayton formed a big band for a brief tenure in 1929, which made one recording, but it was not until 1939 that he fronted his new band in New York City, which had a staff of arrangers, including himself, Deane Kincaide, Bill Challis, and Fulton "Fidgey" McGrath. This band recorded extensively for Vocalion and Decca records. The sidemen included Bunny Shawker, Bill Graham, Bernie Friedland, Walter Mercurio, Dave Barbour, Wendell Delory, Mike Doty, George Jaffre, John Saola, John Dillard, Willard Brady, and Slats Long. He featured singers Linda Keene and Paul Barry. The theme song was "Times Square Scuttle." When Hayton disbanded in the early '40s, he went to Hollywood, where he was music director for Bing Crosby and recorded soundtracks for several MGM pictures. He won an Oscar for his scoring of the movie *On the Town*. Several years later, he married and served as music director for Lena Horne. Hayton died in Palm Springs, California on April 24, 1971.

TINY HILL

(Tiny Hill and His Orchestra) Born in Sullivan, Illinois on July 19, 1906. Tiny Hill (né: Harry Lawrence Hill) was raised by his grandparents and leaned to play banjo and drums while attending Sullivan Township High School in Fort Lupton, Colorado. Lack of funds forced him to drop out of Illinois State Normal University after two years, and he moved to Detroit, where he met an accordion player. In the late '20s, the two of them played for tips in various bars in the Detroit environs. In 1933, Tiny formed a band that he called Harry Hill and His Five Jacks that worked in the Decatur, Illinois area. Tiny continued to gain weight, and by 1934, he weighted more than 365 pounds. That year he disbanded the Five Jacks and joined a band led by Byron Dunbar. In 1935, he left the Dunbar band and formed a Fat Man's Band. After a year, he formed another band that toured, playing at various resorts, and included a long stay at the Ingleterra

Ballroom in Peoria, Illinois. By 1939, the band was heard regularly on radio from the Melody Mill Ballroom in North Riverside, Illinois. That year he recorded "Angry" for Columbia Records, which became the band's theme song and a big hit, and brought the attention of the band to a national audience. In 1943, the band played the *Lucky Strike Hit Parade* radio show, played on ABC's *Soldiers of Production Show* and appeared at the Green Room of the Hotel Edison. In 1945, the band worked at the Trianon and Aragon ballrooms in Chicago. In addition to Columbia Records, the band also recorded extensively for Decca and Vocalion. Tiny worked with many famous musicians and stars, including Muzzy Marcellano, Jack Benny, Ruth Dean, Beryl Davis, Tex Williams, Jimmy Wakely, Margaret Whiting, Eddy Dean, Marie Wilson, Tennessee Ernie Ford, Jerry Lewis and Dean Martin, Roy Rogers and Dale Evans, Fernando Lamas, Debbie Reynolds, and Dennis Morgan. The personnel for the 1965 Tiny Hill Orchestra were Don Carleton and Johnny Hnalko, trumpets; Jesse Stamm, trombone; Art Busch, Danny Windolph and James Van Ostenbridge, saxophones; and Lyle Todd and Rex Bell, drums. Hill died in 1972.

JOHN KIRBY

(John Kirby and His Sextet) Born in Baltimore, Maryland on December 31, 1908. In the early '30s, John Kirby played bass and worked in the Lucky Millinder band with Chick Webb, and with the Fletcher Henderson Orchestra. In 1937, he formed his sextet, which played primarily in greater New York City and which was comprised of the some of the top sidemen of the day: Russell Procope, saxophone; Spencer O'Neil, drums; Charlie Shavers, trumpet; Buster Bailey, clarinet; and Billy Kyle, piano. Kirby's wife, Maxine Sullivan, was the singer and was referred to as Miss Loch Loman. John Kirby recorded for Columbia, Okeh, Vocalion, and Decca records. Kirby died in Hollywood, California on June 14, 1952.

NYE MAYHEW

(Nye Mayhew and His Orchestra) The Mayhew Orchestra was organized in 1937, fronted by tenor saxophonist Nye Mayhew, and was reported to be an excellent organization backed by Hal Kemp with arrangements by John Scott Trotter. Among the band's stars was saxophonist Hugo Winterhalter. The band played extensively at the Hotel Pennsylvania and the Glen Island Casino. By the end of the '30s, the Nye Mayhew Orchestra disbanded for some unknown reason. The Nye Mayhew Orchestra recorded for Vocalion and Perfect records.

GLENN MILLER

(Glenn Miller and His Orchestra) Born in Clarinda, Iowa on March 1, 1904. When Miller (né: Alton Glenn Miller) was a teenager he studied music with Boyd Senter and at the University Of Colorado. After playing with various territory bands in 1926 and 1927, he joined the Ben Pollack Orchestra in 1928. During 1929 and 1930, he played with Paul Ash prior to joining the Red Nichols band in 1931. Moving to New York City in 1934, he became a studio musician, and in 1935, he joined the Dorsey Brothers Band as trombonist and arranger. When Ray Noble came to America, Miller assisted him in organizing his first American band and began to write reed voicings with clarinet lead over the saxophone section, which became his trademark sound later on. In 1937, Miller formed his first band, which proved unsuccessful although they recorded for Brunswick Records. Miller then formed a second band, which became very successful recording for Bluebird Records. The sidemen in that band included sax men Al Klink, Hal McIntyre, and Tex Beneke with singer Marion Hutton. Other sidemen who led their own bands later were Jerry Gray, Claude Thornhill, Charlie Spivak, Ray Anthony, and Billy May, The theme songs of the Miller Orchestra were "Slumber Song" and "Moonlight Serenade." The band also recorded for Victor and Decca Records. When WWII began Miller disbanded, joined the U.S. Army and assembled a big band for the U.S. Air Force. Miller was assumed dead on December 15, 1944, when a flight over the English Channel disappeared.

PHIL NAPOLEON

(Phil Napoleon and His Orchestra) Born in Boston, Massachusetts on September 2, 1901. In 1917, Phil Napoleon and pianist Frank Signorelli formed The Original Memphis Five. This band made many recordings throughout the '20s. The personnel were Napoleon, Frank Signorelli, Jimmy Lytell, Jack Roth, and Charlie Parnelli. Phil also played with McKinney's Cotton Pickers and the Sam Lanin Orchestra. In 1937, Napoleon formed his first big band and Walter

Bloom became his manager. In the early '40s, he joined the Dorsey Brothers and worked as a studio musician in the New York Studios. In 1946, he joined Jimmy Dorsey's band in Los Angeles, California and appeared in the movie *Four Jills and a Jeep* with the band. In 1947, he returned to New York and to his job as a studio musician with NBC. In 1950, he played with a small group at Nick's in New York until the late '50s when he moved to Miami, Florida where he fronted Dixieland groups. Napoleon died in Miami, Florida on September 30, 1990.

LEIGHTON NOBLE

(Leighton Noble and His Orchestra) Born in Pasadena, California on December 25, 1912. Leighton Noble (né: Faye Leighton Jepsen) was taught piano by his mother and sister when he was a child. When Noble was in high school, he organized his first band, the Blue Blazers, and led a college band at Pasadena City College. He won a singing contest held by the Coconut Grove Ballroom in Los Angeles, which was inspired by Phil Harris in order to drum up interest in his new band that was performing at the Ambassador Hotel. Noble's prize for winning was a week-long appearance as vocalist with the Phil Harris Orchestra. During that week, bandleader Hal Grayson offered Noble a job. Noble left the Grayson Orchestra after several months to join the George Hamilton Orchestra that was playing in Los Angeles at the Biltmore Hotel. At this time, Noble also appeared in the movie *Gift of Gab*. Everett Hoagland, who was leading a great band that included pianist Stan Kenton and drummer Spike Jones, offered Noble a job, which he accepted and stayed for nearly a year. In late 1935, Noble joined Orville Knapp's band. When Knapp was killed in a plane crash in 1936, Noble assumed the leadership until 1937 when he and several other band members left to form the Leighton Noble Orchestra. The new band worked from the East Coast playing at the Biltmore and Essex hotels in New York City and the Arcadia Restaurant in Philadelphia. In 1940, Noble took the band to the West Coast where he was eventually rejected for military service and devoted much of his time to USO appearances, including dates at the Stagedoor Canteen in Hollywood. From 1947 to 1952, the band hosted a TV show in Los Angeles featuring stars like pianist Liberace from time to time. In 1957, the Noble Orchestra served as house band at Harrah's Casino in Las Vegas. In 1970, Noble retired moving to British Columbia. During the life of the Leighton Noble

Orchestra, recordings were made for Coral and Vocalion Records. The band's theme song was "I'll See You in My Dreams." Noble's band appeared in many movies, including *There's No Business Like Show Business*, *White Christmas*, *Crazy House*, and *It Ain't Hay*. Noble died on March 5, 1994.

RAY PEARL

(Ray Pearl and His Orchestra) Born on July 24, 1913. After playing in several groups, Pearl formed his first band in Pennsylvania in 1937. The band toured the country, playing extended engagements in Santa Monica, California and at Janzen Beach in Portland, Oregon. After WW II, where Pearl served in the U.S. Army, the band was reorganized and worked at the Melody Mill in Chicago, Illinois. The band made almost two-dozen commercial records as well as a number of transcriptions. Pearl played in Memphis at the Peabody Hotel in 1956 and retired soon after. The Pearl Orchestra had a number of sidemen, including Walter Bloom, Memo Bernabei, Bob Berkey, Sully Walker, Nicky Barile, Buddy Madison, and Walter Link. The most well-known singer was Jean Gordon. The band's theme song was "A Kiss from Me to You."

VAN ALEXANDER

(Van Alexander and His Orchestra) Born in New York City on May 2, 1915. Van Alexander (né: Al Feldman) attended Columbia University and worked for Chick Webb's band in the '30s, where he wrote and arranged "A-Tisket, A-Tasket" for Ella Fitzgerald. In 1938, he left Webb, formed his own band, moved to the West Coast, and arranged and composed for television and movies. The personnel of the Van Alexander band included Si Zentner, Dick Raymong, Ted Nash, Bill Schallen, Shelly Manne, Arnold Fishkind, Irv Cottler, Don Lamond, "Butch" Stone, Charlie Shavers, Ray Barr, "Slam" Stewart, Neal Hefti, and Alvin Stoller. The singers were Phyllis Kenny, David Allen, and "Butch" Stone. The theme song of the Van Alexander band was "Alexander's Swinging." He also composed "I Close My Eyes" and "Got a Pebble in My Shoe." In the mid '40s, he disbanded but continued to write for television and movies scoring for *Andy Hardy Comes Home*, *Straight Jacket*, and *Baby Face Nelson*. He recorded for Victor, Varsity, Bluebird, and Capitol records.

ALBERT AMMONS

(Albert Ammons and His Port of Harlem Jazzmen) Born in Chicago, Illinois in 1907. Ammons studied piano as a child and began playing in small groups and as a soloist in the '20s. During the '30s, he played with the Louis Bank band until 1938 when he moved to New York where he formed his own group. During his New York tenure, he played often with Pete Johnson and Meade Lux Lewis in the boogie-woogie style of the time. Later Johnson and Ammons formed a combo that worked in New York clubs for more than five years, including a long engagement at Café Society Downtown. As Ammons began to age, his son Gene (Jug) Ammons (tenor saxophonist) replaced him on various gigs that had been booked by his father. Ammons died in Chicago, Illinois on December 5, 1949.

LES BROWN

(Les Brown and His Band of Renown) Born in Reinerton, Pennsylvania on March 14, 1912. Les Brown (né: Lester Raymond Brown) was the son of a musician and baker, who played soprano saxophone in a saxophone quartet and taught Les when he was a child. Brown organized his first band, the Royal Seretadore, when he was 14 years old. He entered the Ithaca Conservatory of Music and studied clarinet. He then matriculated at Duke University, where he played with the Duke Blue Devils band for four years, assuming the leadership during the last two years. When the Blue Devils broke up, Brown arranged for Larry Clinton, Isham Jones, Jimmy Dorsey, Red Nichols, and others prior to putting together his first out-of-college band. When the recording strike ended the new band recorded a hit, "Joltin' Joe DiMaggio," which brought positive notoriety to the band. His singer-saxophonist, Butch Stone, and singer Doris Day received national attention; the

Brown recording of "Sentimental Journey" became the number one song in the U.S. for 16 weeks and remained on the *Hit Parade* for many months. Some of the sidemen in the Les Brown band included Frank Comstock, Shelley Manne, Milt Bernhart, Wes Hensel, Dave Pell, Buddy Childers, Jimmy Rowles, Warren Covington, Stumpy Brown, Ted Nash, Randy Brooks, Hal McKusick, Jimmy Zito, Frank Comstock, Ray Linn, Billy Butterfield, Don Jacoby, Si Zentner, and many others. In addition to Doris Day, many singers appeared with the Band of Renown, including Jo Ann Greer, Lucy Ann Polk, Ray Kellogg, Eileen Wilson, Ralph Young, Betty Bonney, and Miriam Shaw. The Brown band was seen and heard on the *Bob Hope Show*, *Spotlight Bands*, *The Fitch Bandwagon*, *The Dean Martin Show*, and *The Rowan and Martin Show*. The band's theme song was "Leap Frog." At the time of Brown's death, the band of Renown still played about 60 gigs a year. Brown's reputation was chiseled in stone due to his affiliation with Bob Hope and his show for more than 50 years. Brown recorded on Coral, Decca, Columbia, Bluebird, and Okeh records. Brown died on January 4, 2001.

SONNY BURKE

(Sonny Burke and His Orchestra) Born in Scanton, Pennsylvania on March 22, 1914. Sonny Burke (né: Joseph Francis Burke) studied piano and violin when he was a child and played in various dance bands while in high school. While attending Duke University, Burke formed his first band and John Hammond, having heard the band, encouraged him to bring the band to New York City, where they played at the Roseland Ballroom. By this time, Sonny Burke had switched to vibes and arranging. Some of Burke's sidemen were Conrad Gozzo, Eddie Webb, Paul Tanner, Milt Bernhart, Milt Raskin, Harry Gozzard, Eddie Webb, Charlie Shavers, Si Zentner, Ray Conniff, and Mitch Paul. The band recorded for Okeh, Decca, and Vocalion Records. Featured singers were Jo Ann Greer and Don Burke. The theme song of the Burke Orchestra was "Blue Sonata." When Gene Krupa hired Sam Donahue, Burke took over Donahue's band, but when Donahue left the Krupa band, he got his old band back by vote of the band. Sonny Burke moved to California and began arranging and conducting for television and writing for bands headed by Charlie Spivak and Jimmy Dorsey. After a time, he also became the music director for Reprise and Warner Brothers records, handling Frank Sinatra's releases. He was later the president of the Daybreak Record Company. Burke died on May 31, 1980.

ERSKINE BUTTERFIELD

(Erskine Butterfield and His Orchestra) Born in Syracuse, New York on February 19, 1913. Pianist-singer Butterfield formed his first band in 1938 and toured the East Coast. Later, while touring the Midwest, the band did a number of radio broadcasts and was signed by Decca Records. Some of the recorded tunes were "Blackberry Jam," "Missouri Waltz," "Salt Butter," "Lovin' Man," and "Because of You." Outstanding sidemen included Jerry Jerome, Yank Lawson, Sal Franzella, and Jimmy Lytell. Still active in the '50s, Butterfield's band continued to record for Decca and Guild Records and appeared on various television shows, including *The Jo Stafford Show*, *The Tony Martin Program*, and *The Nat King Cole Show*. Butterfield died in New York City on July 11, 1961.

SKINNAY ENNIS

(Skinnay Ennis and His Orchestra) Born in Salisbury, North Carolina on August 13, 1909. Skinnary Ennis (né: Robert Ennis) was attending the University of North Carolina when he met Hal Kemp who induced him to become a drummer with Kemp's band. Kemp discovered that Ennis had a breathless way of singing and encouraged him to sing with the band. Before long, the band recorded "Got a Date with an Angel," featuring the voice of Skinnay Ennis. "The Angel Tune" met with great success and became the theme song for the Kemp band. In 1938, Ennis left the Hal Kemp Orchestra and formed his own band that quickly became the official orchestra for *The Bob Hope Show* in Los Angeles and *The Abbott and Costello Camel Show*. Hal Kemp's arranger, John Scott Trotter, left the Kemp band at the same time to become the music director for Bing Crosby. Ennis began playing coast-to-coast and hired singer Janet Blair. Blair eventually left the band and became a famous actress in Hollywood. During WWII, Ennis served in the military, returning to the *Bob Hope Show* on his release from the service. From 1948 until the '50s, the Skinnay Ennis Orchestra toured the Western part of the U.S., played the *Abbott and Costello Show*, and appeared in several movies, including *Follow the band*. During that time, the Ennis band recorded a number of hits, including "Garden of the Moon," "Oh, But I Do," and "Deep in a Dream." The Ennis band recorded for Phillips, Victor, and Signature records. Ennis died in Beverly Hills, California on June 3, 1963.

CHUCK FOSTER

(Chuck Foster and His Orchestra) Born in Jeanette, Pennsylvania on August 26, 1912. Chuck Foster (né: Chuck Fody) organized his first band on the West Coast and toured the Midwest. In the '60s and '70s, the band played west of Chicago, Illinois at the Melody Hill Ballroom, the Biltmore Bowl in Los Angeles, the Peabody Hotel in Memphis, the Roosevelt in New Orleans, the Muehlbach Hotel in Kansas City, and the Aragon Ballroom and the Blackhawk Restaurant in Chicago. The band was labeled "Music in the Foster Fashion" and the theme song was "Oh, You Beautiful Doll." The featured vocalists were Jean Gordon, Dotty Dotson, Dorothy Brandon, and Jimmy Castle. The Foster band recorded for Phillips, Okeh, and Mercury records. Foster wrote the tune "I've Been Drafted, Now I'm Drafting You."

DON GLASSER

(Don Glasser and His Orchestra) Glasser worked with bands led by Art Kassell, Ray Pearl, and Jerry Gray and organized his first band in Derry, Pennsylvania. Eventually, the Glasser Orchestra was based in Chicago, Illinois and toured extensively in the Midwest playing various venues, including the Club in Birmingham, Alabama, the Peabody Hotel in Memphis, Tennessee and as far northeast as the Roseland Ballroom in New York City. Glasser's band featured singers Roger Lopez and Lois Costello. The theme song of the Don Glasser band was "You Call It Madness, I Call It Love." Glasser wrote "I Saw Both Ends of a Rainbow," and "Hey, Pretty Legs." Glasser and his wife, Lois Costello, moved to Florida in the '90s where Glasser had a stroke and Lois leads the band on various state and countrywide tours.

COLEMAN HAWKINS

(Coleman Hawkins and His Orchestra) Born in St. Joseph, Missouri on November 24, 1904. Hawkins played tenor saxophone in the Fletcher Henderson Orchestra from 1924 to 1934, played overseas for five years, and formed his own short-lived band in 1939. He was considered one of the finest musicians of his time and was associated with the tune "Body and Soul" which he played magnificently and became his theme song, along with "Honeysuckle Rose." He recorded for Savoy, Decca, Bluebird, and Apollo records. Hawkins died in New York City on May 19, 1969.

EVERETT HOAGLAND

(Everett Hoagland and His Orchestra) Hoagland played clarinet and led his first band in the '20s, which featured Stan Kenton, his piano player and arranger. In the '30s, after serving as the head music arranger for RKO in Hollywood, Hoagland formed a new band, which was backed MCA, with George Mayes from Orville Knapp's Orchestra.

WILL HUDSON

(Will Hudson and His Orchestra) Born in Barstow, California on March 8. 1908. The theme song of the Hudson Orchestra was "Hobo on Park Avenue." Hudson began as a composer writing for many bands in the late '20s, including McKinney's Cotton Pickers, Erskine Tate, Earl "Fatha" Hines, Jimmy Lunceford, Ina Ray Hutton, Fletcher Henderson, Don Redman, and Cab Calloway. When Hudson's family moved to Detroit, Michigan in the mid-'30s, he formed his first band. From 1936 to 1938, Hudson and Eddie DeLange formed a band but the two severed relations in 1938. In 1939, Hudson formed the Will Hudson Orchestra but disbanded at the end of 1940. In 1941, Hudson and DeLange again formed a band that was disbanded shortly after. During their tenure together Hudson and De Lange wrote a number of tunes, including "Moonglow," "Deep in a Dream," "Remember When," "Sophisticated Swing," "Love Song of a Half-Wit," "Organ Grinder's Swing," "Eight Bars in Search of a Melody," and "Monopoly Swing." Irving Mills published most of their music and much of it was recorded on the Master Records label. The Hudson band recorded for Brunswick, Master, and Decca records. After WWII, Hudson studied composition at the Juilliard School in New York. He was relatively musically inactive after the '50s. Hudson died in South Carolina in 1981.

LOUIS JORDAN

(Louis Jordan and His Tympani Five) Born in Brinkley, Arizona on July 8, 1908. Louis Jordan (né: Louis Thomas Jordan) played clarinet in the Chick Webb band in the early '30s. When Webb died, Jordan remained as Ella Fitzgerald assumed the leadership of the band. In 1938, he formed his first band, which he called Louis Jordan and His Tympani Five. The band played at a small club in Harlem, Elk's Rendezvous, and began recording for Decca Records. In the early '40s, they recorded hits "Caldonia," "Five Guys Names Mo," "Choo Choo Ch'boogie," "I'm Gonna Move to the Outskirts of Town," "Don't Let the Sun Catch You Crying," and "Early in the Morning." The Tympani Five was considered the top R&B group in the '40s and were in the number one position on Billboard for 28 weeks. Many consider Jordan to be the forefather of rock 'n' roll. Jordan died in Los Angeles, California on February 4, 1975.

MILTON LARKINS

(Milton Larkins and His Orchestra) Born in Houston, Texas on October 10, 1910. Larkins, who sang and played both trumpet and trombone, was a self-taught musician who played with Chester Boone in the mid-'30s and led a group of musicians in Chicago in 1938 that included some of the top musicians of the day. Saxophonists Arnett Cobb and Illinois Jacquet and trumpeter Wild Bill Davis were members of the Milton Larkin's Orchestra at that time. In 1943, he started playing trombone in an army band and reformed his earlier band when he was released in 1946. He toured until 1956 when he settled in New York City and worked at the Celebrity Club, fronting his six-piece group. In the mid-'70s, he retired and returned to Houston.

MUZZY MARCELLINO

(Muzzy Marcellino and His Orchestra) Born in San Francisco. As a child, Muzzy Marcellino studied guitar and violin in San Francisco and, by 1932, was playing with the Lofner-Harris Orchestra in the St. Francis Hotel in San Francisco where he began singing as well. In 1935, he joined the Ted Fio Rito band and appeared in several motion pictures with the band, including *Twenty Million Sweethearts*, *The Sweetheart of Sigma Chi*, and *Broadway Gondolier*. In 1938, Marcellino formed his own band and worked at Topsy's Restaurant in San Francisco. His female singer was Gloria De Haven, who later sang with bands led by Jan Savitt and Bob Crosby before becoming a Hollywood star. From 1938 to 1948 the Marcellino Orchestra played colleges, hotels, dance halls, and other venues, including the Florentine Gardens in Hollywood. His band's theme song was "I'll Take an Option on You." Marcellino was also an accomplished whistler in addition to his playing and singing ability and did a lot of whistle gigs for movies, recording companies, and ad agencies. In 1948, Marcellino disbanded his road band, but continued working with local outfits in the Los Angeles area and Reno and Las Vegas, Nevada. He also served as music director for the *Art Linkletter Show* from 1950 until 1969.

ART MOONEY

(Art Mooney and His Orchestra) Mooney formed his first band in Detroit in the mid '30s. He served in the U.S. Army in WW II and, on his release, fronted his best newly formed band that featured singer Fran Warren. In late '40s, the band recorded the hit "I'm Looking Over a Four Leaf Clover That I Overlooked Before." He featured arrangements by George Williams, Jimmy Mundy, and Neal Hefti. In the '50, the band did a lot of unison singing with banjo and had another hit with the theme "Sunset to Sunrise." Although the bands popularity waned they continued to tour through the '60s and '70s. From 1973 to 1974, the Art Mooney Orchestra toured with the Big band Cavalcade. During the life of the Art Mooney Orchestra, records were made for MGM and Victor records. Mooney died in Florida on May 21, 1973.

SPUD MURPHY

(Spud Murphy and His Orchestra) Born in Salt Lake City, Utah on August 19, 1908. Spud Murphy (né: Lyle Murphy) began his professional career playing clarinet in the Jimmy Joy Orchestra while cruising to China in the late '20s. After a short stint with the Ross Gorman band in 1928 he wrote arrangements for the Tracy-Brown Orchestra. From 1930 to 1931 Murphy was the saxo-phonist, clarinetist, and arranger for the Austin-Wylie Orchestra and from 1931 to 1932 worked with Jan Garber. By 1933, he was playing with Mal Hallett and with Joe Haymes in 1934. He arranged for many of the great big bands in the mid-'30s, including Glen Gray and Benny Goodman. From 1938 through 1941, Murphy fronted his own orchestra while writing music for films, including the early cartoons produced by Walt Disney, and arranging for bands led by Segar Ellis and Fletcher Henderson. The theme song of the Spud Murphy Orchestra was "Ecstasy." His singers were Clyde Rogers and Lucy Ann Mathews. In 1940, Murphy hosted a weekly jazz program on WJZ in New York City. In 1941, he moved to Hollywood, developed a unique 12-tone system and taught students, including Gerald Wiggins, Alvin Stoller, Oscar Peterson, and Curtis Counce. In the mid-'50s, Murphy headed jazz groups that worked in Southern California.

DAVID ROSE

(David Rose and His Orchestra) Born in London, England on June 15, 1910. When David was four years old his family moved to the U.S. and he began to study music. While attending the Chicago Musical College at age 16, he left to become a member of the Ted Fio Rito Orchestra. At age 19, he became a pianist, composer, and arranger for NBC radio. In 1936, he wrote the arrangement of "It's Been So Long" for the Benny Goodman recording of the tune. He resigned from NBC in 1938, moved to Hollywood, formed his first orchestra, and was featured on the *California Melodies* program on the Mutual Broadcasting System. That same year, he married actress Martha Raye and backed her on her recording of "Melancholy Mood." That marriage was dissolved after a brief time. He married Judy Garland in 1941 and was named the music director for *The Bob Hope Show* that ran through 1945. During WWII, Rose became a composer and conductor for the U.S. Army and was featured in the Army Air Force musical *Winged Victory* that was filmed in 1944. Rose had a number of hit records, including "Holiday for Strings" (1943) and "Poinciana" (1944). After WWII, he was heard on the *Red Skelton* radio program and was with Red when television became popular. David Rose received several Emmy awards for the television shows *An Evening with Fred Astaire*, *Little House on the Prairie*, and *Bonanza*. Rose died in Burbank, California on August 23, 1990.

ARTHUR ROSEBERRY

(Arthur Roseberry and His Kit Cat Club Dance Band) Roseberry first organized a band in the late '20s that worked at the Kit Cat Club in London. The London office of MCA was informed of the excellent reputation of the band and booked it into the Dolphin Square Restaurant in the early to mid-'30s. By 1938, MCA booked the Roseberry band into the Paradise Club and, according to the English magazine *Melody Maker* (the equivalent to *Down Beat*), Roseberry was fronting "the best swing band in town." It was reported that Roseberry personally trained all of the musicians. When the Paradise Club closed in 1939, Roseberry disbanded.

BENNY STRONG

(Benny Strong and His Orchestra) Born in Chicago, Illinois on March 17, 1911. While a teenager, Strong became a singer in vaudeville when Paul Ashe discovered him while singing at a political convention in Chicago. Ashe brought Benny into his show at the Oriental Theater. When Strong reached puberty his voice changed and he studied drums and tap dancing. In 1938, Strong organized his own band and began playing at the Brown Hotel in Louisville, Kentucky. While fulfilling a three-year engagement, the band played radio broadcasts that drew great popularity to the band throughout the Midwest. During WWII, Strong was drafted and served in the military. Upon his release in 1946 he organized a new band and continued to play the golden oldies. Among other venues, the Stevens Hotel in Chicago gave the band an opportunity to play many remote ballroom television pickups. During one of these programs, the band was seen on live television at the Trianon Ballroom in South Gate, California. By the late '50s, Strong had disbanded and become the manager for a radio station in San Francisco. After serving in that same capacity for a station in Hollywood in the early '60s, he formed a new band that played in various venues in the California area.

MAREK WEBER

(Marek Weber and His Orchestra) Weber was born in Austria and studied violin in Vienna and Berlin. By age 17, he was playing and conducting for a hotel orchestra in Berlin that specialized in performing Viennese waltz tunes. He immigrated to the U.S. where he had immediate success in recordings and radio. Weber recorded for Victor, Decca, Vocalion, and Columbia records. From 1938 to 1939, he served as conductor for *The Contented Hour*, a radio show sponsored by Carnation Brand Condensed Milk. Weber continued to be active into the '40s and became an angel to the Indiana School of Music when he donated his violins and established several scholarships for talented students.

PERCY FAITH

(Percy Faith and His Orchestra) Born in Toronto, Canada on April 7, 1908. Faith was a composer, arranger, pianist, and conductor who was a piano prodigy and by 15 had played a recital at Massey Hall in Toronto. He decided not to pursue a concert career and played for silent movies prior to injuring his hands in a fire in 1926. By 1927, he had become a serious composer and arranger writing for various hotel bands and for radio. The Canadian Broadcasting System was playing music by Faith from 1938 to 1940. He was offered a job with NBC and moved to New York City in 1940, where he conducted and arranged for a number of radio shows, including *The Coca Cola Show*, *The Buddy Clark Show*, and *The Carnation Contented Hour*. At that time he was recording for Victor and Decca records. In 1950, he became a composer and arranger for Columbia Records and wrote "My Heart Cries for You," which was recorded by Guy Mitchell. In 1952, he wrote and produced several hits, including "The Song from the Moulin Rouge" and "Delicado." In the '60s, Percy Faith wrote "Perpetual Notion," "Nervous Gavotte," and "Noche Carib," and was involved in movies like *Love Me or Leave Me*, *Tammy Tell Me True*, *The Love Goddesses*, *The Oscar*, *The Third Day*, and *I'd Rather Be Rich*. Faith died in Encino, California on February 9, 1976.

GENE KRUPA

(Gene Krupa and His Orchestra) Born in Chicago, Illinois on January 15, 1909. Gene Krupa (né: Eugene Krupa) was encouraged to study for the priesthood by his mother but decided to study music. When Krupa was quite young he studied percussion with Roy C. Knapp and spent a lot of time listening to the great drummers of the time: Zutty Singleton, Baby Dodds, and Tubby Hall. While still in his teens, he played with various dance bands in the Chicago area, including bands led by Al Gale, Joe Kayser, and the Benson Orchestra. When Gene was 18, he cut his first record with Eddie Condon's band which was fronted by Red Mckenzie. In 1929, he moved to New York City with Eddie Condon and played in theater bands led by Red Nichols. There were many famous sidemen in those bands, including Benny Goodman and Glenn Miller. During the early '30s, he played with bands led by Russ Columbo, Buddy Rogers, and Mal Hallett. In 1934, he joined the Benny Goodman Orchestra and they recorded "Sing, Sing, Sing," which became a national favorite. Krupa and Dave Tough are credited with stabilizing the size of the drum set (bass drum, snare drum, tom-tom, floor tom, hi-hat, and two to five suspended cymbals) during that period. Shortly after the famous Carnegie Hall Concert in 1938, Benny Gooman and Gene Krupa had a spat and Gene left Goodman's band to form his own big band that opened at the Marine Ballroom on the Atlantic City Steel Pier. The personnel in that first band included Milton Raskin, piano; Horace Rollins, bass, Ray Biondo, guitar; Dalton Rizzotto, Bruce Squires and Toby Tyler, trombones; Tom Goslin, C. Frankhauser, and Nick Prospero, trumpets. The singers were Irene Daye and Leo Watson. By 1941, Roy Eldrige and singer Anita O'Day had joined the band. In 1942, Krupa disbanded and rejoined the Goodman band that was touring various Army bases. Joining the Tommy Dorsey band during an engagement at the Paramount Theater in New York City, Krupa's fans welcomed him with open arms and convinced him to form a new band. By the end of the '40s, Krupa had a staff of wonderful arrangers, including Gerry Mulligan and first-class soloists like Red Rodney, Charlie Ventura, and Don Fagerquist. In 1951, Krupa disbanded and eventually formed a quartet, toured with Jazz at the Philharmonic, and operated a drum school with Cozy Cole. By the '60s, his health started to fail as he contracted leukemia and heart trouble. Krupa died in Yonkers, New York on October 16, 1973.

HAL LEONARD

(Hal Leonard and His Orchestra) Hal Leonard (né: Harold Edstrom) formed his band together with his brother, Everett Leonard Edstrom, in the late '30s in Chicago. A friend, Roger Busdicker, was also an original member of the band. When WWII began, Leonard and his brother disbanded to enter the service. When the war was over Hal and Roger became directors of high school bands while Everett reformed the original band and took it on the road under the name of the Hal Leonard Orchestra. During the same period, Everett founded a music store in Chicago. When the band disbanded, the two brothers, Hal and Everett, and their friend Roger set up a business selling popular music arrangements to various school bands. The original publishing company was formed in 1946. In 1985, Keith Mardak, the current president of the Hal Leonard Corporation, bought the world's largest corporation in the music print industry.

VING MERLIN

(Ving Merlin and the All-Girl Band) The Ving Merlin band was formed in the late '30s. Little is known of the band other than the fact that the harpist was Daphne Hellman. When the All-Girl Band disbanded, Hellman played at the

Village Gate in New York City for 30 years. When her tenure at the Gate was over, she worked at the Ballroom and the Café Figaro. She also played in the 59th Street subway station for many years.

SUNSET ROYAL SERENADERS

(Sunset Royal Serenaders) During the 1930s, the Serenaders were formed in Florida. The owner of the Savoy Ballroom in New York City, Moe Gale, asked Doc Wheeler from Indiana to take control of the band. The band was floundering and Wheeler had considerable experience as a trombonist and music director for several stars, including Ethel Waters. Wheeler brought the band to New York City where it opened at the Savoy Ballroom and eventually went on tour with the Ink Spots. Tommy Dorsey first heard the arrangement of Irving Berlin's "Marie" played by the Sunset Royal Serenaders, the arrangement which catapulted Dorsey to international fame. In the early '40s, the Serenaders recorded several records for Bluebird Records, including "Who Threw the Whiskey in the Well" and "Sorghum Switch."

WILL BRADLEY

(Will Bradley and His Orchestra) Born in Newport, New Jersey on July 12, 1910. Will Bradley (né: Wilbur Schwictenberg) studied trombone in his youth and played in various studio bands, including those led by Victor Young, Raymond Paige, Nat Shilkret, and Jacques Renard. In the early '30s, he joined the Milt Shaw band and met Ray McKinley, who later became the featured drummer in Bradley's first band. By 1935, Bradley was hired by Glenn Miller to play in the Ray Noble Orchestra, which he left after a year to return to studio work. Willard Alexander, who was working for the Walter Morris Talent Agency, suggested that Bradley form his own band, which he did in 1939. Bradley hired Ray McKinley, arrangers Leonard Whitney and Hugo Winterhalter, clarinetist Peanuts Hucko, and pianist Freddie Slack as the nucleus of the band and signed a recording contract with Vocalion/Okeh Records. The band's first appearance was at the Roseland State Ballroom in Boston. Bradley, Jimmy Valentine, Phyllis Miles, and Carlotta Dale handled the vocals. The band's biggest hit, "Celery Stalks at Midnight," was recorded in early 1940 and by the summer of '40 the band played in New York City at the

Famous Door. The Bradley band developed a boogie-woogie style and recorded "Beat Me Daddy," "Eight to the Bar," "Rack-a-Bye Boogie," "Scrub Me, Mama," and "Bounce Me Brother" with a solid four. Ray McKinley and Freddie Slack left the Bradley band in 1942 to form their own bands, leaving Bradley to reform his band. In the reformation, Bradley hired top-notch sidemen like Shelly Manne, drums, and Shorty Rogers, trumpet. Other featured sidemen remaining with the band were pianist Billy Maxted and trumpeter Pete Candoli. The singers were Lynn Gardner and Terry Allen. The theme songs of the Bradley Orchestra were "Strange Cargo," "Fatal Fascination," and "Think of Me." The band ultimately recorded for Beacon/Celebrity and RCA Vicor records. When Bradley disbanded his big band in 1944, he organized a six-piece group called Will Bradley and His Boogie-Woogie Boys. When Bradley retired as bandleader, he worked as a studio musician and played in the *Tonight Show* band on television. He died in 1989.

BOBBY BYRNE

(Bobby Byrne and His Orchestra) Born in Columbus, Ohio on October 10, 1918. Byrne grew up in Detroit. Byrne studied trombone in high school and with his father, who was a music teacher. While still in his teens, Byrne played with the Dorsey Brothers Orchestra. In 1935, when the Dorsey Brothers Orchestra disbanded because of a disagreement between Tommy and Jimmy Dorsey, Byrne replaced Tommy in the new orchestra that was led by Jimmy Dorsey. The band became a huge success playing on the Bing Crosby radio show. In mid 1939, Byrne left the Jimmy Dorsey Orchestra to form his own band. The band featured the tune "Danny Boy" (which became their theme song) and "My Colleen," which was written by Byrne. In 1941, the Byrne band worked at the Glen Island Casino and broadcasted regularly from Frank Dailey's Meadowbrook Ballroom. Singers with the Byrne band included Jimmy Palmer and Dorothy Claire. They recorded for Decca Records. The band was reaching its peak in popularity as Byrne was drafted in WWII. After the war, and although Byrne had reorganized his band after his discharge, the demand for big bands dwindled and Byrne disbanded to work as a studio musician doing record dates, radio, and television shows. He was featured from 1952 to 1954 leading the band on *The Steve Allen Show*. In the early '70s, Byrne retired from music and went into business.

CHUCK CABOT

(Chuck Cabot and His Orchestra) Born in San Fernando, California. Cabot listened to Dixieland, Latin, and swing music as a youngster growing up in San Fernando, California. The Chuck Cabot Orchestra began playing at the University of Southen California in the late '30s, but it was not until Kay Kyser asked his Fitch Bandwagon audience to listen to the Smooth Sounds of Chuck Cabot in September 1940 that many people were aware of the existence of the Cabot band. After the Kyser broadcast, the Cabot Orchestra toured from coast to coast playing extended engagements at the Roosevelt Hotel in New Orleans and at the Peabody Hotel in Memphis. Singers featured with the band were Cabot and Beth Harmon. Other featured performers were John Davenport, Babe Browman, and Cliff Olson. The Chuck Cabot Orchestra recorded for De Ville Records.

JOHNNY CATRON

(Johnny Catron and His Orchestra) Born in Henryetta, Oklahoma on September 24, 1916. Catron led his first band in the late '30s. He disbanded in 1941 and joined the Ben Pollack Orchestra. While with Pollack he began arranging and writing songs. When he began to work for the Union Oil Company in radio, he became the chief arranger. After WWII, Catron was not able to raise enough money to form a new band and took a job in Pomona, California working for a Volkswagen dealership. His loves were writing music and selling cars. His band's theme songs were "Love Day" and "Just a Memory." Many years later he wrote for a California radio station, KFI, which featured Freddy Martin and Lawrence Welk. Catron recorded for Nortac Records. Catron wrote many songs, including the "Volkswagen Song Polka," "There's a Time and a Place for Everything," "Valerie," "Why Did I Let Christmas Get Away from Me?," and a "Little Affection." After President John F. Kennedy was assassinated in Dallas, Texas in 1964, Catron wrote a song entitled "The Big D."

CARMEN CAVALLARO

(Carmen Cavallaro and His Orchestra) Born in New York City on May 6, 1913. Cavallaro studied classical piano as a young boy and played serious concerts while he was a teenager. In the '30s, he became interested in popular music and played piano with the Al Kavelin Orchestra in 1933. In 1937, he joined the

Rudy Vallée Orchestra and played for a brief time with Abe Lyman and Enric Madriguera. In 1939, Carmen Cavallaro formed his own band in St. Louis, Missouri and traveled extensively, including an extended engagement at the Mark Hopkins Hotel in San Fransciso. The Cavallaro band signed a contract with Decca Records and recorded many hits. Cavallaro became known as "the Poet of the Piano." In 1944, the Cavallaro Orchestra was seen in the movie *Hollywood Canteen*. In 1956, Cavallaro recorded the sound track for the movie *The Eddie Duchin Story* and, by the mid-'60s, sold more than a million copies of the record *Sukiyaki*. The theme songs of the Cavallaro Orchestra were "My Sentimental Heart" and "Polonaise." According to a poll conducted by radio station KCEA-FM in San Francisco in 1982, the two top bands, associated with that part of the country over the years, were Paul Whiteman and Carmen Cavallaro. Cavallaro died in 1989.

ELLA FITZGERALD

(Ella Fitzgerald and Her Orchestra) Born in Newport News, Virginia on April 25, 1918. When drummer Chick Webb died in June 1939, the band's vocalist, Ella Fitzgerald, took over the leadership. She fronted the orchestra until its disbandment in 1942 mostly because WWII had caused the draft of many of her fine players. When she took over the Webb band, many of the sidemen were discontent due to small salaries, many seven-nights-a-week gigs, and other wartime inconveniences. Ella's strong musicianship persuaded most of the key players to remain and they did so until 1942. The personnel in the band just prior to its breakup in 1942 included musical director–clarinet Eddie Barefield; Rocks McConnell and Buck Hardy, trombones; Francis Williams, Dick Vance, Irving Randolph, and Taft Jordan, trumpets; Lonnie Simmons, Elmer Williams, Williard Brown, and Chauncey Haughton, saxophones; Bill Beason, drums; Beverly Peer, bass; Ulysses Livingstone, guitar; and Tommy Fulford, piano. The Fitzgerald band was popular at the Savoy Ballroom in New York City and other venues in which they performed. Fitzgerald died in Beverly Hills, California on June 15, 1996.

INTERNATIONAL SWEETHEARTS OF RHYTHM

(International Sweethearts of Rhythm) During WWII, the draft depleted the ranks of male musicians available for the dozens of bands touring throughout the county. This created a wonderful opportunity for women musicians in the U.S. and several all-female bands were formed. Among them, the International Sweethearts of Rhythm was one of the finest. The band was first formed in 1939 in Mississippi at the Piney Woods Country Life School. It first performed at the Howard Theater in Washington, D.C. A high level of professionalism was brought to the unit in 1941 when Anna Mae Winburn assumed the leadership of the Sweethearts. She had been the leader of the Lloyd Hunter Serenaders prior to joining the International Sweethearts. The arrangers were Jesse Stone and Eddie Durham. The band's personnel were Anna Mae Winburn, leader and vocalist; Evelyn McGee, vocalist; Pauline Braddy, drums; Johnnie Mae Rice, piano; Roxanna Lucas, guitar; Lucille Dixon, bass; Ida Bell Byrd, Helen Jones, and Judy Bayron, trombones; Edna Williams, Johnnie Mae Stansbury, Ray Carter, and Ernestine "Tiny" Davis, trumpets; Willie Mae Wong, Viola Burnside, Grace Bayron, Helen Saine, Amy Garrison, and Marge Pettiford, saxophones. The Sweethearts was the first racially integrated women's band in the U.S. The band at the Howard Theater in Washington, D.C. set a new box-office record in 1941 when more than 35,000 listeners filled the theater in one week. The band played in ballrooms and theaters throughout the country for more than ten years before disbanding.

HARRY JAMES

(Harry James and His Orchestra) Born in Albany, Georgia on March 15, 1916. Harry James (né: Harry Hagg James) studied drums when he was seven years old. His father was a circus bandleader and was supportive of James's desire to be a musician. When James was ten he began studying the trumpet with his father. The family moved to Beaumont, Texas when James was 14. During his first year at Beaumont High School, James was awarded a first division when he played a solo with the high school band. After high school, James toured with various bands in Texas, including those led by Herman Waldman, Logan Hancock, Joe Gill, and the Old Phillips Friars. In 1935, he played with Ben Pollack and, in 1937, joined the Benny Goodman Orchestra. In late 1938, he left the Goodman band, formed his own band that opened at the Benjamin Franklin Hotel in Philadelphia and by 1940 had recorded a number of hits. After WW II, he toured the country until 1955 when he appeared in the movie The Benny Goodman Story. During that period he began to discard his commercial style and opted for a swinging type band with arrangements by Neil Hefti, Ernie Wilkins, and Jay Hill. In 1957, the band did a European tour. The personnel of the Harry James Orchestra included Bod Morgan, Steve Davis, Don Baldwin, Skip Stein, Bill King, Jimmy Huntzinger, Dick Carter, Dave Wheeler, Red Kelly, Dave Madden, Jay Corre, Ernie Pack, George Roberts, Buddy Combine, Dick Nash, Joe Comfort, Bob Stone, Gus Bivona, Juan Tizol, Conrad Gozzo, Sam Donahue, Claude Bowen, Dave Mathews, Claude Lakey, Mickey Scrima, Vido Musso, Chuck Gentry, Willie Smith, Corky Corcoran, Buddy Rich, and many others. A host of good singers appeared with the band and included Rita Graham, Ernie Andrews, Joan O'Brien, Buddy DeVito, Buddy Moreno, The Skylarks, Kitty Kallen, Helen Forrest, Lynn Richards, Frank Sinatra, Dick Haymes, Connie Haines, and Bernice Byers. By the '60s, the James band played regularly in Las Vegas, Nevada, and did a Carnegie Hall concert in 1964. James was first married to Louise Tobin, singer on the Benny Goodman band, and secondly to movie star Betty Grable. The James band recorded for Capitol, MGM and Columbia records. James died in Las Vegas, Nevada on July 6, 1983.

JACK JENNY

(Jack Jenny and His Orchestra) Born in Mason City, Iowa on May 12, 1910. Jack Jenny (né: Truman Elliott Jenny) went to school in Cedar Rapids, Iowa and played trombone in his father's band. After attending the Culver City Military Academy, he joined the Austin Wylie band in 1928, the Mal Hallett band in 1933, and the Isham Jones Orchestra in 1934. In the later '30s, he moved to New York City where he worked with Fred Rich, Victor Young, Lennie Hayton, and others in radio. In 1937, he directed a record date for his wife, singer Kay Thompson. From 1938 to 1940, he organized and led his own band that recorded "Star Dust," which had been arranged by Hugo Winterhalter, who was a member of the saxophone section, and which became a big hit. In 1940, Jenny disbanded and joined the Artie Shaw band where he once again was featured on a recording of "Star Dust." In 1942, he left the Shaw band and led a trio until he joined Benny Goodman and appeared in the 1943 movie *Stage Door*

Canteen. When Bobby Byrne entered the service, Jenny fronted his band for a brief period until Byrne himself was drafted. Jack Jenny was the co-composer of tunes "What More Can I Give You" and "Man with a Horn." He recorded for Vocalion, Pan-Am, Victor, and Columbia records. He was discharged in 1944 due to severe health problems. Jenny died in Los Angeles, California on December 16, 1945.

ALVINO REY

(Alvino Rey and His Orchestra) Born in Oakland, California on July 1. 1911. Alvino Rey (né: Alvin McBurney) began to study guitar when his parents moved to Cleveland, Ohio when Rey was a youngster. He met jazz guitarist Eddie Lang who was a big influence on Rey. In 1937, Rey joined the radio band led by Horace Heidt. The featured vocal group was the King Sisters. By 1938, Rey had married one of the sisters, Louise, and formed his own band that included the King Sisters. By 1940, Rey was playing regularly on station KHJ and had added arranger Frank DeVol to the band. Eventually other top arrangers were added, including Billy May, Johnny Mandel, Ray Conniff, and Neal Hefti. The personnel at that time included Bunny Sawker, drums; Gene Traxler, bass; Dick Morgan, guitar; Milt Raskin, piano; Wallace "Blue" Barron and Jerry Ross, trombones; Danny Vanelli, Paul Fredricks, and Frank Strasek, trumpets; Jerry Sanfino, Skeets Herfurt, Bill Shine, and Kermit Levinsky, saxophones. Outstanding sidemen in later bands included Don Lamond, Earl Swope, Bob Greattinger, Zoot Sims, Herbie Steward, Hal McKusick, Chuck Peterson, Kai Winding, and Bob Gordon. The band's theme songs were "Nighty Night" and "Blue Rey." The Rey Orchestra recorded for Bluebird, Capitol, and Victor records. Rey remained active through the '80s, featuring singer Fran Warren. Rey died in Draper, Utah on February 24, 2004.

DICK ROBERTSON

(Dick Robertson and His Orchestra) Born in Brooklyn, New York on July 3, 1903. Robertson was versatile singer who freelanced with various bands during the '20s and early '30s. He used a pseudonym on some recordings and sang in all styles. In 1935, Robertson was featured on a radio show *Music by Gershwin*. From 1937 to 1942 he recorded for Decca Records with his own band that included some of the top jazz players at that time. During that period, his band played throughout the U.S., Canada, France, and England in various theaters and clubs. Robertson wrote "I'd Do It All Over Again," "Why Did It Have to End So Soon?," "A Lovely Rainy Afternoon," "Goodnight, Wherever You Are," "A Lovely Rainy Afternoon," and "A Little on the Lonely Side." Robertson collaborated with Sammy Mysels, James Cavanaugh, Nelson Cogane, and Frank Weldon. Dick Robertson retired from the music business in the late '40s.

TOMMY REYNOLDS

(Tommy Reynolds and His Orchestra) Born in Akron, Ohio on January 17, 1915. Tommy Reynolds (né: Anthony Renaldo) attended the University of Akron, played with Isham Jones and formed his first band in 1938. His bands never became very popular although they were said to be loud and enthusiastic. During the period of 1938–1939, a few of the band members were Tino Isgro, tenor saxophone; Whitey Thomas and Tony Picciotto, trumpet; as well as Bobby Boon and Benny West. In 1940, the Reynolds band gained national attention by way of radio and recordings. They recorded for Okeh, Vocalion, and Derby records. The band traveled extensively throughout the West Coast and Midwest and appeared at the Band Box in Chicago in 1946 where they made a big hit. In the mid '50s, the Reynolds Orchestra toured Canada with Bob Hope. After the tour, Reynolds disbanded and became the music director for WOR radio-TV in New York City. Tommy Reynolds composed "I'll Tell It to the Breeze" and "Once Over Lightly."

CHARLIE SPIVAK

(Charlie Spivak and His Orchestra) Born in Kiev, Ukraine on February 17, 1907. When Spivak was very young, his family immigrated to the U.S. (Connecticut), and Charlie began studying trumpet at age 10. While still in his teens, he played with the Don Cavallaro Orchestra and, from 1924 to 1930, with Paul Specht. From 1931 to 1934, he played with Ben Pollack prior to joining the Dorsey Brothers Orchestra with whom he worked during 1934–1935. After a short stint with the Ray Noble band, Spivak played in New York studios. In 1936, he played with orchestras led by Jack Teagarden, Bob Crosby, and Tommy Dorsey holding down the lead trumpet chair. Glenn Miller encouraged

Spivak to form his own band, which he did in 1939. The first band did not jell and was disbanded; however, shortly thereafter Spivak formed a second band, that had some outstanding sidemen, including June Hutton and Garry Stevens, singers; Davey Tough, drums; and Jimmy Middleton, bass. The Spivak band theme songs were "Let's Go Home" and "Stardreams." The band recorded often and continued to be popular through the '40s, disbanding in the late '50s. Prior to disbanding, the Spivak band added additional outstanding musicians, including Les Elgart, Nelson Riddle, Larry Elgart, Urbie Green, Wayne Andre, and others. Spivak continued playing, featuring his singer and wife Irene Daye, fronting small groups that worked various venues in South Carolina, Florida and Las Vegas. Spivak died in Greenville, South Carolina on March 1, 1982.

JESS STACY

(Jess Stacy and His All-Stars) Born in Bird's Point, Missouri on August 11, 1904. During his teenage years, Stacy played piano with various teenage groups and, in the early '20s, began playing on riverboats in Mississippi and Missouri during the summers. In the winters he lived in Davenport, Iowa playing at the Coliseum Ballroom with Tony Catalano's Iowans. By 1926, he moved to Chicago and joined a band led by Joe Kayser. After a couple of years he played with various groups, freelancing in ballrooms, clubs, and speakeasies. In 1935, he joined the Benny Gooman band, having been recommended by John Hammond. Between 1938 and 1939, Stacy cut a number of albums for Commodore Records under his own name and formed his first band featuring singer Carlotta Dale and instrumental sidemen Irving Fazola, Eddie Miller, and Billy Butterfield. His band was short-lived, breaking up in 1940 when Stacy joined Bob Crosy until 1942 when he rejoined Benny Goodman. In 1945, he played briefly for Tommy Dorsey and Horace Heidt; then organized his second band. The 1945 band featured his wife, singer Lee Wiley, and Muggsy Spanier. The Stacy theme song was "Daybreak Serenade" and was recorded on Victor Records. After a year, he disbanded and rejoined Benny Goodman with whom he remained until moving to California in 1947. Stacy continued playing until 1963, when he sold Max Factor cosmetics. He recorded the soundtrack for the motion picture *The Great Gatsby*, and played at the 1974 Newport Jazz Festival. Stacy died in Los Angeles, California on January 5, 1994.

JOE SULLIVAN

(Joe Sullivan and His Orchestra) Born in Chicago, Illinois on November 5, 1906. Joe Sullivan (né: Dennis Patrick Terence Joseph O'Sullivan) studied at the Chicago Conservatory of Music and played with many of the great musicians in Chicago during the '20s and early '30s, including Eddie Condon, Pee Wee Russell, George Wettling, Frankie Teschemacher, Bud Freeman, Benny Goodman, and Muggsy Spanier. During the '30s, Sullivan played with various commercial bands and jazz groups, including bands led by Eddie Condon, Joe Venuti, Russ Columbo, Ozzie Nelson, Roger Wolfe Kahn, Bob Crosby, Louis Panico, the Coon-Sanders Nighthawks, and Benny Goodman. Sullivan formed his first band and opened at Café Society in New York City in 1939 and at Nick's Nighclub in Greenwich Village in 1940. After disbanding and playing around the country as a single, he played in Louis Armstrong's band for a short while in 1952. Sullivan wrote "Little Rock Getaway" and "Gin Mill Blues." Joe Sullivan died in San Francisco on October 13, 1971.

JACK TEAGARDEN

(Jack Teagarden "Big T" and His Orchestra) Born in Vernon, Texas on August 29, 1905. Jack Teagarden (né: Weldon L. Teagarden) played trombone and sang as a young man. In his teens he played and toured with various bands, including a group led by famous Texas pianist Peck Kelley from 1921 to 1922. Moving to Kansas City, Teagarden briefly led his own band prior to playing with groups led by Willard Robison and Doc Ross. In 1927, he went to New York City, where he recorded with Sam Lanin and Roger Wolfe Kahn and made his debut as a recorded singer with Eddie Condon. He joined the Ben Pollack band in 1928 and gained national prominence as a trombone player. After five years, Teagarden worked with Mal Hallett and, by 1934, had joined the Paul Whiteman Orchestra with whom he played until 1938. At that time, Jack Teagarden formed his own band that included Dave Tough, Charlie Spivak, Lee Castle, and Ernie Caceres. Disbanding in 1947, he became a member of the Louis Armstrong All-Star Band and played with them through 1951. In 1951, Teagarden formed another band that included his sister Norma (piano), and his brother Charlie (trumpet). He also fronted an all-star band, which featured Max Kaminsky, Cozy Cole, and Peanuts Hucko. Teagarden was as famous for his singing as his trombone playing singing tunes like "The Sheik of Araby," "Basin

Street Blues," "Stars Fell on Alabama," "Aunt Hagar's Blues," "If I Could Be with You One Hour Tonight," and "I'm Coming Virginia." Teagarden died in New Orleans, Louisiana on January 15, 1964.

ALEC WILDER

(Alec Wilder and His Octet) Born in Rochester, New York on February 17, 1907. Wilder was basically a studio musician who led and wrote for small studio combos, working with Mildred Bailey and other singers. In 1939, he formed the Alec Wilder Octet that specialized in performing neo-Baroque styled music with unusual instrumentation, including English horn, oboe, bass clarinet and harpsichord. Wilder was a prolific songwriter with a great sense of humor. He penned "Jack, This Is My Husband," "Amorous Poltergeist," "Neurotic Goldfish," and "Bull Fiddles in a China Shop." Wilder died in Gainesville, Florida on December 24, 1980.

GORDON JENKINS

(Gordon Jenkins and His Orchestra) Born in Webster Groves, Missouri on May 12, 1910. In the late '20s, Jenkins played banjo in a St. Louis dance band until 1930 when he became a radio staff pianist. In the early '30s, he played piano and arranged for the Isham Jones Orchestra and then for Vincent Lopez, Paul Whiteman, Andre Kostelanetz, and Benny Goodman. In 1937, he was the arranger and conductor for the Broadway musical *The Show Is On*. Jenkins moved to the West Coast in 1938 and was a music director for NBC radio. He also wrote music for various movies, radio, and nightclub shows in Southern California. In the mid- and late '40s, he conducted the orchestra on the Dick Haymes radio program and, in 1945, became the conductor and musical director for Decca Records. During the remainder of the '40s, Jenkins accompanied a number of singers, including Louis Armstrong and Frank Sinatra. He made many hit records, including *Lonesome Town*, *It's All in the Game*, *You're Mine You*, and *Along Fifth Avenue*. During the '50s and '60s, he continued to record and, by the '70s, Jenkins conducted Sinatra's comeback television special. Jenkins wrote "Blue Prelude," "P.S. I Love You," "You Have Taken My Heart', "When a Woman Loves a Man," "That's All," "Manhattan Tower Suite," "Once Upon a Dream," "I Thought About Marie," and many other tunes. Jenkins recorded for Decca, Capitol, and Victor records.

TEDDY WILSON

(Teddy Wilson and His Orchestra) Born in Austin, Texas on November 24, 1912. In the '30s, Teddy Wilson (né: Theodore Shaw Wilson) played with Benny Gooman who described Wilson as "the greatest musician in music today." When he left Goodman he formed his own band, which made more than three-dozen recordings. After a year, he disbanded and favored small combos for the remainder of his career. One of his groups included singer Thelma Carpenter; J.C. Heard, bass; Al Hall, drums; Al Casey, guitar; Wilson, piano and leader; Ben Webster, Rudy Powell, and Hal Baker, saxophones; Hal Baker and Doc Cheatham, trumpets. Wilson died in New Britain, Connecticut on July 31, 1986.

BOB ZURKE

(Bob Zurke and His Orchestra) Born in Detroit, Michigan on January 17, 1912. Pianist Bob Zurke began playing in the '20s with the Oliver Haylor Orchestra in Philadelphia at the Orient Restaurant and the Palais d'Or. By 1928, he was working with Seymour Simon's band, Thelma Terry and Her Playboys, and at Smokey's Club in Detroit, Michigan. Zurke was also spending considerable time as a music copyist working for Don Redman and the Cotton Pickers. In 1931, Zurke joined the Bob Crosby Bobcats recording "Gin Mill Blues" and "Little Rock Getaway." In 1939, Zurke formed his own orchestra that included singers Gus Ehrman, Evelyn Poe, Sterling Bose, and Claire Martin, and won the *Down Beat* magazine's poll for "best piano player." Zurke's theme song was "Hobson Street Blues" that was recorded on Victor Records. Disbanding in 1940, he played, as a single, in Chicago, Detroit, St. Paul, and Los Angeles. In 1942, while in Los Angeles, he became resident pianist at the Hangover Club, where he recorded the background music for *Jungle Jive*, a Technicolor cartoon film. Zurke died in Los Angeles on February 16, 1944.

RAYMOND PAIGE

(Raymond Paige and His Orchestra) Paige played violin in various theater bands on the West Coast during the '20s. In 1934, he conducted orchestras on radio shows *Pontiac Surprise Party*, *California Melodies*, and *Louella Parsons*. He replaced Ted Fio Rio on the *Hollywood Hotel Show* between 1935 and 1937 and, in fall 1937, worked on the Packard Hour, which starred Lanny Ross. In

1938, he appeared in movies *Hawaii Calls* and *Hollywood Hotel.* He also conducted in the '40s on *Musical Americana, Walter O'Keefe, 100 Men and a Girl,* and *Salute to Youth.* Paige moved to New York City and conducted at Radio City Music Hall during the '50s. Raymond Paige recorded for Victor and Forum records. Paige died on August 7, 1965.

TONY PASTOR

(Tony Pastor and His Orchestra) Born in Middletown, Connecticut on October 26, 1907. Tony Pastor (né: Antonio Pestritto) studied saxophone when he was very young and played with several bands on the East Coast as a teenager. In the early '30s, Pastor organized his first band that failed to meet with success. He disbanded and joined a band led by his Connecticut neighbor, Artie Shaw. Pastor was featured as tenor saxophone soloist and singer while with Shaw. By the mid-'30s, Pastor left the Artie Shaw band and formed his own orchestra that got a lot of exposure via radio and met with great success. The Pastor Orchestra survived through WWII and, by the late '40s, the featured vocalists were the Clooney sisters, Betty and Rosemary. A few of the featured sidemen with the Pastor Orchestra were Max Kaminsky, Chuck Peterson, Bill Robbins, Buddy Morrow, Lou McGarity, and Les Burness. The theme songs for the Tony Pastor Orchestra were "Blossoms" and "Pastoral." The record companies were Columbia, Cosmo, Bluebird, and Victor. The band continued to perform until Pastor disbanded in the late '60s. He died in Old Lyme, Connecticut on October 31, 1969.

MERCER ELLINGTON

(Mercer Ellington and His Orchestra) Born in Washington, D.C. on March 11, 1919. Mercer Ellington was the son of Duke Ellington and attended Columbia University and the Juilliard School of Music in New York City. He formed his own band in 1939 that disbanded after two years. In 1941, he traveled with his father and studied composing and arranging. During WWII, he served in the U.S. military. When he was released in 1948 he reformed his band and traveled for two years. In 1950, he worked briefly with the Duke Ellington Orchestra and formed Mercer Records that he directed for two years. In 1954, he joined Cootie Williams as a sideman manager and from 1955 to 1959, worked once again with his father. He led various groups during the '60s and recorded with all-star sidemen. From

1962 to 1965, he was a disc jockey on a New York radio station. In 1965, he once again joined Duke's band as a sideman-manager and remained until Duke Ellington died in 1974. Mercer then assumed the leadership of the Duke Ellington band. Mercer Ellington was a talented songwriter penning such hits as "Things Ain't What They Used to Be," "Jumpin' Punkins," "The Girl in My Dreams Tries to Look Like You," "John Hardy's Wife," "Blue Serge," and "Moon Mist." The Mercer Ellington band recorded on Coral Records. Mercer Ellington died in Copenhagen, Denmark on February 8, 1996.

Bands directed by the following were known to have organized in the '30s but there was insufficient historical information to include them: Shuffle Abernathy, Jasper "Jap" Allen, Doc Hyder, Johnny Mcghee, Harry Roy, and Raymond Scott.

CHAPTER

THE WAR YEARS
(1940–1949)

Bombings by the Nazis, the London Blitz, forced 170,000 Britishers to camp out in London underground stations. The U.S. Congress instituted the first peacetime draft. Americans began to warm to the idea of lending assistance to the Allies. Hitler marched into the Soviet Union. The average family income was about $5,000 per year. Rationing began. More than 12 million American men left their homes to enter the war. Soldiers were living on Spam, powered eggs, and dried vegetables. June 6, 1944, was D Day and marked the invasion of Normandy; by July the Allies had landed more than one million troops; by August they had freed Paris. On April 12, 1945, President Roosevelt died. Although the Germans surrendered, the war raged on in the Pacific until August 1945 when the Japanese surrendered. After the war there was rebuilding throughout the earth; Levittown was built in the U.S. In 1948, the Marshall Plan, the Berlin airlift, and the Communist threat, which triggered the investigation into un-American activities, began.

1940: The Germans entered Paris. Trotsky was assassinated in Mexico. FDR was elected to a third presidential term. The Leslie Speaker was designed. The Solovox (a small electronic keyboard which could be attached to an acoustic piano) was manufactured.

1941: On December 7, the Japanese attacked Pearl Harbor in Hawaii killing 2,433 American personnel and wounding 1,178 others—President Franklin Delano Roosevelt termed it "a date which will live in infamy." The U.S. entered the war. The deportation of Jewish citizens began in Germany. The FCC authorized the first commercial FM radio stations. The Sonovox (a sound-effects device) was developed. Irving Berlin wrote "White Christmas."

1942: The first nuclear chain reaction by developed by Fermi. The American Federation of Musicians strike (1941–1945) against the record companies paralyzed the record industry.

1943: Race riots were prevalent in Chicago. Roosevelt approved the first withholding income tax. The first wire recorder was developed in Germany.

1944: General MacArthur returned to the Philippines. The Fender (an electric steel guitar) was produced.

1945: World War II ended; sixty million people had died. There were 950 AM radio stations on the air in the U.S. at the end of World War II.

1946: The Nuremberg trials were held as a result of World War II. There were more than 500 additional AM and FM radio stations built in the U.S.

1947: The Truman Doctrine and the Taft-Hartley Act were passed. The Baldwin Organ and Connsonata were designed. The transister was invented.

1948: Gandhi was assassinated. The Alger Hiss case was heard. The long-playing phonograph record, the LP, was introduced. The Miller and Thomas Organs were designed and manufactured.

1949: The U.S.S.R. exploded an atomic bomb. The increasing popularity of television greatly reduced radio advertising and record sales. The Lowrey Organ was manufactured.

BOB ALLEN

(Bob Allen and His Orchestra) Born in Cincinnati, Ohio in 1913. Allen studied music at the Cincinnati Conservatory of Music and sang with the Hal Kemp band in the middle and late '30s. He stayed with the band until Kemp was killed in an automobile accident in December 1940. Allen organized his own band that featured trumpeter and music director Randy Brooks for a year. Bob Allen formed a new band in 1942, again featuring Brooks, and traveled until 1943 when he disbanded and joined the Tommy Dorsey band as vocalist. In 1944, he began his military service. After his release from the service he again joined the Dorsey band and remained until 1947 when he began to freelance as a singer. Allen recorded for Burnswick, Victor, Decca, Banam, and Ara records. Allen retired in California and became a woodworker.

HENRY "RED" ALLEN

(Henry "Red" Allen and His Orchestra) Born in Algiers, Louisiana, on January 7, 1908. Allen studied trumpet and played in his father's brass band as a young-ster. He played with several groups, including George Lewis's during the mid-'20s and traveled to St. Louis in 1927, where he joined King Oliver's Jazz Band and played in New York. From 1928 to 1929, Allen returned to New Orleans and played with Fate Marable on riverboats. During the early '30s, he was featured with the Luis Russell band and during the '30s recorded often. In early 1940, Allen formed a band that featured J. C. Higginbotham, trombone, and played in New York, Boston, Chicago, and California. The Allen band opened at the Metropole in New York in 1954. Allen toured Europe with Kid Ory in late '59 and led his own band through Europe in the '60s. Allen wrote a number of tunes,, including "Ride, Red, Ride," "Angiers Stomp," "Siesta at the Fiesta," "Get the Mop," and "Pleasing Paul." His final important gig was at Jimmy Ryan's in New York in 1966. He did one further tour of Europe in 1967, returned to the U.S., and died on April 17, 1967, in New York City.

ZINN ARTHUR

(Zinn Arthur and His Orchestra) Zinn Arthur led a band that served as the house orchestra for the Roseland Ballroom Ballroom in New York City during the '40s. He was said to have had an unusually good baritone voice and the band featured a song Arthur wrote entitled "Darling." A staff of the best arrangers wrote for the band and alto saxophone player Alvin (Alvy) Weisfeld was the featured soloist. Arthur was drafted, as a result of WWII, and became a star in *This Is the Army*, an Irving Berlin musical. When he was released from the U.S. army he returned to New York where he became a successful photographer, an assistant to the producer Joshua Logan, and a restaurant owner in Long Island, New York. When he retired, he settled in Florida.

CHRISTOPHER COLUMBUS

(Christopher Columbus with Wild Bill Davis and His Orchestra) Born in Greenville, North Carolina on June 17, 1902. Columbus (né: Joseph Christopher Columbus Morris, a.k.a. Joe Morris) was the father of drummer Sonny Payne. He played with many bands in the '20s and '30s and formed his own band in the '40s that played at the Savoy Ballroom Ballroom regularly. He disbanded in 1946 and worked with Louis Jordan. In the late '50s, Columbus played with Wild Bill Davis until he joined Damita Jo in the mid-'60s. By the late '60s, he was playing with Duke Ellington. In the '70s, he formed another band, toured in Europe with Wild Bill Davis, and recorded with Floyd Smith, Milt Buchner, and Al Grey.

TUTTI CAMARATA

(Tutti Camarata and His Orchestra) Born in Glen Ridge, New Jersey on May 11, 1913. Tutti Camarata (né: Salvatore Camarata) grew up and studied music in Verona, New Jersey, and at the Juilliard School of Music in New York City. He studied conducting with Ceare Sodero and composition and orchestration with Bernard Wagenaar. In the early '30s, Camarata arranged for Charlie Barnet and played first trumpet and wrote for the Jimmy Dorsey Orchestra that featured singers Bob Eberly and Helen O'Connell. He wrote the famous arrangements of "Amapola," "Yours," "Green Eyes," and "Tangerine" for Dorsey. After the Dorsey years, he wrote for Paul Whiteman, the Casa Loma Orchestra, and Benny Goodman. Camarata spent a great amount of time doing studio work and at various times was named music director for the American Broadcasting Corporation and Decca Records. He wrote the string backgrounds for the famous Billie Holiday recordings. In the '30s, he worked with George Gershwin writing the score for the movie *Shall We Dance*. During World War II, Camarata was a flight instructor for the U.S. Army Airforce. After the war he traveled to England where he organized and conducted the Kingston Symphony Orchestra. In the late '50s and '60s, he was musical director for the Walt Disney Studios.

RUSS CARLYLE

(Russ Caryle and His Orchestra) Born in Cleveland, Ohio, on July 4, 1921. Caryle began as a singer with the Blue Barron band during the late '30s. In the '40s, he served in the U.S. military during World War II. In 1949 he formed his own orchestra that traveled and played the Peabody Hotel in Memphis, Tennessee, and the Roseland Dance City in New York. The band was considered a very commercial, smooth romantic group and, in 1957, sold more than a million copies of their recording of "In a Little Spanish Town." The band's theme songs were "You Call It Madness," "Miss You," "It Was Wonderful Then," "In the Chapel in the Moonlight," and "If I Ever Love Again." The Caryle Orchestra recorded for Bluebird, Coral, Variety, and Mercury records. Russ Caryle was a prolific songwriter and wrote "Sing a Lumma Lay," "Studola a Pumpa," "Stashu Pandowski," and "Again." The Caryle Orchestra continued performing in the '60s playing in Las Vegas and the Midwest.

JOHNNY WARRINGTON

(Johnny Warrington and His Orchestra) Born in Collingsworth, New York on May 17, 1911. Johnny Warrington (né: John T. Warrington) began to study piano and saxophone when he was six. He received a degree in civil engineering from Duke University and studied theory, harmony, and counterpoint for four years. He then arranged for WCAU radio in Philadelphia, where he served as music director. He joined Jan Savitt's Taphatteres as arranger for a brief time until taking an assignment as conductor of the WABC network in 1945. Warrington wrote for various music publishers in New York from 1946 to 1971. During his career, Johnny Warrington conducted concert band seminars in various universities throughout the U.S. and arranged for Tommy Dorsey, Henry Mancini, Lawrence Welk, Les Elgart, and Lionel Hampton. He conducted the Sound Spectrum and the Ocean City Pops Orchestra. Warrington wrote "Music America 200 Years Young." Warrington died in December 1978.

PHIL CARREON

(Phil Carreon and His Orchestra) Carreon began his band in the '40s and played in Southern California. Some very fine jazz musicians, including Lennie Neihaus, Billy Byers, and Johnny Mandell played and arranged for the band. It was primarily a territory band and had little national exposure. No records indicate recording activity.

EDDIE DURHAM

(Eddie Durham and His Orchestra) Born in San Marcos, Texas on August 19, 1906. Durham's father and six brothers all played music instruments. Eddie played banjo, guitar, and trombone. In the early '20s, he toured with various minstrel shows and co-led the Durham Brothers band throughout the Southwest. In the late '20s, Durham played with Edgar Battle, Walter Page, and Bennie Moten. During the early '30s, he moved to New York City and wrote Moten Swing while experimenting with amplified guitar. During the mid '30s he arranged such tunes as "Avalon," "Pigeon Walk," "Blues in the Groove," and "Lunceford Special" for Jimmie Lunceford and Willie Bryant. From 1935 to 1937, Durham wrote for Count Basie penning tunes like "Topsy," "Time Out," "Swingin' in the Blues," and "Jumpin' at the Woodside." Durham was heard on records with the Kansas City Five and Six, Count Basie, and Lester Young. During the late '30s, he wrote "Wham!," "Glen Island Special," and "Slip Horn Jive" for Glenn Miller. He was the co-composer of the tune " I Don't Want to Set the World on Fire" and "Topsy." He also wrote for Artie Shaw and Ina Ray Hutton during this period. In the '40s, he led the International Sweethearts of Rhythms. During the '50s, Durham freelanced as player and arranger and by the mid-'60s began to sell real estate. Durham died in New York City on March 6, 1987.

ALVY WEST

(Alvy West and His Orchestra) Born in Brooklyn, New York on January 19, 1915. Alvy West (né: Alvin Weisfeld) received a BA degree from New York University and joined the Paul Whiteman Orchestra as a saxophonist. He later conducted and arranged for Andy Williams and conducted and recorded with Bob and Ray. West was heard on NBC radio and seen on CBS television on the *BF Goodrich Show*. West wrote "Charm," "Cathy," "Tony's Guitar," "Hop,

Skip, and Jump," "Papa's Tune," and others. He recorded an album entitled
Originals for the Little Band.

LEE CASTLE

(Lee Castle and His Orchestra) Born in New York City on February 28, 1915.
In the mid-'30s, Castle played trumpet with the Joe Haymes Orchestra. In 1936,
he joined Artie Shaw band, playing first trumpet. He remained with Shaw for
about a year. In 1937, he played with Tommy Dorsey with whom he remained
until 1938 when Dorsey sent him to study with his father in Lansford,
Pennsylvania. After a year he freelanced with bands led by Dick Stabile, Red
Norvo, Jack Teagarden, Glenn Miller, and Will Bradley. In 1940, Castle formed
the Lee Castle Orchestra to play for scheduled events, working with Artie Shaw
and Benny Goodman in the interim. In 1953, he disbanded and played with the
Dorsey Brothers Orchestra. When Tommy and Jimmy Dorsey died, Castle
became the director of the band. Castle recorded for Epic and Musicraft records.
Castle is remembered for his outstanding solos in "So Rare" (with Jimmy
Dorsey), "Basin Street Boogie" (with Will Bradley), "I Never Knew" (with
Tommy Dorsey), and "Sugar Foot Stomp" (with Artie Shaw). Castle died in
Hollywood, Florida on November 22, 1990.

MILTON DELUGG

(Milton Delugg and His Orchestra) Born in Los Angeles, California on
December 2, 1918. Delugg attended the University of California at Los Angeles
and began to work in film and radio studios as a composer and conductor. He
played accordion with the Matty Malneck band in the late '30s and served in the
military during World War II. When he was released from the service in 1946,
he led a small combo and accompanied singer Frankie Laine. In the late '40s,
he conducted and arranged for the *Abe Burrows Show*, initially on radio and
then on television. In the early '50s, he arranged and conducted for the *Herb
Shriner Show* and the *Broadway Open House*. Delugg wrote many popular
songs, including "Orange-Colored Sky," "Hood de Doo," "Shanghai," "Be My
Life's Companion," "Just Another Polka," "Send My Baby Back to Me," and
many others. Delugg recorded on Decca, Victor, Mercury, and Columbia
records. He collaborated with Allan Roberts, William Stein, Sammy Gallop,

Bob Hilliard, and his wife, Anne. During 1966–1967, Delugg was music director for the *Tonight Show*, featuring Johnny Carson. During the late '60s and '70s, Milton Delugg continued composing and conducting on special programs on television.

HAL DERWIN

(Hal Derwin and His Orchestra) Born in 1914, Derwin sang with bands led by Shep Fields, Les Brown, and Boyd Raeburn during the '30s. In 1940, he met Freddy Lange, who had played lead alto saxophone with Glen Gray and Jan Garber. Derwin and Garber formed a new band, recorded for Capitol Records, and played in Los Angeles at the Biltmore Bowl for more than six years, doing nightly radio broadcasts on NBC. In 1950, he signed with Capitol Records as the A&R person and worked with Lee Gillette, his lifelong friend. The theme song of the Hal Derwin Orchestra was "Derwin's Melody." He recorded "That's for Me" with Artie Shaw, "Take Me Back" in a duet with singer Marth Tilton, and "No One But You" and "Blue and Broken Hearted" with his own band. Derwin also sang in movies, dubbing his voice for actor Cliff Robertson and others.

LEO DIAMOND

(Leo Diamond and His Orchestra) Born in New York City on June 29, 1915. Diamond played in Borah Minnevitch's Harmonica Rascals until the '40s when he formed his own band, the Solidaires. His group appeared in several motion pictures during that era, including *Girl Crazy* and *Sweet Rosie O'Grady*. By the '50s, Diamond worked mostly as a solo recording artist, overdubbing all of the various harmonica parts and doing bird calls, jet planes, explosions, and other sound effects. He wrote a number of songs that were recorded, including "Melody of Love," "Skin Diver's Suite," "The Girls of Brazil," and "Off Shore." He recorded for Victor, Roulette, Reprise, Paramount, and Harmony records. Diamond died in Los Angeles, California, on September 15, 1966.

SAXIE DOWELL

(Saxie Dowell and His Orchestra) Born in North Carolina on May 29, 1904. Saxie Dowell (né: Horace K. Dowell) was the tenor saxophone player on the Hal Kemp band until Kemp died. In 1940, Dowell formed his own band that attracted little attention but helped him gain band-leading experience. He was drafted into the service in World War II and led a service band assigned to the ship, the *U.S.S. Franklin* that was torpedoed. The band was saved and assisted in rescuing others. When he was discharged in 1946 he formed a new band, consistent with the Hal Kemp style, and featured himself as singer. The theme song was "Three Little Fishies," which was written by Dowell. He recorded for Brunswick, Victor, and Sonora records. In 1948, he worked mainly as a song plugger for various publishing companies.

LIONEL HAMPTON

(Lionel Hampton and His Orchestra) Born in Louisville, Kentucky on April 12, 1909. Hampton played drums in local bands in Louisville, Birmingham, Alabama, and Chicago when he was a teenager. He moved to California in the mid-'20s and played with Paul Howard, Curits Mosby, and Reb Spikes. In the late '20s, he made his first record with Paul Howard's Quality Serenaders and played with him in Culver City, California at Sebastian's Cotton Club. Les Hite assumed the leadership of the Paul Howard band in the early '30s and backed up Louis Armstrong on many of his records. Hampton began to play the vibes and led a band in California from 1935 to 1936. He also had bit parts in several movies at that time. While playing at the Paradise Club in Los Angeles, he jammed with Benny Goodman and Gene Krupa who were sitting in. In August 1936, he joined Benny Goodman making it the Benny Goodman Quartet, which

became famous almost overnight. When the Goodman drummer was on leave Hampton played drums as well. Hampton made many records during 1937–1940 with small groups of jazz musicians. In 1940, Hampton left the Goodman band and started his own big band that included Milt Buckner, Earl Bostic, Dexter Gordon, Arnett Cobb, and Illinois Jacquet. The featured singer was Dinah Washington. His hit records included "Hamp's Boogie Woogie" and "Central Avenue Breakdown," and his theme song, "Flying Home." In addition to "Flying Home," Hampton wrote "Midnight Sun," "Central Avenue Breakdown," "Vibraphone Blues," "Jack the Bellboy," "Opus 1/2," "Punch and Judy," and many more. The Hampton band recorded for Verve, Columbia, Victor, and Decca Records. Hampton appeared in several movies, including *Hollywood Hotel* (1938), *A Song is Born* (1948), and *The Benny Goodman Story* (1956). In 1973, he rejoined the Benny Goodman Quartet and played several concerts. He escaped a serious fire in 1997. He died in New York City on August 31, 2002. Hampton was 94 years old.

EDDIE HEYWOOD, JR.

(Eddie Heywood and His Sextet) Born in Atlanta, Georgia on December 4, 1915. Heywood took piano lessons from his father and played in theaters in Atlanta when he was 14. He toured with local bands during 1932 to 1935 and traveled with the Wayman Carver and Clarence Love bands out of Kansas City in the mid-'30s. In 1937, he moved to Dallas, Texas, where he led bands until joining the Benny Carter band in 1939. In 1940, Heywood played with Zutty Singleton and accompanied Billie Holiday at the Village Vanguard in New York City. Forming his own band, he recorded *Begin the Beguine* that became a major success. His sidemen included Vic Dicken and Doc Cheatham. He then moved to California where he appeared in movies *High School Kids* and *The Dark Corner*. He suffered partial paralysis of his hands in the late '40s and took early retirement. Through the '50s, Heywood practiced and exercised until he was able to play once again; which he did through the 80's. Heywood wrote a number of tunes, including "I'm Saving Myself for You," "Land of Dreams," "Soft Summer Breeze," and a serious composition entitled "Martha's Vineyard Suite." Heywood played in New York City in 1972.

HENRY LEVINE

(Henry "Hot Lips" Levine and His Chamber Music Society Orchestra of Lower Basin Street) Born in London, England, on November 26, 1907. Levine's family immigrated to the U.S. and moved to New York City where Henry was raised. He studied trumpet in England and New York as his family traveled back and forth. At age 19, he played in the Original Dixieland Jazz band, where he replaced Nick LaRocca, and in England with the Bert Ambrose Orchestra. In 1937, he played for a short time with Vincent Lopez. By 1930 he had established permanent residence in the U.S. and was playing in New York pit bands for various Broadway Shows. He also worked with Rudy Vallée, Cass Hagan, George Olsen, and others. During most of the '30s, he was on NBC staff and directed a show called *The Chamber Music Society of Lower Basin Street*. The singer for the show was Dinah Shore who was replaced later by Dolores "Dodie" O'Neil. Levine appeared in the movie short *When My Sugar Walks Down the Street* with Linda Keene in the '50s and led a band in Las Vegas and Miami in the '60s. Levine recorded for Victor Records. He died in the United States.

MACHITO

(Machito and His Orchestra) Born in Tampa, Florida on February 16, 1909. Machito (né: Frank Raul Grillo) moved to Cuba with his family when he was very young. His father operated a restaurant and Machito sang and played with several Cuban musicians. His future father-in-law, Mario Bauza, went to New York City where he served as musical director for Chick Webb and Cab Calloway and befriended Dizzy Gillespie. Machito followed Bauza to New York and sang with bands led by Xavier Cugat and Noro Morales. Cuban compatriots Bauza and Machito formed a band that specialized in playing Afro-Cuban jazz in 1940. The band joined BMI and recorded for Decca Records. Machito served in the U.S. army during World War II. When he was released because of an injury in 1943, he returned to New York, reformed his band, and was heard in weekly radio broadcasts from the La Conga Club. In 1947 Machito and His Orchestra joined with Stan Kenton and His Orchestra in a joint concert in Town Hall. Charlie Parker and Flip Philips were featured soloists with Machito in a series of 1948 recordings. In 1982, the album *Machito and His Salsa Big band* won a Grammy Award. Machito recorded for Forum, Pablo, Timeless, Tico, Roulette, Harmony, Coral, and Crescendo records. The promotional theme was "El Rey Del Mambo." Machito died in London, England on April 15, 1984.

VAUGHN MONROE

(Vaughn Monroe and His Orchestra) Born in Akron, Ohio, on October 7, 1911. Monroe's family moved to Wisconsin when he was very young where he won a contest playing trumpet. Monroe vacillated in his desire to become a trumpet player, opera singer, or pop singer. He played and sang with Gibby Lockhard's Jazz Orchestra, studied voice at the School of Music at Carnegie Tech and worked with an orchestra led by Austin Wylie. His first big vocal job was with the Larry Funk Orchestra where he recorded on Melotone-Romeo Records. After Funk's band disbanded, he joined the Jack Marchand Orchestra where he recorded "In the Still of the Night" on Brunswick Records. Monroe formed his first band in 1940 and played in Boston at Seller's Ten Acres. Soon after, Willard Alexander, who promoted him and got him an RCA Victor record contract and a gig near New York City at the Glen Island, signed him. He was voted the most popular college band by *Billboard* magazine and hosted The *Camel Caravan* radio program. In 1946, Monroe purchased the Meadows in Farmingham, Massachusetts (a dining-dancing club) where he performed and ran for many years. The theme song of the Vaughn Monroe Orchestra was "Racing with the Moon." Monroe featured various singers and vocal groups over the years, including Rosemary Calvin, the Moon Maids, the Norton Sisters, the 4 Lee Sisters, Ziggy Talent, and Marilyn Duke. A few of the outstanding sidemen were John Pizzarelli, Urbie Green, Ray Conniff, Art Dedrick, Arnold Ross,Warren Covington, and Bobby Nichols. The Monroe Orchestra appeared in several movies, including *Toughest Man in Arizona*, *Singin' Guns*, and *Carnegie Hall*. Monroe recorded for Victor, M and G, and Bluebird Records. Monroe wrote the "Pleasure's All Mine," "Something Sentimental," and "Racing with the Moon." Monroe died in Stuart, Florida, on May 21, 1973.

ORAN "HOT LIPS" PAGE

(Oran "Hot Lips" Page and His Orchestra) Born in Dallas, Texas on January 27, 1908. Page played trumpet with Ma Rainey, working the club circuits and vaudeville, in the mid-'20s. In the late '20s, he moved to Kansas City and played with Walter Page and His Blue Devils Orchestra. From 1930 to 1935, Page worked with an orchestra led by Bennie Moten. When Moten died Count Basie took over his orchestra and Page continued playing with Basie. In 1940,

Page recorded with his own trio prior to joining the Artie Shaw band with whom he worked until 1942. In 1944, Oran "Hot Lips" Page formed his own orchestra and recorded for Savoy and Commodore records. In the late '40s and through the '50s, Oran "Hot Lips" Page and His Orchestra played in Europe. Returning to the United States, Page worked as a single in New York. Page died in New York City on November 5, 1954.

TEDDY POWELL

(Teddy Powell and His Orchestra) Born in Oakland, California on March 1, 1905. Teddy Powell (né: Alfred Paolella) studied at the San Fransisco Conservatory of Music and worked with the Ray West band. He traveled with Abe Lyman, singing and playing banjo and guitar from 1926 until 1934 and served as an executive for Lyman's radio shows. He collaborated with Walter Samuels and Leonard Whitcup in writing the song "Boots and Saddle" that became a big hit. Powell formed his first band in 1939, still another in the mid-'50s, and hired some top-notch sidemen, including Tony Aless, Dave Mathews, Ron Perry, George Paxton, Mickey Folus, Hal Tennyson, Harry Garey, Pete Candoli, Ray Wetzel, Boots Mussulli, Lee Castle, Lee Konitz, Ted Goddard, Jackie Mills, Charlie Ventura, Carmen Mastren, Johnny Austin, and others. From time to time he featured singers, including Ruth Gaylor, Skip Nelson, Mary Ann McCall, Tommy Taylor, and Peggy Mann. The theme song of the Teddy Powell Orchestra was "Blue Sentimental Mood." Powell was a prolific songwriter, penning tunes "My Love Is Yours," "Raindrops," "Am I Proud," "Bewildered," "Love of My Life," "The Lady from Fifth Avenue," "Spring Cleaning," "March Winds and April Showers," "Precious Little One," If I Could Be the Sweetheart of a Girl Like You," and many others. The Teddy Powell Orchestra recorded for Decca, Victor, and Bluebird records. In 1954, Powell retired and became a music publisher.

VIC SCHOEN

(Vic Schoen and His Orchestra) Born in Brooklyn, New York on March 26, 1916. Schoen was an arranger who played trumpet and worked with Gene Kardos in 1934. After playing and writing for Leon Belasco from 1936 to 1937, he wrote for Count Basie, Jimmy Dorsey, Glen Miller, Fred Waring, and Glen Gray.

During that period, he wrote the hit song "Bei Mir Bist Du Schoen." He served as musical director for the Andrews Sisters recordings from late 1937 to early 1942. He led bands, backing up Bing Crosby and the Andrew Sisters in the '40s recordings of "South America," "Take It Away," "Pistol Packin' Mama," and "Don't Fence Me In." In 1942, he wrote the tune "Amen" and, in 1949, "Hopeless Heart." During the beginning of television—in the early '50s—he arranged for and conducted bands on TV for Andy Williams, Pat Boone, Ethel Merman, and Bing Crosby. He served as music director for the TV show *The Big Record*. He recorded for Kapp, RCA, and Decca records. Schoen retired in California.

CLAUDE THORNHILL

(Claude Thornhill and His Orchestra) Born in Terre Haute, Indiana, on August 10, 1909. Thornhill studied music at the Cincinnati Conservatory of Music and the Curtis Institute of Music in Philadelphia. He first played with the Austin Wylie band in the mid-'20s. By the late '20s and '30s, he played with Ray Nobel, Freddie Martin, and Hal Kemp. Thornhill also worked with Benny Goodman, Leo Reisman, Don Voorhees, and Jacques Renard. He also wrote arrangements for various radio shows in New York, including music for André Kostelanetz. In the late '30s, he freelanced in Hollywood and served as music director, arranger, and pianist for Skinnay Ennis's new band. In 1940, Thornhill organized his first band that sponsored Maxine Sullivan's New York debut. She recorded "Loch Lomond" with the Thornhill band that year. In 1941, the Thornhill band worked at the Glen Island Casino. In 1942, he disbanded and joined Artie Shaw's navy band in Pearl Harbor. In 1946, he was discharged from the navy and organized a new band that featured arrangements by Gil Evans, Gerry Mulligan, and Ralph Aldridge, and great soloists, including alto saxophonist Lee Konitz and trumpeters Conrad Gozzo and Billy Butterfield. Thornhill worked as Tony Bennett's musical arranger in the '50s and recorded the tune "A Sunday Kind of Love," which featured singer Fran Warren and became a national hit. Thornhill's theme song was "Snowfall." Claude Thornhill recorded for Victor, Columbia, Okeh, Brunswick, and Vocalion records. Thornhill died in Caldwell, New Jersey on July 1, 1965.

PAUL WESTON

(Paul Weston and His Orchestra) Born in Springfield, Massachusetts on March 12, 1912. Weston attended Darmouth College in New Hampshire and fronted his own band, the Green Serenaders, at the college. He moved to New York, did graduate studies at Columbia University, and sold some arrangements to band-leader Joe Haymes who then sold them to Rudy Vallée. Vallée liked the arrangements and hired Weston to write for the *Fleischman Hour* radio program. In the early '30s, Weston worked with Bing Crosby, and during the mid- to late '30s, he wrote for the Tommy Dorsey band. During that period he met Jo Stafford, a member of the Pied Pipers vocal group, whom he married later. In 1940, Weston left Dorsey and began to freelance as arranger and conductor. He wrote and conducted for Dinah Shore, Jo Stafford, and the Bob Crosby band. Weston wrote the music for the famous film *Holiday Inn* that starred Fred Astaire, Bing Crosby, and Bob Crosby's band. While working at Paramount Pictures, Weston met Johnny Mercer, and the two of them founded Capitol Records; Weston became the A&R musical director. He produced a series of successful albums, including *Music for Dreaming*, *Music for Romacing*, *Music for Memories*, *Music for Quiet Dancing*, and *Music for the Fireside*. During his tenure with Capitol Records, Weston worked with singers Margaret Whiting, Betty Hutton, and Jo Stafford. Weston moved to Columbia Records in 1951, worked with Doris Day, Sarah Vaughan, and Ella Fitzgerald, and had his own CBS radio show. He returned to Capitol Records in 1957 and also became music director for NBC-TV, a division of RCA. By the '70s Weston and Stafford had retired. Weston died in Santa Monica, California in September 1996.

BUDDY COLE

(Buddy Cole and His Orchestra) Born in Irvine, Illinois, on December 15, 1916. Buddy Cole (né: Edwin Lemar Cole) grew up in Los Angeles, California, studied piano, and played in theaters in the early '30s. During the mid-'30s, he played with commercial bands led by Bob Grant, Johnny Bittick, Garewood Van, and Jay Whidden. From 1939 to 1940, he played with Frankie Trumbauer and played organ in Hollywood, California, on NBC radio and at Radio City Music Hall in New York City. Cole was with the Alvino Rey band from 1941 to 1943 and played on radio shows with Phil Harris, Bing Crosby, Ginny Simms, Tony Martin, and Hoagy Carmichael. Cole played piano in many movies and on many record dates as leader of combos, big bands, or accompanying singers. He recorded for Capitol, Columbia and Warner Brothers Records. Cole died in Hollywood, California, on November 5, 1964.

COZY COLE

(Cozy Cole and His Orchestra) Born in East Orange, New Jersey, on October 17, 1909. Drummer Cozy Cole (né: William Randolph Cole) first played with Wilbur Sweatman in New York in 1928 before forming his first band. In 1931, he played with Blanche Calloway and from 1933 to 1934 with Benny Carter. During 1935 and 1936, he worked with Willie Bryant until he joined the band led by Stuff Smith in 1936. He joined Cab Calloway in 1938 and played with his orchestra until 1942. During the years 1942 and 1943, Cole worked with Raymond Scott, Miff Mole, and his own groups in various radio studios. In 1945, Cozy Cole appeared in the Broadway musical *Carmen Jones* and headed the band in Seven Lively Arts. In 1949, Cole joined the Louis Armstrong All-Stars and remained with them until 1954 when he opened a drum school with drummer Gene Krupa in New York. He toured the U.S. and Europe with various groups, including Joe Bushkin, Sol Yaged, Jack Teagarden, and Earl Hines, and recorded "Topsy" in 1958 which became a big hit. In the late '50s and '60s he led a group on the *Arthur Godfrey Show* and, in 1968, played with the Jonah Jones band. Cole died in Columbus, Ohio, on January 31, 1981.

FRANK COMSTOCK

(Frank Comstock and His Orchestra) Born in San Diego, California, on September 20, 1922. Comstock studied music while attending high school and sold some of his arrangements as a teenager. In 1939, he played trombone and arranged for the Sonny Dunham band, in 1941 for Benny Carter, and for Les Brown in 1942. After Les Brown's band, Comstock settled in Hollywood, California and wrote and conducted for the studios. He worked with Doris Day, Rosemary Clooney, the Hi-Lo's, Margaret Whiting, and others. He also arranged for several television shows, including *Steve Allen*, *Bob Hope*, *Pete Kelly's Blues*, *The D.A.'s Man*, *Rocky and His Friends*, *McHale's Navy*, and *Ensign O'Toole*. He recorded for Columbia, Warner Brothers, and Dot records. Comstock remained active through the '60s and into the '70s.

DON COSTA

(Don Costa and His Orchestra) Born in Boston, Massachusetts, on June 10, 1925. Costa began playing in theaters in Boston, played guitar with the Vaughn Monroe band (Ghost Riders in the Sky), and moved to New York where he did studio work during the '40s. In the early '50s, Costa provided an arrangement for Eydie Gorme and Steve Lawrence that was recorded on Coral Records and became a hit. When Lawrence and Gorme signed with ABC-Paramount Records, Costa joined them and became the top A&R person. Again, in the late '50s when Lawrence and Gorme moved to United Artists Records, Costa went with them as a top arranger-conductor. While with ABC, Costa recorded the hit tune "Never on Sunday," which brought him international plaudits. Costa formed Don Costa Productions in the early '60s and developed Trini Lopez and Little Anthony and the Imperials. Shortly thereafter, Costa became Frank Sinatra's main arranger until the early '80s. Costa died in New York City on January 19, 1983.

EMERY DEUTSCH

(Emery Deutsch and His Orchestra) Born in Budapest, Hungary, on September 10, 1906. Deutsch's family immigrated to the U.S. when he was eight years old. He grew up in Cleveland, Ohio, attended Fordham University, and later graduated from the Juilliard School of Music in New York City. He became the music director for a radio station in Queens that was purchased by William S. Paley and became the nucleus for CBS. For 11 years, Deutsch served as music director for CBS and recruited performers, including Bing Crosby, Benny Goodman, and André Kostelanetz. In 1942 Deutsch entered the U.S. Maritime Service as a conductor. On his release and during the remaining '40s, '50s, and '60s, Emery Deutsch and His Orchestra performed throughout the U.S. in clubs and hotels, including the Mayflower in Washington, D.C., and the Ritz Carlton Hotel, Radio City Music Hall, and the Copacobana Nightclub in New York City. Deutsch wrote many songs, including "Play, Fiddle, Play" and his theme song "When a Gypsy Makes His Violin Cry." Deutsch also wrote "Stardust on the Moon," "The Old Gypsy Fiddler," "Budapest Suite," "My Gypsy Rhapsody," and many other tunes. He recorded for Brunswick, ABC, and Majestic records. In the early '70s, Deutsch moved to Miami, Florida where he played at various clubs and hotels until his retirement in 1995. Deutsch died in Miami, Florida on April 16, 1997.

JERRY JEROME

(Jerry Jerome and His Orchestra) Born in Brooklyn, New York, on June 19, 1912. Tenor saxophonist Jerry Jerome spent many years studying to be a medical doctor, but chose to be a professional musician. He played with Harry Reser in 1935 and with Glenn Miller's first band in 1937. In 1938, he worked with Benny Goodman, Red Norvo, and in the New York studios. Jerome is heard prominently on 1939 recordings with Ziggy Elman. In 1940, Goodman became ill and disbanded. Jerome joined Artie Shaw and worked with him until he became a radio staff conductor and musician from 1942 until 1946. In the late '40s, Jerry Jerome served as the recording director for Apollo, played in various venues, and led groups, backing singers for local dates and recordings. During the '50s and '60s, Jerome was active in New York on radio and television. In the early '70s, he played at the New York Athletic Club. Jerome recorded on MGM, ABC-Paramount, Stintson, and Camden records.

JOEY KEARNS

(Joey Kearns and His Orchestra) Tenor saxophonist Kearns played with and wrote for the Bob Crosby band from 1938 to 1940 and fronted a band working out of Philadelphia, Pennsylvania during early '40s. He had also played with a band led by Jan Savitt called the Tophatters Orchestra during the '30s. Kearns's Orchestra played on station WCAU in Philadelphia. Kearns's wife was a popular singer and his daughter, a cellist.

"PREACHER ROLLO" LAYLAN

(Preacher Rollo and His Five Saints) Laylan contracted polio at a young age and studied drums to help strengthen his right arm. He worked with several bands prior to playing with Jack Teagarden and Paul Whiteman. He was basically a Dixieland drummer but studied classical percussion as well. He formed his band during the '40s and played in and out of Miami Beach, Florida where he was heard on regular broadcasts over WKAT and the mutual radio network. Some of his sidemen were Tommy Justice, trumpet; Tony Parenti, clarinet; Ernie Goodson, clarinet; Jerry Gorman, trombone; and Marie Marcus, piano.

MARTY MARSALA

(Marty Marsala and His Orchestra) Born in Chicago, Illinois on April 2, 1909. Marty Marsala (né: Mario Salvatore Marsala) played trumpet (occasionally drums) and was the younger brother of clarinet player Joe Marsala. He played drums in Chicago in the late '20s and studied trumpet. In the early '30s, he joined his brothers' band, playing trumpet in New York, and recorded with the Bob Howard band and Tempo King from 1936 to 1937. In the early '40s, Marsala toured with the Chico Marx big band. During the latter part of 1943, he led a band in Chicago. Marsala served in the military during World War II (1944–1945), and played with Tony Parenti and Miff Mole in 1946 on his release from service. During the remaining '40s and through the '50s, Marsala led small groups in Chicago and on the West Coast. In the late '50s, he had a serious illness that nearly terminated his playing activity. He once again led a band during the '60s but became inactive and retired. Marsala recorded for ABC, Brunswick, and Riverside records. Marsala died in Chicago, Illinois on April 27, 1975.

MITCH MILLER

(Mitch Miller and His Gang) Born in Rochester, New York on July 4, 1911. Mitch Miller (né: Mitchell William Miller) studied piano when he was six and the oboe when he was 12. He attended the Eastman School of Music in Rochester, New York, and played with various symphony orchestras in the area. He joined CBS radio in 1932 and through 1943 played with the Budapest String Quartet, the Saidenburg Little Symphony, Percy Faith, and André Kostelanetz. After World War II, he was named the director of the popular division of Mercury Records, where he conducted and helped to produce hits for Frankie Laine, Hank Williams, and Jo Stafford. Moving to Columbia Records in the early '50s, he worked with Tony Bennett, Guy Mitchell, Rosemary Clooney, Jo Stafford, and Frank Sinatra. In the 1950s, Miller conducted his own orchestra in a series of successful recordings. During the '60s, he conducted a large all-male chorus in a series of sing-along television programs which used simple choreography and featured Dick Hyman on piano and solo singers Victor Griffin, Diana Trask, Louise O'Brien, and Leslie Uggams. Miller recorded for Mercury and Columbia records.

CLAUS OGERMAN

(Claus Ogerman and His Orchestra) Born in Ratibor, Germany on April 27, 1930. Ogerman attended the gymnasium in Nurnberg and studied classical piano. His first gig was with a big German jazz band led by Kurt Edelhagen, followed by a five-year tenure with the Max Greger Orchestra. He also did some arranging and composing for films at that time and led several groups of his own. Ogerman immigrated to the U.S. in 1959 and worked in recording studios and television. In 1963, he became a music director for Verve Records and worked with Bill Evans, Oscar Peterson, Cal Tjader, and Antonia Carlos Jobim on some albums. Ogerman than became the A&R man for A&M Records headed by Herb Alpert, where he worked with Paul Desmond and others. He ultimately recorded for Victor and Warner Brothers records.

GLENN OSSER

(Glenn Osser and His Orchestra) Born in Munising, Minnesota, on August 28, 1914. Glenn Osser (né: Abe Arthur Osser). Little is known of Osser's early life. Osser received the B.M. degree from the University of Michigan. Most of his work as we know it, was as music director and conductor for various orchestras on television. He was staff conductor on ABC from 1947 to 1968 and was musical director for the TV program *Your Big Moment* (aka, *Blind Date*) beginning in 1949 and for Pinocchio in 1957. He was the orchestra leader for the TV program music for a *Summer Night* commencing in 1959 (retitled in 1960 as *Music for a Spring Night*). Osser wrote "Ah Yes, There's Good Blues Tonight," "Young Man with the Blues," "Holiday for Winds," "Music for a Summer Night," "Look at Her," "Roseanne," and many others.

NELSON RIDDLE

(Nelson Riddle and His Orchestra) Born in Oradell, New Jersey on June 1, 1921. Riddle studied piano and trombone while still a teenager and during the mid- to late '30 played with several bands, including Charlie Spivak, Jerry Wald, Bob Crosby, and Tommy Dorsey. He worked for NBC for two years beginning in 1940 when Buddy DeSylva, Glen Wallach, and Johnny Mercer offered him a job conducting and arranging for Capitol Records, which had just been formed. With Capitol, Riddle directed and arranged for Nat "King" Cole,

Frank Sinatra, Ella Fitzgerald, Judy Garland, and Peggy Lee. In the '50s, Riddle worked in television and films, including the programs *Route 66* and *The Untouchables*, for which he wrote the theme song. Movies included *The Great Gatsby*, *The Pajama Game*, *A Hole in the Head*, and *St. Louis Blues*. He recorded three albums with singer Linda Ronstadt in the '80s. Riddle died on October 6, 1985.

TERRY SNYDER

(Terry Snyder and His Orchestra) Born in 1916, Snyder was a drummer who began working in the Bert Black Orchestra as a percussionist. In 1940, he was featured on WNEW, a New York radio station, and became Perry Como's drummer on Como's radio and television shows. During the '50s, he was heard on the harpsichord album with Stan Freeman, Bill Clifton's band, and the pianist Shura. He played with Lew Davies and Enoch Light on the Persuasive Percussion records and the Wall-to-Wall Sound series for United Artists Records. He also recorded for Columbia, United Artists, and King records. Snyder died in New York City on March 17, 1963.

LU WATTERS

(Lu Watters and His Yerba Buena Jazz band) Born in Santa Clara, California on December 19, 1911. Watters (né: Lucious Watters) began playing on cruise ships when he was quite young. In the '30s, he worked with the Carol Lofner Orchestra that later became the Phil Harris band. In the early '40s, Watters formed the Yerba Buena Jazz band, a New Orleans–type band. In 1942, he began serving in the U.S. military during World War II. When he was released from service in 1945, he reformed his band and worked until 1950. His latter band featured Bob Helm on clarinet, Bob Scobey on trumpet, Wally Rose on piano and Turk Murphy on trombone. In the early '50s, Watters retired from music but quickly organized another band and worked until he retired when he studied geology. Watters died in Santa Rosa, California on November 5, 1989.

GEORGIE AULD

(Georgie Auld and His Orchestra) Born in Toronto, Canada on May 19, 1919. Georgie Auld (né: John Altwerger) first played tenor saxophone in the '30s with the Bunny Berigan Orchestra. In 1939, he played with Artie Shaw and assumed the directorship of the Shaw band, when Shaw left for Mexico in 1940, and made his first record with his orchestra for Varsity Records. After several months, Auld disbanded and joined the Benny Goodman Orchestra that featured Charlie Christian and Cootie Williams. In 1941, Auld rejoined Artie Shaw, who had returned from Mexico, and played with Shaw until 1942. At that time Shaw joined the U.S. navy during World War II. In 1943, Georgie Auld formed a new band that featured sidemen like Billy Butterfield, Errol Garner, Trummy Young, and Dizzy Gillespie. After a bout with tuberculosis, Auld fronted a combo that played at the Three Deuces in New York City until 1950 when he joined the Count Basie Sextet. Shortly thereafter he moved to California and opened a club, the Melody Room. In the later part of his career Auld led studio orchestras and worked as Tony Martin's music director. Georgie Auld recorded for Guild, Musicraft, Discovery, Roost, and Apollo records. Auld's theme song was "I've Got a Right to Know." Auld died in Palm Springs, California on January 8, 1990.

BILL CLIFFORD

(Bill Clifford and His Orchestra) Clifford played violin with bands led by Griff Williams and Anson Weeks in the '30s. He organized his first big band in San Francisco in 1941. Bill Clifford sang, as well as played violin, and the band traveled throughout the country doing many radio broadcasts. The Clifford Orchestra played in Las Vegas at the Flamingo and El Rancho through the mid-'60s when Clifford disbanded. He then went on to sing with the Gary Nottingham big band. The theme song for the Bill Clifford band was "My Bill." When Clifford retired from the music business he moved to Phoenix, Arizona were he worked as general manager of radio KUPD and served as music director for Jim Bailey. Clifford died in 1984.

JOE GARLAND

(Joe Garland and His Orchestra) Born in Norfolk, Virginia, on August 15, 1903. Joe Garland (né: Joseph Copeland) studied saxophone and composition at the Aeolian Conservatory of Music in Baltimore, Maryland. He played with the Seminole Syncopators in 1924 and worked as a sideman for a long period of time with the orchestras of Elmer Snowden, Leon Abby, Lucky Millinder, Don Redman, and Louis Armstrong. When the U.S. entered World War II in late '42, Garland took over the Luis Russell Orchestra and led the band into the '50s. Garland wrote the tunes "In the Mood (Glenn Miller's Theme)" and "Leap Frog (Les Brown's Theme)." He also wrote a tune that was recorded as "Hot and Anxious" by Fletcher Henderson's Orchestra, "Congo Caravan," "Serenade to a Savage," and "There's Rhythm in Harlem." Garland retired and died in Teaneck, New Jersey on April 21, 1977.

CARL HOFF

(Carl Hoff and His Orchestra) Born in Oxnard, California, in 1905. Hoff played with Paul Ash and arranged for Paul Whiteman and Vincent Lopez in the early '30s. He formed his first band in 1934 and played in the Chicago area. In the mid '30s, Hoff was heard on network radio and remained active through the decade. Hoff broadcasted on *The Lucky Strike Parade* from 1936 to 1941 and on the *Al Pearce Show* from 1937 to 1940. Hoff's singers were Bob Haymes and Louanne Hogan. He had a good band with good arrangements, which he wrote, but the band never gained much popularity. Carl Hoff was the co-composer of "Vaya con Dios." Hoff recorded for Okeh Records.

SPIKE JONES

(Spike Jones and His City Slickers) Born in Long Beach, California on December 14, 1911. Jones (né: Lindley Armstrong Jones) played drums and organized his first band, the Five Tracks, while attending high school. He worked for the Southern Pacific Railroad and was given the nickname "Spike" as a result of that affiliation. Jones played with various territory bands in the '30s, including Everett Hoagland, Earl Burtnett, and Ray Robbins. In 1941, he formed his own band to do funny songs and song parodies. This band became well known for various noises it produced, including gunshots, cowbells, and honking car horns. During this period, Jones continued playing drums in the studios with various groups of musicians. In 1942, two hits, "Der Fuehrer's Face" and "Clink, Clink, Another Drink," brought positive notoriety to the group. At that time Spike Jones also played drums on Bing Crosby's international hit "White Christmas." From 1943 to 1944, the Jones Slickers toured throughout the U.S. In 1944, during World War II, they entertained troops in Europe. When the A F of M ban on recording was over the Spike Jones City Slickers recorded three big sellers: "The Jones Polka," "Chloe," and "Cocktails for Two." By 1947, Jones led two bands, the City Slickers and Spike Jones and His Other Orchestra that specialized in commercial dance music. The singer on both bands was Helen Grayco, who was married to Spike. After a year the dance band folded and in 1948 Spike formed a different version of the City Slickers and was heard on the popular radio show *The Spotlight Revue* (which later became *The Spike Jones Show*). In 1948, the band recorded "All I Want for Christmas Is My Two Front Teeth" and, in 1954, "I Saw Mommy Kissing Santa Claus." The Spike Jones Slickers appeared in a number of movies, including *Fireman, Save My Child*; *Ladies' Man*; *Variety Girl*; *Breakfast in Hollywood*; *Bring on the Girls*; *Meet the People*; and *Thank Your Lucky Stars*. They recorded for Liberty, Warner Brothers, and Kapp records. Jones's theme songs were "Cocktails for Two," "The Sheik of Araby," and "Pass the Biscuits, Mirandy." Jones died in Los Angeles, California on May 1, 1965.

HAL McINTYRE

(Hal McIntyre and His Orchestra) Born in Cromwell, Connecticut, on November 29, 1914. McIntyre studied saxophone and organized his first band in his hometown. He left to play in the Benny Goodman Orchestra for a brief time temporarily replacing a sax man who had taken a short leave. He then joined the Glenn Miller band, where he played for four years. In 1941, he left Miller and formed his own band, which was supported financially by Glenn Miller, and opened in New Rochelle, New York, at the Glen Island Casino. The original McIntyre band featured bass player Eddie Safranksi and singers Al Nobel, Ruth Gaylor, and Gloria Van. The band ultimately played at the Commodore Hotel in New York, at the Palladium Ballroom in Hollywood, at the Meadowbrook Club in New Jersey, at the Paramount Theater in New York, and many other venues. Some additional writers, sidemen, and singers with the

Hal McIntyre band through the years were Danny Hurd, Billy May, Dave Mathews, Carl Denny, and Jeanne McManus. The theme songs of McIntyre band were "Moon Mist" and "Ecstasy." Hal McIntyre recorded for Cosmo and Victor records. McIntyre died in California on May 5, 1959.

BOBBY SHERWOOD

(Bobby Sherwood and His Orchestra) Born in Indianapolis, Indiana on May 30, 1911. Sherwood grew up in a musical family and played in vaudeville when he was a child. He learned to play various instruments, including piano, guitar, trombone, and trumpet, He played guitar for Bing Crosby and moved to Hollywood, where he worked for MGM and began playing in studios as both a sideman and leader. He led the orchestra on the *Eddie Cantor* radio program and, in 1940, played with Artie Shaw for a brief time. In 1942, Sherwood formed his first orchestra that recorded "Moonlight Becomes You" that featured singer Kitty Kallen and "The Elk's Parade," which became a million-record-seller. A national tour ensued with the Sherwood band that had Flip Philips and Dave Pell in the saxophone section. The Broadway show *Hear That Trumpet* featured Sherwood in 1946. In 1947, the Sherwood band played at the Casino Gardens and featured saxophonist-arranger Dave Cavanaugh. Other prominent musicians who were heard on Sherwood recordings at a later date included Babe Russin, Hymie Shertzer, and Kai Winding. Various singers appeared with the band from time to time and included Jay Johnson, Gale Landis, Ginny Gibson, and Lynne Stevens. The theme songs of the Orchestra were "Waiting" and "The Elk's Parade." The band recorded for Capitol, Victor, Coral, Mercury, and Monogram records. Sherwood died in Auburn, Massachusetts, on January 23, 1981.

FREDDIE SLACK

(Freddie Slack and His Orchestra) Born in Westby, Wisconsin on August 7, 1910. Freddie Slack (né: Frederick Charles Slack) began as a drummer, moved to Chicago in 1927, and studied piano. In 1931, after playing with an orchestra led by Johnny Tobin, Slack moved to Los Angeles, California and played with Earl Burnett, Lennie Hayton, Archie Rosate, and Henry Halsted. From 1934 to 1936, he worked with the Ben Pollack band and joined Jimmy Dorsey in 1936 as pianist. In 1939, he played with the Will Bradley/Ray McKinley Orchestra and recorded the famous "Beat Me Daddy, Eight to the Bar." During the same period, Slack also recorded with Big Joe Turner and T-Bone Walker for Capitol Records. In 1941, Slack left the Bradley-McKinley band and was replaced by Billy Maxted. In 1942, Slack formed his first orchestra and was signed to Capitol Records where he recorded "Cow Cow Boogie" and "Strange Cargo." Ella Mae Morse was the band's singer. Although Slack became less popular in the early '50s, he continued to appear occasionally. The Slack Orchestra appeared in a number of motion pictures in the '40s, including *High School Hero*, *Babes on Swing Street*, *Take It Big*, *Seven Days Ashore*, *Hat Check Honey*, and *Reveille with Beverly*. Slack wrote the big hit "House of Blue Lights," which was recorded by nearly a dozen top artists of the day. Slack died in Hollywood, California on August 19, 1965.

MUGGSY SPANIER

(Muggsy Spanier and His Orchestra) Born in Chicago, Illinois, on November 9, 1906. Muggsy Spanier (né: Francis Joseph Spanier) studied cornet and played with bands led by Sig Meyers and Elmer Scheobel in Chicago, Illinois in the early '20s. He then recorded with the Bucktown Five and, from 1925 to 1928, played with Floyd Towne, Charley Straight, Gene Green, Charles Pierce, and Joe Kyser. In late 1928 and 1929, he worked with Ray Miller. Spanier left Chicago in late 1929 and joined Ted Lewis, with whom he played until 1936. While with Lewis, he appeared in the movies *Here Comes the Band* and *Is Everybody Happy?* In 1936, Spanier worked with Ben Pollack and remained with his band until 1938. In 1939, Spanier formed his own Dixieland group that made 16 Bluebird recordings and played at the Hotel Sherman in Chicago and Nick's in New York. After a short stint with Ted Lewis he played with Bob Crosby until 1941, when he formed a big band with arrangements by Deane

Kincaide. Vernon Brown, trombone, and Irving Fazola, clarinet, were members of that band which played at the Arcadia Ballroom in New York City and was heard on regular radio broadcasts. Spanier disbanded in 1943 and freelanced around the city. He rejoined Ted Lewis momentarily in 1944 and, for the remaining years of the '40s, played with various groups in and around New York City. During the '50s, Spanier played in San Francisco and did various jobs with Earl Hines. He played the Newport Jazz Festival in 1964 and retired soon thereafter. Spanier died in Sausalito, California on February 12, 1967.

JERRY WALD

(Jerry Wald and His Orchestra) Born in Newark, New Jersey, on January 15, 1918. Jerry Wald (né: Jervis Wald) was a clarinet player who was a big fan of Artie Shaw and tried to emulate Shaw's playing. Wald formed his first band in 1941 with excellent personnel like saxophonists Bob Dukoff, Larry Elgart, and Les Robinson. The arrangers for the band were Jerry Gray, Ray Coniff, and Bill Challis. World War II and the draft suspended activity of the band until 1949 when Wald formed a band along the "progressive" lines. In the latter part of 1949 and because of the relative failure of the new band, Wald led a combo in Hollywood at the Studio Club. From 1951 to 1952, Jerry Wald formed a new big band that played in California and New York, backing up Patti Paige, Frankie Laine, Mel Tormé, Perry Como, Frank Sinatra, and others. The band also played the *Donn Arden Ice Revues* and was heard on the *Robert Q. Lewis Show*. Television appearances included the *Jackie Gleason Show* and the *Kate Smith Show*. The theme songs of the Jerry Wald Orchestra during the years were "The Moon's on Fire," "Trains in the Night," "Summer Moon," "Laura," "Clarinet High Jinx," and "Call of the Wild." The Wald band recorded for Columbia, Majestic, and Decca records. Wald died in Las Vegas, Nevada, in 1973.

DICK WICKMAN

(Dick Wickman and His Orchestra) Born in 1916. Wickman organized his first band in 1941 in Omaha, Nebraska. After one year, Wickman drafted into the armed services due to the beginning of WWII. When he was discharged from the army, he went into business until the late '40s when he started a new band that played the ballrooms and various venues in the Dakotas, Nebraska, and

Iowa and began recording for a record label founded by Wickman. By 1965, the Wickman Orchestra was heard regularly from a Lincoln, Nebraska radio station on a half-hour show. The band continued playing into the '70s under Wickman's part-time leadership. The theme song of the Dick Wickman band was "I Want to Be Happy." He took on additional business interests and rarely traveled. Wickman died in 1988.

COOTIE WILLIAMS

(Cootie Williams and His Orchestra) Born in Mobile, Alabama, on July 24, 1910. Cootie Williams (né: Charles Melvin Williams played trombone in his high school marching band, switched to tuba temporarily, and then took trumpet lessons from Charles Lipskin, a member of the New Orleans Excelsior Jazz band. He joined the Calvin Shields Orchestra in Florida when he was 15 and played with them for a year. In 1926, he joined the Alonzo Ross Deluxe Syncopators and traveled to New York City with the band. In 1928, he left the Syncopators and played with Jabbo Smith, Chick Wenn, and Fletcher Henderson. In 1929, he replaced Bubber Miley with Duke Ellington's band and remained there for 11 years. In 1940, he left Ellington and played with Benny Goodman for a year until he formed Cootie Williams and His Orchestra in 1941. In 1942, the Williams band featured Eddie Vinson, Arnett Cobb, and Pearl Bailey and recorded "Tess's Torch Song" and "Now I Know." After World War II, in 1948, Williams reduced the size of his band to a sextet and played at the Savoy Ballroom until it closed in 1959. Williams rejoined the Ellington band and played there until Duke died in 1974. The Williams band recorded for RCA, Mercury, Savoy, Majestic, Hit, and Okeh records. The band's theme song was "Round Midnight," which was co-written by Williams and Thelonius Monk. Williams died in Long Island, New York on September 15, 1985.

PAUL LaVALLE

(Paul LaValle and His Orchestra) Born in Beacon, New York on September 6, 1908. LaValle attended the Juilliard School of Music in New York City and played in several bands during the '30s in the U.S. and Cuba. He played with the NBC Symphony Orchestra and was a staff musician on NBC for several years. In the '40s, he worked in various bands in and around New York City and was heard on several radio programs, including the *Chamber Music Society of Lower Basin Street* on station WEAF, which featured Diana Shore as the female singer. LaValle also conducted a 50-piece orchestra on the Cities Service radio show. He was active in various band concerts, including the Mall Show in 1945 and the band of America in 1948. Paul LaValle conducted the official band of the New York World's Fair in 1964–1965 and guest conducted various symphony orchestras and bands throughout the U.S. In the '70s, LaValle was musical director of the Radio City Music Hall in New York and directed McDonald's All-American High School Band. Paul LaValle wrote several novelty and concert tunes, including "Deep Melody," "Memoirs of a Dilemma," "Dance of the Woodwinds," "Good Fellowship," "United States Overture," "The Merrymakers," and "Big Joe the Tuba." LaValle recorded with MGM, Metro, Victor, and Musicraft records.

BOB ASTOR

(Bob Astor and His Orchestra) Astor former his band in California in 1940 and, although the band never recorded or did radio broadcasts, was considered a very musical organization featuring future stars, including Tommy Allison, Zoot Sims, Illinois Jacquet, Neal Hefti, Les Elgart, and Shelly Manne. Astor formed the band as a way of hearing his arrangements and compositions played. Some of those were "You're My Baby You," "Here Comes the Judge," "Blue Lights" (the band's theme song), "Fat Sam," "If You Don't Believe I'm Leaving," "Count the Days," "In the Cool of the Evening," and "I Remember Harlem." When Astor disbanded, he became a radio disc jockey.

D'ARTEGA'S ALL-GIRL ORCHESTRA

(D'Artega and His Orchestra) D'Artega (né: Alphonso D'Artega) was born in Spain. His parents immigrated to the U.S. when D'Artega was 11 and he studied music composition and orchestration with Boris Levenson, who had been a pupil of Rimsky-Korsakov. D'Artega graduated from the Strassberger Conservatory and tried to popularize classical music. He conducted, arranged, and composed for many different groups and, at one time played the role of Tchaikovsky in a movie produced by United Artists entitled *Carnegie Hall.* He originated the Pop Concerts at Carnegie Hall in New York City and guest conducted with the symphony orchestras in Long Island, at the Lewisohn Stadium in New York, and in Long Island, Buffalo, and Miami. D'Artega recorded for Epic Records.

CHARLIE FISK

(Charlie Fisk and His Orchestra) Charlie Fisk graduated from the University of Missouri and organized his band in the early '40s. He was a big fan of Harry James and emulated his trumpet playing. His singer was Ginny Coon, his wife. The band was booked by the Music Corporation of America (MCA) and played primarily in the Midwest. Favorite venues included the Pla-Mor in Kansas City, the Pleasure Pier in Port Arthur, Texas, the Tunetown Ballroom in St. Louis, the Indiana Roof in Indianapolis, the New Casino in Fort Worth, and the Nu-Elm Ballroom in Youngstown, Ohio. The band prospered during the '40s but disbanded in the early '50s.

EDDIE HOWARD

(Eddie Howard and His Orchestra) Born in Woodland, California, on September 12, 1914. Eddie Howard (né: Edward Evan Duncan Howard) sang on local radio stations and attended San José State University and Stanford Medical School. He soon discovered that music was his true love and sang on various radio stations in Los Angeles and San Francisco. He joined the Eddie Fitzpatrick Orchestra for a brief time before joining the Tom Gerunovich Orchestra. In the early '30s, he left school and joined the Ben Bernie band. In 1933, he signed with the Dick Jurgens Orchestra and played trombone as well as being the featured singer. Howard joined Dick Jurgens in writing several popular songs. Among them were "Careless," "A Million Dreams Ago," "My Last Good-Bye," and "If I Knew Then What I Know Now." In 1940, Eddie Howard left the Jurgens Orchestra and joined George Olsen's band. In 1941, he took over the Buddy Baer Orchestra and opened at the Casa Loma Ballroom in St. Louis, Missouri. The Howard Orchestra also worked regularly at the Aragon Ballroom in Chicago and did many national radio broadcasts. During World War II, when most of the sidemen in the Howard Orchestra were drafted, Eddie Howard worked as a solo act until 1946, when he reformed his big band and began recording for Majestic Records (which later became Mercury Records).

Howard recorded two tunes that made the band a hit: "It's No Sin" and "To Each His Own." The band stayed together until 1960 when Howard moved to Las Vegas where he made a comeback and played at Catalina Island in the summers. Howard died in Palm Desert, California on May 23, 1963.

STAN KENTON

(Stan Kenton and His Artistry in Rhythm Orchestra) Born in Wichita, Kansas on December 15, 1911. Stan Kenton (né: Stanley Newcomb Kenton) was raised in Colorado; however, his family moved to California when Stan was 15 years old. He studied piano with Frank Hurst and played during high school. In 1930, Kenton toured with the Flack Brothers band in California and Nevada. From 1933 to 1934, he played with the Everette Hoaglund Orchestra and, in 1935, with the Russ Plummer band. After a short stint with the Hal Grayson Orchestra in San Francisco, he joined the Gus Arnheim band. In 1938, Kenton played with Vido Musso at the Villa Venice in Los Angeles. From 1939 to 1940, he was the pianist in the pit band of the Earl Carroll Vanities. In 1941, Kenton formed a rehearsal band, named Artistry in Rhythm Orchestra that eventually played at the Hollywood Palladium. The band attracted some great arrangers, players, and singers, including Bob Cooper, Art Pepper, Buddy Childers, Kai Winding, Shelly Manne, Laurindo Almeida, Gene Roland, Pete Rugolo; singers June Christy, Anita O'Day, Chris Connor, and others. In the early '50s, Kenton organized a 43-piece orchestra that included a string section and named it the Innovations in Modern Music Orchestra. Some of the outstanding new players were Maynard Ferguson, Shorty Rogers, Bud Shank, and arranger Bob Graettinger. By the mid-'50s, Kenton's band was the only American big band allowed to work in Great Britain without restriction. In the late '50s, Kenton organized an "Orchestra in Residence" program that took his band for two-week residencies to various campuses to work with students. They were typically called "Kenton Camps." In the '60s, Kenton organized two new bands. One was the "mellophonium" orchestra entitled New Era in Modern Music and the other, a larger orchestra, the Neophonic Orchestra, which played heavier symphonic jazz. In the '70s, band took on some "rock" characteristics that Kenton led unenthusiastically sticking to his lifelong belief that the future of modern jazz remained in the colleges and universities to which he had dedicated so much of his time and talent. Later in the '70s, and after a serious operation, his health began to wane and one of his final concerts was held at the Newport Jazz Festival. Kenton died in Los Angeles, California on August 25, 1979.

RONNIE KEMPER

(Ronnie Kemper and His Orchestra) Born in Missoula, Montana on August 1, 1912. Kemper first sang, wrote arrangements, and played piano with the Dick Jurgens Orchestra in 1934 and remained with that band until 1940 when they recorded the hit "Cecilia." He joined the Horace Heidt band in 1941, appeared in the movie *Pot of Gold*, and organized his own band in 1942. Soon after, Kemper was drafted into military service and served until early 1946 when he worked as a single. He was one of the musicians on early television, directing his own show, *Kemper's Kapers*, for seven years. He was also heard on his own radio show. Kemper wrote several tunes, including "Dine and Dance," "Doodle Bug Song," "In a Blue Canoe," "Knit One, Purl Two," and "It's a Hundred to One." He recorded for Columbia and Vocalion records. The theme song of the Ronnie Kemper Orchestra was "Cecilia." Kemper died in Dayton, Ohio on December 19, 1993.

RAY McKINLEY

(Ray McKinley and His Orchestra) Born in Fort Worth, Texas, on June 18, 1910. McKinley began playing drums in the Fort Worth–Dallas area. He joined the Smith Ballew band in 1933 with sideman Glenn Miller. McKinley and Miller left Ballew to join the Dorsey Brothers band in 1934. McKinley remained with the Dorsey Brothers until they split up in 1935 and Jimmy took over the band. Ray McKinley then stayed on the Jimmy Dorsey band until 1939, when he went to work for Will Bradley as co-leader of that band. McKinley left to form his own band in 1942 and opened at the Hotel Commodore in New York City. Dick Cathcart was one of the trumpet players and the featured singer was Imogene Lynn. The McKinley band was featured in the movie *Hit Parade of 1943* and recorded for Capitol and Hit Records. The band disbanded when McKinley received his draft notice and joined Captain Glenn Miller in his Air Force band. When Miller disappeared over the English Channel, McKinley took over the band. When the war ended and McKinley was discharged, he formed a new band which featured Mundell Lowe, guitar; Rusty Dedrick, trombone; Peanuts Hucko, clarinet; and Eddie Sauter, arranger. The band played at Hotel Commodore and was billed as "the most versatile band in the land". This McKinley band was the most successful and recorded for Majestic and Victor Records. McKinley disbanded in 1952 and headed an all-star studio big band that recorded for Dot Records. In 1956, McKinley became the leader of a new Glenn MIller Orchestra, which toured and recorded for Epic, Majestic, Camden, and Victor Records. McKinley theme song was "Howdy, Friends." Some of the featured sidemen with McKinley were Curly Broyles, Nick Travis, Johnny Carisi, Billy Ainsworth, Deane Kincaide, Pete Condoli, Peanuts Hucko, and Mundell Lowe. Various singers were featured with the McKinley bands over the years, including Joan Shepherd, Debbie Land, Lorrie Peters, Artie Malvin, Dale Nunally, Jean Friley, Marcie Lutes, Ann Hathaway, and Imogene Lynn. McKinley died in Largo, Florida on May 7, 1995.

HERB MILLER

(Herb Miller and His Orchestra) Born in North Platte, Nebraska. Herb Miller (né: John Herb Miller) was the younger brother of Glenn Miller and played trumpet while attending college. After playing in his brother's band for a brief time Herb Miller joined the Charlie Spivak Orchestra. In the '40s, Miller organized his own band that toured the U.S. and was featured at the Aragon Ballroom in Ocean Park, California, the Jerry Jones Ballroom, and the Rendezvous Ballroom in Salt Lake City, Utah. Herb formed his own record label Millertone and made one album. In the late '40s, Miller moved to Pacific Grove, California, where he lived for about 25 years. In the late '60s, Miller moved to England and formed a new band that he fronted until he retired. Miller died in the late '80s.

BILLY VAUGHAN

(Billy Vaughan and His Orchestra) Vaughan was a hairdresser who had a great interest in singing and arranging. When he was in the U.S. army during World War II, he was based in Mississippi and formed his first orchestra. When he was released in 1945, he gave up the beauty business and pursed his dream of a career in music. He was the first artist to receive a platinum record for the three-million-seller "Sail Along, Silv'ry Moon" that also earned gold medals in the Netherlands and in Germany. He obtained a second three-million-seller by arranging and conducting the recording of Pat Boone's "Love Letters in the Sand." He constantly researched new sound (e.g. a guitar quartet, twin saxophones, etc.) won awards for Best Studio Orchestra, Most Programmed Orchestra, Best-Selling Orchestra, the Golden Tulip Award (the Netherlands), the Gold Cow Bell Award (Switzerland), among others. All of his recordings (albums) were on Dot Records and included *Mexican Pearls, Blue Velvet and 1963 Great Hits, As Requested, Alfie, A Swinging Safari, Michelle, Josephine, Great Country Hits, Memories in Gold, Orange Blossom Special, Wheels, Berlin Melody*, and many more.

JOHNNY RICHARDS

(Johnny Richards and His Orchestra) Born in Toluca, Queretaro, Mexico on November 2, 1911. Johnny Richards (né: Juan Cascales) moved with his family to Schenectady, New York when he was a teenager. He studied violin and piano with his mother, who was a concert pianist. In 1932, when he graduated from Syracuse University, he moved to London, England, and began writing music for movies. In 1934, he returned to the U.S., moved to Hollywood, and began writing music for Paramount Pictures as Victor Young's assistant. At that time he, also studied composition with Arnold Schoenberg. From 1940 to 1945, he fronted his own big band, after which he settled in Los Angeles and arranged for the Boyd Raeburn Orchestra from 1946 to 1948. During the early '50s, he conducted studio orchestras recording with Sarah Vaughan and Helen Merrill and arranged for Dizzy Gillespie and Ben Webster. From 1952 to 1957, he wrote for Stan Kenton penning such works as "Cuban Fire," a six-part suite. In 1956, Richards formed a new band that he fronted through 1960, which recorded for Capitol, Coral, and Bethelem records. In 1961, Richards rejoined the Stan Kenton Orchestra as arranger and wrote music for the LP *The West Side*

Story. In 1964, Richards once again left Kenton to form his own band that recorded for Roulette Records. Richards was the co-composer of his theme song "Young at Heart." Richards died in New York City on October 7, 1968.

SID BASS

(Sid Bass and His Orchestra) Born in New York City on January 22, 1913. Sid Bass (né: Sidney Bass) attended New York University, formed his own band, and worked for Muzak. After disbanding his orchestra, he joined RCA as a composer and arranger, writing music, conducting, and recording. He wrote "Music," "Soft Shoe Song," "One-Man Woman," "Greatest Feeling in the World," "More of Everything," and "The Story of Man." He recorded pre-stereo hi-fi albums, including *With Bells On*, *Sound and Fury*, *Moog Expana*, *Funny Bones*, *From Another World*, *Blue Bells*, and *Bells Are Swinging* on Vik and Camden records.

"BULL MOOSE" JACKSON

("Bull Moose" Jackson and His Buffalo Bearcats) Born in Cleveland, Ohio on April 22, 1919. "Bull Moose" Jackson (né: Benjamin Clarence Jacon) studied the violin as a child and alto saxophone as a teenager. While in high school Jackson and a close friend, Freddie Webster, formed a band called the Harlem Hotshots and by 1943 were playing in a Buffalo, New York nightclub. Jackson joined the Lucky Millinder band in 1944 as a singer and saxophone player. It was while he was with Millinder that a band member gave him the name "Bull Moose" that stuck with him throughout his career. Jackson soon formed his own band that he called the Buffalo Bearcats inasmuch as they played on a regular basis at a Buffalo club. The newly formed Jackson band quickly recorded for the Queen Record label and succeeded with the big hit "Who Threw the Whiskey in the Well." During the remainder of the '40s and through the '50s the Jackson Buffalo Bearcats recorded a number of hits, including "I Can't Go On Without You," "I Want a Bowlegged Woman," "Sneaky Pete," "I Love You, Yes, I Do," "All My Love Belongs to You," "Why Don't You Haul Off and Love Me," and "Little Girl, Don't Cry." Other records labels recording the Jackson Buffalo Bearcats were King and 7Arts Records. In the '60s they recorded "I Love You, Yes, I Do," and, in the '80s, "Get Off the Table, Marbel (The Two Dollars Is the Beer)." Jackson died in Cleveland, Ohio on July 31, 1988.

BOB STRONG

(Bob Strong and His Orchestra) Born in Kansas City, Missouri in 1902. Strong graduated from Kansas State University in 1924 and joined a band at the Rendezvous Café in Chicago led by Charlie Straight. Bix Beiderbecke was in the band at that time. Strong also conducted the orchestra and was the music director for *The Avalon Time* radio program featuring Red Skelton and the *Buddy Clark's Treat Time* show. In the early '40s, Strong organized his first band and played at the Glen Island Casino in New York. Strong wrote the theme song of the band, "Tonal Color Serenade." The Strong band was often heard on the radio during Saturday afternoon broadcasts from Chicago although there were few recordings due to the AF of M recording ban.

LEROY ANDERSON

(Leroy Anderson and His Orchestra) Born in Cambridge, Massachusetts, on June 29, 1908. Anderson took music lessons when he was a small child, attended the New England Conservatory of Music and Harvard University and composed and arranged music that caught the attention of Arthur Fiedler, the conductor of the Boston Pops Orchestra. Fiedler often played Anderson's compositions and arrangements and allowed him to guest-conduct the orchestra on occasion. In 1940 Anderson formed his own orchestra playing semi-classical music, which had become popular. During World War II and the Korean War, Anderson served in the U.S. Military. In the late '40s he wrote the hit "Fiddle Faddle" for large wind and percussion groups that also used strings. In the late '50s, Anderson wrote the music for the Broadway show *Goldilocks* that included tunes "Save a Kiss," "Pussyfoot," "Lazy Moon," "Who's Been Sitting in My Chair?," as well as others. During his career, Leroy Anderson wrote many "serious" compositions that became popular among the symphonic crowd. "The Typewriter," "The Penny-Whistle Song," "Sleigh Ride," "Pink, Plank, Plunk," "Horse and Buggy," and "Blue Tango" were among his most popular. Anderson died in Woodbury, Connecticut on May 18, 1975.

JOHN BENSON BROOKS

(John Benson Brooks and His Orchestra) Born in Houlton, Maine, on February 23, 1917. Brooks attended the New England Conservatory of Music and worked in Boston in various venues. Pianist Brooks arranged for Les Brown, Tommy Dorsey, Boyd Raeburn, Eddie DeLange, and Randy Brooks in the early '40s, prior to organizing his own band in 1944. His band opened at the Howard Theater in Washington, D.C. and, by 1946, was featuring some superb musicians like Eddie Kane (alto saxophone), Shorty Allen (vibes), and Stan Getz (tenor saxophone). During the mid-'40s, Brooks was married to bandleader Ina Ray Hutton and they moved to the West Coast. In the early '50s, Brooks played with Miles Davis's band that included Gerry Mulligan, Gil Evans, John Carisi, John Lewis, George Russell, Dave Lambert, Billy Exiner, Joe Shulman, Barry Galbraith, Specs Goldberg, Sylvia Goldberg, and Blossom Dearie. Brooks wrote the tune "You've Come a Long Way from St. Louis," which was sung by Peggy Lee, Johnny Mercer, and Perry Como, among others. Brooks recorded for Vik Records. Brooks died in the '60s from a series of strokes.

FRANKIE CARLE

(Frankie Carle and His Orchestra) Born in Providence, Rhode Island on March 25, 1903. Pianist Carle (né: Francis Nunzio Carlone) began playing in his uncle's band for $1 a week in 1916. In the early '20s, he joined the Edwin McEnelley band and recorded for Victor Records. In the mid-'30s, he played with the Mal Hallett band and formed his own band in the late '30s and worked as a territory band in the greater New England area. At that time he wrote and performed the hit tune "Sunrise Serenade." In the early '40s, he disbanded and joined Horace Heidt who featured him and brought him national attention. When Eddie Duchin joined the U.S. navy in 1941, he asked Carle to assume the leadership of his band and offered him 25 percent of the gross income to do so. Carle told Heidt about this offer and Heidt, in turn, offered him a thousand dollars a week plus fiver percent of the gross income to stay with him. Carle elected to remain with Heidt and did so until 1944, when he organized his own band. Carle band featured singers Greg Lawrence, Paul Allen, Marjorie Hughes, and Phyllis Lynn. In addition to "Sunrise Serenade," Carle wrote "Estelle," "Roses in the Rain," "Oh! What It Seemed to Be," "Falling Leaves," "Don't You Remember Me?" and "Carle Boogie." He recorded for Victor and Columbia records. Carle died on March 7, 2001.

SID CATLETT

("Big Sid" Catlett and His Orchestra) Born in Evanston, Indiana on January 17, 1910. Sid Catlett (né: Sidney Catlett) studied drums and played his first gig at the age of 17 at the Club Arlington in Chicago with the Darnell Howard band. In the late '20s and early '30s, he played with several bands in various styles before joining Benny Carter's band in New York City in 1931. He joined the Louis Armstrong band for a stint prior to playing with the Benny Goodman Orchestra in 1941. At that time, Goodman's band included Tommy Morgan, guitar; Mel Powell, piano; Sid Weiss, bass; Al Davis, Jimmy Maxwell and Billy Butterfield, trumpets; Cutty Cutshall and Lou McGarity, trombones; Chuck Gentry, Julie Schwartz, George Berg, Clint Neagley, and Vito Musso, saxophones; and singers Art Lund and Peggy Lee. The Catlett style of drumming helped to set the style of bands led by Louis Armstrong ("Jeepers Creepers") and Fletcher Henderson ("Stealin' Apples" and "Jangle Nerves"). After the Goodmand band, Catlett played with Eddie Condon, Roy Eldridge, and Don Redman. He formed his own band in 1944, did a national tour, and recorded in Los Angeles. In the late '40s, Catlett played with the Louis Armstrong All-Stars. Sid Catlett recorded for Commodore, Music Shop, Decca, Victor, Columbia, Capitol, Swing, Keynote, and Regis records. Catlett died in Chicago, Illinois, on March 25, 1951.

CARMEN DRAGON

(Carmen Dragon and His Orchestra) Born in Antioch, California on July 28, 1914. Dragon studied at San Jose State College and was known as a complete musician with a total reputation as a radio and television personality, educator, composer, arranger, and conductor. Most of his work was done on the West Coast in the '40s and '50s where he wrote and conducted for Hollywood studios, record dates, radio and television performances, and performed many concerts at the Hollywood Bowl. He did numerous arrangements of popular tunes and semi-classical pieces that were very identifiable and original. He worked on numerous movies, including *Mr. Winkle Goes to War*, *The Young Widow*, *Out of the Blue*, *Dishonored Lady*, *The Time of Your Life*, *Kiss Tomorrow Goodbye*, *Night into Morning*, *The Law and the Lady*, *The People Against O'Hara*, *When in Rome*, *At Gunpoint*, and *Invasion of the Body Snatchers*. Dragon died on March 28, 1984.

BILLY ECKSTINE

(Billy Eckstine and His Orchestra) Born in Pittsburgh, Pennsylvania, on July 8, 1914. Singer Billy Eckstine (né: William Clarence Eckstine) attended Howard University in Washington, D.C. and began his singing career doing solo work in Washington, D.C., Detroit, Buffalo, and Chicago venues. In the mid-'30s, he sang in the Tommy Myles band prior to joining the Earl Hines band in 1939 where he remained until 1943. After working as a single and with the help of saxophonist Buddy Johnson, he formed his own big band in 1944 that was an important contributor to the new music, bebop. At various times, the following played in the Billy Eckstine Orchestra: Charlie Parker, Dizzy Gillespie, Dexter Gordon, Fats Navarro, Miles Davis, Leo Parker, Art Blakey, Lucky Thompson, Gene Ammons, Jerry Valentine, Kenny Durham, Howard McGhee, and many other contributors to the bebop movement. The female singer was Sarah Vaughan. The principal arrangers were Tadd Dameron, Budd Johnson, and Dizzy Gillespie. The band was an instant musical success and toured the U.S. In 1947, Eckstine disbanded the big band and toured as a single. During his career, Eckstine recorded for Bluebird, Deluxe, National, MGM, Roulette, Mercury, Lion, Regent, and Emarcy records. Eckstine remained active into the '70s, touring Asia, Australia, and Europe. Eckstine died in Pittsburgh, Pennsylvania on March 8, 1993.

JERRY MURAD AND THE HARMONICATS

(Jerry Murad and the Harmonicats) Born in Turkey, Murad and colleague Al Fiore (né: Al Fiorentino), born in 1923, played with a harmonica band, begin-ning in 1940, called Borah Minnevitch's Harmonica Rascals that appeared in Hollywood and on various vaudeville stages. In 1944, they left to form their own trio, the Harmonicats, by adding Don Les (né: Dominic Leshinski), born in 1915, and began to record for Columbia Records. In 1947 they recorded the number one tune "Peg O' My Heart," which became a national success. In the mid-'50s, they recorded for Mercury Records for a short Harmonicats before returning to Columbia. In 1966 they recorded an album, *What's New, Harmonicats?*, that contained hit tunes "Get Off of My Cloud" and "Blowin' in the Wind." The original pair, Murad and Fiore, played many duets with the Richard Hayman Orchestra and upon retirement, Murad wrote a number of harmonica books. A few of the albums recorded by the Harmonicats were *Try a Little Tenderness*; *The Love Songs of Tom Jones*; *The Cat's Meow*; *That New Gang of Mine*; *South American Nights*; *Sentimental Serenade*; *In the Land of Hi-Fi*; *Harmonica Rhapsody*; *Forgotten Dreams*; *El Cid & Moon River; Fiesta!*; *Dolls, Dolls, Dolls*; *Cherry Pink and Apple Blossom White*; and *Cats Around the Horn*. Murad died in Liberty Township, Ohio on May 11, 1996; Fiore died in Chicago, Illinois on October 25, 1996; and Don Les in Madison, Wiscosin on August 25, 1994.

TED HEATH
(Ted Heath and His Orchestra) Born in Wandsworth, S.W., London, England on March 30, 1900. Ted Heath (né: Edward Heath) played trombone in the early '20s with Jack Hylton, Bert Firman, and Al Starita. He played from 1927 to 1935 with the Ambrose Orchestra and with various groups in the later '30s. During the period of 1940 to 1945, he played with the Geraldo band until he formed his own orchestra that achieved great success at the London Palladium and toured England. His band worked with Toots Camarata on the musical movie *London Town* and played a number of engagements at Hammersmith Palais de Danse. The Heath Orchestra had a number of great soloists, including trumpets Bobby Pratt and Kenny Baker, drummer Jack Parnell, saxophonists Ronnie Scott and Les Gilbert and trombonist Don Lusher. The singers included Lita Roza and Beryl Davis. In the '50s, the Heath band, which was described as a great group of well-trained musicians who could really swing, concluded a very successful American tour. The band recorded for London and Decca records. It was considered a band that was great for listening and dancing. Heath died in Surrey, England on November 18, 1969.

BUDDY JOHNSON
(Buddy Johnson and His Orchestra) Born in Darlington, South Carolina, on January 10, 1915. Buddy Johnson (né: Woodrow Wilson Johnson) studied arranging and moved to New York City in 1938. In 1939 he toured Europe with the Cotton Club Revue. He arranged for various bands and toured the South until 1944 when he organized his own big band and featured his sister, Ella Johnson, as singer. The Buddy Johnson band was a hit when it recorded "Please,

Mr. Johnson." The band worked for long periods at the Savoy Ballroom in New York and featured Arhtur Prysock as vocalist in the late '40s and early '50s. The band was well known for a rhythm and blues style. In the '60s, Buddy Johnson disbanded the big band and formed a combo. Johnson wrote "Southern Exposure" and "Troyon Swing." The Buddy Johnson band recorded for Decca and Mercury records.

EDDIE MILLER

(Eddie Miller and His Orchestra) Born in New Orleans, Louisiana on June 23, 1911. Miller first played the saxophone and clarinet with the New Orleans Owls and Billy Lustig's Orchestra in New Orleans. In the late '20s, he moved to New York City and played with Julie Wintz's band that had a Columbia Record contract. He played with Ben Pollack and His Orchestra when he was 19 and remained with him until 1934. Matty Malneck, Gil Rodin, Ray Bauduc, and Nappy Lamare were also on the Pollack band at the time. This same group served as the nucleus for the Bob Crosby band when Pollack disbanded. Miller served in the armed forces from 1943 to 1944. When he was released, he moved to California, doing studio work and leading his own orchestra. The theme song of the Eddie Miller Orchestra was "Lazy Mood." The band disbanded in 1946. During the heyday of the Miller Orchestra, the sidemen included Nappy Lamare, Nick Fatool, and Artie Shapiro. Matty Malneck and Joe Haymes wrote arrangements for the band and the singers included Penny Parker and Mickie Roy. When Miller disbanded he went to work for 20th Century Fox. After 1950, Miller played with Bob Crosby and toured with the World's Greatest Jazz Band. Miller died in Van Nuys, California on April 8, 1991.

GEORGE PAXTON

(George Paxton and His Orchestra) Born in Jacksonville, Florida, on March 4, 1916. Saxophonist Paxton's family moved to New Jersey when he was very young. He formed a six-piece band while in high school with his classmates Herbie Haymer and Tony Mottola and played at Frank Dailey's Meadowbrook. Haymer, Mottola, and Paxton soon moved to New York City and Frank Dailey hired Paxton as his arranger. Tony Mottola became a studio guitar player and Haymer, who played tenor saxophone, played with Red Norvo and then with

Woody Herman. In the late '30s, George Paxton wrote arrangements and played saxophone with the George Hall Orchestra and Dolly Dawn's Patrol. The Hall Orchestra soon went on the road while Paxton remained in New York and wrote for Bea Wain who had just joined Bunny Berigan, having been with the Larry Clinton Orchestra. Charlie Spivak and his newly formed Cincinnati band hired Paxton along with Sonny Burke and Nelson Riddle to write arrangements for his new band until Paxton was lured back to New York City by Ina Ray Hutton who guaranteed Paxton 50 percent of her new all-male band's profits. During that same period, Paxton also wrote for the bands of Sammy Kaye and Vaughn Monroe. In 1944, George Paxton formed his own band that played for a year at the Roseland Ballroom in New York City and gained national exposure through regular radio broadcasts. The band toured extensively in the U.S. during 1945 and dropped the string section. His singers included Alan Dale and Liza Morrow and he featured sidemen Nick Fatool and Boomie Richmond. The Paxton Orchestra recorded for MGM, Guild, Hit, V-Disc, and Majestic records. When Paxton disbanded he founded his own music publishing company and an unsuccessful record company.

DON REID

(Don Reid and His Orchestra) Reid studied the banjo as a child and switched to trombone in high school. In 1934, he graduated from Allegheny College in Pennsylvania and joined the Jan Garber Orchestra, playing trombone. After ten years with Garber, he organized his own band, after being encouraged by Gracie Allen and Tony Martin, for which he wrote arrangements. The sidemen in the band were Don Bennett, Floyd Waltz, Art Compratt, and Chuck Moony, saxophones; Charlie Claycomb and Chris Mischoff, trumpets; Don Reid, Fred Sherwood and Stan Pilacki, trombones; Chuck Loufele, piano; Ed Schneider, tuba; and Phil Reed, drums. The Don Reid Orchestra played on tour and in residence at venues, including the Aragon and Trianon Ballrooms in Chicago, the Merrill and Muehlebach in Kansas City, the Rainbow Ballroom and Turnpike Casino in Denver, and the Skyway and Peabody Hotels in Memphis. In 1946, Reid disbanded and moved to California where he wrote arrangements for Art Kassell and Jan Garber. In 1947, he formed a new band, retaining only Charlie Clay, trumpet and Art Compratt, saxophone from his 1944 band. The new personnel included Floyd Waltz, Don Bennett, and Art Compratt, saxophones;

Chris Mischoff and Charlie Clay, trumpets; Don Reid and Stanley Diask, trombones; Charles Lovfek, piano; Ed Schneider, bass; Don Sheldon, drums; and Bill Howard and Gwen Parke, singers.

GERALD WILSON

(Gerald Wilson and His Orchestra) Born in Shelby, Michigan on September 4, 1918. Gerald Wilson (né: Gerald Stanley Wilson) studied piano as a child and attended school in Memphis, Tennessee, and the Cass Technical College in Detroit, Michigan. He studied trumpet while in Detroit with Bobby Byrne's father and met Sam Donahue. His first band job was with the Chich Carter band at the Plantation Club in Detroit and on the road with Carter. He moved to Los Angeles, played with Phil Moore, and worked on sound film tracks. When Sy Oliver left the Jimmy Lunceford band in 1941, Wilson replaced him. At that time, the trumpet section in the Lunceford band was Snooky Young, Freddie Webster, and Gerald Wilson. Eventually Wilson and Young left Lunceford and joined Les Hite's band. Benny Carter moved to Los Angeles in 1943 and formed a band that included trumpets Gerald Wilson and Snooky Young and J.J. Johnson on trombone. The singer was Savannah Churchill. Gerald Wilson served in the U.S. Navy during WWII, from 1943 until his discharge in late 1944 when he joined the Lee Young Quartet. After a brief period Wilson fronted a small band prior to organizing his own big band. The new Gerald Wilson Orchestra disbanded in late 1944 and Wilson played as a sideman with orchestras led by Dizzy Gillespie and Count Basie. In the '60s, Wilson once again formed a big band that became one of the most significant bands of the decade. In the '70s, Wilson was active in jazz education, broadcasting and writing large symphonic pieces. He continued to flourish in the '80s and '90s.

MIFF MOLE

(Miff Mole and His Orchestra) Born in Long Island, New York on March 11, 1898. Miff Mole (né: Irving Milfred Mole) studied piano and violin as a child and played piano in movie houses when he was 14. He switched to trombone and played in a Brooklyn Café when he was sixteen. In the early '20s, he played with Sam Lanin and the Original Memphis Five. In 1924 he worked with Ray Miller and with Ross Gorman in 1925. That year he also played the Broadway show *Earl Carroll's Vanities*. During the remainder of the '20s, Mole played with Bix Beiderbecke, Red Nichols, and Roger Wolfe Kahn prior to working with the Red Nichols/Don Voorhees group on WOR radio. During the '30s, Mole played classical and popular music on NBC radio until 1938, when he joined the Paul Whiteman Orchestra where he remained until 1940. For three years he taught and did studio work until he joined Benny Goodman in 1943 when he left Goodman and formed his own band. He worked at Nick's in New York until 1947 when he disbanded and went with Muggsy Spanier. A hip operation curtailed his activities although he resumed playing in 1956. Mole died in New York City on April 29, 1961.

JOHNNY OTIS
(Johnny Otis and His Orchestra) Born in Berkeley, California, on December 28, 1924. Johnny Otis (né: John Veliotes) was born to Greek parents and changed his name while still in his teens. Otis studied drums at an early age and joined the Count Otis Matthews Orchestra in Oakland, California where he traveled extensively and played for other territory bands as well. He moved to Los Angles in 1940 and played with Harland Leonard Rockets at the Club Alabam. When the Rockets left town, Otis formed his own big band and by 1945 was recording for Excelsior Records. Jimmy Rushing joined the band, and they recorded "Harlem Nocturne," which became a big hit. Otis also played drums for Wynonie Harris and Charles Brown during that period. Otis and Bardu Ali opened their own club, the Barrelhouse Club, in 1947 in the Los Angeles Watts section and Otis began playing R&B. In the early '50s, Otis recorded for Mercury Records and served as a record producer for Peacock Records from 1953 to 1955. His band backed singer Big Mama Thornton on her hit recording of "You Ain't Nothing But a Hound Dog" and discovered singers Etta James, Little Willie John, and Hank Ballard. In 1955, Otis formed his own record company, Dig Records, and, in 1957, signed with Capitol Records and recorded "Willie" and "The Hand Jive." In the late '50s, Otis appeared on his own TV program in Los Angeles and, in the early, '60s recorded for Kent Records. By the early '90s, Otis had disbanded and ran a health food store in California.

JAN AUGUST

(Jan August and His Orchestra) Born in New York, New York, on September 24, 1912. Jan August (né: Jan Augustoff) studied piano as a youngster and played in Paul Specht's Orchestra. In the '30s, he played piano and xylophone with Ferde Grofé and Paul Whiteman. By the '40s, he soloed in various clubs playing piano, appeared in the Broadway show *Pal Joey*, and recorded with Jerry Murad and the Harmonicats and Richard Hayman. He recorded for Mercury and Diamond Records in the mid-'40s, recording hit tunes "Malaguena," "Oye Negra," and "Misirlou." In the late '40s and early '50s, August accompanied singer Roberta Quinlan on NBC-TV and recorded the hit tune "Buffalo Billy." During his career he also recorded albums *Plays Songs to Remember*, *Plays Great Piano Hits*, *Piano Roll Blues*, *Music for the Quiet Hour*, *Jan August Styles the Great Pop Piano Classics*, *Cha Cha Charm*, and *Accent! Latin Piano*. August died in New York City on January 9, 1976.

RAY BAUDUC

(Ray Bauduc and His Orchestra) Born in New Orleans, Louisiana, on June 18, 1906. When he was very young he played drums with Bob Crosby, Ben Pollack, and the Dorsey Brothers. While with Crosby, he gained quick fame for the recording of "Big Noise from Winnetka" that featured him and bassist Bob Haggert, his co-writer. He formed his own band on the West Coast in 1945, after WWII, and hired arrangers Billy May and Joe Reisman. His band quickly became very popular and remained so through 1947. When Bauduc disbanded, he played with Jack Teagarden and Jimmy Dorsey from 1952 through 1956. Baduc and Nappy Lamare formed a jazz band that appeared in the movie *The Fabulous Dorseys* in the late '50s. In 1966, Bauduc moved to Houston, Texas, and appeared at various reunions. Bauduc died on January 8, 1988.

PANAMA FRANCIS

(Panama Francis and His Savoy Sultans) Born in Miami, Florida on December 21, 1918. Francis (né: David Francis) began to play drums when he as eight years old and made his professional debut at 13. In 1934, he joined the George Kelly band and toured the country. When he was 19, he moved to New York City and played with Roy Eldridge and Tab Smith. In 1940, he joined the Lucky

Millinder band that was playing regularly at the Savoy Ballroom in Harlem. He stayed with Millinder for five years. In 1945, Francis formed his own band and toured the Southern states. He disbanded in 1947, and joined the Cab Calloway Orchestra, where he remained until 1952. At that time, he became a studio musician, backing up artists like John Lee Hooker, Eubie Blake, Ella Fitzgerald, Mahalia Jackson, and Ray Charles. In the late '70s, he left the studios and played with an all-star big band led by Lionel Hampton. He then formed the Savoy Sultan band, patterned after Al Cooper's Savoy Sultans that had worked thirty years before. The new Sultan band included sidemen Norris Turney, George Kelly, and Francis Williams. Francis was still playing in the '90s at Fat Tuesday's in New York City.

EARL BOSTIC

(Earl Bostic and His Orchestra) Born in Tulsa, Oklahoma on April 25, 1913. Bostic studied saxophone and clarinet as a youngster and was a professional by age 18, playing on riverboats with Fate Marable and with Ernie Fields, Joseph Robichant, Clarence Olden, and Charlie Breath. Turning to jazz, he played with bands led by Don Redman, Lionel Hampton, Cab Calloway, Hot Lips Page, and Cousin Joe. In the early '40s, he played at Minton's in New York City with Charlie Parker, Kenny Clarke, Thelonious Monk, Dizzy Gillespie, and Charlie Christian. He also wrote arrangements for Gene Krupa, Alvino Rey, Paul Whiteman and Louis Prima. In the mid-'40s, Bostic formed his own band that recorded for King Records. His sidemen included Joe Pass, Earl Palmer, Al McKibbon, Jackie Byard, Sir Charles Thompson, Tiny Grimes, John Coltrane, Stanley Turrentine, Blue Mitchell, Don Byas, Cozy Cole, Teddy Charles, Johnny Coles, Benny Carter, Groove Holmes, Jimmy Cobb, Benny Golson as well as many other famous jazz musicians. Bostic wrote "Let Me Off Uptown," "Brooklyn Boogie," and "The Major and the Minor." Bostic died in Rochester, New York on October 28, 1965.

RANDY BROOKS

(Randy Brooks and His Orchestra) Born in Sandford, Maine on March 28, 1917. Brooks took trumpet lessons when he was a very young child. When he was a 12-year-old Rudy Vallée contracted him to play a classical trumpet solo on the *Fleischmann Hour* radio program. When he was 20, he moved to New York City and worked with Ruby Newman at the Rainbow Grill in Rockefeller Center. He left Newman to join the Hal Kemp Orchestra, playing first trumpet. When Kemp died in a car accident, Art Jarrett took over the band until it disbanded in 1942. Brooks immediately went to work for Bob Allen, Artie Shaw, and Claude Thornhill until he joined the U.S. navy. When he was discharged from the navy, due to a medical problem, he joined the Les Brown band. In 1945, he left Brown and formed his own band that recorded for Decca Records. The theme songs of the Randy Brooks Orchestra were "Harlem Nocturne" and "Holiday Forever." Brooks died in Springfield, Maine, on March 21, 1967.

BILLY BUTTERFIELD

(Billy Butterfield and His Orchestra) Born in Middleton, Ohio on January 14, 1917. Billy Butterfield (né: Charles William Butterfield) played trumpet with Bob Crosby & the Bobcats from 1937 to 1940. When he left Crosby he worked briefly with Artie Shaw and then with Benny Goodman for two years. He served in the U.S. army during WWII and when he was discharged in 1945 formed his own band that worked at Eddie Condon's and Nick's in New York during the

remainder of the '40s and '50s. He recorded for Capitol Records. His theme song was "Moonlight in Vermont," which he recorded with Margaret Whiting in the mid-'40s. In 1968, he toured with the World's Greatest Jazz Band until he retired in Florida. Butterfield died in North Palm Beach, Florida, on March 18, 1988.

RAY EBERLY

(Ray Eberly and His Orchestra) Born in Hoosick Falls, New York on January 19, 1919. Ray Eberly (né: Raymond Eberle) did not study music but was able to sing at an early age. His older brother Bob Eberle, was the singer for the Jimmy Dorsey band, and recommend Ray to Glenn Miller, who hired him and featured him on the *Chesterfield* radio show. His recordings of "Moonlight Cocktails" and "At Last" brought him to prominence. He remained with Miller until Miller disbanded and joined the U.S. service. In 1942, he sang with the Gene Krupa band for a short while before entering the U.S. army. In 1943, Ray Eberly acted in several movies, including *This Is the Life* and *Follow the Band*. In 1945, Eberly formed his band and featured Glenn Miller–type arrangements. The band gradually evolved its own style with arrangements from Billy Maxted and worked until the mid-'50s. The theme song of the Ray Eberly band was "Serenade in Blue." Eberly then appeared on numerous television programs until 1970, when he joined the Tex Beneke band and toured the U.S. The Beneke band, featuring Ray Eberly, also appeared at the Sahara and Desert Inn in Las Vegas and at Madison Square Garden in New York. Eberly died on August 28, 1979.

LES ELGART

(Les Elgart and His Orchestra) Born in New Haven, Connecticut, on August 3, 1918. Les Elgart played trumpet with the Raymond Scott band in 1941. At that time the Scott band featured Specs Powell, drums; Israel Crosby, bass; Tony Mattola, guitar; Benny Morton, trombone; and Ben Webster, tenor saxophone. During the latter part of 1941 and 1942 Elgart played first trumpet with the Charlie Spivak Orchestra the Harry James band, and groups led by Bunny Berigan, Muggsy Spanier, and Woody Herman. The original Elgart band (the Les and Larry Elgart Orchestra) was formed in 1945 with arrangements by Bill Finegan and Nelson Riddle. Les was not an enthusiastic bandleader as opposed to his brother, Larry, who was very animated. By 1952, the band was signed to a Columbia Record contract and appeared at many colleges and universities. The band's theme song was the "Dancing Sound." In 1953, Elgart launched his own band with arrangements by Charles Albertine. The band quickly rose to popularity recording for Columbia Records. The theme songs of the Les Elgart Orchestra were "Heart of My Heart" and "Sophisticated Swing." Elgart wrote "Bandstand Boogie." During the '60s, the band appeared on television, recorded, and played some of the top venues in the country. Elgart died in Dallas, Texas on August 2, 1995.

DIZZY GILLESPIE

(Dizzy Gillespie and His Orchestra) Born in Cheraw, South Carolina on October 21, 1917. Dizzy Gillespie (né: John Birks Gillespie) studied music in his early life and attended the Laurinburg Institute in North Carolina. Moving to Philadelphia, Pennsylvania he began to play with local bands in the mid '30s. He played with the Teddy Hill band beginning in 1937 and toured Europe with him. Returning to America, Gillespie freelanced in New York until he joined the Cab Calloway band in 1939. Gillespie played with Calloway until 1941 when he began experimenting

with the new music bebop. During the early '40s, he wrote for the Woody Herman Orchestra, Earl Hines, Jimmy Dorsey and others. He worked for a short time with Ella Fitzgerald, Charlie Barnet, Benny Carter, Lucky Millinder, and Les Hite. Gillespie met Charlie Parker, when they both played on the Earl Hines band in late 1942, and began to formulate the bebop style, for which they both became known. In 1943, Gillespie co-led a combo with Oscar Pettiford and, in 1943, joined Billy Eckstine's big band as writer, player, and musical director. He and Parker worked together on the Eckstine band until 1944, when Gillespie formed a combo featuring Charlie Parker. In 1945, Gillespie formed his own big band that played in the U.S. and abroad until 1950. He also toured with his band and played with Jazz at the Philharmonic. For a brief period, he was a partner in the Deegee Records company. Through the '50s, '60s, and '70s, he led various combos, recorded, and appeared in this country and throughout the world. He led big bands that toured for the U.S. Department of State in the late '50s. Gillespie continued to do clinics at various schools and colleges through the '70s and '80s and was admired by all knowledgeable musicians throughout the world. He wrote "Con Alma," "A Night in Tunisia," "Woody 'n' You," "Groovin' High," "Manteca," "Cool Breeze," "Blue 'n' Boogie, "Swing Low Sweet Cadillac," and many other compositions. Gillespie died in Englewood, New Jersey, on January 6, 1993.

JERRY GRAY

(Jerry Gray and His Orchestra) Born in Boston, Massachusetts, on July 3, 1915. Jerry Gray (né: Graziano) studied music and led a local band when he was a teenager. Known as an excellent arranger, he worked briefly with the Artie Shaw band in 1936 and rejoined in 1938 as head arranger eventually arranging the big Shaw hit "Begin the Beguine." After a short period of writing for Andre Kostelanetz he joined Glenn Miller in 1939 and arranged several of that bands bit hits, including "Pennsylvania 6-5000," "A String of Pearls," "Carribean Clipper," "I Dreamt I Dwelt in Harlem," "Sun Valley Jump," "Here We Go Again," and "The Spirit Is Willing." When Miller disbanded in late 1942, to join the U.S. Air Force, Gray wrote for Jerry Wald. When Miller disappeared over the English Channel and through the '40s, Gray worked as music director for the Philip Morris, Bob Crosby, Patti Clayton radio programs. In 1950, he led a band on radio and toured the U.S. From 1951 to 1952, Gray played the *Club 15* radio show with outstanding personnel. Gray recorded frequently during the '50s using the Glenn Miller sound and backing various singers on recordings. In the mid-'60s, he moved to California and did studio work before relocating in Dallas, Texas. Gray wrote "Introduction to a Waltz," "Jeep Jockey Jump," "Crew Cut," "V-Hop," and "Flag Waver." He recorded for Decca, Golden Tone, Victor, and Vocalion records. Gray died in Dallas, Texas on August 10, 1976.

RED INGLE

(Red Ingle and His Orchestra) Ingle played violin and tenor saxophone with Ted Weems from 1931 to 1939. He worked with Spike Jones in the '40s, recording hits such as "Tim-Tayshun (Temptation)" in corny style with Jo Stafford. In 1947, he left Jones and organized his own band that specialized into turning popular tunes into hillbilly tunes. The Ingle band recorded for Mercury, V-Disc, and Capitol records and played through the '50s.

DON JACOBY

(Don "Jake" Jacoby and His Orchestra) Born in York, Pennsylvania, on May 28, 1920. Don Jacoby grew up in York, Pennsylvania, and studied trumpet as a child. When he was nine, he appeared with the Spring Garden band in New York playing a classical trumpet solo and during his teenage years played on various radio programs, played with several orchestras and studied with Ernest Williams. In the '30s and early '40s, he played with Les Brown, Claude Thornhill, and Van Alexander. In 1942, he joined the U.S. Armed Forces and played with several world-renowned figures, including John Charles Thomas, Vladimir Horowitz, and Fritz Keisler. After his discharge in 1945, he rejoined the Les Brown band prior to playing with Benny Goodman. He subsequently moved to Chicago where he joined ABC as a studio musician and became a conductor, music director, and trumpet soloist. In 1957, Jacoby joined the CBS network. Soon after, he began to travel and do solo performances and music clinics for the Conn Music Instrument Company. In the late '70s, he retired as a trumpet performer and moved to Dallas, Texas, where he taught privately. Jacoby died in Dallas, Texas, in December 1992.

JIMMY PALMER

(Jimmy Palmer and His Orchestra) Jimmy Palmer studied music in high school, entered a Paul Whiteman singing contest and won. The prize was a sustaining contract on a Pittsburg radio station, KDKA. This gave him the exposure needed to get into the music business. Jimmy Palmer played trumpet and sang during the '30s and early '40s, with bands led by Bobby Byrne, Lou Breese, and Blue Barron. He took over the Dick Stabile band in 1944 when Stabile went into the U.S. Coast Guard and led the band into the '70s. Palmer was known as "Dancing

Shoes" and wrote a song called "Dancing Shoes." The band's theme song was "It's a Lonesome Old Town," The Palmer band recorded for Mercury and United Artists Records. Jimmy Palmer and His Orchestra were still active into the '70s.

BILL PANNELL

(Bill Pannell and His Orchestra) Pannell led a West Coast band that played often in Fresno, Los Angeles, and Hollywood. He had previously played in an Air Force band during WWII. Pannell played at various times at the Roosevelt Hotel for more than ten years in the interim playing in Phoenix at the Westward Ho, at various lounges in Las Vegas, Catalina Island, and throughout the Southwest and West Coast. In the early '70s, Pannell disbanded. During his career Pannell recorded for Val, Fanfare, Amco, and London records. His theme song was "Twilight Time."

RAY ROBBINS

(Ray Robbins and His Orchestra) Born in Gardenia, California, on January 1, 1912. Trumpeter Robbins (né: Ray Jurgens) formed a dance band during his senior year at Gardenia High School and sang and played trumpet in various movie theaters. In 1934, he moved to Los Angeles and played with a local band until joinging the George Hamilton Orchestra at that time. After touring with the band, he returned to Los Angeles and joined the Russ Plumber band that was working at the Rendezvous Ballroom. Members of the Plumber band at that time were Stan Kenton, Spike Jones, Lumpy Brannon, and Vido Musso. When Everett Hoagland took over the Plumber band, Robbins joined Garwood Van. He then joined the Gus Arnheim Orchestra and toured the East Coast. When the band returned to Los Angeles, Robbins left and rejoined the George Hamilton band. In the late '30s, Jurgens changed his name to Ray Robbins as he joined the Dick Jurgens Orchestra. When Dick Jurgens was drafted in WWII, he turned the band over to Ray Robbins who led it until he was drafted in 1943. Returning to Los Angeles, after WWII, Robbins played for a short time with Al Donahue and Joe Reichman until he formed another band of his own. In 1945, Stan Kenton got Robbins a recording contract with Capitol Records. In 1950, the Robbins Orchestra alternated with Lawrence Welk on television and at the Aragon Ballroom in Chicago. In 1962, Robbins disbanded and moved to Lake Tahoe.

SHORTY SHEROCK

(Shorty Sherock and His Orchestra) Born in Minneapolis, Minnesota on November 17, 1915, Shorty Sherock (né: Clarence Francis Cherock) studied trumpet and spent his childhood in Gary, Indiana. He first played with Ben Pollack in 1936, and ultimately spent time with orchestras led by Frankie Masters, Jack Pettis, Seger Ellis, Santo Percora, and Jacques Renard. From 1937 to 1939, he played with Jimmy Dorsey and joined the Bob Crosby band in late 1939. After playing with Gene Krupa from 1940 to 41, he played with Raymond Scott and Tommy Dorsey. In 1942, he played briefly with Bob Strong, Alvino Rey, and Max Miller. In 1944 and 1945, he worked with Horace Heidt prior to forming his own band that he led from 1945 until 1949. He then disbanded and rejoined Jimmy Dorsey with whom he worked until 1952. During 1954, Sherock played with Georgie Auld, then settled in California where he worked as a studio musician during the remainder of the '50s and '60s. He was often seen with the Mort Lindsay band on Merv Griffin's television show in the '70s.

ART VAN DAMME

(Art Van Damme and His Quintet) Born in Norway, Michigan, on April 9, 1920. Art Van Damme studied piano in Iron Mountain, Michigan, and accordion with Andy Rizzo in Chicago where he was raised. From 1939 until 1943, he played with the Ben Bernie band and some small combos in and around Chicago. In 1945 Van Damme formed his own quintet consisting of Max Mariash, drums; Lou Shakinder, bass; Fred Rundquist, guitar; Chuck Calzaretta, vibes; and himself on accordion. The jazz-influenced group recorded for Columbia Records and created a lot of interest. While Van Damme continued to lead his quintet, he also worked as an NBC staff musician and played with other musicians, including pianist Frank Melrose, cornetist Pete Dailey, and tenor saxophonist Bud Freeman. The Art Van Damme Quintet recorded the big hit "Buttons and Bows," sang by the Dinning Sisters. The Quintet recorded for Capitol and Columbia Records. The group won the Down Beat Poll from 1952 through 1958. In 1970 Van Damme took an all-star group to Germany, which included Kenny Clarke on drums and Joe Pass on guitar. That group recorded for the MPS Records.

GEORGE WINSLOW

(George Winslow and His Orchestra) Born in Jamestown, New York, in 1916. Winslow graduated from Wooster College and played with and wrote for various groups in the territory, including Ray Herbeck, Art Kassel, Blue Barron, Sammy Watkins, Hank Biagini, Sammy Kaye, and Blue Steele. Moving to Chicago, Winslow organized his band, Music with a Smile, and toured the Midwest from 1945 to 1950. During this period, his band was featured on radio stations WGN and WBBM from the Martinique and O'Henry Ballrooms. The band also worked at the Trianon and Aragon Ballrooms in Chicago and at hotels Shroeder in Milwaukee and Peabody in Memphis. The theme song of the George Winslow band was "You've Got to Smile Awhile." Winslow was a prolific songwriter, penning "I'm Going to Copyright Your Kisses," "Ruth," "Rhythm on the Farm," and "When Twilight Falls." Winslow lives in Monroe, New York and is writing, playing and singing with the Winslow Three.

BARCLAY ALLEN

(Barclay Allen and His Orchestra) Born on September 27, 1918. In 1946, pianist Barclay Allen replaced Murray Arnold in the Freddy Martin band. After a brief period, Allen left the Martin Orchestra and formed his own band. Unfortunately Allen had a terrible automobile accident in 1949 that left him paralyzed and unable to play. Allen died on December 7, 1966.

RAY ANTHONY

(Ray Anthony and His Orchestra) Born in Bentleyville, Pennsylvania, on January 20, 1922. Trumpeter Ray Anthony (né: Raymond Antonini) received music lessons from his father and played in the Antonini Family Orchestra when he was only five. He worked with local bands in Cleveland, Ohio, while he attended high school and after graduation joined the Al Donahue (Low Down Rhythm in a Top Hat) band. In the late '30s, he joined the Glenn Miller Orchestra and in the early '40s worked with Jimmy Dorsey. During WWII, Anthony joined the navy and led a navy band in the South Pacific for four years. When he was released from the navy, after WWII in 1946, Anthony formed his own band and recorded for Capitol Records. During the late '40s and '50s, the Ray Anthony band was considered one of the top bands in the U.S. Big recorded hits included "Harbor Lights," "At Last," "The Bunny Hop," "Peter Gunn," and "Dragnet." The band also appeared in several motion picture, including *Daddy Long Legs* and *This Could Be the Night*. Ray impersonated Jimmy Dorsey in the film the *Five Pennies: The Biography of Red Nichols*. In the '60s, and with the advent of the end of the big-band era, Ray Anthony led a sextet and featured a female vocal duo called the Bookends. Several female singers served as the Bookends, including Vikki Carr, Anita Ray, and Diane Hall. Anthony still tours with various size groups and continues to use his theme song "The Man with the Horn."

TEX BENEKE

(Tex Beneke and His Orchestra) Born in Fort Worth, Texas on February 12, 1914. Beneke studied saxophone and clarinet as a youngster in his hometown and played with the Ben Young band from 1935 to 1937. He joined the Glenn Miller Orchestra in 1938. When Miller disbanded, to join the service, in 1942 Beneke played with Jan Savitt and Horace Heidt. During WWII, Beneke played in a U.S. navy band until his discharge at the end of the war. In 1946 Glenn Miller's widow asked Beneke to lead the Glenn Miller band and people who were still enamored with the sound of the Miller band flocked to hear and dance to the Miller sounds. During the '60s, Beneke formed his own band that was billed as Tex Beneke and His Orchestra, playing the music made famous by Glenn Miller. In the '70s and '80s, he continued to utilize the Miller style but added new tunes to the library. In the '90s, Beneke retired to the West Coast. Beneke died in Costa Mesa, California, in 2000.

JOHNNY BOTHWELL

(Johnny Bothwell and His Orchestra) Born in Gary, Indiana on May 26, 1917. Bothwell played with the Max Miller group in Chicago in 1940. He played with Gene Krupa, Woody Herman, Bob Chester, Sonny Dunham, and Tommy Dorsey in the early '40s. From 1944 to 1945, he played lead alto saxophone with the famous Boyd Raeburn band. In 1945, he left Raeburn and formed a small combo expanding to a large band in 1946. The band featured the singers Claire Hogan and Don Darcy and recorded for Signature Records. Arrangements for the band were written by Villepeigh. The band's theme song was "Sleep Alto." In early 1948, Bothwell disbanded and became a salesman for General Electric in Connecticut. When he retired he moved to Lakeland, Florida, and ran a video/photography production company. Bothwell died in Florida in August 1995.

ZEV CONFREY

(Zev Confrey and His Orchestra) Born in Peru, Illinois, on April 3, 1895. Zev Confrey (né: Edward Eleazar Confrey) studied piano and composition at the Chicago Musical College and recorded piano rolls for player pianos after graduation. He served in the U.S. armed forces during WWI and worked at various radio stations when he was discharged. At that time, he adopted the first name "Zev" and fronted his own large band. During Paul Whiteman's famous Aeolian Hall concert, Confrey introduced his composition, "Kitten on the Keys." Joe "Fingers" Carr and Bob Crosby and the Bob Cats recorded his most successful composition, "Stumbling." Mary Tyler Moore and Julie Andrews revived the song in the 1967 movie *Thoroughly Modern Millie*. Confrey recorded for Victor, Brunswick, and Banner Records. He also wrote "Dizzy Fingers," "Charleston Chuckles," "Sittin' on a Log," and "Grandfather's Clock." Confrey died in Lakewood, New Jersey, on March 18, 1972.

JACK FINA

(Jack Fina and His Orchestra) Born in Passiac, New Jersey, on August 13, 1913. Fina studied piano as a child and attended the New York College of Music. In the mid-'30s, he played with Clyde McCoy and was a radio staff pianist. In 1936, he joined the Freddy Martin Orchestra where he did some arranging and was featured on piano. He played with Martin until the early '40s, when WWII temporarily tabled his playing. In 1946, he formed his own big band and recorded his composition "Bumble Boogie" that he had also arranged. The band played venues that included the Aragon Ballroom in Chicago, the Balinese Room in Galveston, Texas, the Chase Hotel in St. Louis, Elitch's Gardens in Denver, and the Waldorf-Astoria in New York. Fina was a boogie-woogie ragtime piano player who also composed "Chango," "Rhumbaner," "Samba Caramba," "Dream Sonata," and "Piano Portrait." Alto saxophonist Paul Desmond played in the Jack Fina band. The Jack Fina Orchestra recorded for MGM Records. Fina died in California on May 14, 1970.

ILLINOIS JACQUET

(Illinois Jacquet and His Orchestra) Born in Broussard, Lousiana on October 1922. Jacquet (né: Jean-Baptiste Illinois Jacquet) grew up in Houston, Texas, and was the younger brother of trumpeter Russell Jacquet. He played alto and soprano saxophone locally until the late '30s when he moved to California and played with the Floyd Ray Orchestra. From 1941 until 1942, he played tenor saxophone with the Lionel Hampton band and gained fame playing "Flying Home." In 1943 to 1944, Jacquet played with Cab Calloway and, in late 1944, led his brother's band. From 1944 and 1945, he toured with Jazz at the Philharmonic and fueled his reputation as a wild exhibitionist. Cooling down, he joined Count Basie and played with his band until the end of 1946. He led combos during the '50s, and formed a big band with which he toured in 1955. Jacquet began playing bassoon in the mid-'60s, and wrote many songs, including "Don'cha Go 'Way Mad," "Robbins Nest," and "Black Velvet." He recorded for Alladin, Mercury, Victor, Verve, Cadet, Roulette, and Prestige records. Jacquet died in Las Vegas, Nevada, on July 6, 1983.

ELLIOT LAWRENCE

(Elliot Lawrence and His Orchestra) Born in Philadelphia, Pennsylvania, on February 14, 1925. Elliot Lawrence (né: Elliot Lawrence Broza) played piano in his father's *Children's Hours Theater* when he was four years old and led a children's band on radio in Philadelphia from 1937 to 1941. Lawrence attended the University of Pennsylvania and led a big jazz band that played for dances in the area. Lawrence wrote many of the band's arrangements. In 1946, he took the band to New York City, played at the Hotel Pennsylvania, and recorded "You Broke the Only Heart That Ever Loved You." Various famous musicians played with the band from 1946 to 1949, including trumpeter Alec Fila and baritone saxophonist Gerry Mulligan, who also wrote arrangements. In the early '50s, Lawrence disbanded and became an arranger-conductor for radio and television. He had a daily CBS radio show, where he led a jazz combo and served as musical director for a number of Broadway shows, including *How to Succeed in Business Without Really Trying*, *Golden Boy*, *The Apple Tree*, *Here's Love*, and *Bye, Bye Birdie*. He was active into the '70s, and arranged for the 1974 Broadway musical *Music! Music!* Elliot Lawrence wrote a number of jazz tunes, including "Five O'Clock Shadow," "Once Upon a Moon," "Sugar Beat," "Hunter," and "Three Dears," "Box 155," "Heart to Heart,"and "Sugartown Road." Lawrence recorded for Fantasy, Decca, Columbia, V-Disc, King, and VIK records.

RALPH MARTERIE

(Ralph Marterie and His Orchestra) Trumpeter Ralph Marterie formed his first orchestra in Chicago in 1946, after playing with bands in Chicago and on the road with Percy Faith and Paul Whiteman. He gained much positive exposure through various radio programs and particularly while playing at the Melody Ballroom. In 1951, he signed with Mercury Records and was promoted nationally. The Marterie Orchestra appeared at Frank Dailey's Meadowbrook and the Hollywood Palladium and featured singers Lou Prano, Janice Borla, and Bill Waters. The Marterie Library was written by some of the great arrangers of the time. The band was featured on the *Marlboro Cigarette* radio program and appeared on the television show the *Cavalcade of Bands*. When the Ralph Marterie Orchestra left Mercury Records, they recorded for Musicor and United Artists Records. The band's theme song was "Carla," written by Marterie. Marterie died on October 8, 1978.

SY OLIVER

(Sy Oliver and His Orchestra) Born in Battle Creek, Michigan on December 12, 1910. Sy Oliver (né: Melvin James Oliver) was raised in Zanesville, Ohio and his father was a concert singer. His father and mother taught music in Zanesville and Sy studied trumpet while attending high school. In 1928, Oliver graduated from high school and joined the Zach White band in Cincinnati, Ohio. After traveling on the road he returned to Zanesville where he played with local groups, taught music, and studied arranging. Oliver joined the Jimmy Lunceford Orchestra in 1933, playing and writing for the Lunceford band until 1939, when he went with Tommy Dorsey. He remained with Dorsey until he was drafted into WWII in 1943. When he was released from service in 1945, he rejoined the Dorsey band but also began writing for other groups as well. In 1946, he organized his own band that he led for two years before disbanding and becoming staff arranger, music director, and recording supervisor for Decca Records. Oliver's theme songs, which were written by him, were "For Dancers Only," "Well Git It," and "Opus No. 1." In 1954 and 1955, he worked for Bethelem Records and, in 1958, for Jubilee Records. He wrote for nearly every outstanding recording artist during the '60s and '70s. Oliver died in New York City on May 28, 1988.

TEDDY PHILLIPS

(Teddy Phillips and His Orchestra) Born in Chicago, Illinois on June 15, 1916. Teddy Phillips [né: Teddy Steve Phillips (Tedd Simms)] took private lessons on saxophone while attending Oak Park High School. He played with Lawrence Welk, Ted Weems, and Ben Bernie and was employed by ABC prior to WWII. When Phillips was discharged from the U.S. army at the end of WWII in 1945, he worked at CBS as a staff musician. In 1946, he formed a pit band in a downtown theater in Chicago, and by 1947, MCA had contracted the band to tour through the South and Southwest for a year. During that period, the band, originally jazz-oriented, became quite commercial and geared for dancers. He eventually wound up in Chicago and played at the Trianon and Aragon Ballrooms for more than a year. In the interim, the band worked on the road for two to four week dates at the Golden West Ballroom and Myron's Ballroom in Los Angeles; and the Baker, Muehlbach, Roosevelts; and Peabody Hotels. In the '70s, while touring in the Midwest, the band was in an automobile accident, causing Phillips to disband and concentrate on arranging, composing, and playing in Los Angeles, where he made his home. The theme song of the Teddy Phillips Orchestra was "Thankful." Trombonist Bobby Burgess once played with the Teddy Phillips band. Phillips wrote the songs "Open House," "Camel Hump," "Wishin'," "Little Canole," and "Don't Call Me Sweetheart Anymore." The Phillips band recorded for Coral, Liberty, London, Mercury, Decca, Brunswick, Tower, Dot, and MGM records.

HAL PRUDEN

(Hal Pruden and His Orchestra) Hal Pruden played with the bands of Bob Crosby and Chuck Foster in the '30s and early '40s. Pianist Pruden formed his band in 1946. When he was quite young he lost control of his hands due to scarlet fever and rheumatism but, over a period of time, was able to exercise his fingers, gain flexibility, and became a very fast piano player. The Music Corporation of America (MCA) booked the Pruden Orchestra on tour throughout the country spending weeks at venues such as the Shamrock Hotel in Houston, the Baker Hotel in Dallas, the Peabody Hotel in Memphis, the Statler Hotel in Boston, and the Mapes Hotel in Reno. The theme song of the Pruden Orchestra, which was written by Pruden, was "Busy Body." Pruden also wrote "Powder Blue" and "Ivory Mischief." In 1953, Pruden's band disbanded.

TOMMY REED

(Tommy Reed and His Orchestra) Tommy Reed played saxophone and clarinet and worked with Russ Morgan, Dick Jurgens, Jimmy Dorsey, Joe Venuti, Ernie Hecksher, Richard Himber, Del Courney, and Henry King, during the late '20s, '30s, and early '40s. After WWII, in 1946, Reed formed his band in San Francisco, California, and toured the U.S., ending up at the Lexinton Hotel in New York City. The Reed Orchestra built up a big following playing at rooms such as the Roosevelt Hotel in New Orleans, the O'Henry Ballroom and Chase Hotel in St. Louis, and the Peabody Hotel in Memphis. The band's singer was Sue Mouro. The Tommy Reed band theme song was "Two Clouds in the Sky." The band featured songs that Reed had written: "Fishin' for Love," "Two Heavens," and "After All," and recorded for MGM and Camelback Records. During the '50s, Reed continue to cut back the size of the band until 1961 when he completely disbanded, moved to Phoenix, Arizona, and formed a talent agency known as Southwest Booking Agency, Inc. with fellow bandleader Al Trace.

BUDDY RICH

(Buddy Rich and His Orchestra) Born in Brooklyn, New York, on June 30, 1917. Buddy Rich's parents acted in vaudeville as Wilson and Rich. When Buddy (né: Bernard Rich) was 18 months old, he was on stage and by age four was on Broadway, tap dancing and playing drums. When he was six, he toured Australia as a solo artist and, at 11, formed his first band and sat  in with various groups in New York City venues. He played with Joe Marsala in 1937 and, prior to WWII, worked with bands led by Artie Shaw, Tommy Dorsey, Bunny Berigan, and Harry James. Rich served in the armed forces during WWII and returned to the Tommy Dorsey band at the end of the war. He formed a short-lived big band in the late '40s, worked with Les Brown, and toured with Jazz at the Philharmonic. In the early '50s, he formed another band and recorded for Norman Granz until he had a heart attack that momentarily derailed his career. In the early '60s, he rejoined the Harry James band and worked there until forming a new big band in 1966. The theme song of the Rich band was "Rain on the Roof." That band was active for about 12 years, until Rich disbanded and formed a combo. In the late '70s, Rich formed another big band that toured until his final illness. Many well-known sidemen played with the Buddy Rich band through the years, including Herb Ellis, Ernie Watts, Mary Flax, Jay Corre, Sam Most, Benny Golson, Phil Woods, Sonny Russo, Sam Marowitz, Terry Gibbs, Harvey Leonard, Allen Eager, Eddie Caine, Red Rodney, Bitsy Mullins, Earl Swope, Johnny Mandel, and many others. The singers included Lynn Warren, Jean Weeks, Dorothy Reid, Marjorie Dean, Linda Larkin, and Muriel James. The Buddy Rich Orchestra recorded for Victor, Mercury, Liberty, Pacific, and Verve records. Rich died on April 2, 1987.

EARLE SPENCER

(Earle Spencer and His Orchestra) Born on December 9, 1926. Trombonist Earle Spencer studied trombone and played in a navy band during WWII. He had a heart problem and was discharged from the navy. He was also told to discontinue playing trombone but formed his big band on his release in 1946. He loved the sounds of bands under the directions of Boyd Raeburn, Johnny Richards and Stan Kenton and emulated them. Some of his sidemen on that 1946 band were Ray Linn and Wilber Schwartz. In 1949, when Stan Kenton temporarily disbanded, a few of his sidemen joined the Spencer band, including Laurindo Almeida, Buddy Childers, Harry Betts, and Art Pepper. The Spencer band recorded for Black and White Records. The featured singers were Bob Haywood and Toni Aubin. Spencer disbanded in 1952. Spencer died in California on September 23, 1991.

TOM TALBERT

(Tom Talbert and His Orchestra) Born in Crystal Bay, Minnesota, on August 24, 1924. During WWII, Tom Talbert became the head arranger for the U.S. army dance band at Fort Ord, California, although he had very little formal musical training. When he was discharged in 1946, he played piano with several bands in California prior to meeting with Johnny Richards in Boston. Richards was leading and writing for his own band and encouraged Talbert to form and write for his own band, which Talbert organized when he returned to California. Talbert band was patterned after the Stan Kenton band, and had in its ranks many sidemen who had become prominent in such famous bands as Benny Goodman's. Jack Cascales, the brother of Johnny Richards, recorded the band for Paramount Records and the band toured various clubs on the West Coast. Various musicians played and sang with the band in 1946 and 1947, including Dod Marmarosa, Anita O'Day, Steve White, and Warne Marsh. The band worked at Lake Tahoe and the Trianon Ballroom. In 1949, more changes took place in personnel as Art Pepper joined the band on alto saxophone. The band recorded for Sea Breeze Records. During the '50s, Talbert disbanded and wrote for bands led by Oscar Pettiford, Charlie Ventura, Tony Pastor, Boyd Raeburn, Buddy Rich, Claude Thornhill, and Stan Kenton. In 1956, he formed a new band and recorded *Bix Duke Fats* for Atlantic Records. In the '60s, Talbert led a band in the Midwest until he returned to Los Angeles in 1975. There he worked as a studio musician writing for many television shows, including *Emergency, Mulligan's Stew*, and *Serpico*. In 1976, he recorded "Lousiana Suite" with a new band and, in 1986, recorded "Things as They Are." Talbert continued to record in the 1990s in California and New York. Some of the titles were "Warm Café," "Duke's Dream," and "This Is Living." Talbert died in 2005.

TURK MURPHY

(Turk Murphy and His Orchestra) Born in Palermo, California on December 16, 1915. Murphy Murphy (Melvin E. Murphy) was raised in Williams, California, and studied trombone as a youngster. When he finished high school, he joined the Merle Howard band until the mid-'30s when he left to go with Val Bender. He worked with Bender, Mal Hallett, and Will Osborne, playing trombone and arranging until the late '30s when he studied and jobbed around Oakland. In 1940, he joined Lu Watters and the Yerba Buena Jazz Band in San Francisco until he was drafted into military service, where he remained until 1945. When he was released, he rejoined Watters, with whom he played until forming his own band in 1947. In 1951, he disbanded and joined Marty Marsala. By the mid-'50s, he organized another band that became quite popular featuring soloists Clancy Hayes, Wally Rose, and Bob Scobey. Murphy opened his own club, Earthquake McGoon's, in San Francisco in 1960. He wrote "Ballad for Marie Brizzard" and "Something for Annie." The Turk Murphy Orchestra recorded for Good Time Jazz and Jazz Man Records. The Murphy band performed into the '70s.

CHARLIE VENTURA

(Charlie Ventura and His Orchestra) Born in Philadelphia, Pennsylvania on December 2, 1916. Charlie Ventura (né: Charles Venturo) studied saxophone when he was in high school and played with local bands in Philadelphia in the '30s. From 1942 to 1946, he was featured with Gene Krupa's band, playing momentarily with Teddy Powell (1943–1944). He formed a group called Bop for the People with Jackie Cain and Roy Kral in 1947. The group also contained Bennie Green on trombone, Conte Candoli on trumpet, and Boots Mussulli on alto saxophone. In 1951, he joined the Big Four consisting of himself, Chubby Jackson, Marty Napoleon, and Buddy Rich. During the remaining '50s and '60s he played with Krupa and guitarist Johnny Smith. He retired to Las Vegas in the early '70s, and worked as a deejay. From 1972 to 1975, Ventura led a house band at Sheraton Tobacoo Valley Inn in Windsor, Connecticut, which featured a number of guest performers, including Dave McKenna and Bobby Hackett. During the '80s, he freelanced until his retirement. Ventura died in Pleasantville, New Jersey, on January 17, 1992.

PÉREZ PRADO

(Pérez Prado and His Orchestra) Born in Matanzas, Cuba on December 11, 1916. Pérez Prado (né: Damaso Pérez Prado) studied classical piano at school. As a youngster he played organ and piano in various movie houses in Cuba. In the late '30s, he moved to Havana, played in various nightclubs, and eventually joined Orquestra Casino de la Playa, one of Cuba's most popular bands. Prado claimed to have gotten the idea for Mambo rhythm from playing jam sessions after the regular gig. In 1947, he toured South America performing Mambo-style rhythm with various local musicians. He formed his first big band in Mexico City in 1948 and was based at the Club 1-2-3. He recorded for a Cuban record company in 1948 but, by 1949, was recording for RCA. At that time, his big featured tune was "Mambo #5," which brought him and his band to the attention of the North American public. Prado first toured the U.S. in 1951 and sold out major venues, including the Puerto Rican Theater in New York and the Zenda Ballroom in Los Angeles. By 1954, the Prado band appeared at the Waldorf-Astoria Hotel in the Starlight Room. In 1955, the band recorded "Cherry Pink and Apple Blossom White" that was number one on the charts for ten weeks. In addition, the song was also in the movie *Underwater*, which featured Jane Mansfield, Richard Egan, and Jane Russell. In 1956, Columbia Pictures released the movie *Cha-Cha-Cha Boom*, featuring Perez Prado, the Mary Kaye Trio, Helen Grayco, and Luis Alcarez. In 1958, "Patricia," another number one tune, was recorded for RCA. In 1970, Prado left the U.S. and returned to Mexico. He did return to the U.S. in 1987 for a date at the Hollywood Palladium before returning permanently to Mexico. Prado died in Mexico City, Mexico on September 15, 1989.

TED B. BUCKNER

(Teddy Buckner and His Orchestra) Born in Sherman, Texas on July 16, 1909. Teddy Buckner (né: John Edward Buckner) was raised in Los Angeles and studied trumpet as a youth. He joined Sonny Clay in the early '30s and played with the Buck Clayton band in the mid-'30s. The Clayton band traveled to Shanghai, China and featured Buckner on several solos. When the band returned to Los Angeles, Buckner joined the orchestra led by Lionel Hampton. Benny Goodman heard Hampton playing at the Paradise Club and took him to New York. Buckner then took over the Hampton band, but most of the members were soon drafted into the U.S. service during WWII, and the band was dissolved. When the war was over, Buckner recorded with Kid Ory and Benny Carter. In 1954, he formed a new band and recorded three *Dixieland Jubilee* albums. During the mid-'50s, Kid Ory was heard on a broadcast from the Club Hangover and Buckner was featured on "Just a Closer Walk with Thee." Buckner died in Los Angeles, California on September 22, 1994.

JOHNNY AUSTIN

(Johnny Austin and His Orchestra) Johnny Austin played solo trumpet with the Jan Savitt band in the mid-'30s. In 1938, Johnny Austin was the lead trumpet player with the Glenn Miller band. After a year, and prior to the band's great success, Austin played with Abe Lyman, Larry Clinton, and Jan Savitt. After WWII, he formed the Johnny Austin Orchestra, based out of Philadelphia and traveled throughout the country playing at various venues, including dates at many colleges and universities. Austin continued to lead the band throughout the '60s, playing in the Philadelphia area. The Johnny Austin Orchestra recorded for Decca Records.

ZIGGY ELMAN

(Ziggy Elman and His Orchestra) Born on May 26, 1914. Ziggy Elman (né: Harry Finkelman) was raised in Atlantic City, New Jersey, where he learned to play trombone at an early age. As a teenager he joined the Alex Bartha band playing trombone at the Steel Pier in Atlantic City. In the late '20s and early '30s, he switched to trumpet and played with various groups in the New Jersey area. In 1935, he replaced Pee Wee Erwin with the Benny Goodman band and remained with Goodman until 1940. It was during his stay with Goodman that he recorded "And the Angels Sing," which he had written, for Bluebird Records that became a national hit. While with Goodman, Elman recorded 20 records for Bluebird Records using members of Goodman's band but crediting Elman as the leader. In 1941, he played with Joe Venuti until he joined Tommy Dorsey as Bunny Berigan's replacement. In 1944, he was drafted into the U.S. army and rejoined Dorsey when he was released in 1946. In 1947, Dorsey disbanded his orchestra and Elman moved to California and organized his own band. He used the tune "And the Angels Sing" as his theme song. After a few months, Dorsey reorganized and Elman disbanded and joined the new Dorsey band. In 1948, Elman formed his second band that traveled and recorded until 1951. At that time, Elman did studio film work, recordings, and appeared with various bands. Elman died in George Nuys, California on June 26, 1968.

SKITCH HENDERSON

(Skitch Henderson and His Orchestra) Born in Halstad, Minnesota, on January 27, 1918. Skitch Henderson (né: Lyle Henderson) studied at the London Conservatory of Music when he was seven and at the University of California and Juilliard School of Music in New York City. In the late '30s, he was active on the West Coast playing in radio, theaters and with various dance bands. From 1939 to 1940, after accompanying Judy Garland on tour, he did studio work. During WWII, he served in the U.S. armed forces and, in 1946, was the featured soloist on the Bing Crosby and Frank Sinatra radio shows. He organized and led his own band from 1947 until 1950 that featured two French horns, good arrangements, and spotlighted singer Nancy Reed. The theme song of the Skitch Henderson Orchestra was "Anita." In 1950, he disbanded and became the musical director on Frank Sinatra's radio show. Henderson was one of the first active musicians on television appearing on *The Dave Garroway Show* and his own show that featured Henderson's piano performance with strings. In 1954 and 1956, he was the bandleader for *The Steve Allen Tonight Show*. Henderson continued on television during the '60s, and led the band on the *Tonight*'s summer show with different hosts when Jack Paar left the show. Henderson continued when Johnny Carson took over the *Tonight Show* in the fall of 1962. In the late '60s, Skitch Henderson left the show and did freelance conducting and arranging, including the Tulsa Symphony (1971–1972). Henderson wrote "Come Thursday," "Curacao," "Skitch in Time," "Skitch's Blues," "Skitch Boogie," and "Minuet on the Rocks."

BUDDY MORENO

(Buddy Moreno and His Orchestra) Born in California. Moreno began as a singer in a San Francisco trio in 1929 and studied guitar. He worked with the Griff Williams Orchestra from 1933 to 1940. He then joined the band led by Dick Jurgens until Jurgens disbanded to join the U.S. marines in 1943 and Moreno joined the Harry James band. In 1944, Moreno left for military service and returned in 1947, when he formed his own band. The Buddy Moreno band was heard regularly on broadcasts from St. Louis at the Casa Loma Ballroom featuring singer Perri Mitchell. In the early '50s, the Moreno band was featured on its own television show in California until it disbanded. Moreno than became a disc jockey with Ted Weems on a Memphis, Tennessee radio station. After a year, Moreno returned to St. Louis, fronted an orchestra, and hosted a music variety show on KMOX-TV. The theme song of the Buddy Moreno Orchestra was "It's That Time Again." The band recorded for Victor Records. When the show was cancelled the band was booked into the Chase Hotel in St. Louis. After Moreno once again disbanded, he worked as a radio disc jockey through the '80s.

SALTY DOG ORCHESTRA

(The Salty Dog Orchestra) There is little information available on this group although it is known that they were originally organized by students at Purdue University and played for school functions, but eventually performed in greater Chicago at clubs, hotels, and other venues. Gradually, the band was made up of personnel other than those who had attended Purdue and featured Lou Green and others. They eventually toured with the Kingston Trio, George Shearing, and other top names. The Red Arrow Club was the main venue in Chicago, where the band appeared. The Dixieland-oriented band recorded tunes, including "Brush Stomp," "Let's Get Drunk and Strut," "Sweet Lorraine," "Mobile Stomp," "Down in Honky Town," "Black Bottom Stomp," "Coal Cart Blues," and others. The band recorded for Stomp Off Records.

PUPI CAMPO

(Pupi Campo and His Orchestra) Pupi Campo led an orchestra in the Latin big band style of Tito Puente, Jose Cabello, and Noro Morales. The Campo band was heard on radio during the latter part of the '40s and seen and heard on television in the early '50s. The Pupi Campo band joined Jack Paar's television program in the latter part of 1953 and appeared for three years. During that period singer, Betty Clooney (Rosemary's sister) joined the show, and she and Pupi Campo were eventually married.

PAUL NEIGHBORS

(Paul Neighbors and His Orchestra) Neighbors organized his first big band in 1948 and played at the Mapes Hotel in Reno, Nevada. He traveled the West Coast, playing from Washington State to California, and completed a long engagement at the Claremont Hotel in Berkeley, California. Neighbors relocated to Houston, Texas, in the early '50s and began to travel the Midwest with his band playing the Shamrock-Hilton in Dallas, the Schroeder in Milwaukee, and the Peabody and Chase hotels. Traveling northeast, the Neighbors Orchestra played in New York City at the Hotel Pennsylvania. He always returned to the Shamrock Hotel in Houston, where the band played an average of six months per year. Neighbors died in Houston, Texas, on August 26, 1983.

RALPH FLANAGAN

(Ralph Flanagan and His Orchestra) Born in Loraine, Ohio, on April 7, 1919. While still in his teens, Ralph Flanagan played piano with various local bands. In 1940, he joined the Sammy Kaye Orchestra as pianist-arranger. In 1942, Flanagan joined the U.S. merchant marines and arranged for a service band. When he returned to civilian life, he arranged for Blue Barron, Alvino Rey, Boyd Raeburn, Gene Krupa, Hal McIntyre, Tony Pastor, Charlie Barnet, Sammy Kaye, *The Perry Como Supper Club* radio program, and for singers Mindy Carson and Tony Martin. In 1949, he formed his own big band, and through live performances, broadcasts, and record dates the band rose to quick prominence. Flanagan utilized the Glenn Miller sound and recorded "Nevertheless," "Harbor Lights," "Slow Poke," "Rag Mop," "Hot Toddy," and others for Victor, Bluebird, and Rainbow Records. The band featured singer Harry Prime. The theme song was "Singing Winds." The Flanagan Orchestra played through the '60s, when Flanagan disbanded and became a full time writer-arranger. Flanagan wrote "Singing Winds" "Albuquerque," "Flanagan's Boogie," and "Hot Toddy." The Ralph Flanagan Orchestra recorded for Victor Records.

LESTER LANIN

(Lester Lanin and His Orchestra) Lester Lanin led and booked bands beginning in the late '40s. Although he began in Philadelphia, Pennsylvania, he branched out to other major cities as well, doing most of his work out of New York City. Although his bands were primarily hotel, social-type bands, the personnel included some of the top jazz players of the time as well. Lanin booked many bands on the same night and continued to be active through most of the remaining 20th century. The Lanin Orchestra recorded for Epic, Pick, Phillips, Mercury, Harmony, and Audio Fidelity records.

TITO PUENTE

(Tito Puente and His Orchestra) Born in New York City on April 30, 1923. Tito Puente (né: Ernest Anthony Puente Jr.) wanted to become a dancer but had a torn ankle tendon early in life and studied piano. He ultimately played piano, saxophone, vibes, and conga and bongo drums. During WWII, Puente served in the U.S. Navy and met Charlie Spivak who gave Puente music lessons while they sailed on the *U.S.S. Santee*. When Puente was discharged from the service, he studied at the Juilliard School of Music in New York City. While attending Juilliard, Puente played with several Latin bands, including Machito, Noro Morales, and Pupi Campo. In 1949, he formed a group called Picadilly Boys that eventually became the Tito Puente Orchestra. The band featured Willie Bobo, Mongo Santamaria, Johnny Pacheco, and Ray Barretto. Puente loved the sounds of the Count Basie, and Stan Kenton bands and combined American big band sounds with a Latin feel. In the '60s, he promoted the cha-cha and played Broadway show tunes in a Latin style. Puente toured Europe in the '70s and recorded with Ray Barretto and Cal Tjader. The band appeared in a TV film, *Salsa '79*, and recorded for Atlantic and Fantasy records. By 1980, Puente had cut the band down to eight pieces and won several Grammys. In the early '90s, Tito Puente was seen in a film entitled *The Mambo King*. Tito Puente died in New York City in 2000.

BOB SCOBEY

(Bob Scobey and His Frisco Jazz band) Born in Tucumcari, New Mexico, on December 9, 1916. Bob Scobey was raised in Stockton and Berkeley, California, and studied trumpet as a youth. He finished high school and worked in the Bay Area in ballrooms, pit bands, and on radio. In 1940 he joined Lu Watters and the Yerba Buena Jazz band and played with them through the '40s before and after serving in the U.S. military during WWII. He formed his own band in 1949, playing mostly on the West Coast in Oakland and San Francisco but also in Las Vegas and Chicago. During the '50s, he played and recorded with Turk Murphy. In the early '60s, he worked in New Orleans and Chicago. During his career Scobey recorded for Trilon, Ragtime, Jazz Man, West Coast, and Good Time Jazz records. Scobey died in Montreal, Canada, on June 12, 1963.

Bands directed by the following were known to have been organized in the '40s but there was insufficient historical information to include them: Johnny Addini, Will Back, Louise Carlyle, Joy Cayler, the Darlings of Rhythm, Peter Dean, Samuel Jacob, Ada Leonard, Dick McIntyre, Prairie View Co-eds, Maurice Rocco, Sharon (Wright) Rogers, Freddie Shaffer, Ted Steele, Just in Stone, and Virgil Whyte.

CHAPTER

TELEVISION REIGNS
(1950–1959)

The '50s were a period of enormous physical and psychic transformation. The U.S. farm population dropped from 4.5 million (in 1950) to 2.75 million (in 1960). It was the beginning of the Joseph McCarthy Era and the McCarthy hearings. President Harry Truman fired General Douglas MacArthur. When Joseph Stalin died, Nikita Khrushchev took over as leader of U.S.S.R. Television sets were everywhere and credit cards became popular. People in the U.S. became intrigued with Christianity. The phrase "one nation under God" was added to the Pledge of Allegiance. Swanson created the "TV dinner" and Disneyland opened in California. "In God We Trust" was added to American currency. America experienced a deep recession.

1950: Korean War began. U.S. planned the hydrogen bomb. The Minshall, Radareed, Vierling, and Wobble electronic organs were designed and developed.

1951: Truce talks began in Korea. The first digital computer was marketed. The first major electronic music studio, Radio Cologne, was established. The Polychord III, an electronic organ, was developed.

1952: King George VI died. Dwight F. Eisenhower was elected president of the U.S. The Columbia-Princeton Electronic Music Center was founded. The Univox, a monophonic piano attachment, was developed and manufactured.

1953: Armistice was declared in Korea. The rapid growth of television greatly impacted network radio eliminating most live music and radio staff orchestras. Electrical transcriptions and disk jockeys began to dominate radio. Tuttivox, an electronic organ, was developed.

1954: The first atomic submarine, the *Nautilus*, was developed. Electronic pianos, Clavier and Pianophon, were developed and manufactured.

1955: The Montgomery, Alabama, boycott was held. The Salk serum was perfected. Great Britain's Winston Churchill (80 years old) was succeeded by Anthony Eden as prime minister. Phonograph Record Clubs were begun by Columbia, followed by RCA and Capitol. The RCA electonic music synthesizer was developed and produced. The Illiac computer, a computer used in music composition, was produced. The Gulbransen organ was manufactured.

1956: Elvis Presley's first album was released. The great uprising in Hungary occurred. The ANS, a photoelectric composition machine, was developed.

1957: The first man-made satellite, Sputnik I (Russian for "fellow traveler") orbited Earth. The rack jobbing of phonograph records began. The first experiments were carried out on Computer Sound Synthesis. The first integrated circuit was crafted. The Diemens synthesizer, an electronic composition machine, was designed.

1958: Boris Pasternak's *Doctor Zhivago* won the Nobel Prize for literature. Stereo was introduced in commercial phonograph records. The Rogers organ was manufactured.

1959: In Cuba, Fidel Castro defeated Fulgencio Batista Zaldívar. Nikita Kruschhev visited the U.S. Investigations into the legitimacy of quiz shows began. Classical music had its first million-seller—Van Cliburn's performance of Tchaikovsky's Concerto for Piano and Orchestra.

BANDS FIRST ORGANIZED DURING
1950–1959

LUTHER HENDERSON

(Luther Henderson and His Orchestra) Born in Kansas City, Missouri on March 14, 1919. Henderson studied piano in his youth and became a prominent conductor and arranger during the '50s and '60s. He attended the Juillard School of Music in New York City and played piano with Leonard Ware from 1939 to 1944. He served in the U.S. military during WWII and when he was discharged played piano with Mercer Ellington prior to assuming the musical directorship with Lena Horne from 1947 to 1950. He then became an active arranger and teacher. During the '50s and '60s, Henderson organized an orchestra and conducted a number of television shows and record dates accompanying various singers in New York. In the early '70s, he wrote music for the Broadway revival of *No, No, Nanette* and arranged music for the shows *Do-Re-Mi* and *Funny Girl*. Luther Henderson wrote the tunes "Ten Good Years," "Solitaire," and "Hold On." The Luther Henderson Orchestra recorded the albums *Clap Hands* and *The Greatest Sound Around* for Columbia Records.

STEVE ALLEN

(Steve Allen and His Orchestra) Born in New York City on December 26, 1921. Allen's parents were vaudeville performers. His career began on a radio station in Phoenix, Arizona, and he learned to play piano and began to play in small venues and write popular songs. From radio he progressed to television and served as the host of *I've Got a Secret*. Allen was the founder and first host of *The Tonight Show*, which hosted a number of bands, including Les Brown, Bobby Byrne, and Skitch Henderson, and discovered many young talents, like Steve Lawrence, Eydie Gorme, and several major comedians during the '50s. Allen led several bands for recordings and played piano with the Donn Trenner All-Stars. During the '50s and '60s, Allen recorded more than 20 piano-based mood record albums, including *Music for Swingers*, *Jazz for Tonight*, *Let's Dance*, and *Music for Tonight*. During the course of his career, he wrote hundreds of songs, including "The Bell Book and Candle," "This Could Be the Start of Something Big," "Houseboat," and "Picnic." Allen and his wife, Jayne

Meadows, appeared on many television programs during the '60s, '70s, and '80s and he continued to write songs and books. Allen died in 2000.

JAMES ARCHEY

(James Archey and His Orchestra) Born in Norfolk, Virginia on October 12, 1902. Archey was a trombone player who played with Louis Armstrong, Thomas "Mutt" Carey, Henry Allen, and King Oliver. During the '30s and early '40s, Archey played and recorded with Claude Hopkins, Ella Fitzgerald, Benny Carter, Willie Bryant, and Luis Russell. In 1948, he joined the Bob Wilber Dixieland Band and fronted the band when Wilber left in 1950. Archey led the band through 1954 when he took the group on a European tour. In 1955, he disbanded and joined the Earl Hines Orchestra in San Francisco, where he worked until 1962. Archey continued to tour overseas with various all-star groups and with the Muggsy Spanier band until 1967. Archey died in New Jersey on November 16, 1967.

DICK HYMAN

(Dick Hyman and His Orchestra) Born in New York Cityon March 8, 1927. Dick Hyman studied classical piano when he was young and served in the military during WWII (1945–1946). After attending Columbia University, he played in various clubs in New York in 1948 and with Eddie Shu and Tony Scott in 1949. In 1950 he joined Benny Gooman and toured Europe. In 1951, Hyman played with Flip Phillips, Lee Castle, Alvy West, and then formed his own band. After disbanding, Hyman served as a studio musician for several years sometimes recording and playing harpsichord. During the late '50s and early '60s, he was music director for Arthur Godfrey's radio and television shows, and worked with Leonard Feather directing and writing for various record sessions and concert dates. He also played and conducted for Mitch Miller and Percy Faith on television shows. In 1962, Hyman was the pianist-conductor for singer Johnny Desmond and, during the remainer of the '60s, arranged for various jazz groups and singers. He did a number of freelance recordings with Toots Thielemans and others in the '70s. Hyman made a number of recordings, including albums *Unforgettable, Fabulous Dick Hyman & His Orchestra, Plays Kurt Weill*, and *Great All-Time Songs*. Hyman recorded for Proscenium, Command, and MGM records. Hyman eventually retired and lives in Florida.

BUDDY MORROW

(Buddy Morrow and His Orchestra)
Born in New Haven, Connecticut, on February 8, 1919. Buddy Morrow (né: Muni "Moe" Zudekoff) studied at the Juilliard School of Music in New York City in 1934. From the middle to late '30s, he played first trombone with Artie Shaw, Paul Whiteman, and Eddy Duchin. Morrow played with Tommy Dorsey from 1939 to 1941, when he left to be a full time studio musician in New York City. He also played for a short while with Vincent Lopez and again with Artie Shaw. He played with Bob  Crosby in 1942 prior to serving in the military during WWII. When he was released in 1945 he joined Jimmy Dorsey prior to forming his own band in 1946 that failed to meet with much success. He formed another band in 1951 that gained considerable fame. It was considered a smooth, swinging group and recorded the big hit "Night Train" that became their theme song. Pat Collins sang with the Buddy Morrow Orchestra. During the '60s, Morrow disbanded and returned to the studios where he appeared on the Tonight Show (featuring Johnny Carson) and, during the '70s, on the Big Band Cavalcade tour. In 1974, Morrow led a revived Glenn Miller Orchestra. Morrow wrote "Our Song of Love," "When the Moon Is Gone," and "Should I Believe My Heart?" The Buddy Morrow Orchestra recorded for CMS, Victor, Epic, Mercury, and Camden records. In 1979, Morrow took to the road once again as the leader of the Tommy Dorsey Orchestra.

GENE WILLIAMS

(Gene Williams and His Orchestra) Williams began his career as a singer with the Claude Thornhill Orchestra in the '40s. Williams formed his own band in 1950, in New York City, at a time when the big band era was waning. The Gene Williams band was hailed by musicians and worked college dates and other club one-nighters. Sidemen included Jack Moots, Don Josephs, Mel Zelnick, Mickey Folus, Sam Marowitz, Harry Divito, and Buddy Arnold. The arrangers were Chico O'Farrell, Hubie Wheeler, Joe Reisman, and Gil Evans. In addition to Williams, the other featured singer was Adele Castle. The band worked at the Glen Island Casino and made several recordings prior to its demise.

LES BAXTER

(Les Baxter and His Orchestra) Born in Mexia, Texas, on March 14, 1922. Les Baxter studied classical piano as a teenager and attended the Detroit Conservatory of Music and Pepperedine College in Los Angeles. He was a member of Mel Torme's vocal group, Mel Torme and the Mel-Tones, in the mid-'40s and developed as an arranger and conductor. In the late '40s, he served as music director for various radio shows, including *The Bob Hope Show*, *The Abbott and Costello Show*, and *Halls of Ivy*. He did some arranging for Nat "King" Cole, Frank Devol, and Margaret Whiting. In the early '50s, Capitol Records signed him as a producer and recording artist and recorded many albums with a large orchestra featuring Latin-American and jungle drum themes as well as popular tunes. He recorded "I Love Paris," "April in Portugal," "Blue Tango," "The Poor People of Paris," "La Sacre du Sauvage," "A Day in Rome," "Brandy," "Ceremony," "The High and the Mighty," "Shooting Star," "Fiesta Bravo," "Unchained Melody," "Coffee Bean," "Sunshine at Kowloon," and many others, some of which he had written. Baxter retired in California and died in Newport Beach, California on January 15, 1996.

HUGO MONTENEGRO

(Hugo Montenegro and His Orchestra) Born in New York City in 1925. Montenegro grew up in New York City. During WWII, he served in the U.S. Naval Reserve and arranged for several service bands. When WWII was over, he enrolled at Manhattan College. In 1955, he began recording, serving as a staff manager for André Kostelanetz. He also conducted and arranged for several artists, including Harry Belafonte, and made some albums under his own name. He moved to California in 1967, and scored music for the film *Hurry Sundown*, directed by Otto Preminger. In 1968, his orchestra and chorus recorded the theme for the Italian motion picture *The Good, the Bad and the Ugly*, composed by Ennio Morricone. The recording hit number two on the charts and sold more than one million copies. Montenegro continued to write and conduct in Hollywood through the '60s and '70s.

JOE BUSKIN

(Joe Buskin and His Orchestra) Born in New York City on November 7, 1916. He studied piano as a teenager and played in local groups in New York City. In the mid-'30s, he worked at the Famous Door and with Eddie Condon and Joe Marsala. From 1938 to 1939, he played with the Bunny Berigan Orchestra and then briefly with Joe Marsala and Muggsy Spanier. In early 1940, he joined the Tommy Dorsey band where he played through 1942. During that period with Dorsey, Buskin wrote "Oh, Look at Me Now," which was a big feature by Dorsey in 1941. Buskin served in the U.S. Military during WWII where he directed some service shows. When he was discharged he joined the Benny Goodman band in late 1946 and was featured by Goodman. While with Goodman, Buskin composed "Man Here Plays Fine Piano" and "Benjie's Bubble." In 1947, Buskin joined Bud Freeman and worked awhile as a radio staff musician. From 1949 to 1950, he acted in a Broadway play, *The Rat Race*, and also appeared in the movie version. During the '50s and '60s, Buskin led his own bands primarily in New York, Las Vegas and California. He also made occasional appearances on television during that period. During the mid-'60s, Buskin moved to Hawaii where he played on a part-time basis. Buskin wrote "Serenade in Thirds," "There'll Be a Hot Time in the Town of Berlin," "Something Wonderful Happens in Summer," "Whatcha Doin' After the War?," "Lovely Weather We're Having," "Every Day Is Christmas," "Lucky Me,"

"Love Is Everything," "If I Knew You Were There, and "Portrait of Tallulah." Buskin recorded for Decca, Victor, Capitol, Camden, Epic, Columbia, and Atlantic records.

GEORGE FEYER

(George Feyer and His Orchestra) George Feyer studied with Szekely, Kodaly, and Dohnanyh at Hungary's Budapest Conservatory of Music. He was considered one of the finest young pianists in Hungary. When he matured, he began playing popular music and appeared at the top venues, including hotels and clubs in the Hague, St. Moritz, Geneva, Monte Carlo, Nice, Deauville, and Paris, and became one of the most famous and well-paid entertainers in Europe. In 1951, he moved to the U.S. and debuted at Gogi's La Rue in New York. He organized a band that played the classics in a commercial style and catered to the well-to-do. He had a limitless repertory. It was said that he "played the classics with a touch of Broadway." He wrote a series of tunes that he referred to as his Echoes Series that included "Echos of Paris," "Echos of Childhood," "Echos of Spain," "Echos of Budapest," "Echos of Italy," "Echos of Hollywood," "Echos of Latin America," etc.

SHORTY ROGERS

(Shorty Rogers and His Orchestra) Born in Great Barrington, Massachusetts on April 14, 1924. Shorty Rogers (né: Milton Michael Rajonsky) attended the High School of Music and Art in New York City, where he spent his teenage years. Moving to California, he attended the Los Angeles Conservatory of Music. During the early '40s, he played trumpet with, and wrote for, Red Norvo, Will Bradley, and Woody Herman. During the later '40s, he worked with bands led by Charlie Barnet and Butch Stone, prior to rejoining Woody Herman who had formed a new "herd." In 1950, he joined the Stan Kenton Orchestra where he remained for a year. In 1951, he played at Howard Rumsey's Lighthouse. He formed the group Shorty Rogers and the Giants in 1953, and continued composing and arranging. His studies with Dr. Wesley Laviolette resulted in many experimental works written by Rogers and were reflected during the '50s in his work with Kenton, the Giants, and with Teddy Charles. During the '60s, '70s, and '80s, Rogers wrote music for several movies and toured extensively throughout the U.S. and Europe. Rogers's compositions include "Round Robin," "Back Talk," "The Sweetheart of Sigmund Freud," "More Moon," "Keeper of the Flame," "Be As Children," "Not Really the Blues," "Curbstone Scuffle," "Cerveza," "Jolly Rogers," "Wake Up and Shout," "That's Right," "Jazz Waltz," "So Voce," "Samba Do Lorinho," "Freedom's Coming," "Keen and Peachy," and many others. Rogers died in Van Nuys, California, on November 7, 1994.

NEAL HEFTI

(Neal Hefti and His Orchestra) Born in Hastings, Nebraska on October 29, 1922. Hefti studied arranging and trumpet in the beginning of his teenage years in his hometown. He played with Bob Astor in 1941 and traveled to Cuba with the Les Lieber band. When he returned, he joined Chalie Barnet, then Bobby Byrne, and arranged for the Earl Hines Orchestra. He then joined the Charlie Spivak band in 1943 and traveled to Los Angeles. After a brief stint with Horace Heidt, he joined the Woody Herman band in 1944 and wrote the famous charts "The Good Earth" and "Wildroot." In 1945, he married Woody's singer, Frances Wayne. In 1946, he left the Herman band and joined Charlie Ventura. From 1948 to 1949, Hefti played and wrote for the Harry James band. He also wrote and recorded "Repetition" for the *Jazz Scene* album produced by Norman Granz that featured Charlie Parker. Beginning in 1950, Hefti wrote for the Count Basie band, penning tunes like "Kid From Red Bank," "Whirly Bird," "Little Pony," "Li'l Darlin'," and "Cute." In 1952, Hefti formed his own big band, which he led for several years. The theme song of the Neal Hefti Orchestra was "Coral Reef." During the '60s, Hefti wrote for various film and television series, including *Batman, The Odd Couple, Barefoot in the Park, Sex and the Single Girl, How to Murder Your Wife, Boeing Boeing, Synanon,* and many others. Hefti's other compositions include "Bag-A' Bones," "Pony Tail," "A Little Tempo, Please," "It's Awfully Nice to Be with You," "Has Anyone Here Seen Basie?," "Why Not?," and "Fancy Meeting You." Hefti continued to write and edit throughout the '70s, '80s, and '90s.

LEO ADDEO

(Leo Addeo and His Orchestra) Leo Addeo's family moved from their home in Italy to Brooklyn, New York when Addeo was a child. He studied violin, clarinet, and saxophone, and began to arrange music as well. In the '40s, he worked with Gene Krupa, Larry Clinton, and Frankie Carle. In the early '50s, he was orchestrating for Hugo Winterhalter, when Winterhalter was appointed to RCA Victor Records, taking Addeo with him. Addeo wrote and produced for Victor, conducting various instrumental groups and specializing in Hawaiian instrumental music. He recorded albums *Musical Orchids from Hawaii*, *Songs of Hawaii*, *More Hawaii in Hi-Fi*, *Hello Dolly!*, *Hawaii's Greatest Hits*, *Hawaiian Paradise*, *Hawaii in Stereo*, *Great Standards with a Hawaiian Touch*, *Far Away Places*, and *Blue Hawaii*.

LENNY HERMAN

(Lenny Herman and His Orchestra) Herman organized his band in New York City in the early '50s. His commercial band played dance music in various New York hotels, including the New Yorker, Hotel Astor, Hotel Roosevelt, Waldorf-Astoria, and Hotel Edison. In Dallas, the Herman band worked at the Baker Hotel; in Virginia Beach, the Cavalier; in Atlantic City, the Straymore. The Herman Orchestra moved to Nevada in the mid-'60s and worked the Lake Tahoe and Reno hotels. The band was billed as "the mightiest little band in the land." The theme song of the Lenny Herman band was "No Foolin'."

BILLY MAY

(Billy May and His Orchestra) Born in Pittsburgh, Pennsylvania, on November 10, 1916. Billy May (né: William E. May) studied trumpet, piano, and arranging when he was very young. His early big band experience included jobs with Baron Elliott in Pittsburgh and on CBS radio. In 1938, he arranged for Charlie Barnet and played trumpet in his band until 1939 when he joined the Glenn Miller Orchestra. He remained with Miller until 1942, writing arrangements on "Take the 'A' Train," "Serenade in Blue," "At Last," "Always in My Heart," "Long Tall Mama," "Ida," and "Sweeter Than the Sweetest." May played on NBC radio in New York from late 1942 through 1943, and wrote for bands led by Les Brown, Alvino Rey, and Woody Herman. During WWII, May worked in a defense plant and was active on the West Coast in studio work. He played and wrote for the radio shows *Ozzie & Harriet*, *Bing Crosby*, and *Red Skelton*, and arranged for Phil Harris, Alvino Rey, and Woody Herman. In fall 1951, he organized a big band and made a number of popular recordings. The singers on the Billy May band were the Encores and Peggy Barrett. His theme song was "Lean Baby." In 1954, he sold his band to Ray Anthony. During the '50s and '60s, May served as arranger and conductor for several singers, including Frank Sinatra, and conducted studio recordings under his own name. He wrote for the TV shows and films *The Naked City*, *Johnny Cool*, *Tony Rome*, *Duffy's Tavern*, *Sergeants Three*, *Bob Crosby*, *Ozzie & Harriet*, and *Red Skelton*. May recorded on Capitol, Victor, Reprise, and Bluebird records. He died on January 24, 2004, in Juan Capistrano, California.

ERNIE RUDY

(Ernie Rudy and His Orchestra) Born in Altoona, Pennsylvania, in 1912. Ernie Rudy (né: Ernie Rudisill) played drums and joined the Sammy Kaye Orchestra in the 1930s. He was featured as "Cecil, the Daffy Drummer" in an early Kaye routine. In 1952, Rudy and a dozen of Kaye's sidemen, including Rudy's son, Ernie Rudy Jr., on drums; Frank Haendle, arranger; Charley Wilson, saxophone; and Butch Oblak, trumpet. He left the Kaye Orchestra and formed the Ernie Rudy Orchestra. The Rudy band copied the Kaye style and toured the U.S., recording for Lion and Derby records. The cooperative venture dissolved after time and Rudy retained leadership of the band and kept the name. The band remained active into the '60s, when Rudy disbanded and became an automobile salesman. Rudy died in Palm Springs, California, in December 1997.

SAUTER-FINEGAN

(The Sauter-Finegan Orchestra) Eddie Sauter (né: Edward Ernest Sauter) was born in Brooklyn, New York, on December 2, 1914. Bill Finegan (né: William J. Finegan) was born in Newark, New Jersey, on April 3, 1917. Sauter studied at Juilliard School of Music and Columbia University. As a teenager he played trumpet and arranged with Archie Bleyer and on various ship cruises and various dance bands in the mid-'30s. In the mid-'30s, he played and wrote for Charlie Barnet and Red Norvo. From 1939 to 1940, Finegan wrote for the Glenn Miller Orchestra and for Benny Goodman, for whom he wrote "Benny Rides Again," "Clarinet à la King," "All the Cats Join In," and "Superman." In the mid-'40s, he wrote for Artie Shaw, Benny Goodman, Woody Herman, Tommy Dorsey, and Ray McKinley, and led the new Glenn Miller Orchestra in the early '50s. In 1952, Sauter joined with Bill Finegan to form the Sauter-Finegan Orchestra. Bill Finegan had extensive music studies, including attending the Paris Music Conservatory. Glenn Miller was so impressed with Finegan's music score on *The Lonesome Road* that he had written for Tommy Dorsey that he hired Finegan to write for his band from 1939 to 1942. Between 1942 and 1949, Finegan wrote for Horace Heidt and Les Elgart. Finegan wrote the music for the two movies that featured the Miller band, *Orchestra Wives* and *Sun Valley Serenade*. Finegan also wrote the music for *The Fabulous Dorseys* that was shown in 1947. When Glenn Miller was called into the U.S. service in 1942, Finegan rejoined the Dorsey Orchestra and worked with him until 1950. During that period, he went to England and France and completed more advanced music study. When he joined with Eddie Sauter to form the Sauter-Finegan Orchestra in 1952, the band did extensive recordings for Victor Records. The Sauter-Finegan Orchestra recorded albums *New Directions in Music, Inside Sauter-Finegan, Memories of Goodman and Miller, Adventure in Time, Concert Jazz, Inside Sauter-Finegan Revisited*, and others. The theme song of the Sauter-Finegan Orchestra was "Doodle Town Fifers." Eddie Sauter wrote "Concerto for Jazz Band and Symphony Orchestra," "Superman," "All the Cats Join in," "Clarinet à La King," and others. Bill Finegan wrote "Pussywillow" and others. When the Sauter-Finegan Orchestra disbanded in 1957, Eddie Sauter arranged for a house band in Baden Baden and wrote for Stan Getz. Finegan worked as a freelance arranger for jingles, radio, and television until retirement. Sauter died in Nyack, New Jersey, on April 21, 1981.

AL HIRT

(Al Hirt and His Orchestra) Born in New Orleans, Louisiana on July 7, 1922. Al Hurt (né: Alois Maxwell Hirt) began to play trumpet at the age of six, when his parents bought him his first horn at a pawnshop. When he was 17, he played at the Louisiana Fairgrounds (racetrack), calling the horses to the post. During the early '40s, Hirt attended the Cincinnati Conservatory of Music until he was called to enter the U.S. Army. While in the service, he played with the 82nd Army Air Force band. When he was discharged, he joined the Jimmy Dorsey Orchestra and, prior to returning to New Orleans in the early '50s, played with Ray McKinley, Horace Heidt, and Benny Goodman. When he arrived back home in New Orleans, he formed his first band that included Bob Havens, trombone; Paul Edwards, drums; Ronnie Dupont, piano; Harold Cooper, clarinet; Bob Coquille, bass; and himself on trumpet. In the mid-'50s, he joined with clarinetist Pete Fountain and made a number of hit records, including "Java" and "Cotton Candy," for Victor Records. In 1965, the band played at Carnegie Hall and received a Grammy for the recording of "Java." During his career, Hirt recorded more than 50 albums and appeared in a number of motion picture films, including *New Orleans Jazz Brunch*, *Sass and Brass: A Jazz Session*, *Number One*, *What Am I Bid?*, *Electric Showcase*, *Fanfare for a Death Scene*, *Rome Adventure*, and the CBS television series *Touched by an Angel*. Hirt also recorded for Monument, Intersound, Projazz, and Novus records. Hirt died in New Orleans, Louisiana, on April 27, 1999.

FRANK DeVOL

(Frank DeVol and His Orchestra) Born in Moundsville, West Virginia, on September 20, 1911. DeVol grew up in Ohio and attended Miami University, where he studied music. He played with orchestra's lead by George and Gill Olsen and played lead alto saxophone and arranged for Horace Heidt in the mid-to late '30s. In the '40s, he played violin in his father's orchestra, worked in radio and television studios, and was the staff conductor in Los Angeles. During the '50s, he recorded mood music albums conducting a studio orchestra using the label Music by DeVol and was musical director for the shows of Johnny Carson, Jack Smith, and Ginny Simms. He appeared as an actor in early television, and arranged and wrote original compositions for various television shows, including *My Three Sons*. DeVol also wrote the music title songs for movies *Hush, Hush,*

Sweet Charlotte and *Lylah* and background music for *Pillow Talk, Big Knife, Boys' Night Out, The Bramble Bush, Whatever Happened to Baby Jane, The Dirty Dozen, Guess Who's Coming to Dinner, Cat Ballou, The Glass Bottom Boat, Sweet Charlotte, Send Me No Flowers, Good Neighbor Sam,* and *Under the Yum Yum Tree*. His compositions include "My Chinese Fair Lady," "Friendly Tavern Polka," "I and Claudie," and "The Chaperone." DeVol recorded for Columbia, ABC Paramount, and Capitol records.

ROBERT DRASNIN

(Robert Drasnin and His Orchestra) Born in Charleston, West Virginia on November 17, 1927. Robert Drasnin grew up in Los Angeles, California, studied the saxophone, and played with Les Brown and Tommy Dorsey during the early '40s. He played flute with the Red Norvo band in the late '50s and worked in L.A. as a studio musician. In the early '50s, Drasnin worked as an arranger and studio musician while attending advanced music classes at the University of California at Los Angeles (UCLA). While at UCLA, he served as associate conductor of the university symphony orchestra. When he graduated from UCLA, he worked full time in the studios, conducting and scoring for various CBS television shows, including *Lost in Space* and *The Wild, Wild West*. He also wrote music for the movie studios, including *The Kremlin Letter, The Hot Angel, Ride the Whirlwind,* and *Picture Mommy Dead*. He was invited to teach composition at UCLA and accepted the invitation.

SID FELLER

(Sid Feller and His Orchestra) Born in New York City on December 24, 1916. Feller studied the trumpet in his youth and played "Reveille" on the bugle for his Boy Scout troupe. In his teens, he played with local bands in New York and joined Jack Teagarden in the late '30s and early '40s. He served in the U.S. military during WWII, and continued playing with local territory bands after the war. In the early '50s, he joined the Carmen Cavallero Orchestra and became one of the musical directors at Capitol Records. Serving as conductor, arranger, and producer, he worked with Peggy Lee, Jackie Gleason, Nancy Wilson, and Mel Torme. In addition, he conducted the orchestra on the CBS's *Jane Froman Show*. The new ABC Paramount Records invited Feller to join its staff in the

331

mid-'50s. By 1960, he was working with Ray Charles and they recorded the hit record album *Modern Sounds*. In the mid-'60s, Feller resigned from ABC-Paramount Records, moved to California and became a freelance conductor, writer, and producer. From 1969 to 1974, he served as music director for *The Flip Wilson Show* and on TV specials with John Davidson, Andy Williams, John Denver, Pat Boone, and several others. He also produced records albums reflecting the soundtracks of Broadway shows, including *Mack and Mabel* and *Fade in, Fade Out*. Feller also recorded "Music to Break a Lease By" and "More Music to Break a Lease."

RICHARD MALTBY

(Richard Maltby and His Orchestra) Born in Chicago, Illinois on June 26, 1914. Maltby attended Northwestern University and played in several local dance bands before working at WBBM, a local radio station. He wrote for Paul Whiteman's band in the late '30s and was with Benny Goodman in the early '40s. While with Goodman, he wrote "Six Flats Unfurnished," one of Goodman's hit tunes. When Goodman left New York, Maltby remained and worked in various radio stations until the '50s. In the early 1950s, Maltby formed his own big band and recorded for Vik and X record labels for RCA prior to receiving a Columbia Record deal. When he disbanded he arranged for the Lawrence Welk television program. During his career Maltby recorded the following albums: *Threnody*, *Swingin' Down the Lane*, *Manhattan Bandstand*, *Music from Mr. Lucky*, *Just a Minute!*, *Hi-Fi Moods by Maltby*, *Hello, Young Lovers*, and *A Bow to the Big Name Bands*.

EDDIE GRADY

(Eddie Grady and the Commanders) Eddie Grady played with several bands and was a child drummer. The Grady Commanders was organized in the early '50s and rehearsed in the Decca Record studios. Tutti Camarata rehearsed the band which consisted of Mario Bonofidi and Willie Gillette, trumpets; Felix Mayerhofer, Morty Trautmaun, Porky Cohen and Al Lorrain, trombones; Lou Lindholm and Paul Gaglio, saxophones; George Cooper, piano; Rudy Berser, bass; Griff Howe, guitar; and Eddie Grady, drums. The singer was Lucia Roberts. The Grady Commanders made their first record in 1953. The trombone section was featured in the band that played the major ballrooms from coast to coast during its three-year existence. They appeared on *The Jackie Gleason Show* with the Tommy Dorsey band. In 1956, Grady left the band to enroll in college. He finished in 1958 and moved to New York City, where he worked with combos. In 1957, Warren Covinton assumed the leadership of the Commanders for a brief period. In 1959, Grady played with a group in Reno, Nevada at the Mapes Hotel. The Commanders eventually disbanded.

ALEX STORDAHL

(Alex Stordahl and His Orchestra) Born in New York City on August 8, 1913. Alex Stordahl studied trombone and arranging, when he was a teenager and played and wrote for Bert Block in 1934 and 1935. He joined Tommy Dorsey in 1936 and sang in the vocal trio. He wrote for Dorsey until 1943. At that time, he joined with Frank Sinatra and worked with him from 1943 to 1949. During that period, he conducted on Sinatra's radio shows, including *Your Hit Parade* (1947–1949), and Sinatra's recordings for RCA Victor Records. During the '50s, Stordahl arranged and conducted for singers Dinah Shore, Gisele MacKenzie, Nanette Fabray, Eddie Fisher, Dean Martin, and Bing Crosby. Stordahl wrote the songs "Jasmaine and Jade," "Return to the Magic Islands," "Night After Night," "Day by Day," "I Should Care," "Talking to Myself," "Ain'tcha Ever Comin' Back?," and "Recollections." Stordahl recorded for Capitol, Decca, Columbia, Dot, and Victor records. Stordahl died in Encino, California, on August 30, 1963.

MARTIN DENNY

(Martin Denny and His Orchestra) Born in New York City on April 10, 1911. Martin Denny took piano lessons as a child and by 1930 was working professionally. In the early '30s, he played with the Don Dean Orchestra that toured North and South America. During WWII, he enlisted in the U.S. Army Air Force. When the war ended and he was released from service, he enrolled in the Los Angeles Conservatory of Music, where he studied arranging and composition with Wesley La Violette. During his studies, he played in various combos in Los Angeles and, in 1954, began a long tenure in Hawaii at Don the Beachcombers and the Hawaiian Village. The outdoor bars were inhabited with many frogs and Denny began to include their sounds in his arrangements. In 1956, Denny returned to the mainland, organized a band, and toured the West Coast and the various venues in Las Vegas. He also recorded for Liberty Records, appeared on television, and continued to tour. During his career, Denny recorded dozens of LPs, including *Hypnotique, 20 Golden Hawaiian Hits, Exotic Love, Hawaii Tatoo, A Taste of Honey, Exotica, Latin Village, The Versatile Martin Denny, Paradise Moods, Spanish Village*, and many more.

GEORGE CATES

(George Cates and His Orchestra) Born in New York City on October 19, 1911. George Cates graduated from New York University and worked in vaudeville with the team of Olsen and Johnson in *Hellzapoppin*. He played saxophone and arranged for Russ Morgan, Henry Busse, and Dick Stabile, during the mid to late '40s. By the mid-'50s, he worked with Coral Records as A&R director. While at Coral, he conducted and wrote for Danny Kaye, Bing Crosby, the Andrew Sisters, and Teresa Brewer and joined ABC. One of his hit records with Coral was Steve Allen's "Moonglow" from Picnic. In 1971, Cates left the ABC radio network and joined Lawrence Welk as music director. He stayed with Welk for more than 25 years and produced many record albums, including *Under European Skies, Hit Songs-Hit Sounds, Take Five, Exciting, Polynesian Percussion*, and *Moonglow (Theme from Picnic)*. Cates wrote the songs "Champagne Time," "Adios," "Fantastic, That's You," "My North Dakota Home," "Auf Wiedersehen," and "Au Revoir."

DICK SCHORY

(Dick Schory and His Orchestra) Dick Shory studied classical percussion and played with various local groups. He auditioned and was accepted into the Chicago Symphony Orchestra and, at the same time, wrote music for radio and TV commercials. He ultimately founded The New Percussion Ensemble and commissioned new works. In the late '50s and early '60s, he worked as educational director for the Ludwig Drum Company in Chicago and began to record for RCA Victor Records that featured pieces for big band and percussion. Schory also worked in various schools in an effort to bring to realization the importance and versatility of the percussion family of instruments. Among the many albums he recorded for Victor are *Music for Bang, Baaroom and Harp*; *Happy Hits*; *Wild Percussion and Horns A'Plenty*; *Runin' Wild*; *Holiday for Percussion*; *Supercussion*; *Movin' On*; *Roar of the Greasepaint*; *Repercussion*; *Music to Break Any Mood*; *Resurrection*; and many others.

MAYNARD FERGUSON

(Maynard Ferguson and His Orchestra) Born in Montreal, Quebec, Canada, on May 4, 1928. Ferguson studied the trumpet as a child in his hometown. He played in various local bands and attended the French Conservatory of Music in Montreal. He led his own band as a teenager and greatly impressed all of the visiting U.S. bands. Entering the U.S. in 1948, he played with Boyd Raeburn, Jimmy Dorsey, and Charlie Barnet. In January 1950, he joined the Stan Kenton Orchestra and moved to Los Angeles, California, where he played with the top bands in the area and did studio movie work. In 1956, he led an all-star band on the road and at Birdland in New York City. After traveling throughout the U.S., he moved to England and traveled the continent for the next ten years. While there he made, and continues to make, annual trips to India as visiting professor of Western music at the Rishi Valley School near Madras. He moved to Ojai, California, in the '70s, organized a big American band and recorded hits "MacArthur Park" and "Gonna Fly Now." In the '80s, he formed a funk-jazz group, High Voltage, until the late '80s, when he disbanded and formed his present band, Big Bop Nouveau. Many noted sidemen have worked on the Maynard Ferguson band through the years, including Bill Watrous. Urbie Green, Don Ellis, Art Pepper, Shorty Rogers, Bill Chase, Nick Travis, Joe Burnett, Georgie Auld, Bob Burgess, Bill Holman, and others. During his career, Ferguson has made many hit records and played on the movie sound-track *The Ten Commandments*. He has recorded for Emarcy, Mainstream, Cameo, Capitol, Vik, Mercury, Roulette, and Concord records.

JONAH JONES

(Jonah Jones and His Orchestra) Born in Louisville, Kentucky on December 31, 1909. Born Robert Elliott Jones, Jonah leaned to play trumpet and sat in with local bands in Louisville when he was growing up. He played alto saxophone in a Sunday school band that also included trombonist Dickie Wells. Deciding to devote his life to trumpet, Jones traveled on a riverboat with the Othello Tinsley's Royal Aces and Wallace Bryant's Syncopators. In the late '20s, he joined the Horace Henderson band that traveled the Midwest and played in Indianapolis with the Hardy Brothers band. In the early '30s, he joined Jimmie Lunceford and then Stuff Smith's band. While with Smith, Jones was seen in a Hollywood movie *Thanks for Listening* that starred Maureen O'Sullivan and the bandleader and composer Pinky Tomlin. After a brief stint with Lil Armstrong's Big Band and McKinney's Cotton Pickers, Jones moved to New York City and worked at the Onyx Club on 52nd Street. From 1930 to 1937, Jones recorded on Vocalion Records with the Dick Porter Orchestra. In the early '40s, Jones played with Fletcher Henerson and Benny Carter and then played for 11 years with Cab Calloway. In the early '50s, Jonah Jones played with Earl Fatha Hines for two years. In 1954, Jones traveled through Europe as a soloist. In 1955, he organized his band and went into the Embers in New York, where he remained for more than ten years. During that period, he recorded "On the Street Where You Live" and "Baubles, Bangles and Beads" that sold millions of copies. Jones recorded for Columbia, Mercury, Capitol, and Hep records. Jones died in New York City on April 29, 2000.

STAN RUBIN

(Stan Rubin and His Tigertown Orchestra) Born in New Rochelle, New York in 1934. Stan Rubin graduated from Princeton University in 1955. During his freshman year he organized a Dixieland band called the Tigertown Five that played college dates at Princeton and other universities, including Dartmonth and Cornell. After graduation, he played on the Paul Whiteman radio and television programs and on many disc jockey shows. In the early '60s, the band toured Europe and met with great success. They played their way over and back from Europe on the steamship liner *S.S. Groote Beer*. Once in Europe, they worked at great venues, including the St-Germain section of Paris, and other French spots like Harry's New York Bar, the Academie du Ven, the Vieux Columbier, and the Carlton Hotel in Cannes. They also played at Maxims' on the Riviera and at one of Elsa Maxwell's gay bars. In Italy, the group played at the Excelsior Palace in Venice and at the Elbow Beach Surf Club in Bermuda. Returning to the States, the Stan Rubin band played at the Palisades Amusement Park in New Jersey. The band recorded many songs, including "Margie," "After

You're Gone," "San," "St. James Infirmary Blues," "Basin Street Blues," "Tiger Rag," "Tin Roof Blues," "Yes, Sir," "That's My Baby" and many others. The original band featured Ed White, bass; Dick Shallberg, guitar; Rich Herbrook, drums; Norm Osheroff, trumpet; and Bill Spilka, trombone.

RAY CONNIFF

(Ray Conniff and His Chorus and Orchestra) Born in Attleboro, Massachusetts, on November 6, 1916. Conniff was raised in a musical home. His mother played piano and his father trombone. When Conniff was attending high school, he formed a local band. After graduation, Conniff went to Boston and joined Dan Murphy's Musical Skippers, where he arranged, played trombone, and drove the bus. Conniff moved to New York City in the mid-'30s and played with several combos for several years. He joined the Bunny Berrigan band in 1937, and the Bob Crosby Bobcats in 1939. In 1940, he joined the Artie Shaw band followed by a time with Glen Gray and the Casa Loma Orchestra. About this time Conniff took a correspondence course in arranging. In 1942, he joined the U.S. Navy and played and wrote for Artie Shaw's Navy band. After WWII, in 1945 he wrote and played trombone in Shaw's civilian band. In 1946, he worked for the Harry James band, playing and writing; during the remainder of the '40s, he studied conducting and music theory. He moved to Hollywood, California, and began writing for films. Returning to New York in 1951, he was hired by Mitch Miller to write for Columbia Records vocal groups which he did for about four years. In 1955, he wrote an arrangement of "A Band of Gold" for singer Don Cherry that became a top-seller. Soon after, he arranged "Chances Are" for Johnny Mathis, "Singing the Blues" for Guy Mitchell, "Just Walking in the Rain" for Johnnie Ray, "A White Sport Coat" for Marty Robbins, and "Moonlight Gambler" for Frankie Laine, all million-sellers. By 1956, Columbia commissioned him to write and conduct instrumentals and vocals, including "S'Wonderful" and others. By the end of the '50s, Conniff had recorded gold albums, including *Concert in Rhythm* and *S'Marvelous*, which sold millions of copies. During the '60s and '70s, Conniff continued to write and conduct for groups like the Fifth Dimension, Lambert, Hendricks & Ross, Simon and Garfunkel, the Carpenters, etc. Conniff was the first American to record in the U.S.S.R. He ultimately recorded for Columbia, Victor, Blue Note, Asch, and Brunswick records.

ARTHUR LYMAN

(Arthur Lyman and His Orchestra) Arthur Lyman was the son of a vibes player and studied music with his dad. Lyman joined Martin Denny in the 1940s, and worked with him for a long tenure. In the mid-'50s, Lyman left to move to Hawaii and worked at Don The Beachcomber's in Honolulu. In 1956, he worked at the Hawaiian Village at the Shell Bar, owned by Henry J. Kaiser. In the late '50s, Lyman returned to the mainland and scored the music for Les Baxter's hit "Quiet Village" that was in the Top 40 having been recorded on the Hi-Fi Record Label. That same record company then hired Lyman to record his own album and, by 1958, recorded *Taboo*, which also hit the charts and sold millions of copies. Lyman's use of bird calls, the sound of his vibes, and the use of various percussion instruments, including conch shells, boo-bam drums, and conga drums, created an interest in "exotica" music throughout the country. Lyman retired to Honolulu, Hawaii, and is still playing at the New Otani Hotel at last report.

DON SWAN

(Don Swan and His Orchestra) Born in Manitowoc, Wisconsin on June 28, 1904. Don Swan (né: Wilbur Clyde Schwandt) studied music and graduated from the University of Chicago where he worked with Sigvart Holland and Emil Soderstrom. After graduation, he orchestrated and arranged for various groups, including the touring show of Bob Hope. In the early '40s, he began writing for various Latin bands, including Xavier Cugat and other bands seeking Latin-styled arrangements. He eventually also wrote for Freddie Martin, Harry James, and Skinnay Ennis. In the late '50s, Swan formed his own band in New York City that toured extensively before appearing in Las Vegas. He signed with Liberty Records in 1957 and recorded five albums of Latin music. The Don Swan Orchestra went on to play at the Hollywood Palladium and other West Coast venues. Swan wrote "Dream a Little Dream of Me," "Hokey Joe," "Ay, Que Merengue," 'Betita," "What's the Meaning of It All," and "Sheila Shesa."

SI ZENTNER

(Si Zentner and His Orchestra) Born in Brooklyn, New York, on June 13, 1917. SI Zenter (né: Simon H. Zentner) studied trombone at an early age and played with various local bands. His first professional gig was with the Van Alexander band that he joined in the late '30s. In the early '40s, he played with Les Brown, Jimmy Dorsey, Harry James, and Abe Lyman. In the later '40s, he moved to California and played with various studio musicians at clubs and other venues. In 1951, he joined the Sonny Burke band and worked at MGM. In 1957, Zenter formed his first big band in Los Angeles and did extensive touring. By 1959, they played the Hollywood Palladium and received rave notices in *Down Beat* magazine. The Si Zentner band recorded "Up a Lazy River" for Liberty Records, and it quickly became a big hit and was the theme song of the orchestra. This record kept the band in the public eye for more than a decade. He also recorded for Victor, Smash, and Bel Canto records. Famous sidemen who appeared with the Si Zentner band included Mel Lewis, Tom Scott, Lanny Morgan, Dick Hurwirx, Bob Florence, Bob Edmundson, Dick Hurwitz, Bob Edmundson, and others. Zenter moved to Las Vegas in 1965, and played at the Tropicana Hotel. He continued to live and work in Las Vegas until he retired. Zentner died in Las Vegas, Nevada on January 31, 2000.

MEMO BERNABEI

(Memo Bernabei and His Orchestra) Born in Pittsburg, Pennsylvania in 1917. Bernabei studied the saxophone as a young man and played with the Ray Pearl Orchestra from 1936 to 1939. He worked with Jan Garber after a short stint in the military and formed his own band in 1958. His first job with his own orchestra was at the Chateau Ballroom in Los Angeles, California followed by other hotel-type jobs. The Bernabei band was said to be similar to the Jan Garber Orchestra in style and tempi. In the mid-'50s Bernabei signed with Windsor Records and recorded "Bernabei's Bounce," which became a local dance hit. In the '60s, the Memo Bernabei Orchestra was the house band for the Golden West Ballroom in Norwalk, where they remained for 15 years. The theme song of the Memo Bernabei Orchestra was "Memories of You." The Bernabei Orchestra settled in Southern California and continues to work out of Los Angeles.

CLAUDE GORDON

(Claude Gordon and His Orchestra) Gordon studied music as a youngster and learned to play the trumpet as a teenager. He worked with bands led by Frankie Masters, Matty Malneck, and Ronnie Kemper in the '40s and as a staff musician at CBS. His major love was teaching trumpet at the Los Angeles Conservatory of Music and he had many successful students. He organized his own big band in Los Angeles in the late 1950s, and featured the singer Darts Alexander. In an attempt to restart the big band movement, the American Federation of Musicians sponsored a contest in 1959 to discover the best big band at that time. The final "play-off" was held in the Roseland Ballroom in New York City. The Claude Gordon band won the national title. As a reward, the band members won new instruments and the band received an appearance on a network television show, a record contract with Alma Records, and a coast-to-coast tour of one-nighters arranged by Frank Monte (the manager of the Benny Goodman and Harry James bands). Gordon eventually returned to teaching and played locally on a part-time basis.

LOUIS BELLSON

(Louis Bellson and His Orchestra) Born in Rock Falls, Illinois, on July 26, 1924. Louie Bellson (Né: Luigi Paulino Alfredo Francesco Antonio Balassoni) studied drums at an early age and won a contest for best young drummer sponsored by Gene Krupa. When he was 17 years old, he played with the Tel Fio Rito band. In the late '30s, he played with Benny Goodman until he was drafted into the U.S. Army during WWII. He rejoined the Goodman band after the war and played with him until 1947 when he joined the Tommy Dorsey Orchestra. He stayed with Dorsey until 1949 when he left to go with small groups headed by Terry Gibbs and Charlie Shavers. He toured extensively with Jazz at the Philharmonic during the '50s and played with the Harry James band until he, with Juan Tizol and Willie Smith, left to go with Duke Ellington. While with Ellington, Bellson wrote some great big band compositions, including "Skin Deep," "Ortseam," and "The Hawk Talks." In 1953, Bellson married singer Pearl Bailey and, in 1955, left Ellington to rejoin the Dorsey band. In 1962, Bellson joined Count Basie, worked with the Dorsey ghost band in 1964 and rejoined Ellington in 1965. Bellson played with Harry James in 1966; he formed his first big band during the '50s and has led a big band, on and off, for

40 years. A few of his star sidemen over the years have included Joe Romano, Sam Noto, Blue Mitchell, Bobby Shew, Ross Tompkins, Cat Anderson, Ted Nash, Pete Christlieb, and Don Menza. Bellson has recorded for Columbia, Verve, Roulette, Hep, Pablo, and Prestige records.

QUINCY JONES

(Quincy Jones and His Orchestra) Born in Chicago, Illinois on March 14, 1933. Quincy Jones (né: Quincy Delight Jones Jr.) moved, with his family, to Seattle when he was ten. His family got him a trumpet when he was 14 and he began to study with Clark Terry when he was seventeen. He attended the Berklee School of Music in Boston prior to joining the Lionel Hampton Orchestra in 1951. After freelancing for two years, he arranged for Oscar Pettiford, Art Farmer, James Moody, Count Basie, Ray Anthony, and others. In the late '50s, he joined the trumpet section in the Dizzy Gillespie band and traveled to South America. He then traveled to Paris, where he studied composition with Nadia Boulanger. In 1958, Jones organized his first big band and toured with the opera Free and Easy. When that tour ended, the band toured the U.S. and Europe. In the '60s, Jones was appointed A&R head of Mercury Records, where he eventually became vice president. He then took on the musical directorship for Peggy Lee, Billy Eckstine, Frank Sinatra, and others. Jones began writing for motion pictures, winning Oscars and praise for such films as *Cactus Flower, In Cold Blood, In the Heat of the Night, The Color Purple*, etc. In the '70s, he had two brain aneurysms, but recouped and toured Japan with an orchestra. In the '80s, Jones founded his own record label, Quest, and began producing for several companies, including Columbia; he's worked for pop stars Aretha Franklin and Michael Jackson, and jazz artists Sarah Vaughan, Joe Zawinul, and others. During the '90s, Jones produced films, records, television, etc., with Time Warner.

Bands directed by the following were known to have been organized in the '50s, but there was insufficient historical information to include them: Manny Album, Dean Elliot, The Hormel Girls, Sal Salvadore and Bill Snyder.

CHAPTER 6

EXIT THE BANDS
(1960–1969)

In the early '60s, the Peace Corps was founded and the Bay of Pigs invasion of Cuba was deemed a failure. James Meredith enrolled at the University of Mississippi, furthering the integration effort. In 1963, President John F. Kennedy was assassinated. In the mid-'60s, the Beatles performed on *The Ed Sullivan Show* and Martin Luther King Jr. was awarded the Nobel Peace Prize. African-Americans marched in Selma, Alabama; there was a riot in the Watts section of Los Angeles; Malcolm X was assassinated. By 1967, the protests of the Vietnam War heated up and there was a march on the Pentagon. The Soviets rolled their tanks into Prague. In the late '60s, the spaceship *Columbia* launched its lunar module, the Eagle, and it landed on the moon. There were killings at Kent State University as students protested the Vietnam War.

1960: A U-2 plane was shot down in the U.S.S.R. John F. Kennedy was elected president. The Clavinet, an electronic keyboard instrument, was manufactured. The Sideman, an electronic percussion instrument, was manufactured.

1961: First manned space flights took place. The FCC authorized multiplex broadcasting. FM stations greatly increased in numbers .

1962: Direct synthesis was developed. NARM (National Association of Record Merchants) was formed by record wholesalers. An electric piano, Planet, was designed. A computer program language, SNOBOL, was developed.

1963: President Kennedy was assassinated. MUSICOMP (Music Simulator-Interpreter for Composition Procedures) was developed.

1964: Congress passed a bill establishing the National Guard Center. The Buchla synthesizer was designed. The Moog synthesizer was developed. The Mellotron, an electromechanical keyboard instrument, was developed.

1965: *Gemini VI* and *VII* were launched. The Rhodes electronic piano was designed. The MIR (Musical Information Retrieval) was developed.

1966: Russians placed first un-manned space vehicle in "soft" landing on the moon. The Wyvern organ, an electronic organ, was designed.

1967: Three American astronauts died in the *Apollo* at Cape Canaveral. The first digital organ was developed. Billy Strayhorn and Paul Whiteman died.

1968: The manned spaceship, *Apollo VIII*, circled the moon. Cassettes achieved a significant market breakthrough. Robert F. Kennedy and Martin Luther King Jr. were assassinated. Korg electronic instruments (Synthesizer, Polysix, Delta, Lambda, Trident) were developed. The string synthesizer was developed.

1969: "One giant leap for mankind"—Neil A. Armstrong was the first man to walk on the moon. Paris peace talks on Vietnam. Moog synthesizer named "instrument of the year." Founding of EMS (Electronig Music Studios) in England. Putney synthesizer was developed. Release of the historic recording with voltage-controlled equipment—*Switched on Bach*.

BANDS FIRST ORGANIZED DURING
1960–1969

KEN McINTYRE

(Ken McIntyre and His Orchestra) McIntyre served in the U.S. Military during WWII. After the war, he graduated from the Boston Conservatory of Music. In 1960, he moved to New York City and worked with Eric Dolphy in a small jazz group. McIntyre and Dolphy recorded for New Jazz Records and he began to make a name for himself. By 1961, he was teaching in the public schools of New York while continuing to play in the area. In 1962, he organized his own band and recorded an album, *Way, Way Out*, for United Artists Records. In 1966, he made an album with Cecil Taylor. By the mid-'70s, McIntyre was recording an album entitled *Hindsight* for Steeple Chase Records. By the mid-'80s, he had recorded with Craig Harris and, in the early '90s, was heard on *Prestigious: A Tribute to Eric Dolphy*.

CHARLES MUSSEN

(Charlie Mussen and the Queen City Stompers) Born in Vallejo, Callifornia, on October 25, 1933. Mussen learned to play trombone, bass, guitar, banjo, and ukulele when he was quite young, growing up in Buffalo, New York. When he was in college he hoped to become a Dixieland jazz musician. Soon after graduation, his dreams were answered as he took advantage of various opportunities that came his way and opened the door for performances with Pete Johnson, Muggsy Spanier, Vic Dickenson, Jimmy McPartland, Spike Jones, and Clyde McCoy. Right after he graduated in 1960, he began teaching and playing with Bob Scobey's Frisco Jazz Band and Clyde McCoy's Dixielanders. Mussen organized the Queen City Stompers in the early '60s. This provided opportunities for the group to play with the Buffalo Philharmonic and the professional football team, The Buffalo Bills. The Stompers also played at a number of jazz festivals, including the New York State Dixieland Jazz Festival, the All that Jazz Festival, the Potomac River Jazz Club, the Sacramento Dixieland Jazz Jubilee, the Pennsylvania Jazz Society and many others. The band ultimately worked at Eddie Condon's club in New York and recorded albums *I Love Jazz*, *Blue Prelude*, and several others.

DOMINIC FRONTIERE

(Dominic Frontiere and His Orchestra) Born in New Haven, Connecticut, on June 17, 1931. Frontiere's parents all played instruments and he studied accordion with Joseph Biviano in New York City when he was seven years old. Frontiere played at Carnegie Hall when he was twelve and studied the classics, arranging and composition. In the late '40s, he was hired by Horace Heidt to arrange and replace accordionist Dick Contino. In the early '60s, Frontiere left the Heidt band, moved to Hollywood, California and studied with Felix Slatkin and Mario Castelnuovo-Tedesco. After a few months, he was hired at 20th Century Fox Studios as music director. He worked with Lionel Newman and his brother Alfred Newman writing for films. In the early '60s, Frontiere formed his own band that recorded for Liberty Records. In the mid-'60s, the Frontiere band recorded an album entitled *Pagan Festival* for Columbia Records and, by the end of the '60s, Frontiere was writing and producing albums for Capitol Records. One album featured 20 accordions and was entitled *The Mighty Accordion Band*. Frontiere also wrote music for films and television, including *Hang 'Em High*, *Cancel My Reservation*, *Hammersmith Is Out*, *The Stunt Man*, and *The Invaders* series. During his career, Frontiere recorded for Liberty, Columbia, Capitol, United Artists, Bell, and American International records.

BILLY MAXTED

(Billy Maxted and His Orchestra) Born in Racine, Wisconsin, on January 21, 1917. Maxted played piano in New York in the late '30s and studied at the Juilliard School of Music in New York City. He played with Teddy Powell and Ben Pollack prior to joining the Red Nichols big band from 1939 to 1940. In the early '40s, he played and wrote for Will Bradley prior to starting military service in WWII. When he was discharged he led a combo in New York before joining the Ray Eberle band in 1947 and 1948. During the late '40s and early '50s, he wrote for bands led by Claude Thornhill, Will Bradley, and Benny Goodman. In the '50s, he served as the house pianist with bands fronted by Phil Napoleon, Pee Wee Erwin, and Bobby Hackett. In the '60s, Maxted formed his own band that featured excellent sidemen Jack Lesberg and Ed Hubble. The group was basically a Dixieland band but played most styles appearing at various venues in New York. Maxted moved to Florida in the '70s, and led several groups there. Maxted and His Orchestra recorded for Liberty, Seeco, Cadence, and K&H records.

GERRY MULLIGAN

(Gerry Mulligan and His Orchestra) Born in New York City on April 6, 1927. Mulligan's (né: Gerald Joseph Mulligan) parents played piano and Gerry studied piano in his youth. When he was very young his family moved to Ohio and Michigan before settling down in Philadelphia, Pennsylvania. He studied saxophone with Sam Cortenti in Reading, Pennsylvania, but taught himself the basics of arranging. He later studied arranging with Johnny Warrington and Gil Evans. Mulligan's first playing jobs, playing tenor saxophone, were with Chuck Gordon, Alex Bartha, George Paxton, and Harvey Marburger in the mid-'40s. He arranged for Elliot Lawrence, Tommy Tucker, and Johnny Warrinton in 1945, before moving to New York City in 1946. In New York he joined the Gene Krupa band and wrote arrangements on "How High the Moon" and "Disc Jockey Jump." In 1947, he played baritone saxophone and arranged for Kai Winding and Claude Thornhill. During 1948–1949, Mulligan played with the Miles Davis "Birth of the Cool" group and wrote tunes "Godchild," "Venus de Milo," "Boplicy," and "Rocker." In the early '50s, Mulligan wrote for Thornhill and Lawrence prior to moving to California where he wrote for Stan Kenton and formed his "piano-less" quartet with Chet Baker. In the mid-'50s, he traveled to Europe, leading a combo that included musicians Zoot Sims, Art Farmer, etc. Mulligan formed his big band, the Concert Jazz Band, in New York City in 1960, which traveled in the U.S. and Europe to standing-room-only audiences. In the '70s, he was artist-in-residence at the University of Miami and played with Dave Brubeck. During the '80s, he won a number of prizes and received recognition from Yale University and the Philadelphia Music Association Hall of Fame. During his career, Mulligan recorded for Prestige, New Jazz, A&M, Chiaro, Columbia, Accord, Verve, Victor, Evid, GRP, Concord, Telefunken, Blue Note, and Riverside records. Mulligan died in Darien, Connecticut on January 20, 1996.

FRANK BETTENCOURT

(Frank Bettencourt and His Orchestra) Bettencourt played trombone and arranged for Jan Garber for more than twenty years. In 1962, he formed his own band in Dallas, Texas and played in the North Texas area. He was then booked into the Shamrock Hotel in Houston, Texas before touring the South and Midwest. The band played venues from the St. Anthony Hotel in San Antonio to the Willowbrook in Chicago, Illinois and many place between. By 1968, the Bettencourt Orchestra spent the year at the Conrad Hilton Hotel (Boulevard Room). In the early '70s the band traveled to New York City and became the house band at the Roseland Dancehall. The Bettencourt Orchestra theme song was "Dreams of You." The featured singers on the band were Julie Vernon and Frank Bettencourt. Bettencourt wrote many songs, including "The Magic Fire of Love," "Clodhopper," "Call to the Post Cha-Cha," "Pflugerville Pflip," and "Blue Room Bounce."

PETER DUCHIN

(Peter Duchin and His Orchestra) Born in New York City on July 28, 1937. Peter Duchin (né: Peter Oelrichs Duchin), the son of pianist Eddy Duchin, attended Hotchkins School and graduated from Yale University in 1958, where he majored in music and political science. During the summer 1957, Duchin studied music at the Paris Conservatory of Music in France. In 1962, Peter Duchin formed his orchestra and played at the St. Regis Hotel in New York City emulating the move of his father 30 years before him. He quickly made a name for himself and traveled to Miami, Florida where he opened at the famed Fontainebleu Hotel in Miami Beach. His third opening was in Los Angeles at the Cocoanut Grove. When he returned to New York he organized a service titled Peter Duchin's Orchestras, which books various sized orchestras throughout the United States. The theme song of the Peter Duchin Orchestra is "My Twilight Dream." The band records for Decca Records.

DON ELLIS

(Don Ellis and His Orchestra) Born in Los Angeles, California on July 25, 1934. Don Ellis (né: Donald Johnson Ellis) studied music with his mother who was a church organist. Ellis began leading his own bands when he was in junior high school. He studied trumpet and composition at Boston University where he was granted the Bachelor of Music degree. He played with Ray McKinley in 1956 and in U.S. Army dance bands in Germany in 1957–1958. Ellis worked for Charlie Barnet in 1958, Maynard Ferguson in 1959 and the George Russell sextet during 1961–1962. He formed an improvisation workshop orchestra for television appearances and toured Poland and the Scandinavian countries in 1962–1963 and was the soloist with the New York Philharmonic in 1963, performing Larry Austin's "Improvisations." In 1964, he performed Gunther Schuller's "Journey Into Jazz" and moved to Los Angeles where he did graduate work at UCLA, and formed a sextet and a new 23-piece band. In 1964 and '65, he was assistant to Lukas Foss at SUNY-Buffalo under a Rockefeller grant and in the late 1965 returned to Los Angeles and re-formed his orchestra. In L.A., he taught arranging and introduction to jazz courses at UCLA and San Fernando State College but suffered a heart attack which terminated his activities. Don Ellis recorded for Enja, Riverside, GNP, Crescent, Rhino and Columbia records. Ellis died in Los Angeles, California on December 17, 1978.

JACKIE GLEASON

(Jackie Gleason and His Orchestra) Born in Brooklyn, New York, on February 26, 1916. When Gleason was a child he worked as a master of ceremonies as a disc jockey and at various amateur shows and carnivals. In the early '40s he was a nightclub comic and began to do small roles in movies in 1941 and 1942. He appeared in several unsuccessful Broadway shows, including *Artists and Models* (1943), and in a hit show in 1944 called *Follow the Girls*. During the remainder of the '40s, he appeared in various nightclubs until he once again acted in the 1949 show *Along Fifth Avenue*. In the early '50s, he made a hit on television playing a character part in *The Life of Riley*. He got his own TV show as a result and featured *The Honeymooners* with Joyce Matthews, Audrey Meadows, and Art Carney. In the mid-'60s, the actresses were replaced temporarily by Betty Kean and Sheila MacRae. Gleason wrote the theme of the show, "Melancholy Serenade," as well as "Lovers' Rhapsody," "Glamour," "To a Sleeping Beauty", and "On the Beach." Many records were released featuring the Jackis Gleason Orchestra, including albums *Music for Lovers Only*; *Music, Martinis and Memories*; *Plays Romance Jazz*; *Music to Change Her Mind Presents Velvet Brass*; *Taste of Brass*; *Doublin' in Brass*; and *Take Me Along*. The Gleason Orchestra, directed by Sammy Spears, had some of the nation's outstanding sidemen, including Billy Butterfield, Milt Hinton and Bobby Hackett. The Gleason Show ultimately moved to Miami Beach, Florida, and Gleason established residence in South Florida. He died in Fort Lauderdale, Florida on June 25, 1987.

BOB THOMPSON

(Bob Thompson and His Orchestra) Born in San Jose, California, on August 22, 1924. Bob Thompson attended the University of Califonia at Berkeley, and the Juilliard School of Music in New York City. In the '50s, he wrote for the Hi Los ("Clap Yo Hands"), Judy Garland ("Live at Carnegie Hall"), Bill Crosby ("Holiday in Europe"), and Rosemary Clooney ("Love and Clap Hands"). In the '60s Thompson wrote and conducted orchestras for more than 2,000 commercial radio and television jingles for such companies as General Motors and Colt 45 Malt Liquor. He conducted many instrumental record albums, including The *Sound of Speed* and *Mmm, Nice*. During his career, Bob Thompson worked with Dwayne Eddy, Phil Ochs, Van Dyke Parks, Warren Zevon, Randy Newman, and Jack Sheldon, who performed Thompson's song "What Goes Around."

HUGO WINTERHALTER

(Hugo Winterhalter and His Orchestra) Born in Wilkes-Barre, Pennsylvania, on August 15, 1909. Hugo Winterhalter graduated from St. Mary's College and the New Enland Conservatory of Music with a degree in violin and woodwinds. In the mid-'30s, he worked with Count Basie, Raymond Scott, Tommy Dorsey, and Claude Thornhill. He also wrote arrangements for Billy Eckstine and Dinah Shore. In the late '40s, he worked as musical director for MGM Records and, by 1950, had taken the same position with Columbia Records. While at Columbia, he arranged and conducted "Blue Christmas" that became a big hit. In the late '50s, he joined RCA Victor Records as A&R and wrote and conducted for the Ames Brothers ("The Naughty Lady of Shady Lane"), Eddie Arnold ("Cattle

Call"), Eddie Fisher, and Perry Como. In 1963, Winterhalter was appointed to the Kapp Record Company and recorded *The Best of '64 and the Best of '65*. In 1965, Winterhalter resigned from Kapp and began to write and conduct for Broadway and for films, including *Diamon Head*, for which he also wrote the music. During the late '60s, he began releasing record albums under his own name and produced a number of gold record singles, including "The Third Man Theme," "Vanessa," "Canadian Sunset," and "Blue Tango." Wintehalter worked with many stars during his career, including Joe Carlton, Sarah Vaughan, Perry Como, Babe Russin, Billy Butterfield, Frank Sinatra, Bernard Kaufman, Joe Reisman, Rubin Zarchy, Axel Stordahl, Henry Ross, Nuncio Mondello, Russ Case, Dave Kapp, Harold Feldman, Gordon Driffin, Frederick Buldrini, and Art Drelinger. Winterhalter composed "Far Away Blues," "How Do I Love Thee?," "Melody of Spain," "Eyes of Love," and "La Muñeca Español." Winterhalter retired in the late '60s and died in Greenwich, Connecticut, on September 17, 1973.

NORMAN LEE

(Norman Lee and His Orchestra) Born in Danbury, Iowa on March 24, 1921. Norman Lee (né: Norman Francis Uehle) studied saxophone and played and sang in his mother's band, in Correctionville, Iowa, when he was in the eighth grade. It was at that time that Lee wrote "What America Means to Me," his first song. The band played every night and, as a result, Lee spent little time in school. When he graduated from high school he attended Morning Side College in Sioux City, Iowa for a brief time until he joined the Jimmy Barrnet band, a territory orchestra, which played out of Omaha, Nebraska. In the early '40s, Lee played with the Eddy Howard Orchestra in Chicago. During WWII, Lee joined the Army Air Force. Upon his release, in 1945, he joined the Lawrence Welk Orchestra and co-wrote "The Champagne Polka." By 1947, he had resigned from the Welk band and rejoined the Eddy Howard Orchestra. When Howard died in 1963, Lee took over the leadership of the group, calling it the Norman Lee and the Eddy Howard Orchestra. As time went by, Lee dropped the Eddy Howard Orchestra title and the band simply became known as the Norman Lee Orchestra, but the band continued to use the arrangements from the Howard library. The band remained, primarily, in the Midwest but traveled to Hawaii occasionally. Lee died in Wichita, Kansas on December 6, 1978.

CARL "DOC" SEVERINSEN

(Doc Severinsen and His Orchestra) Born in Arlinton, Oregon on July 7, 1927. Doc Severinsen (né: Carl Hilding Severinsen) was nicknamed after his father who was an MD. When Severinsen was in school he was called little Doc, his father always being referred to as Big Doc. Doc studied trumpet with his father and won various state and national contests playing the cornet. He joined the Ted Fiorito band in 1945 and played with Charlie Barnet from 1947 through 1949, playing short stints with Sam Donahue and Tommy Dorsey in the interim. During 1954–1955, he was featured on the *Steve Allen Show* and was a member of Billy Taylor's house band in *The Subject Is Jazz*.

He was assistant conductor to Skitch Henderson on NBC's *Tonight Show* from 1962 until he became the conductor in 1967. When the show moved in 1972 from New York City to Burbank, California, Doc moved with the show and retained the job at conductor. In 1992, he left the show, continued to perform with his own band, Xebron, and worked as guest conductor and clinician. Some of the LPs recorded by Severinsen include *Doc Severinsen's Closet*, *Big Band's Back in Town*, *Command Performances*, *Torch Songs for Trumpet*, *The New Sound of Today's Big Band*, *Swinging & Singing*, *Tempestuous Trumpet*, *Fever! Live! High!*, *Wide and Wonderful*, *16 Great Performances*, and *The Great Arrival*. He recorded on Passport, BB, Verve, ABC, Capitol, Coral, Victor, Roulette, Imperial, and Command records.

TONY BARRON

(Tony Barron and His Orchestra) Born on January 6, 1943. Barron organized his first band in 1967 when he graduated from high school in South Bend, Indiana. Tony sang and directed the band in the local area. He eventually added Steve Rice to do the singing as the band took to the road doing one-nighters throughout the Midwest area. The band earned the reputation as a great sweet music-dance band and played venues like the Colliseum Ballroom in

Davenport, Iowa. The Barron band made a recording, which the band members paid for, which was sold at the various places they played. The theme song of the Tony Barron band was "How I Miss You When the Summer Is Gone." Barron died in 1998.

ERNIE CARSON

(Ernie Carson and the Castle Jazz Band) Carson studied trumpet while attending grammar school and worked in theater pit bands while in junior high and high school. In 1954, he played in the Castle Jazz Band until he joined the U.S. Marines in 1956, where he played in various bands in the Los Angeles area, including those led by Jig Adams, Ray Bauduc, and Dave Wierbach. In the early '60s, he played with the Turk Murphy band and, in 1972, moved to Atlanta, Georgia and formed the Capital City Jazz Band. Carson remained in Atlanta and in 1992 reformed the Castle Jazz band which worked in that area until he moved to Oregon in 1995. The band recorded for Stomp Off, Good Time Jazz, Fat Cat's Jazz, GHB, Jazzology, and Pearl records.

DON HOY

(Don Hoy and His Orchestra) Hoy started his band in the '60s and became most active in the '70s and '80s. Working out of Des Moines, Iowa the band traveled to Arkansas, Colorado, Oklahoma, Missouri, Kansas, Wisconsin, Illinois, and Minnesota. Occasionally, the band toured the East Coast as far south as Atlanta and as far north as New York City, Don sang and the drummer Rick Wynant was also a singer. Don eventually retired, moved to Kansas City, and sold his library to John Morgan in Des Moines, Iowa.

CHUCK MANGIONE

(Chuck Mangione and His Orchestra) Born in Rochester, New York on November 29, 1940. Chuck Mangione (né: Charles Frank Mangione) Studied piano when he was eight years old. His father was a musician and introduced him to Kai Winding, Dizzy Gillespie, Jimmie Cobb, Horace Silver, and Art Blakey in the early '50s. Mangione studied music at the Eastman School of Music in Rochester, New York and led a bebop band with his brother Gap Mangione and Sal Nistico in the late '50s. He taught music from 1963 to 1964, moved to New York City in 1965, and played with Kai Winding, Woody Herman, and Maynard Ferguson, before joining the Art Blakey Jazz Messengers, with whom he played until 1967. Returning to Rochester, he taught at the Eastman School from 1968 until 1972. While there, he organized and conducted a large orchestral group that gave a concert of his music and, as a result, got him an invitation to conduct the Rochester Philharmonic. That concert was broadcasted on PBS and attracted the attention of Mercury Records. After that success, Mangione recorded for Mercury and formed Sagoma Records that recorded his smaller group as well as those led by his brother Gap, Esther Satterfield, Gerry Niewood and others. Mangione's successful records included *Children of Sanchez* and *Feels So Good.*

CHAPTER

FINALE
(1970–1999)

For almost one-hundred years, the American big bands provided entertainment, dancing pleasure, listening enjoyment, background music for live shows, radio, and television, and exposed a variety of commercial, popular, and jazz music to millions of Americans. Jazz began in the early 19th century with slave dances and ring shouts in New Orleans by many Africans who had been moved to America. The man most responsible for interpreting the beginnings of jazz in written music notation was Louis Moreau Gottschalk (1829–1869). Gottschalk, born in New Orleans, pulled together African polyrhythms, banjo gigs, spirituals, gospel music, Scottish and Irish folk melodies, combined them with European harmonies, and produced the beginnings of American jazz. He was a child prodigy who went to Paris, France, before his 16th birthday (Chopin predicted that he would become "the king of pianists"), and wrote pieces, including "La Mamboula," "La Savane," and "La Bananier," which contain melodies and syncopated rhythms that help to define jazz. During the 19th century, American pianists—including Scott Joplin, Tom Turpin, Artie Matthews, and others—developed ragtime as a continuance to Gottschalk's music. During the next 100 years, blues, Dixieland, swing, bebop, third stream, etc. followed ragtime. Many electronic music instruments were developed and used. The computer was adapted to performance and music composition.

Since the beginning of the 20th century, jazz spun off various subcultural music art forms in the United States: hillbilly, country, race music, gospel, western swing, R&B, and rock 'n' roll. and continuined to grow and develop as a true art form. Further spins offs during the '70s, '80s, and '90s included fusion, new age, funk, rap and hip-hop.

During the era of the big bands (1900–1970), there were bands of every description. Dance bands, show bands, jazz bands, Mickey Mouse bands, hotel bands, tenor bands, stage bands, ballroom bands, radio bands, television bands, theater bands, sweet bands, swing bands, society bands, country and western bands, hillbilly bands, Latin bands—each band strived to seek its own identification. Each band needed arrangers who could write music in the style they wished to purvey. Ballrooms were located in every nook and cranny of the U.S., from the Mark Hopkins Hotel in San Francisco, to the Apollo Theater and Roseland in New York City, to the Hotel Roosevelt in New Orleans, to the Raymor Ballroom in Boston, to the Steel Pier in Atlantic City, to the Aragon and Trianon Ballrooms in Chicago, to the Palomar Ballroom in Hollywood, to the

Adophus Hotel in Dallas—every city had at least one! The leaders of the bands varied from those who were superb musicians to those who were strictly showbiz folks. Salaries were low; traveling conditions were hazardous; accommodations were inconsistent. Many musicians lived dissipated and short lives. Female vocalists had to travel on buses with a dozen or more men on a daily and nightly basis. Alcohol and drugs were plentiful and used by many. The glamour that the general public saw on the outside was continued by the unhappiness and disappointment lived by those who performed. Few made great artistic and financial successes—many met unhappiness and despondency. The only joy was the prospect of performance on a daily (nightly) basis and the prospect of performing better each time.

THE '40s, '50s, AND '60s

Small jazz groups began to emerge in the 1940s as a result of WWII, the American Federation of Musicians recording strike, the economy, and a great change in America's listening habits. Again, jazz took the lead in moving the art form forward with the advent of bebop and stellar groups led by Charlie Parker, Dizzy Gillespie, Thelonious Monk, and others. The '40s movement continued through the '50s with the Modern Jazz Quartet, Miles Davis, Gerry Mulligan/Chet Baker, and others making up the Cool School. In the '60s, great jazz orchestras like the Thad Jones-Mel Lewis Big Band stormed the country playing where they could find intelligent listeners. During the latter part of the '60s fusion bands began to gain great popularity. Fusion bands consisted of seven to 12-piece groups that featured rock 'n' roll, played with a jazz-feel, and highlighted some of the greatest soloists of the period. Groups such as Blood, Sweat & Tears, Chicago, and Dreams took the nation by storm, selling millions upon millions of records.

THE '70s AND '80s

1970: The first "rock" opera *Tommy*. Johnny Hodges died. The Minimoog, a monophonic synthesizer, was designed.

1971: The John F. Kennedy Center for the Performing Arts opened in Washington, D.C. Louis Armstrong died. The Digital computer organ was manufactured.

1972: Watergate. Duke Ellington's *Memories of Jacksonville*. Recording enginérs began to use 16- and 24-track consoles. The Roland Company was founded. The Synclavier, a polyphonic digital synthesizer, was developed.

1973: Donald Byrd's *Black Byrds*. Ceasefire in Vietnam. The Dartmouth digital synthesizer was developed.

1974: American Music Awards. Skylab (84 days) ends. Duke Ellington died. The Qasar and Oberheim synthesizers were developed.

1975: *Saturday Night Live* premiered. Financial crisis in music and arts **[AU: vague. Define.]**. The Lyricon, an electronic wind instrument that controls a synthesizer, was developed.

1976: George Benson's *Breezin'*. The U.S. Congress passed the 1976 copyright statute. There were 4,497 commercial AM radio stations; 2,873 commercial FM stations; 870 non-commercial FM stations; 8,240 total stations in operation with revenues of $1.8 billion and TV revenues of $4.2 billion.

1977: The birth of punk rock. Bing Crosby, Paul Desmond, Errol Garner, and Guy Lombardo died. The first guitar synthesizer was introduced. The sophistication of technology increases, including use of synthesizers, computer-assisted mixing, and digital recording.

1978: First "test tube" baby was born in England. Louis Prima died. The record business increased rapidly with multinational conglomerates forming and 5,000 industry leaders from 52 countries attending the international music conference. The Prophet synthesizer was developed.

1979: The birth of new wave music. Death of John Wayne and Charles Mingus. The Con Brio, a polyphonic digital synthesizer, was developed.

THE COLLEGES AND UNIVERSITY

The '70s saw the rise of other big jazz bands like the Wildlife Refuge led by trombonist Bill Watrous. Great movement took place in the colleges and universities that were emulating the lead taken by Westlake College of Music and the Berklee College of Music, both founded in 1945 at the end of WWII. Much activity in jazz studies took place in many colleges and universities, including the Manhattan School of Music in New York City, the University of North Texas in Denton, Texas, the University of Southern California in Los Angeles, California, and the University of Miami in Coral Gables, Florida. The largest music association in the United States, the Music Educators National Conference, encouraged students in all grades to improvise. The International Association of Jazz Educators, which had been formed with six members in 1968, presented annual conferences drawing more than 8,000 attendees. The IAJE had members in more than 40 countries and was the world leader in modern music education.

1980: World Saxophone Quartet. John Lennon, Jimmy Durante died. The Casiotone, C-Ducer, The Kit, Chroma, Linn Drum, Polysix, Simmons Electronic Drums, and Touche were developed.

1981: MTV debuts. President Reagan and Pope John Paul II were wounded. Other electronic instruments continued to develop—including the Emulator, GDS, Omnichord, Soundchaser.

1982: Compact discs were developed. John Belushi died. Snergy, a polyphonic digital synthesizer, was developed. The Synsonics drums, an electronic percussion instrument, was manufactured.

1983: Count Basie and Sonny Rollins received the Jazz Masters awards from the NEA. Ira Gershwin and Muddy Waters died.

1984: The New Romanticism, a program mixing computer, synthesizer, and performance art, was developed. Count Basie and Meredith Wilson died. The Drumulator, an electronic percussion unit, was manufactured.

1985: VH1 premieres. Forty-three musicians record "We Are the World." The 4X, a polyphonic digital synthesizer, was developed.

1986: Rock and Roll Hall of Fame founded in Cleveland, Ohio. Jimmy Durante, Benny Goodman, Rudy Vallée died.

1987: Death of Woody Herman and Buddy Rich.

1988: Death of Chet Baker.

1989: The birth of rap music. Death of Irving Berlin.

Since the '80s, the television bands providing music for live audiences in the studios continue to thrive. *The NBC Tonight Show*, featuring the music of the Kevin Eubanks Orchestra, and on CBS, *The Late Night Show with David Letterman* with music by Paul Shaffer and His Orchestra, represented the major airings. Other contemporary big bands included those lead by Bill Watrous, Bob Florence, Louis Bellson, Doc Severinson, Maria Sneider, John Fedchock, the Vanguard Orchestra, Mike Vax (who led his own band and another band comprised of Stan Kenton alumni), etc. Commercial bands led by Meyer Davis, Lester Lannin, Peter Duchin, Ray Bloch, etc. were still active and playing in various venues for dances, weddings, bar mitzvahs, etc.

Clockwise from top left: Kevin Eubanks, Paul Shaffer, and Maria Sneider.

THE '90s

1990:   Deaths of Pearl Bailey and Sarah Vaughan.

1991:   Persian Gulf War. Death of Miles Davis

1992:   Sales of compact discs surpass those of cassette tapes.

1994:   Twenty-fifth anniversary of Woodstock. Death of Cab Calloway.

1996:   Death of Ella Fitzgerald.

1997:   Wynton Marsalis's *Blood on the Fields* won the Pulitzer Prize
        for music.

1998:   Death of Frank Sinatra.

1999:   Deaths of Al Hirt and Mel Torme.

During the '80s and '90s, two excellent women's bands were organized—Maiden
Voyage and Diva. Toshiko Akiyoshi (pianist, composer, arranger) led a high-spirited
big band with great musical success. In Southern
California, the American Jazz Philharmonic
combined the traditional large jazz ensemble with
an orchestral string compliment to broaden the
sound possibilities and make jazz more palatable to
the general audience. In the larger cities—New
York, Los Angeles, Chicago, Houston,
Philadelphia, etc.—local and territory bands
continued to organize and perform. It seemed as
though dancers had turned into listeners.

Toshiko Akiyoshi

There were rehearsal bands (kicks bands) in
nearly every town in the U.S.; bands that were reading their own arrangements or
arrangements of the famous big bands that had disbanded. There was continuing
interest on the part of musicians, aged six to 96, in the sound of big band music
and the thrill of performing it.

GHOST BANDS

"Ghost bands"—bands who played the music of the bands of the '20s, '30s, and '40s, appeared at various conventions, business meetings, etc. Ghost bands, in the minds of the people who led them, were attempts to pay tribute to the great leaders who have died and to keep alive the music that they created in the era of the big bands. In the concept of booking agents and people of the estate, the reason for the ghost band was two-fold: to keep the name alive and to provide a source of revenue for the estate.

The most famous ghost band was the Glenn Miller ghost band. When the concept of having a Glenn Miller ghost band was presented to the Glenn Miller estate, it was initially rejected, and then over a period of time Dave McKay Sr., who controled the Glenn Miller estate, was convinced by Williard Alexander to keep Miller's music alive by forming a ghost band. It was between the two of them. The Glenn Miller ghost band, to pay tribute to Glenn Miller's music, was formed; drummer Ray McKinnley was hired as the leader and it was a natural because Ray McKinnley had played with the Miller Air Force Band. McKinnley led the band for a number of years and then decided to leave the road (due to vigorous traveling, around 50 weeks per year), and then the long-time leader was clarinetist Buddy DeFranco. After several years Jim Henderson took over the band and led it for a number of years. In 1981, the Glenn Miller ghost band was so popular in the U.S. that people in Europe requested a tour of the band. Inasmuch as the Glenn Miller band, under the leadership of Jimmy Henderson, was fully booked in the states, Dave McKay Jr., who had taken over the estate from his father, decided to create a number two Glenn Miller ghost band and chose Clem DeRosa to lead the band. DeRosa took the second Glenn Miller ghost band on tour through Europe with great success. In 1982, the bookers requested the same band for another European tour. So there existed two Glenn Miller ghost bands, one in Europe and one in America.

With the success of the Glenn Miller ghost bands concept, Lee Castle organized and fronted a Jimmy Dorsey ghost band; which was very successful. Other ghost bands began to surface, as various established leaders began to die, as the estates wanted to keep the music alive and be provided with a revenue source. Clem Derosa had been doing some Jimmy Dorsey dates, when two Jimmy Dorsey Ghost bands were called for, and when Lee Castle died Derosa covered for Lee Castle until the estate was purchased. At the end of the 20th century there was the Benny Goodman ghost band, the Les Brown ghost band, the Nelson Riddle Orchestra (led by his son Christoper Riddle), the Sammy Kaye Orchestra, the Guy Lombardo Orchestra, the Woody Herman band (led by saxophonist Frank Tiberi), the Harry James band, the Artie Shaw Orchestra (led by Dick Johnson, although Shaw was still alive), the Count Basie band (led by Grover Mitchell), the Duke Ellington band, and several others under various names and leaders. Serious leaders of ghost bands considered it a tremendous responsibility to be chosen to conduct the music of a deceased leader. They carefully researched what the leaders did, as well as their music, keeping true to the concept that they had originally wanted and trying to maintain the quality of performance established by them.

IS THERE A FUTURE FOR THE BIG BANDS?

The big bands that were very popular in the '20s, '30s, '40s, and '50s served us well. With the advent of the computer, advanced sound systems, and other sophisticated electronic equipment, the need for large instrumental groups became passé. We exited the period in the early part of the century when we were obliged to travel to hear a big band to today's sophisticated selection of electronics that allow us to hear the very best on compact disc in our own home surroundings. The basic economics of sustaining more than a dozen traveling musicians has escalated to the point where such organizations have become financially less than feasible. The attitude was "Why spend money traveling to hear something less than first-rate when the best is available on my own home sound system?" Also, we became accustomed to hearing quality music, of all kinds, reproduced on radio, television, and in movie theaters. To sum up: American ears for music consumption became more sophisticated in terms of quality of sound. It is for this reason, and the fact that few of them are outstanding musically and play the music of Western Europe, that the traditional symphony orchestras, as we have known them, are disappearing in the U.S. Recent figures indicate that nationally 66 percent of online ticket sales for symphony orchestras come from new customers annually, indicating that only a small percentage of music lovers subscribe for more than one season.

We believe that jazz, which has become an international music, will survive as it allows for individual expression and that was what music was all about in the centuries preceding the 19th. There will always be an informal interest in the big bands, i. e. the kicks bands (rehearsal bands). These groups have proven to be of inestimable value in middle schools, high schools, colleges and universities. The various military units in the U.S. (army, airforce, navy, marines, etc.) have found value in sustaining the big bands and will, most likely, continue to do so. There were more than 50,000 such bands in schools and the military as the 20th century ended.

Will they come back? In America. anything can happen!

BIBLIOGRAPHY

ASCAP Biographical Dictionary (Fourth Edition). New York: Compiled by Jaques Cattell Press, R. R. Bowker Company, 1980.

Blesh, Rudi, and Janis, Harriet. *They All Played Ragtime*. New York: Oak Publications, 1871.

Cuney-Hare, Maud. *Negro musicians and Their Music*. New York: Da Capo Press, 1974.

Driggs, Frank, and Lewine, Harris. *Black Beauty, White Heat: A Pictorial History of Classic Jazz*. New York: William Morrow and Company, Inc., 1982.

Feather, Leonard, and Gitle, Ira. *The Biographical Encyclopedia of Jazz*. New York: Oxford University Press, 1999.

Ferrett, Gene. *Swing Out: Great Negro Dance Bands*. New York: Da Capo Press, Inc., 1993.

Gourse, Leslie. *Madame Jazz: Contemporary Women Instrumentalists*. New York: Oxford University Press, 1995.

Hitchcock, H. Wiley and Sadie, Stanley (Ed.). *The New Grove Dictionary of American Music*. London, England: MacMillan Press Limited, 1986.

Jennings, Peter, and Brewster, Todd. *The Century*. New York: Doubleday, 1998.

Kimball, Robert, and Bolcom, William. *Reminiscing with Sissle and Blake*. New York: The Viking Press, 1973.

Kinkle, Roger D. *The Complete Encyclopedia of Popular Music and Jazz, 1900–1950*. New Rochelle, New York: Arlington House Publishers, 1974.

Kornfeld, Barry (Ed.). *The New Grove Dictionary of Jazz*. London, England: MacMillan Press Limited, 1988.

Lee, Bill. *People in Jazz: Jazz Keyboard Improvisors of the 19th and 20th Centuries*. Hialeah, Florida: Columbia Pictures Publications, 1984.

Lee, William. *Music in the 21st Century: The New Language.* Miami, Florida: Belwin Mills Publishing Corp., 1994.

Lee, William F. *Music Theory Dictionary.* Miami, Florida: Charles Hansen Educational Music and Books, 1965.

McCarthy, Albert. *The Dance Band Era: The Dancing Decades from Ragtime to Swing, 1910–1950.* Radnor, Pennsylvania: Chilton Book Co., 1971.

Rose, Al, and Souchon, Edmond. *New Orleans Jazz.* Baton Rouge, Louisiana: Louisiana State University Press, 1984.

Simon, George T., et al. *The Best of the Music Makers.* New York: Doubleday & Company, Inc., 1979.

Simon, George T. *The Big Bands.* New York: The Macmillan Company, 1967.

Simon, George T. *The Big Bands Trivia Quiz Book.* New York: Barnes & Noble Books, 1985.

Simon, George T. *Simon Says: The Sights and Sounds of the Swing Era, 1935–1955.* New Rochelle, NY: Arlington House, 1971.

Tucker, Sherrie. *Swing Shift: "All-Girl" Bands of the 1940s.* Durham, N.C.: Duke University Press, 2000.

Walker, Leo. *The Big Band Almanac.* New York: Da Capo Press, 1989.

Walker, Leo. *The Wonderful Era of the Great Dance Bands.* New York: Da Capo Press, 1990.

Wood, Ean. *Born to Swing.* London: Sanctuary Publishing Ltd., 1996.

Woods, Bernie. *When The Music Stopped: The Big Band Era Remembered.* New York: Barricade Books, 1994.

Bands Alphabetically

A

Irving Aaronson, 94
Leon Abbey, 135
Shuffle Abernathy, 244
Leo Addeo, 327
Johnny Addinni, 316
Bernard Addison, 86
Charlie Agnew, 87
Harry Akst, 179
Manny Albam, 341
Don Albert, 152
Jack Albin, 135
Van Alexander, 219
Barclay Allen, 299
Bob Allen, 248
Henry "Red" Allen, 248
Jasper "Jap" Allen, 244
Steve Allen, 320
Danny Alvin, 179
Bert Ambrose, 59
Albert Ammons, 219
Harry Archer, 113
James Archey, 321
Louis Armstrong, 133
Leroy Anderson, 281
Ray Anthony, 299
Luis Arcaraz, 133
Arden and Ohman, 95
Gus Arnheim, 104
Zinn Arthur, 248
Paul Ash, 59
Bob Astor, 274
Jan August, 290
Georgie Auld, 267
Johnny Austin, 311
Mitchell Ayres, 186
Don Azpiazu, 126

B

Will Back, 316
Ken Baker, 186
Smith Ballew, 63
Bud Barclay, 199
Walter Barnes, 87
Charlie Barnet, 172
Blue Baron, 199
Tony Barron, 354
Count Basie, 187
Sid Bass, 280
Ray Bauduc, 290
Charles Baum, 211
Les Baxter, 323
Phil Baxter, 104
Sidney Bechet, 88
Bix Beiderbecke, 55
Leon Belasco, 114
Louis Bellson, 340
Tex Beneke, 300
Bunny Berigan, 200
Memo Bernabei, 339
Ben Bernie, 64
Vic Berton, 115
Don Bestor (Benson), 56
Frank Bettencourt, 348
Henry Biagini, 109
Paul Biese, 26
Billy Bishop, 144
Frank Black, 152
Ted Black, 126
Jerry Blaine, 212
Eubie Blake, 56
Archie Bleyer, 180
Buddy Bolden, 15
Sharkey Bonano, 200
Earl Bostic, 291

Johnny Bothwell, 301
Perry Bradford, 140
Will Bradley, 231
Tiny Bradshaw, 180
Brady's Clarinet Orch., 65
Mario Braggiotti, 143
Nat Brandwynne, 153
Lou Breese, 201
Ace Brigode, 55
Lou Bring, 188
John Benson Brooks, 282
Randy Brooks, 292
Les Brown, 220
Brown's Dixieland Jass Band, 19
Willie Bryant, 1014
Teddy Buckner, 201
Ted B. Buckner, 311
Bucktown Five, 40
Chick Bullock, 188
Sonny Burke, 221
Earl Burtnett, 65
Joe Buskin, 324
Henry Busse, 145
Billy Butler, 96
Billy Butterfield, 292
Erskine Butterfield, 221
Bobby Byrne, 232

C

Chuck Cabot, 233
California Ramblers
  (Ted Wallace), 89
Cab Calloway, 115
Tutti Camarata, 249
Buddy Campbell, 145
Pupi Campo, 313